JINK!™

Book 14 in the  *ELFQUEST* Reader's Collection

WOLFRIDER BOOKS

**Poughkeepsie
New York**

Reprinting **Elfquest: Jink**
comic book issue numbers 1 through 6

Story by
John Ostrander with Wendy Pini

Art by
Art by David Boller, Terry Beatty, Craig Taillefer,
Dennis Fujitake, Charles Barnett and Paul Abrams

About the ELFQUEST Reader's Collection

The twenty year — and ongoing — saga that is Elfquest has been told in many different comic book titles. The Elfquest Reader's Collection is our attempt to collect all the core stories in book form, so that readers new and old can follow the entire tale from its beginnings on up to the most recent work.

As planned the Elfquest Reader's Collection series will include the following volumes:

#1 - Fire and Flight
#2 - The Forbidden Grove
#3 - Captives of Blue Mountain
#4 - Quest's End

    The story of Cutter, chief of the Wolfriders, and his tribe as they confront the perils of their primitive world, encounter new races of elves, and embark on a grand and dangerous quest to unveil the secret of their past.

#5 - Siege at Blue Mountain
#6 - The Secret of Two-Edge

    The adventures of the Wolfriders some years after the end of the first quest, as they face the machinations of a villainess from their past and her enigmatic half-elf, half-troll son.

#7 - The Cry from Beyond
#8 - Kings of the Broken Wheel

    The Wolfriders face their most daunting challenge when one of their number kidnaps Cutter's mate and children into future time, to prevent the accident that first brought the elves to this world.

#8a - Dreamtime

    The visions of the Wolfriders as they slept for ten thousand years, waiting for the time when Cutter and his family can be united once more.

#9 - Rogue's Challenge

    Tales of the "bad guys" who have caused the Wolfriders so much trouble over the centuries.

#9a - Wolfrider!

    The tale of Cutter's sire Bearclaw, and how he brought two things to the Wolfriders — the enmity of humans and a monstrous tragedy, and a chief's son like no elf the tribe had ever known.

#10 - Shards
#11 - Legacy
#11a - Huntress
#12 - Ascent
#12a - Reunion

    Cutter and family are together again, but now a ruthless human warlord threatens the elves' very existence. The Wolfriders must become two tribes — one to fight a terrible war, the other to flee to ensure that the tribe continues. Volume #10 sets the stage; volumes #11 and #11a follow Cutter's daughter Ember as she leads the Wild Hunt elves into new lands; volumes #12 and #12a take Cutter and his warriors into the flames of battle.

#13 - the Rebels
#13a - Skyward Shadow
#14 - Jink!
#14a - Mindcoil

    In the far future of the World of Two Moons, human civilization has covered the planet — and the elves have disappeared. Where did they go? Volumes #13 and #13a follows a group of young adventurers as they seek the answer. Volumes #14 and #14a tell the story of a mysterious woman who is more than she seems — for she may be the last surviving descendant of the missing elves.

JINK!™

Book 14 in the *ELFQUEST* **Reader's Collection**

Published by Warp Graphics, Inc.
under its Wolfrider Books imprint.

Entire contents
copyright © 1999
Warp Graphics, Inc.
All rights reserved worldwide.

43 Haight Avenue
Poughkeepsie, New York 12603

ISBN 0-936861-48-7
Printed in USA

www.elfquest.com

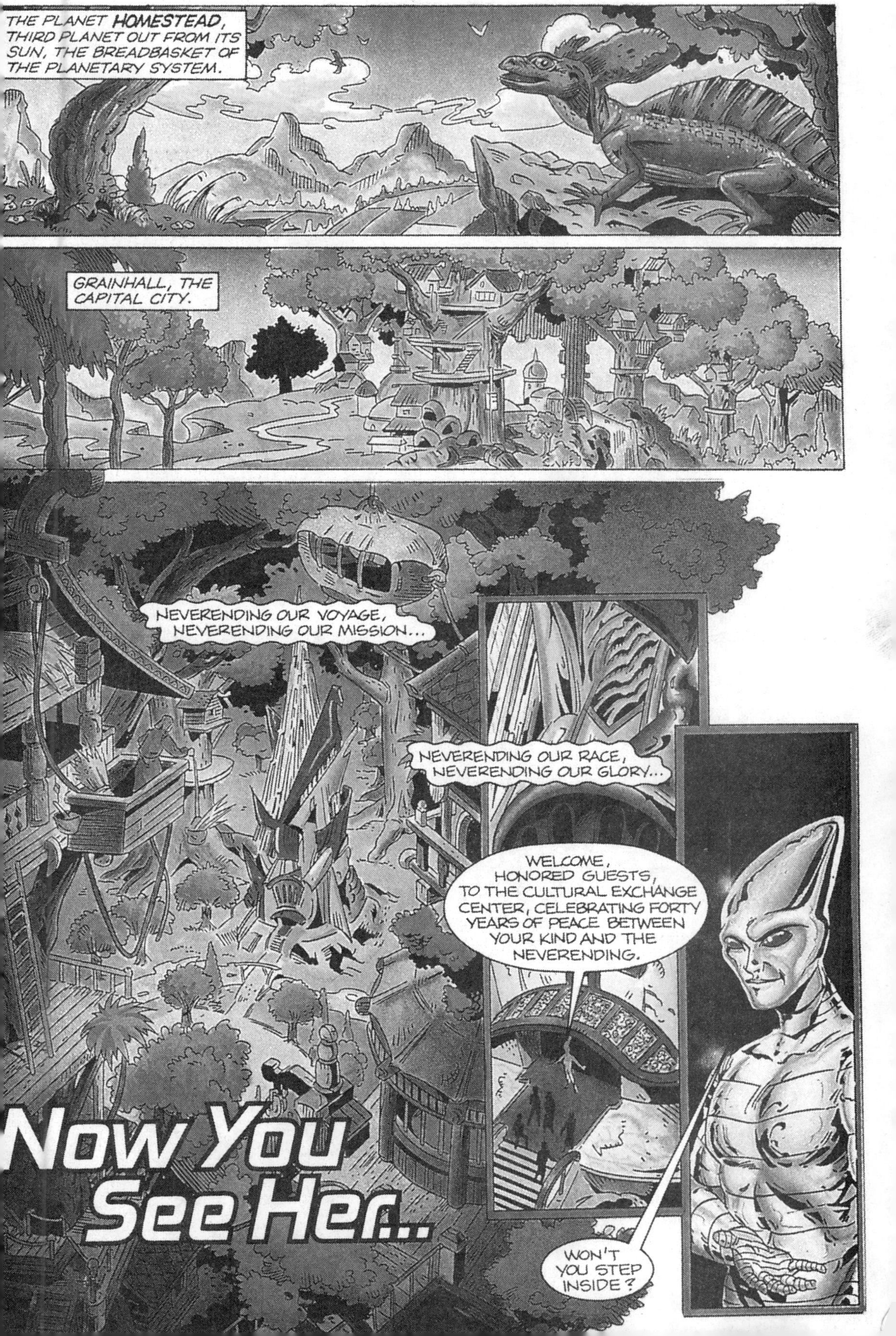
THE PLANET HOMESTEAD, THIRD PLANET OUT FROM ITS SUN, THE BREADBASKET OF THE PLANETARY SYSTEM.
GRAINHALL, THE CAPITAL CITY.
NEVERENDING OUR VOYAGE, NEVERENDING OUR MISSION...
NEVERENDING OUR RACE, NEVERENDING OUR GLORY...
Now You See Her...
WELCOME, HONORED GUESTS, TO THE CULTURAL EXCHANGE CENTER, CELEBRATING FORTY YEARS OF PEACE BETWEEN YOUR KIND AND THE NEVERENDING.
WON'T YOU STEP INSIDE?

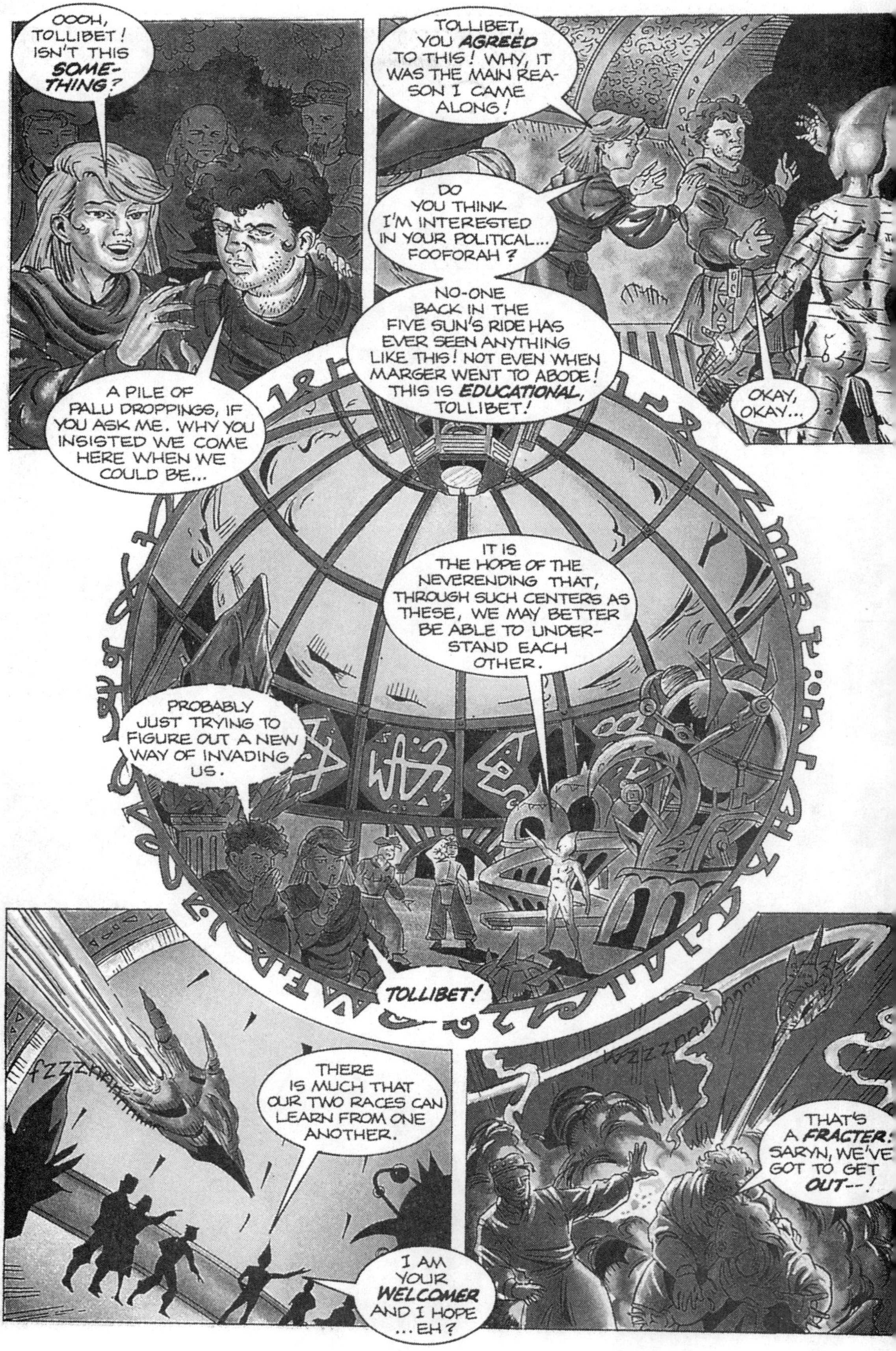

OOOH, TOLLIBET! ISN'T THIS SOME-THING?
A PILE OF PALU DROPPINGS, IF YOU ASK ME. WHY YOU INSISTED WE COME HERE WHEN WE COULD BE...
TOLLIBET, YOU AGREED TO THIS! WHY, IT WAS THE MAIN REA-SON I CAME ALONG!
DO YOU THINK I'M INTERESTED IN YOUR POLITICAL... FOOFORAH?
NO-ONE BACK IN THE FIVE SUN'S RIDE HAS EVER SEEN ANYTHING LIKE THIS! NOT EVEN WHEN MARGER WENT TO ABODE! THIS IS EDUCATIONAL, TOLLIBET!
OKAY, OKAY...
IT IS THE HOPE OF THE NEVERENDING THAT, THROUGH SUCH CENTERS AS THESE, WE MAY BETTER BE ABLE TO UNDER-STAND EACH OTHER.
PROBABLY JUST TRYING TO FIGURE OUT A NEW WAY OF INVADING US.
TOLLIBET!
fzzznnn
THERE IS MUCH THAT OUR TWO RACES CAN LEARN FROM ONE ANOTHER.
I AM YOUR WELCOMER AND I HOPE ...EH?
wzzznnn
THAT'S A FRACTER! SARYN, WE'VE GOT TO GET OUT--!

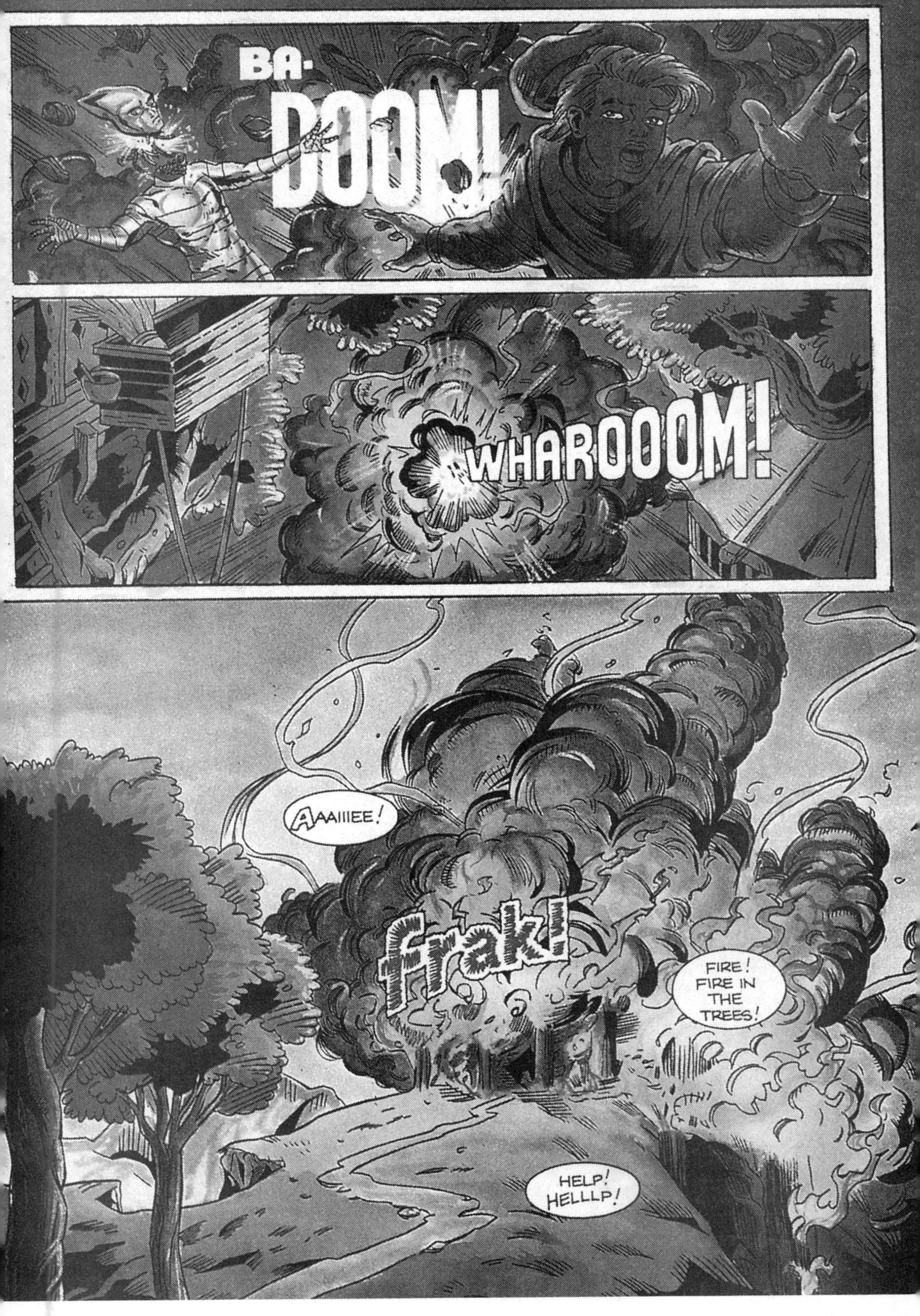
BA-
DOOM!
WHAROOOM!
AAIIIEE!
frak!
FIRE! FIRE IN THE TREES!
HELP! HELLLP!

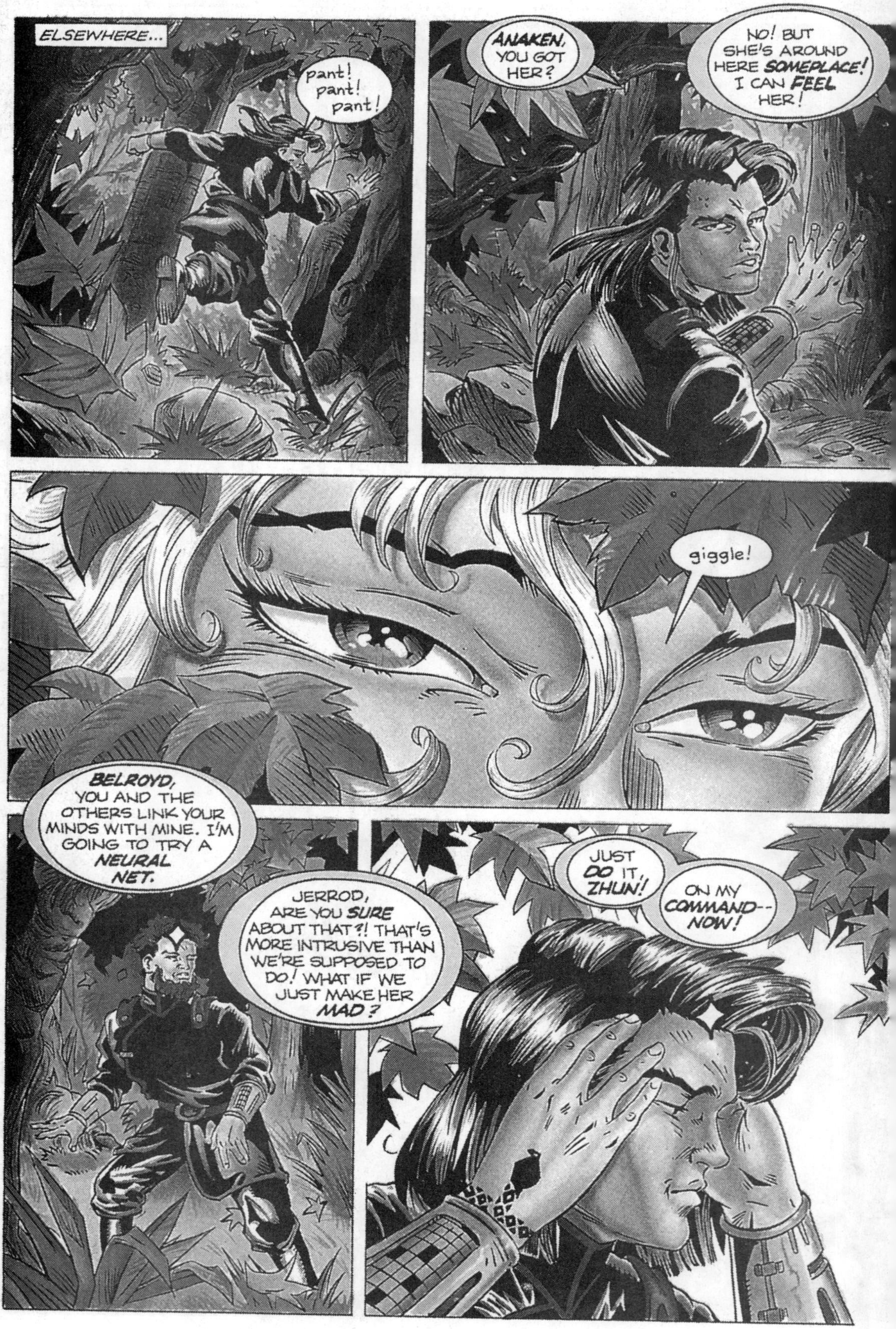
ELSEWHERE...
pant! pant! pant!
ANAKEN, YOU GOT HER?
NO! BUT SHE'S AROUND HERE SOMEPLACE! I CAN FEEL HER!
giggle!
BELROYD, YOU AND THE OTHERS LINK YOUR MINDS WITH MINE. I'M GOING TO TRY A NEURAL NET.
JERROD, ARE YOU SURE ABOUT THAT?! THAT'S MORE INTRUSIVE THAN WE'RE SUPPOSED TO DO! WHAT IF WE JUST MAKE HER MAD?
JUST DO IT, ZHUN!
ON MY COMMAND--NOW!

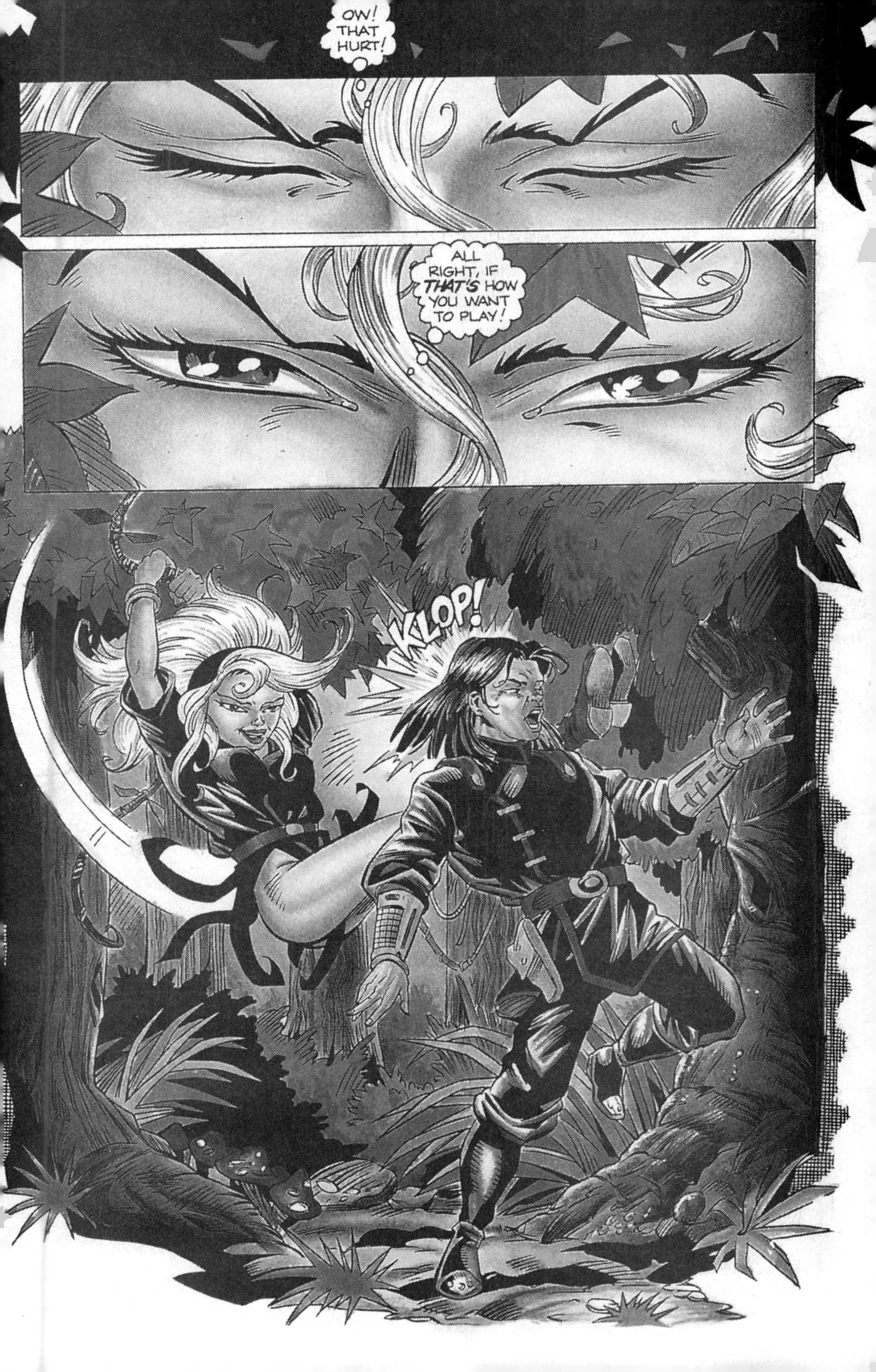
OW! THAT HURT!
ALL RIGHT, IF THAT'S HOW YOU WANT TO PLAY!
KLOP!

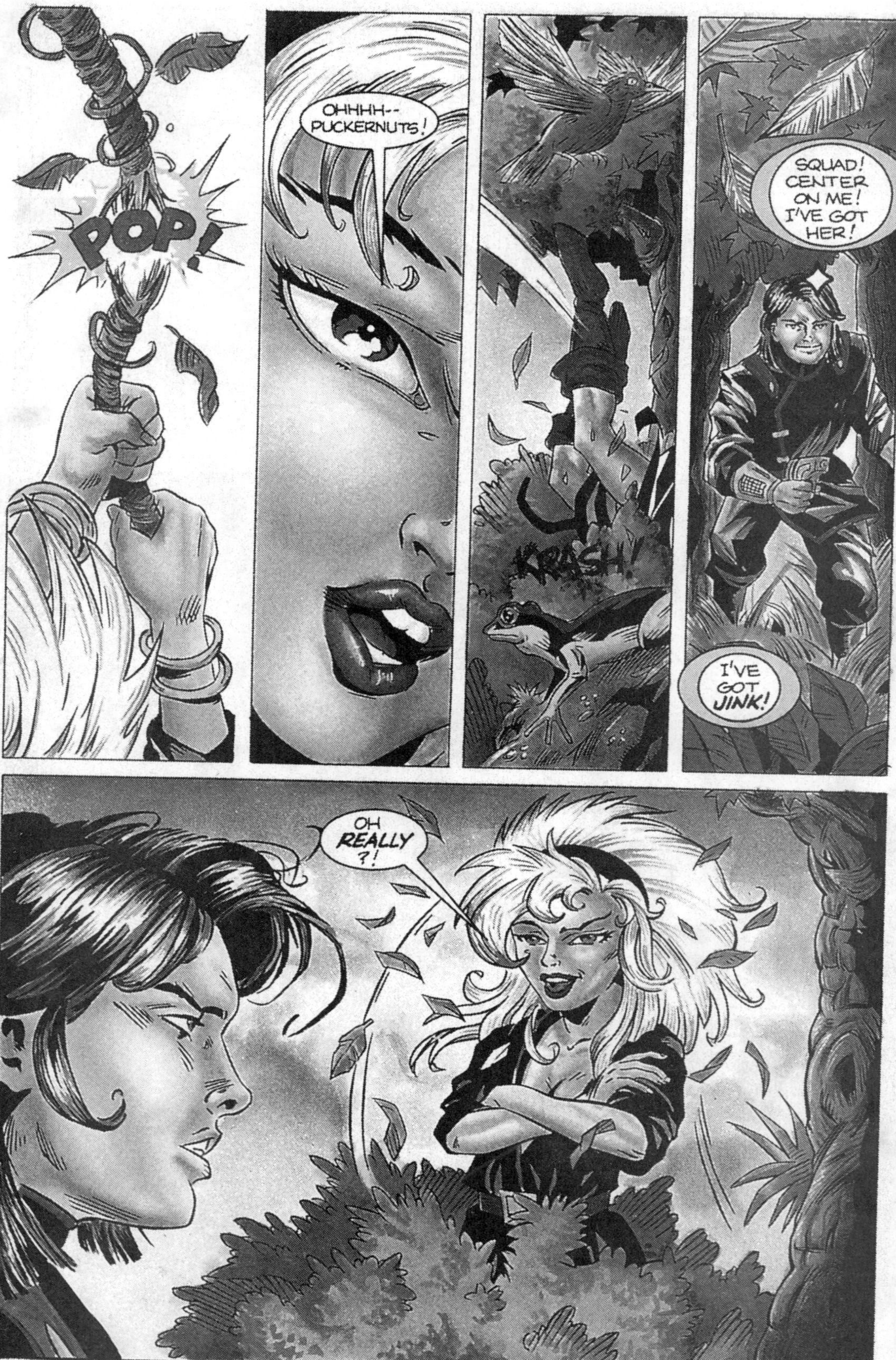
POP!
OHHHH--
PUCKERNUTS!
KRASH!
SQUAD!
CENTER
ON ME!
I'VE GOT
HER!
I'VE
GOT
JINK!
OH
REALLY
?!

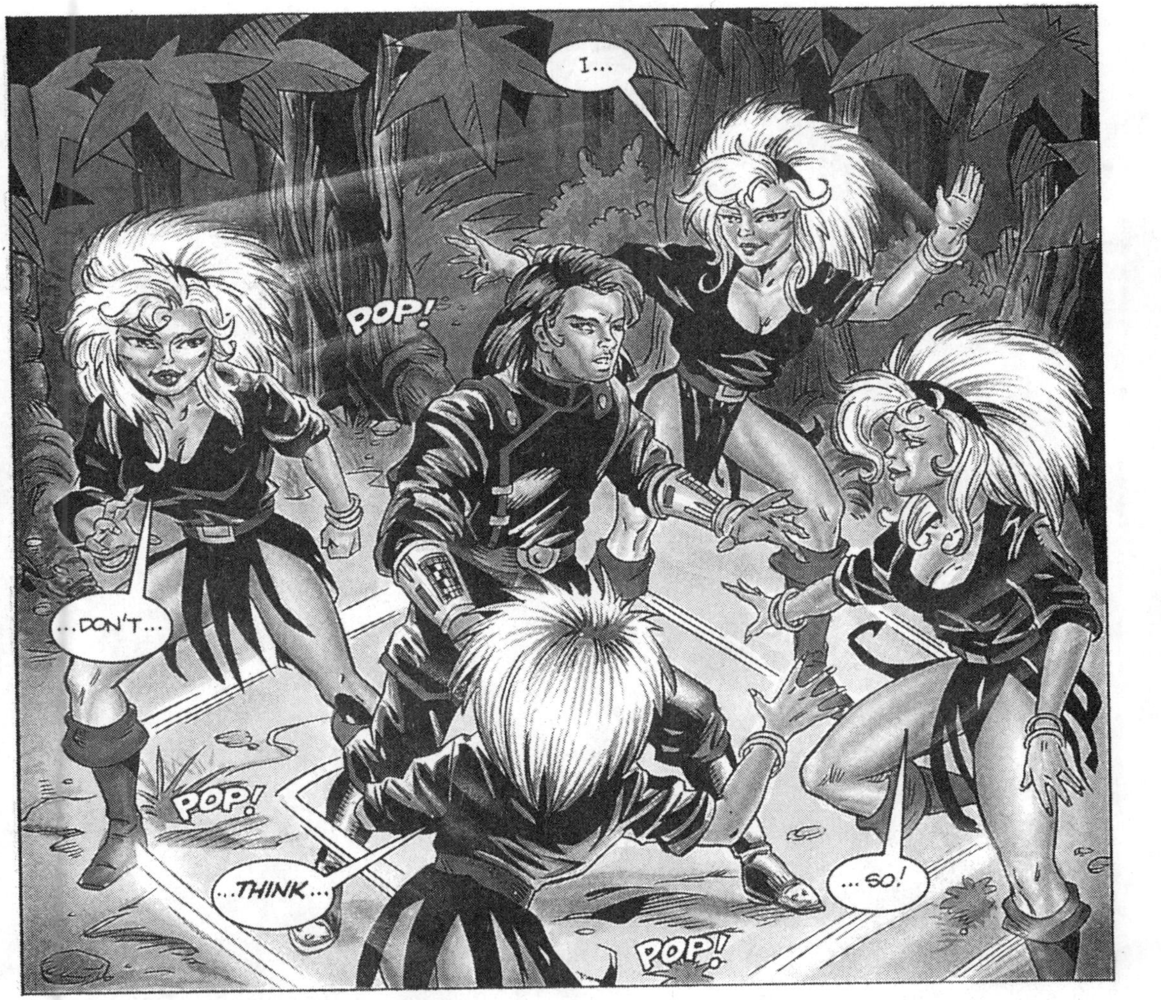
I...
POP!
...DON'T...
POP!
...THINK...
...SO!
POP!

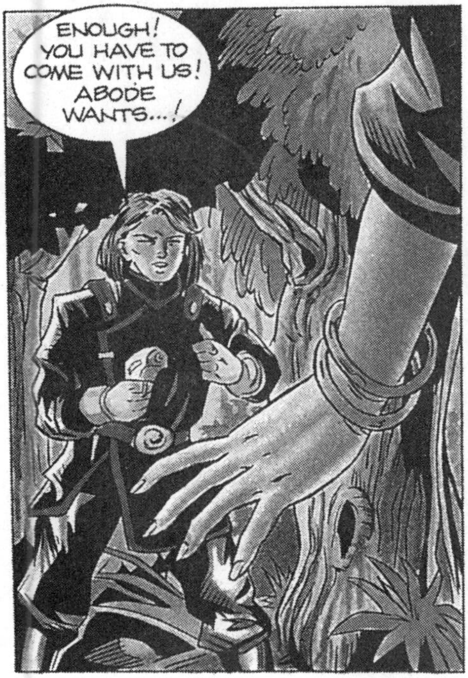
ENOUGH! YOU HAVE TO COME WITH US! ABODE WANTS...!

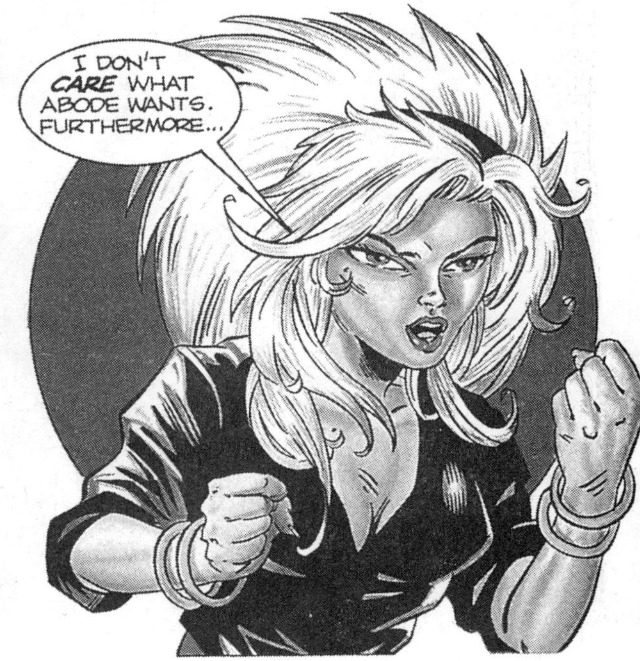
I DON'T CARE WHAT ABODE WANTS. FURTHERMORE...

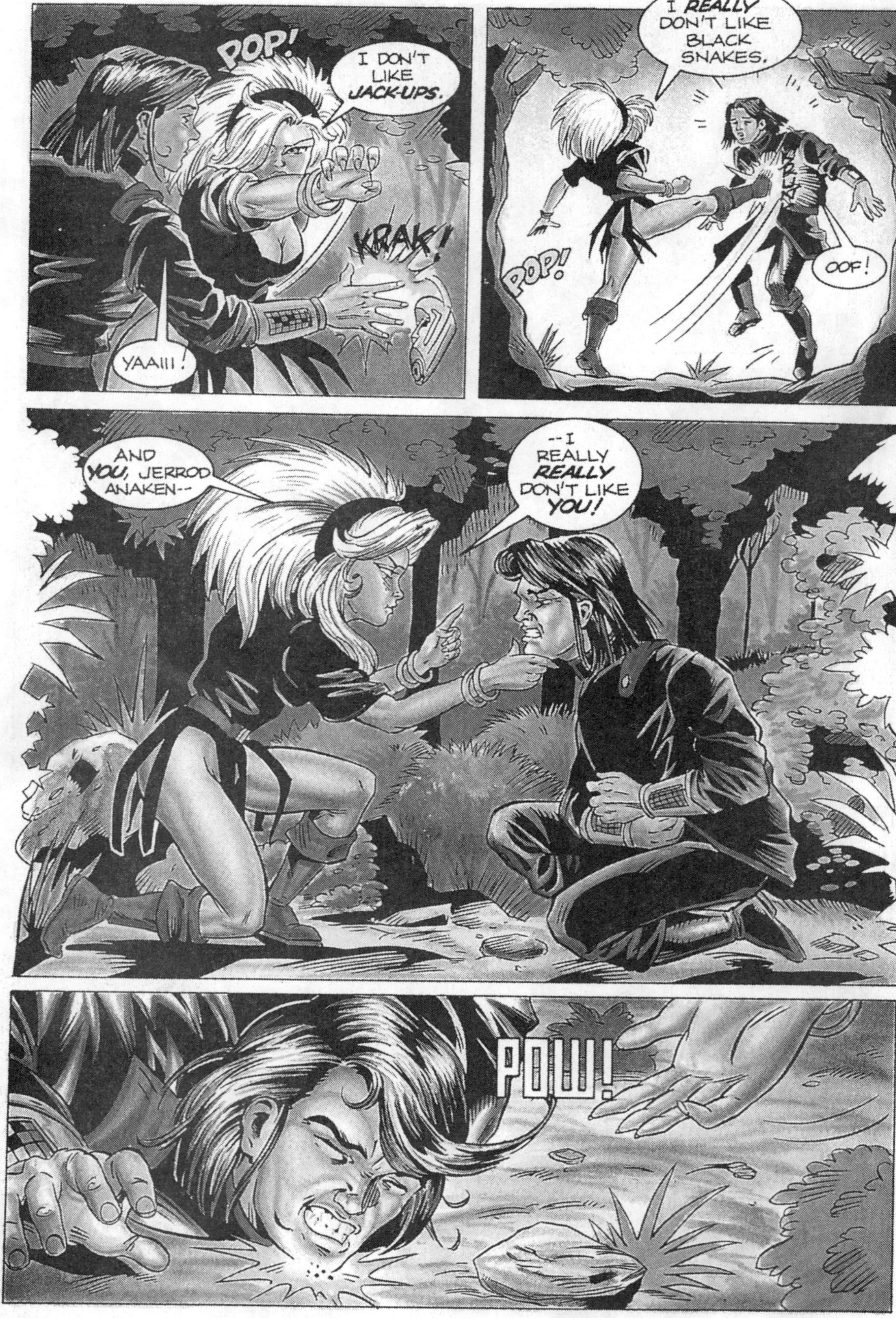
POP!
I DON'T LIKE JACK-UPS.
KRAK!
YAAIII!
I REALLY DON'T LIKE BLACK SNAKES.
POP!
OOF!
AND YOU, JERROD ANAKEN--
--I REALLY REALLY DON'T LIKE YOU!
POW!

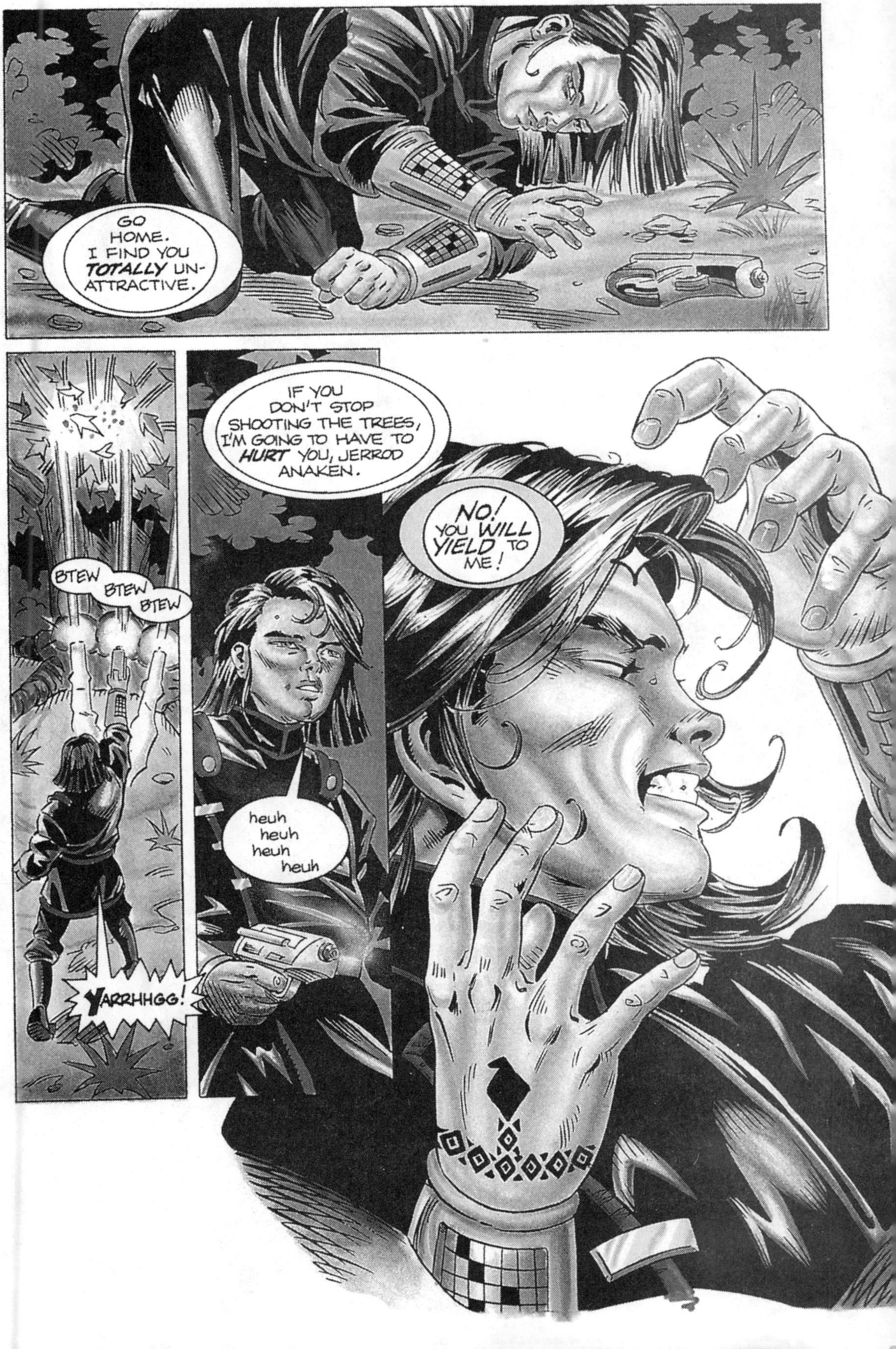
GO HOME. I FIND YOU TOTALLY UN-ATTRACTIVE.
IF YOU DON'T STOP SHOOTING THE TREES, I'M GOING TO HAVE TO HURT YOU, JERROD ANAKEN.
BTEW BTEW BTEW
YARRHHGG!
heuh heuh heuh heuh
NO! YOU WILL YIELD TO ME!

AND IF YOU EVER TRY *THAT* AGAIN, I WILL *KILL* YOU, JERROD ANAKEN.

C'MON, JERROD. WE'RE PACKING IT UP.

...N-NO!... ...MISSION... ...NOT... ...COMPLETED...!

YEAH, IT IS. WE'RE WHUPPED. SHE NEARLY TOOK *ALL* OUR HEADS OFF.

"WE'RE PULLING OUT, JERROD. THEY'LL HAVE TO FIND ANOTHER WAY OF BRINGING THE *MINX* IN."

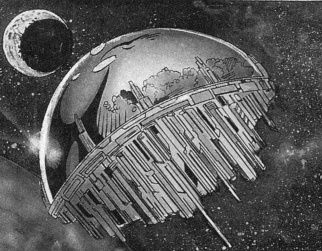

"THOUGH IT BEATS ME *WHY* ABODE WANTS HER."

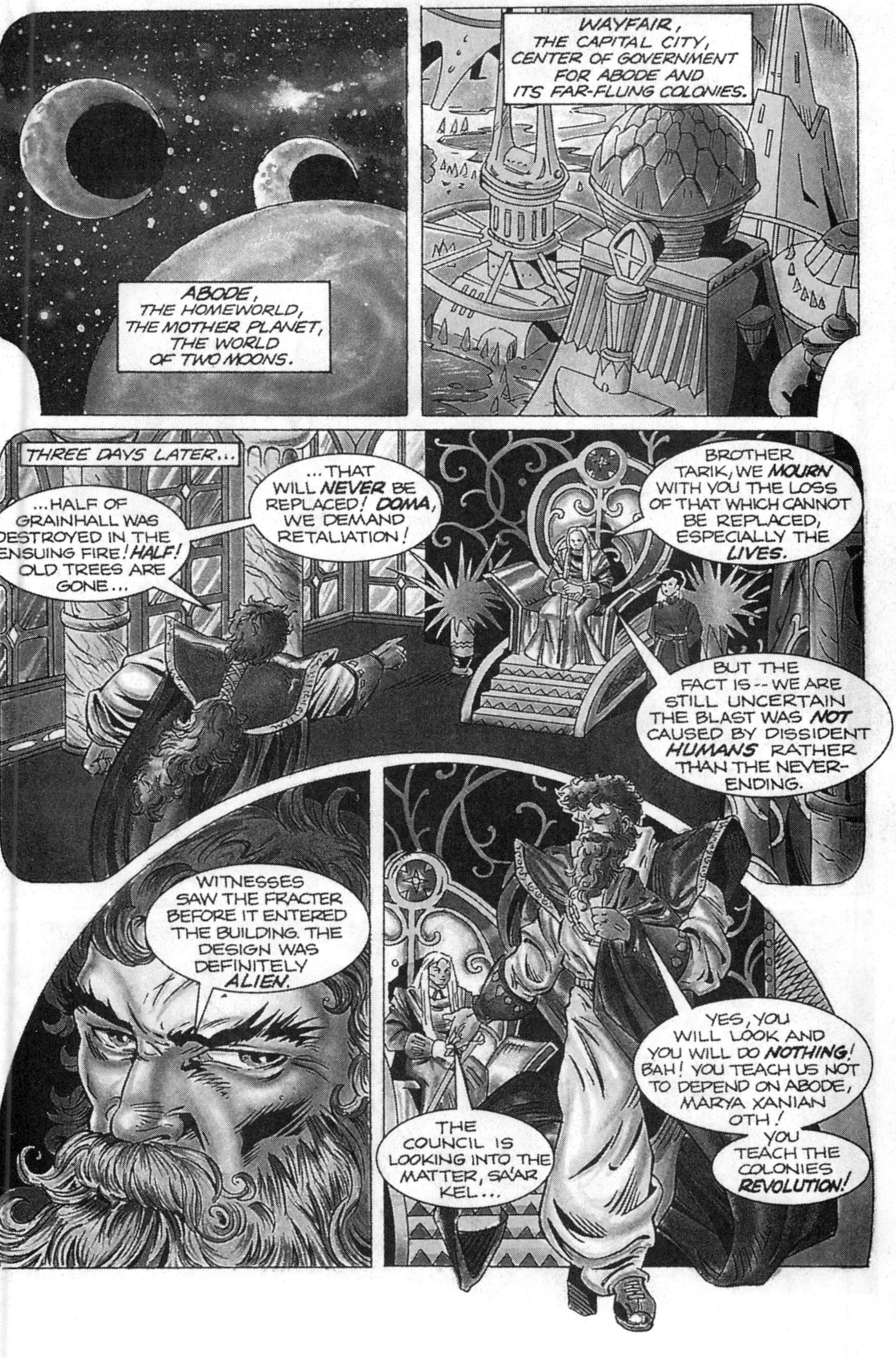
ABODE, THE HOMEWORLD, THE MOTHER PLANET, THE WORLD OF TWO MOONS.
WAYFAIR, THE CAPITAL CITY, CENTER OF GOVERNMENT FOR ABODE AND ITS FAR-FLUNG COLONIES.
THREE DAYS LATER...
...HALF OF GRAINHALL WAS DESTROYED IN THE ENSUING FIRE! HALF! OLD TREES ARE GONE...
...THAT WILL NEVER BE REPLACED! DOMA, WE DEMAND RETALIATION!
BROTHER TARIK, WE MOURN WITH YOU THE LOSS OF THAT WHICH CANNOT BE REPLACED, ESPECIALLY THE LIVES.
BUT THE FACT IS--WE ARE STILL UNCERTAIN THE BLAST WAS NOT CAUSED BY DISSIDENT HUMANS RATHER THAN THE NEVER-ENDING.
WITNESSES SAW THE FRACTER BEFORE IT ENTERED THE BUILDING. THE DESIGN WAS DEFINITELY ALIEN.
THE COUNCIL IS LOOKING INTO THE MATTER, SA'AR KEL...
YES, YOU WILL LOOK AND YOU WILL DO NOTHING! BAH! YOU TEACH US NOT TO DEPEND ON ABODE, MARYA XANIAN OTH! YOU TEACH THE COLONIES REVOLUTION!

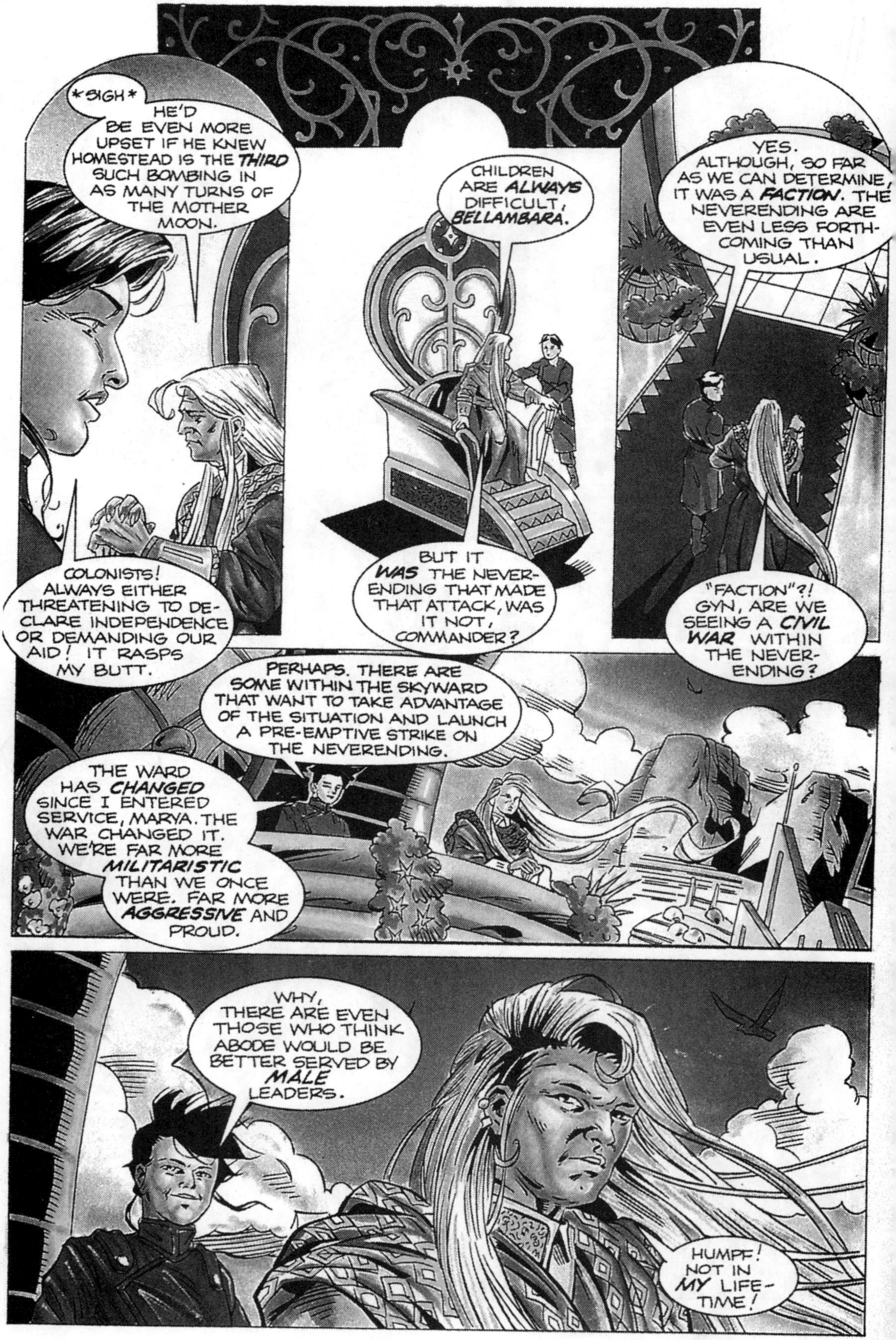
SIGH HE'D BE EVEN MORE UPSET IF HE KNEW HOMESTEAD IS THE THIRD SUCH BOMBING IN AS MANY TURNS OF THE MOTHER MOON.
COLONISTS! ALWAYS EITHER THREATENING TO DECLARE INDEPENDENCE OR DEMANDING OUR AID! IT RASPS MY BUTT.
CHILDREN ARE ALWAYS DIFFICULT, BELLAMBARA.
BUT IT WAS THE NEVERENDING THAT MADE THAT ATTACK, WAS IT NOT, COMMANDER?
YES. ALTHOUGH, SO FAR AS WE CAN DETERMINE, IT WAS A FACTION. THE NEVERENDING ARE EVEN LESS FORTHCOMING THAN USUAL.
"FACTION"?! GYN, ARE WE SEEING A CIVIL WAR WITHIN THE NEVERENDING?
PERHAPS. THERE ARE SOME WITHIN THE SKYWARD THAT WANT TO TAKE ADVANTAGE OF THE SITUATION AND LAUNCH A PRE-EMPTIVE STRIKE ON THE NEVERENDING.
THE WARD HAS CHANGED SINCE I ENTERED SERVICE, MARYA. THE WAR CHANGED IT. WE'RE FAR MORE MILITARISTIC THAN WE ONCE WERE. FAR MORE AGGRESSIVE AND PROUD.
WHY, THERE ARE EVEN THOSE WHO THINK ABODE WOULD BE BETTER SERVED BY MALE LEADERS.
HUMPF! NOT IN MY LIFETIME!

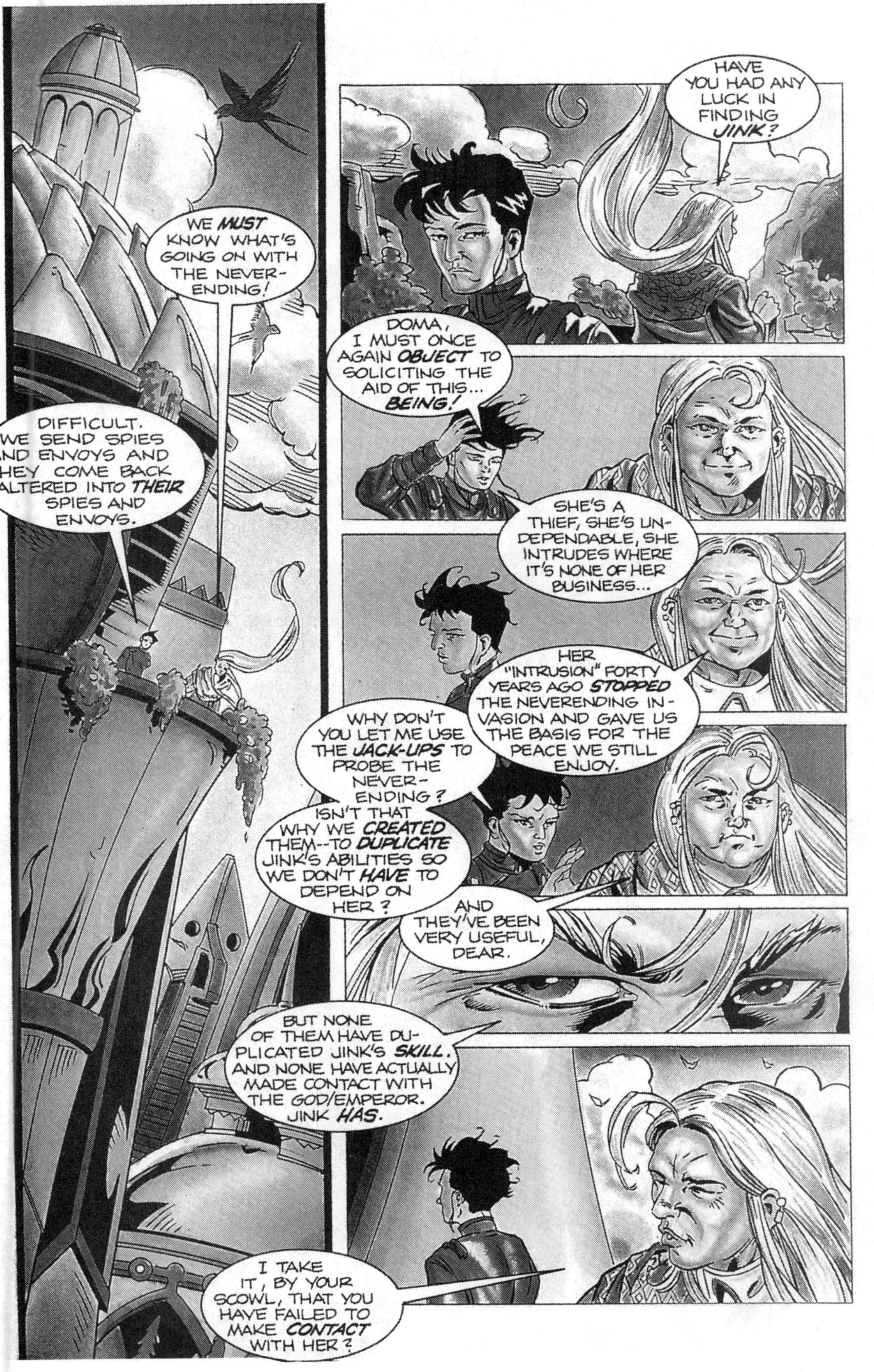
WE MUST KNOW WHAT'S GOING ON WITH THE NEVER-ENDING!
DIFFICULT. WE SEND SPIES AND ENVOYS AND THEY COME BACK ALTERED INTO THEIR SPIES AND ENVOYS.
HAVE YOU HAD ANY LUCK IN FINDING JINK?
DOMA, I MUST ONCE AGAIN OBJECT TO SOLICITING THE AID OF THIS... BEING!
SHE'S A THIEF, SHE'S UN-DEPENDABLE, SHE INTRUDES WHERE IT'S NONE OF HER BUSINESS...
HER "INTRUSION" FORTY YEARS AGO STOPPED THE NEVERENDING IN-VASION AND GAVE US THE BASIS FOR THE PEACE WE STILL ENJOY.
WHY DON'T YOU LET ME USE THE JACK-UPS TO PROBE THE NEVER-ENDING? ISN'T THAT WHY WE CREATED THEM--TO DUPLICATE JINK'S ABILITIES SO WE DON'T HAVE TO DEPEND ON HER?
AND THEY'VE BEEN VERY USEFUL, DEAR.
BUT NONE OF THEM HAVE DU-PLICATED JINK'S SKILL. AND NONE HAVE ACTUALLY MADE CONTACT WITH THE GOD/EMPEROR. JINK HAS.
I TAKE IT, BY YOUR SCOWL, THAT YOU HAVE FAILED TO MAKE CONTACT WITH HER?

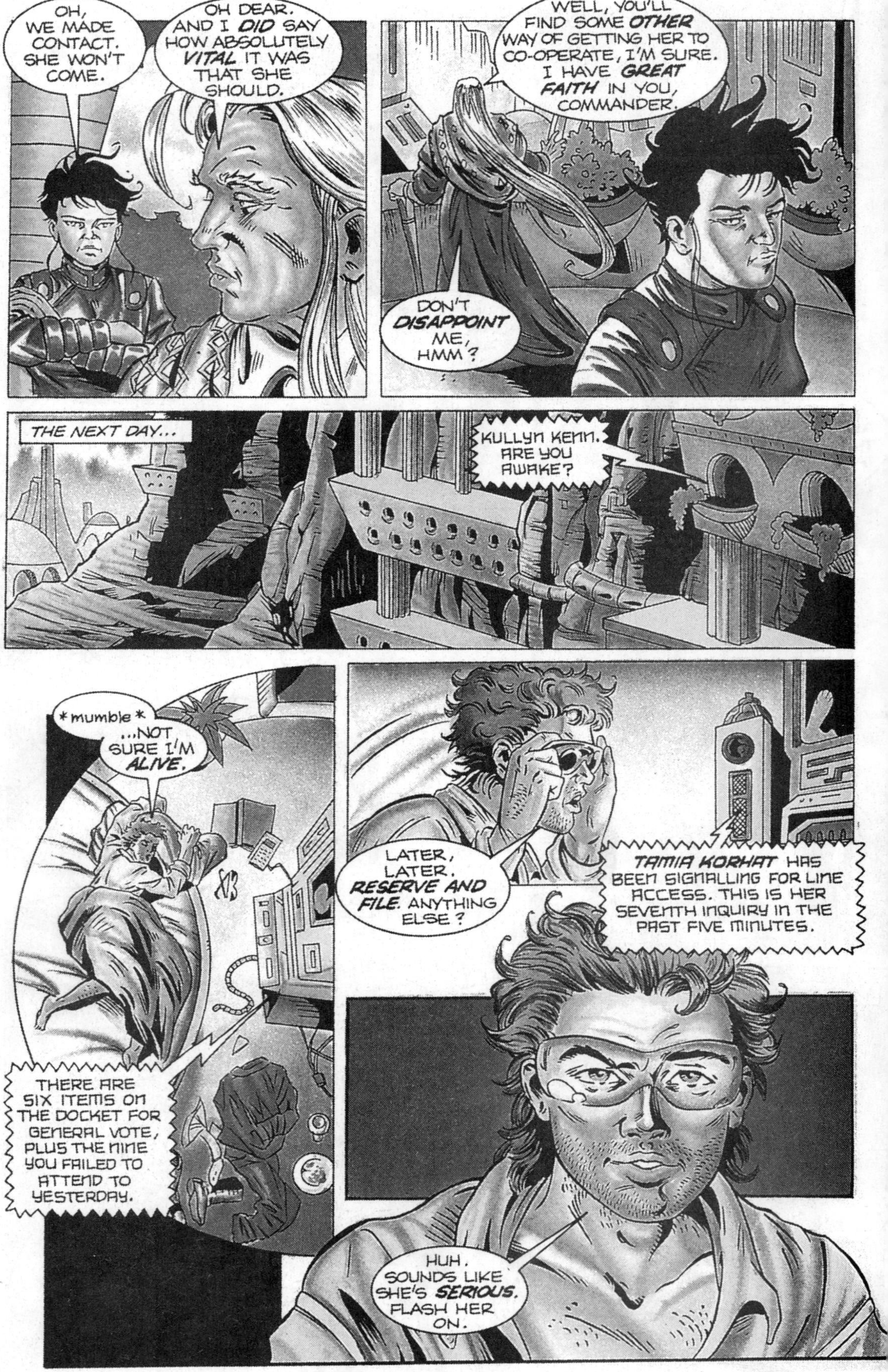
OH, WE MADE CONTACT. SHE WON'T COME.
OH DEAR. AND I DID SAY HOW ABSOLUTELY VITAL IT WAS THAT SHE SHOULD.
WELL, YOU'LL FIND SOME OTHER WAY OF GETTING HER TO CO-OPERATE, I'M SURE. I HAVE GREAT FAITH IN YOU, COMMANDER.
DON'T DISAPPOINT ME, HMM?
THE NEXT DAY...
KULLYN KENN. ARE YOU AWAKE?
mumble ...NOT SURE I'M ALIVE.
THERE ARE SIX ITEMS ON THE DOCKET FOR GENERAL VOTE, PLUS THE NINE YOU FAILED TO ATTEND TO YESTERDAY.
LATER, LATER. RESERVE AND FILE. ANYTHING ELSE?
TAMIA KORHAT HAS BEEN SIGNALLING FOR LINE ACCESS. THIS IS HER SEVENTH INQUIRY IN THE PAST FIVE MINUTES.
HUH. SOUNDS LIKE SHE'S SERIOUS. FLASH HER ON.

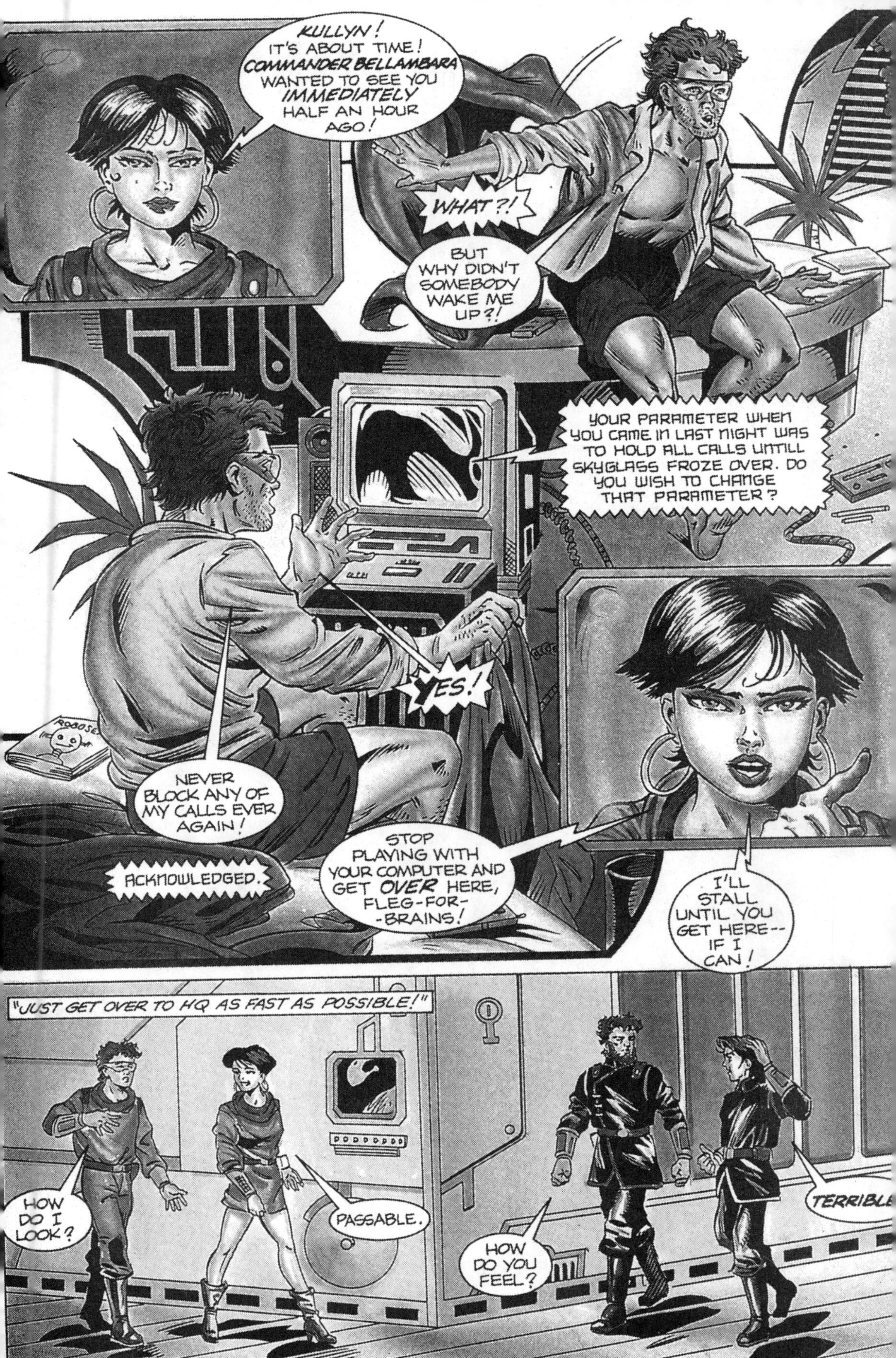
KULLYN! IT'S ABOUT TIME! COMMANDER BELLAMBARA WANTED TO SEE YOU IMMEDIATELY HALF AN HOUR AGO!
WHAT?!
BUT WHY DIDN'T SOMEBODY WAKE ME UP?!
YOUR PARAMETER WHEN YOU CAME IN LAST NIGHT WAS TO HOLD ALL CALLS UNTILL SKYGLASS FROZE OVER. DO YOU WISH TO CHANGE THAT PARAMETER?
YES!
NEVER BLOCK ANY OF MY CALLS EVER AGAIN!
ACKNOWLEDGED.
STOP PLAYING WITH YOUR COMPUTER AND GET OVER HERE, FLEG-FOR-BRAINS!
I'LL STALL UNTIL YOU GET HERE-- IF I CAN!
"JUST GET OVER TO HQ AS FAST AS POSSIBLE!"
HOW DO I LOOK?
PASSABLE.
HOW DO YOU FEEL?
TERRIBLE

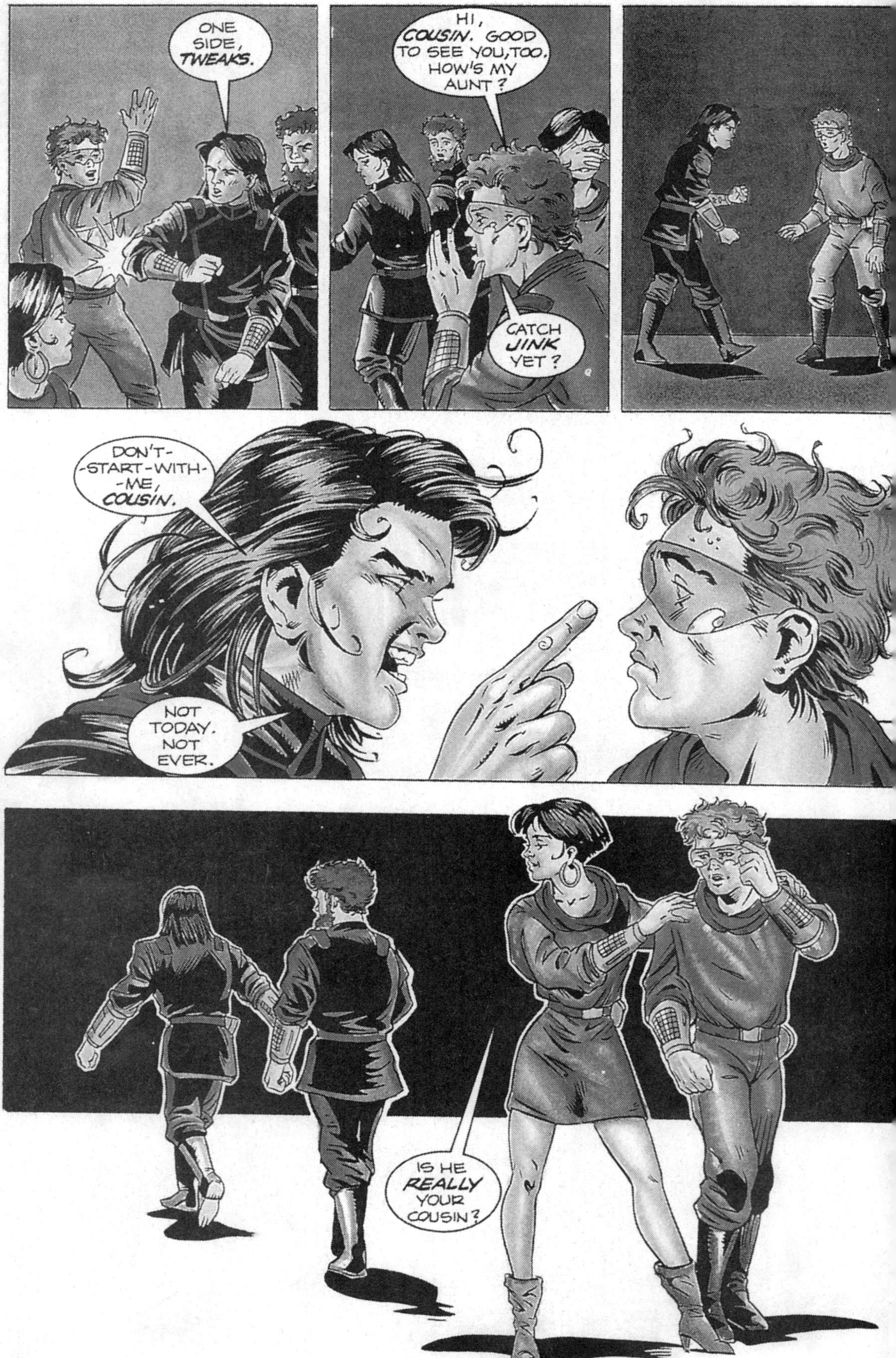
ONE SIDE, TWEAKS.
HI, COUSIN. GOOD TO SEE YOU, TOO. HOW'S MY AUNT?
CATCH JINK YET?
DON'T-START-WITH-ME, COUSIN.
NOT TODAY. NOT EVER.
IS HE REALLY YOUR COUSIN?

OHHH YEAH. THERE'S NO ENEMY LIKE FAMILY. WE'VE LOATHED EACH OTHER SINCE WE WERE GROWING UP. NEVER KNEW EXACTLY WHY...

THE TALENT--PSIONIC ABILITY--SEEMS TO RUN IN OUR FAMILIES. JERROD AND I BOTH TESTED STRONG FOR IT.

THE COMPUTERS WERE ABLE TO "JACK-UP" JERROD TO WHERE HE'S AMONG THE BEST-- IF NOT *THE* BEST-- THE WARD HAS.

MINE GOT ONLY "TWEAKED"-- REAL LOW LEVEL STUFF. AND HE'S NEVER LET ME FORGET IT.

LISTEN, SOME OF THE NICEST PEOPLE ARE "TWEAKS". IF YOU HADN'T TWEAKED OUT, WE MIGHT NEVER HAVE MET. AND *YOU* WOULD'VE MISSED SOMETHING.

I'D [BET]TER GET IN [C]RONE'S OFFICE [BEFOR]E SHE ASSEMBLES [A FI]RING SQUAD [T]O LOOK FOR ME.

WELL, WELL.

AH... I BELIEVE YOU SENT FOR ME, COMMANDER?

GET ...*IN*.

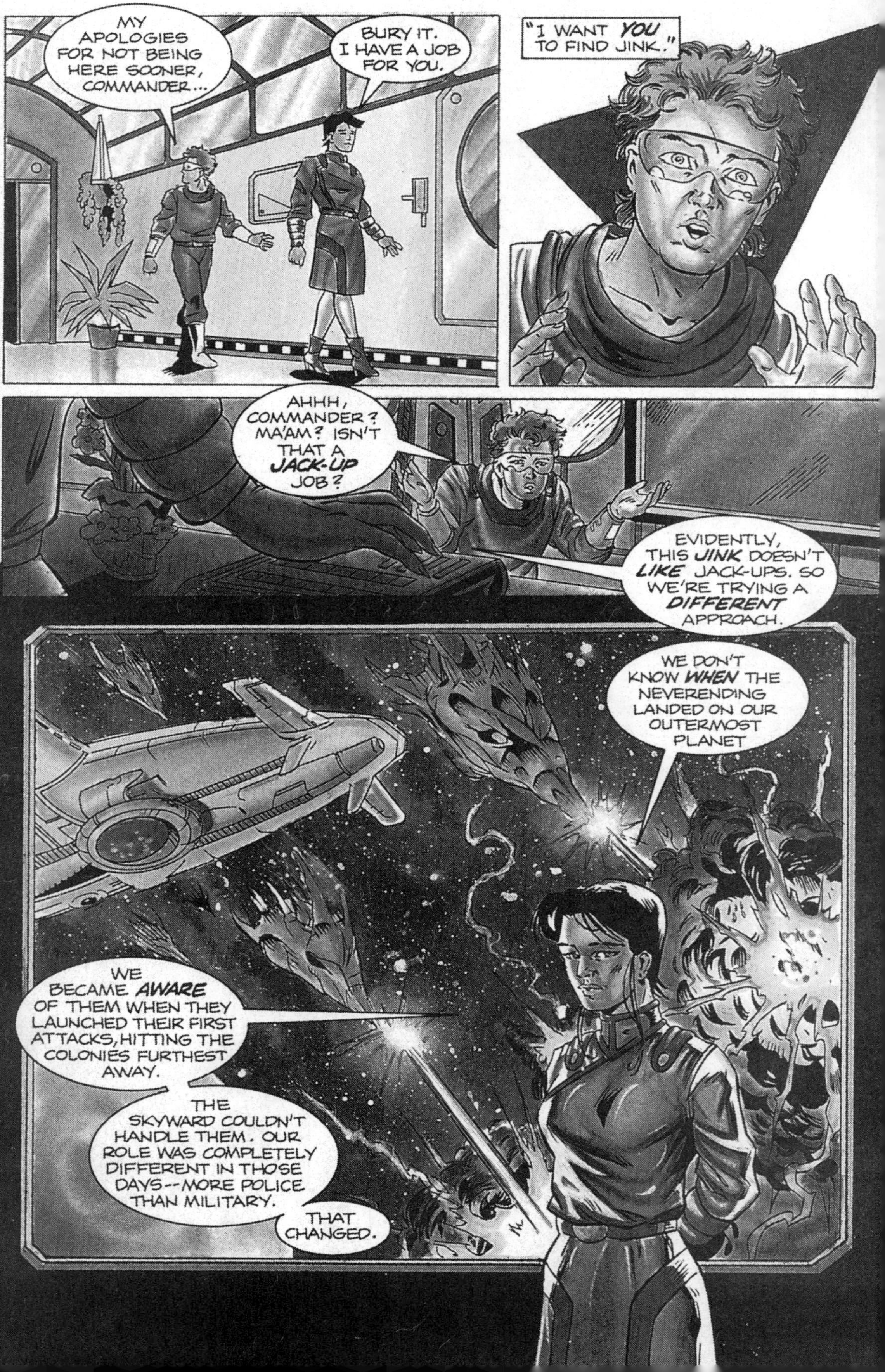

MY APOLOGIES FOR NOT BEING HERE SOONER, COMMANDER...
BURY IT. I HAVE A JOB FOR YOU.
"I WANT YOU TO FIND JINK."
AHHH, COMMANDER? MA'AM? ISN'T THAT A JACK-UP JOB?
EVIDENTLY, THIS JINK DOESN'T LIKE JACK-UPS. SO WE'RE TRYING A DIFFERENT APPROACH.
WE DON'T KNOW WHEN THE NEVERENDING LANDED ON OUR OUTERMOST PLANET
WE BECAME AWARE OF THEM WHEN THEY LAUNCHED THEIR FIRST ATTACKS, HITTING THE COLONIES FURTHEST AWAY.
THE SKYWARD COULDN'T HANDLE THEM. OUR ROLE WAS COMPLETELY DIFFERENT IN THOSE DAYS--MORE POLICE THAN MILITARY.
THAT CHANGED.

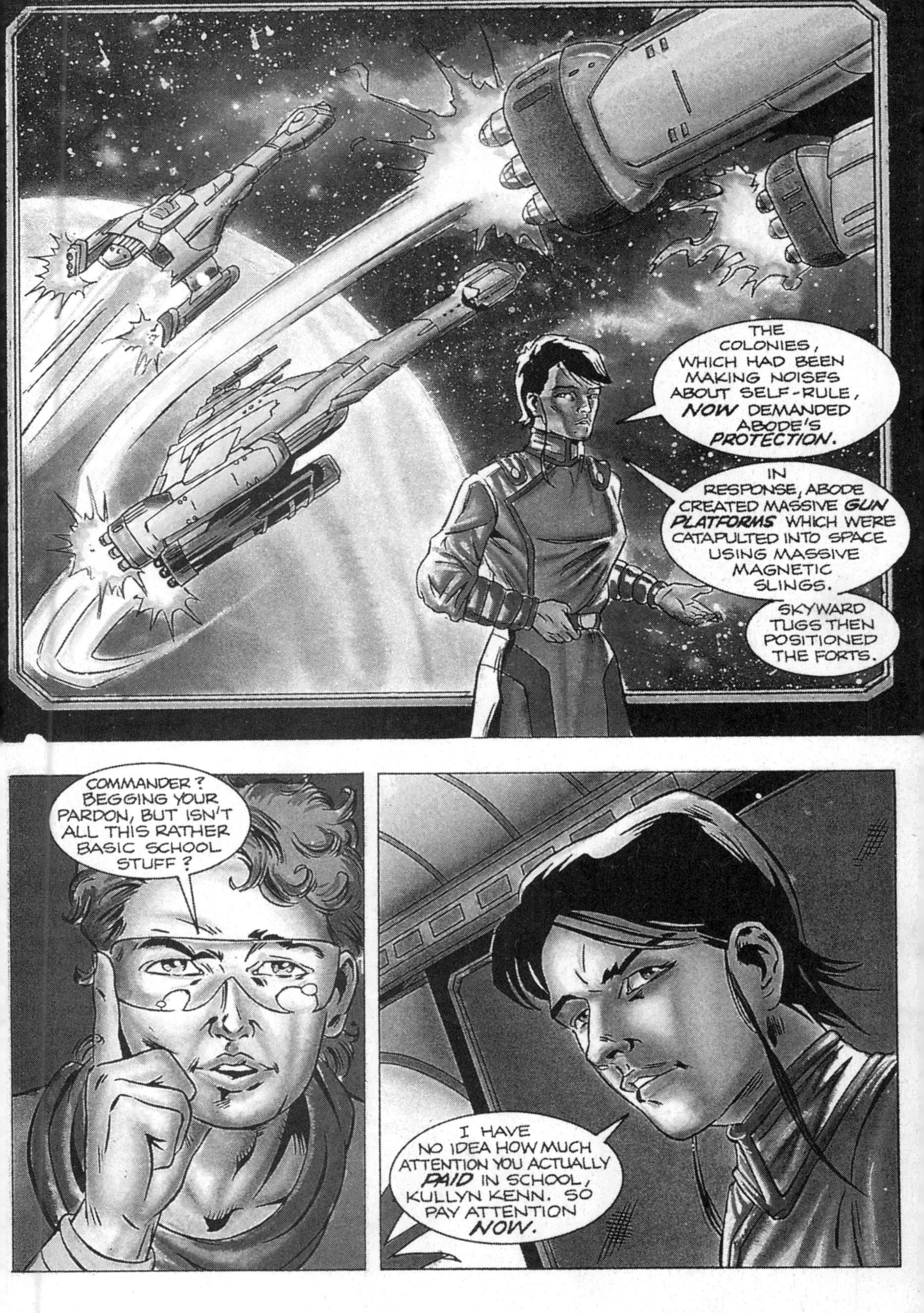
THE COLONIES, WHICH HAD BEEN MAKING NOISES ABOUT SELF-RULE, NOW DEMANDED ABODE'S PROTECTION.
IN RESPONSE, ABODE CREATED MASSIVE GUN PLATFORMS WHICH WERE CATAPULTED INTO SPACE USING MASSIVE MAGNETIC SLINGS.
SKYWARD TUGS THEN POSITIONED THE FORTS.
COMMANDER? BEGGING YOUR PARDON, BUT ISN'T ALL THIS RATHER BASIC SCHOOL STUFF?
I HAVE NO IDEA HOW MUCH ATTENTION YOU ACTUALLY PAID IN SCHOOL, KULLYN KENN. SO PAY ATTENTION NOW.

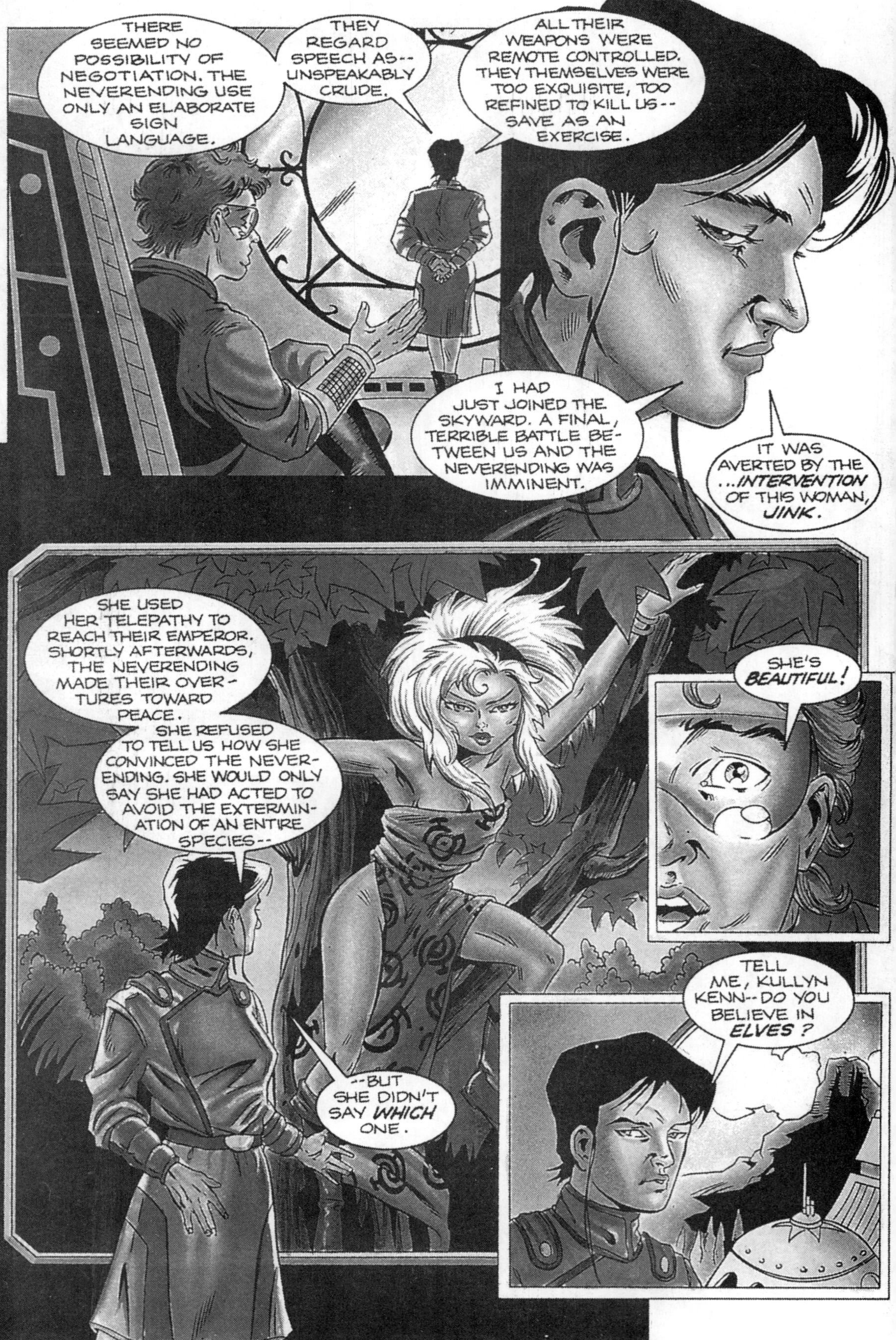

THERE SEEMED NO POSSIBILITY OF NEGOTIATION. THE NEVERENDING USE ONLY AN ELABORATE SIGN LANGUAGE.
THEY REGARD SPEECH AS-- UNSPEAKABLY CRUDE.
ALL THEIR WEAPONS WERE REMOTE CONTROLLED. THEY THEMSELVES WERE TOO EXQUISITE, TOO REFINED TO KILL US-- SAVE AS AN EXERCISE.
I HAD JUST JOINED THE SKYWARD. A FINAL, TERRIBLE BATTLE BETWEEN US AND THE NEVERENDING WAS IMMINENT.
IT WAS AVERTED BY THE ...INTERVENTION OF THIS WOMAN, JINK.
SHE USED HER TELEPATHY TO REACH THEIR EMPEROR. SHORTLY AFTERWARDS, THE NEVERENDING MADE THEIR OVERTURES TOWARD PEACE.
SHE REFUSED TO TELL US HOW SHE CONVINCED THE NEVERENDING. SHE WOULD ONLY SAY SHE HAD ACTED TO AVOID THE EXTERMINATION OF AN ENTIRE SPECIES--
SHE'S BEAUTIFUL!
--BUT SHE DIDN'T SAY WHICH ONE.
TELL ME, KULLYN KENN--DO YOU BELIEVE IN ELVES?

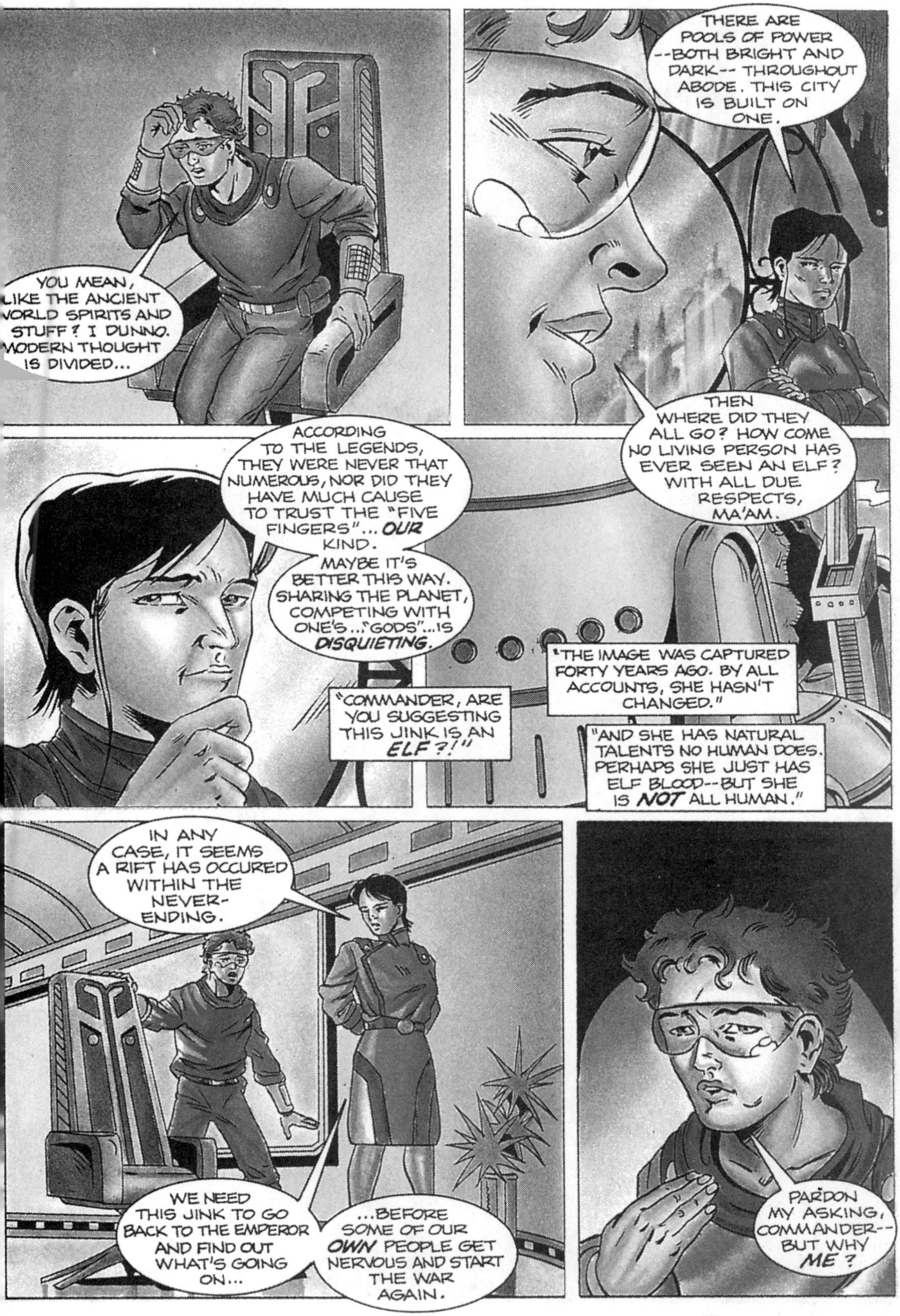
YOU MEAN, LIKE THE ANCIENT WORLD SPIRITS AND STUFF? I DUNNO. MODERN THOUGHT IS DIVIDED...
THERE ARE POOLS OF POWER --BOTH BRIGHT AND DARK-- THROUGHOUT ABODE. THIS CITY IS BUILT ON ONE.
THEN WHERE DID THEY ALL GO? HOW COME NO LIVING PERSON HAS EVER SEEN AN ELF? WITH ALL DUE RESPECTS, MA'AM.
ACCORDING TO THE LEGENDS, THEY WERE NEVER THAT NUMEROUS, NOR DID THEY HAVE MUCH CAUSE TO TRUST THE "FIVE FINGERS"... OUR KIND.
MAYBE IT'S BETTER THIS WAY. SHARING THE PLANET, COMPETING WITH ONE'S..."GODS"...IS DISQUIETING.
"COMMANDER, ARE YOU SUGGESTING THIS JINK IS AN ELF?!"
"THE IMAGE WAS CAPTURED FORTY YEARS AGO. BY ALL ACCOUNTS, SHE HASN'T CHANGED."
"AND SHE HAS NATURAL TALENTS NO HUMAN DOES. PERHAPS SHE JUST HAS ELF BLOOD--BUT SHE IS NOT ALL HUMAN."
IN ANY CASE, IT SEEMS A RIFT HAS OCCURED WITHIN THE NEVER-ENDING.
WE NEED THIS JINK TO GO BACK TO THE EMPEROR AND FIND OUT WHAT'S GOING ON...
...BEFORE SOME OF OUR OWN PEOPLE GET NERVOUS AND START THE WAR AGAIN.
PARDON MY ASKING, COMMANDER-- BUT WHY ME?

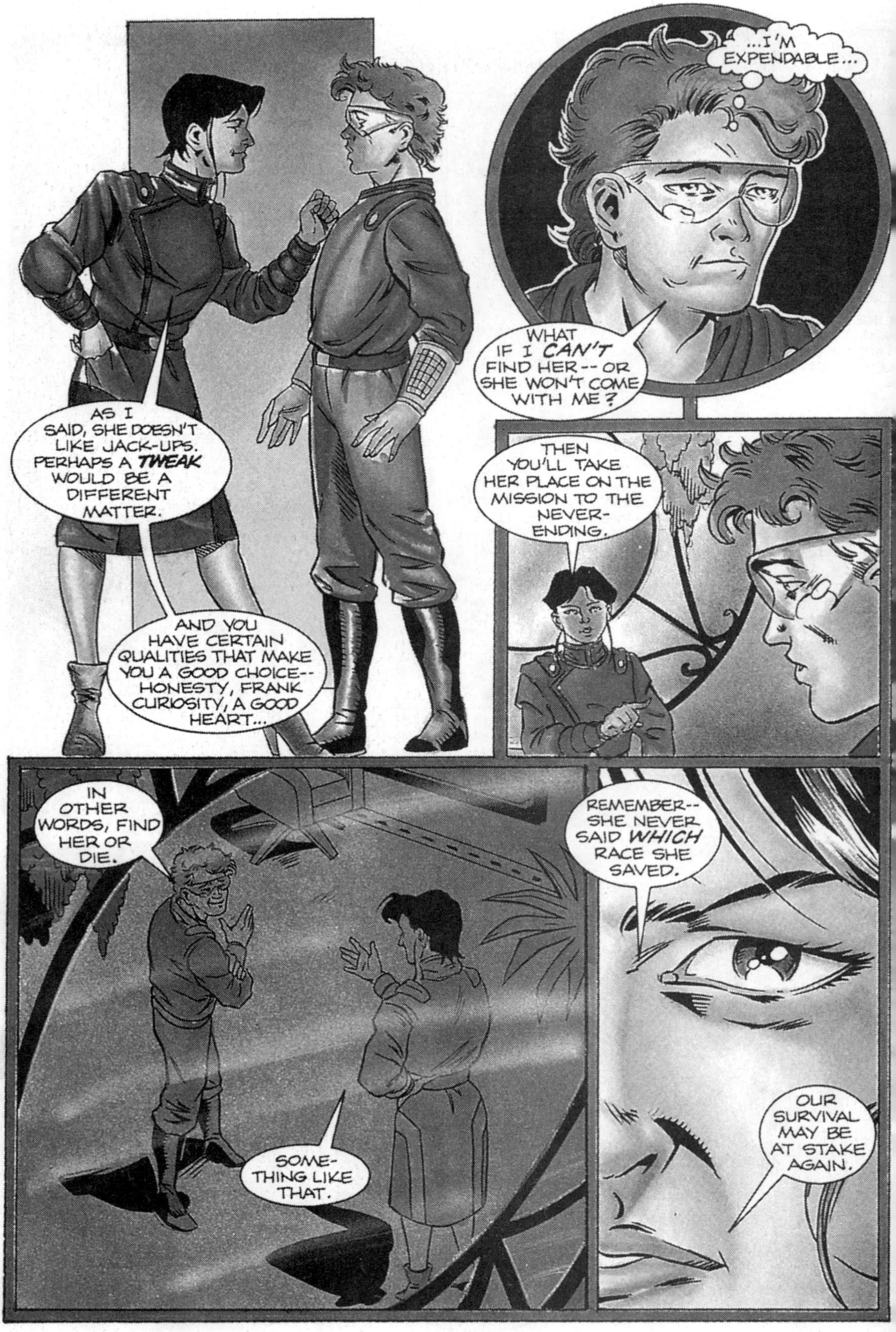
AS I SAID, SHE DOESN'T LIKE JACK-UPS. PERHAPS A TWEAK WOULD BE A DIFFERENT MATTER.
AND YOU HAVE CERTAIN QUALITIES THAT MAKE YOU A GOOD CHOICE-- HONESTY, FRANK CURIOSITY, A GOOD HEART...
...I'M EXPENDABLE...
WHAT IF I CAN'T FIND HER-- OR SHE WON'T COME WITH ME?
THEN YOU'LL TAKE HER PLACE ON THE MISSION TO THE NEVER-ENDING.
IN OTHER WORDS, FIND HER OR DIE.
SOME-THING LIKE THAT.
REMEMBER-- SHE NEVER SAID WHICH RACE SHE SAVED.
OUR SURVIVAL MAY BE AT STAKE AGAIN.

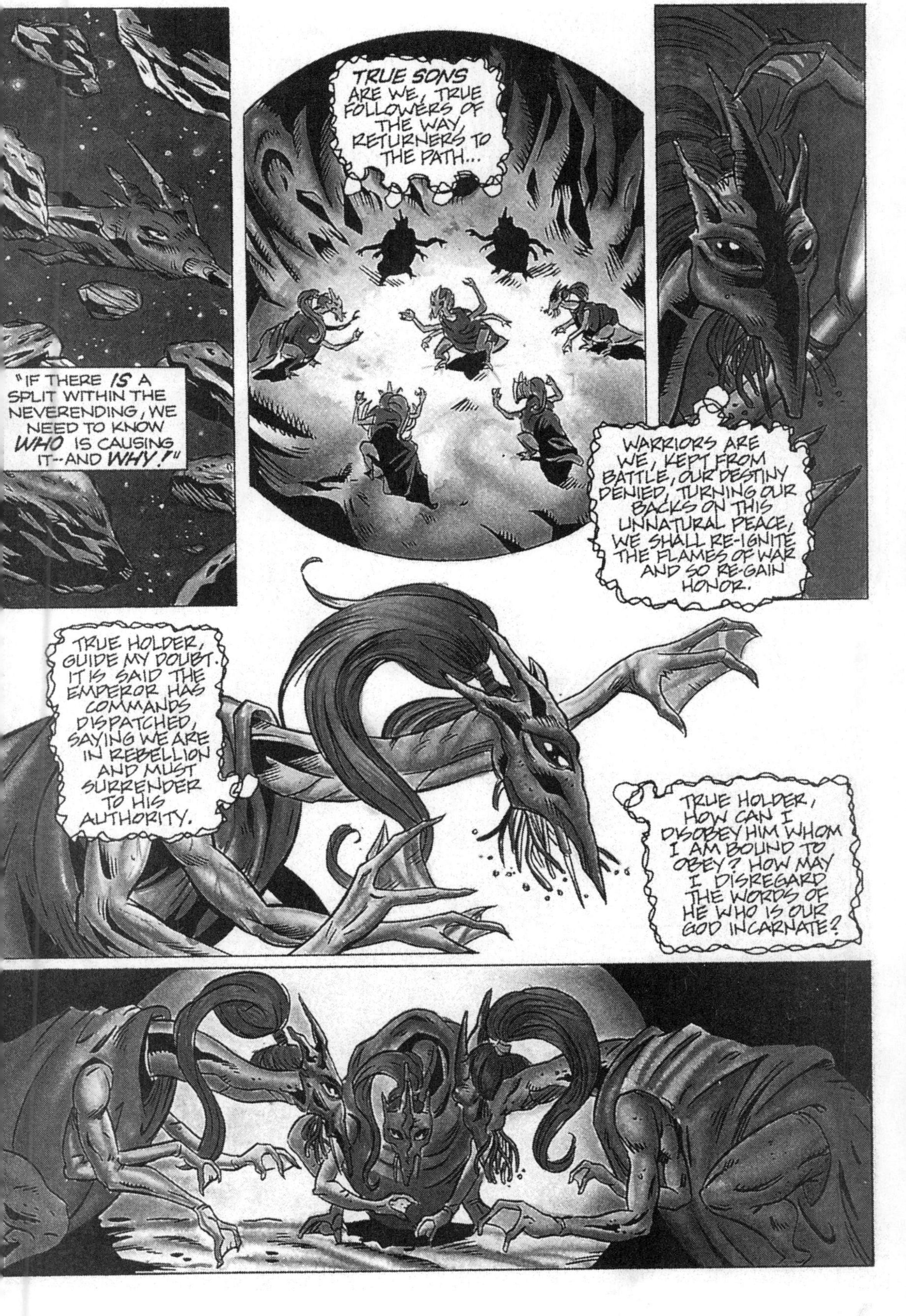

"IF THERE IS A SPLIT WITHIN THE NEVERENDING, WE NEED TO KNOW WHO IS CAUSING IT--AND WHY!"
TRUE SONS ARE WE, TRUE FOLLOWERS OF THE WAY, RETURNERS TO THE PATH...
WARRIORS ARE WE, KEPT FROM BATTLE, OUR DESTINY DENIED, TURNING OUR BACKS ON THIS UNNATURAL PEACE, WE SHALL RE-IGNITE THE FLAMES OF WAR AND SO RE-GAIN HONOR.
TRUE HOLDER, GUIDE MY DOUBT. IT IS SAID THE EMPEROR HAS COMMANDS DISPATCHED, SAYING WE ARE IN REBELLION AND MUST SURRENDER TO HIS AUTHORITY.
TRUE HOLDER, HOW CAN I DISOBEY HIM WHOM I AM BOUND TO OBEY? HOW MAY I DISREGARD THE WORDS OF HE WHO IS OUR GOD INCARNATE?

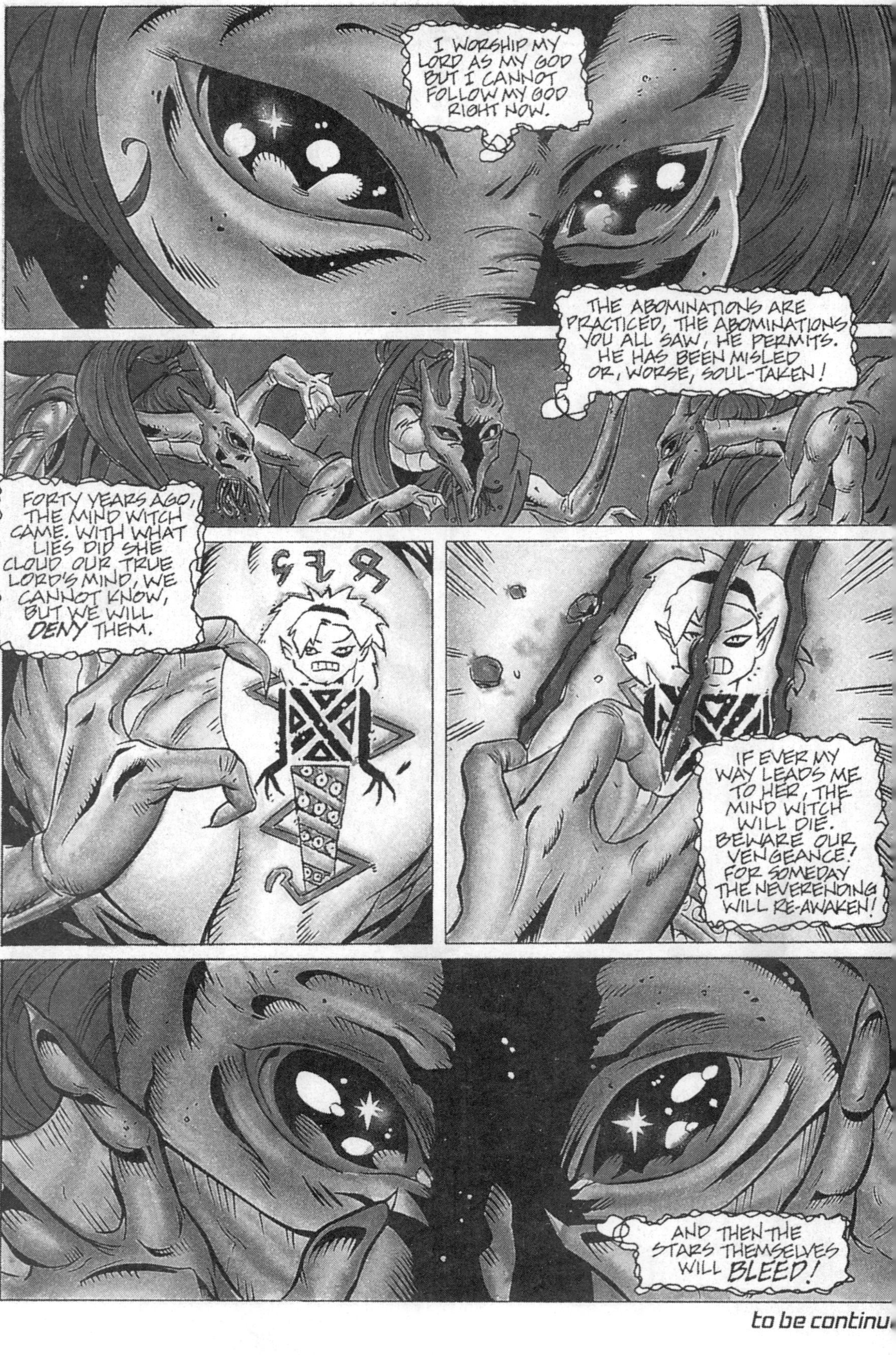
I WORSHIP MY LORD AS MY GOD BUT I CANNOT FOLLOW MY GOD RIGHT NOW.
THE ABOMINATIONS ARE PRACTICED, THE ABOMINATIONS YOU ALL SAW, HE PERMITS. HE HAS BEEN MISLED OR, WORSE, SOUL-TAKEN!
FORTY YEARS AGO, THE MIND WITCH CAME. WITH WHAT LIES DID SHE CLOUD OUR TRUE LORD'S MIND, WE CANNOT KNOW, BUT WE WILL DENY THEM.
IF EVER MY WAY LEADS ME TO HER, THE MIND WITCH WILL DIE. BEWARE OUR VENGEANCE! FOR SOMEDAY THE NEVERENDING WILL RE-AWAKEN!
AND THEN THE STARS THEMSELVES WILL BLEED!

to be continu

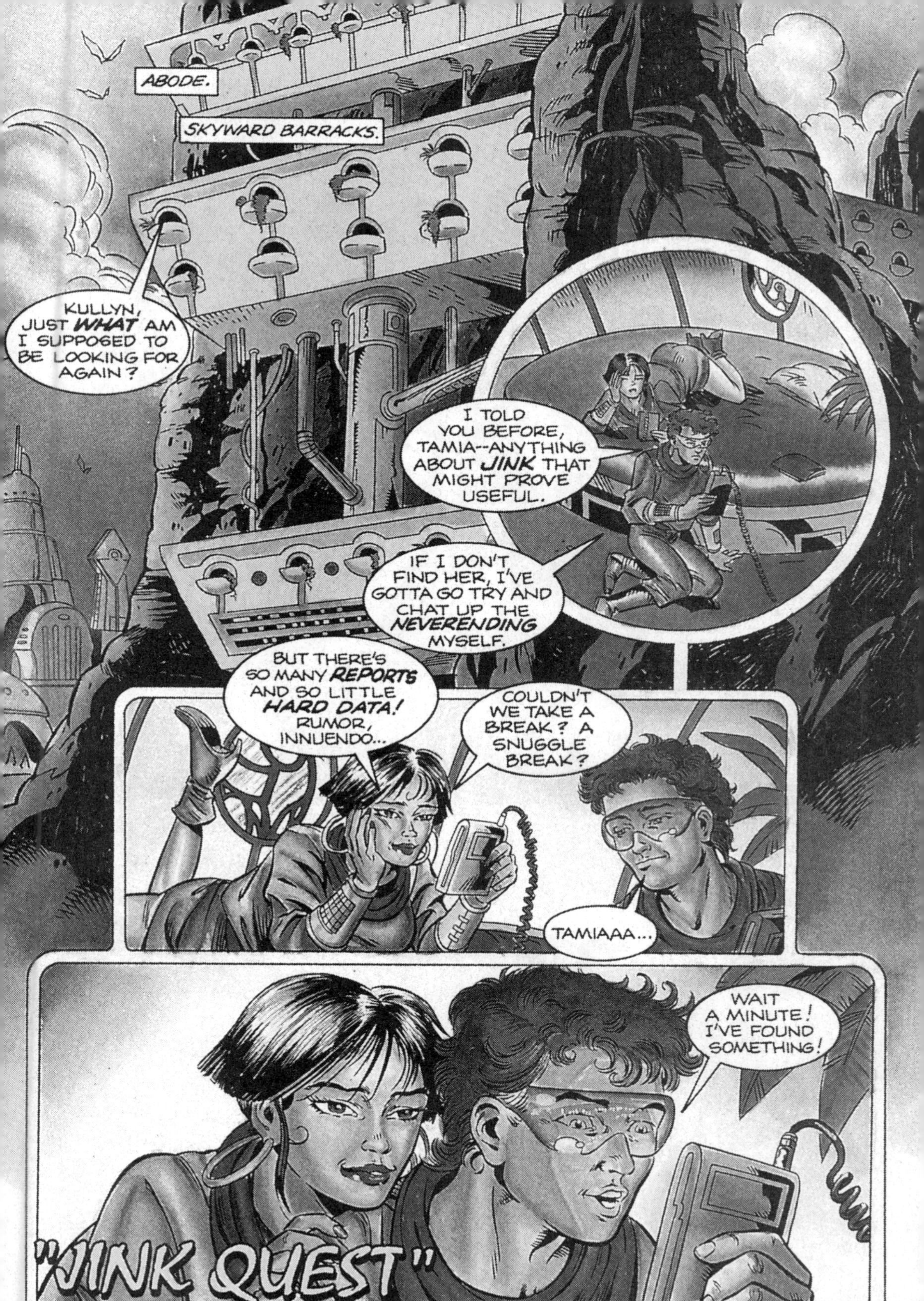
ABODE.
SKYWARD BARRACKS.
KULLYN, JUST WHAT AM I SUPPOSED TO BE LOOKING FOR AGAIN?
I TOLD YOU BEFORE, TAMIA--ANYTHING ABOUT JINK THAT MIGHT PROVE USEFUL.
IF I DON'T FIND HER, I'VE GOTTA GO TRY AND CHAT UP THE NEVERENDING MYSELF.
BUT THERE'S SO MANY REPORTS AND SO LITTLE HARD DATA! RUMOR, INNUENDO...
COULDN'T WE TAKE A BREAK? A SNUGGLE BREAK?
TAMIAAA...
WAIT A MINUTE! I'VE FOUND SOMETHING!
"JINK QUEST"

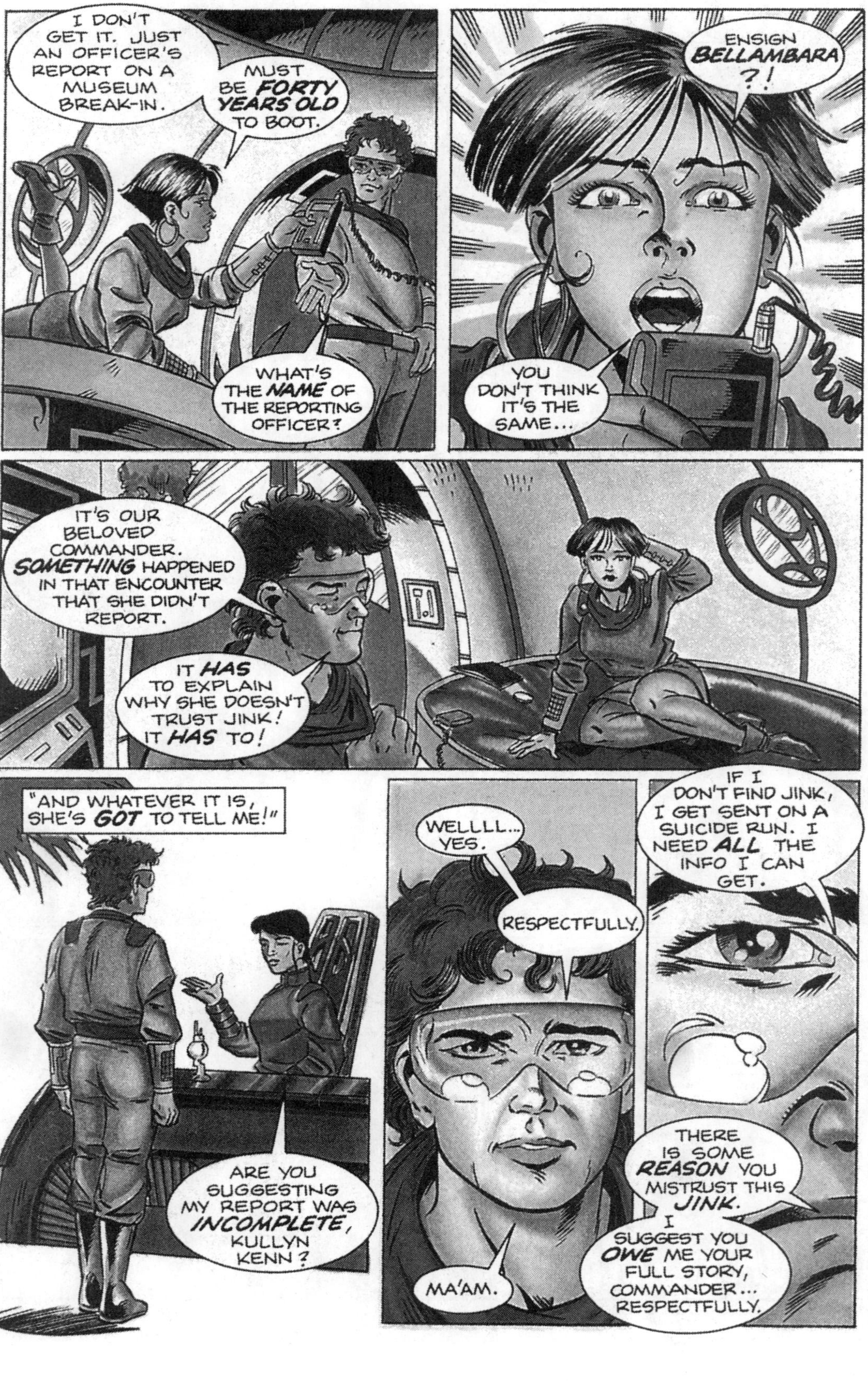
I DON'T GET IT. JUST AN OFFICER'S REPORT ON A MUSEUM BREAK-IN.
MUST BE **FORTY YEARS OLD** TO BOOT.
WHAT'S THE **NAME** OF THE REPORTING OFFICER?
ENSIGN **BELLAMBARA** ?!
YOU DON'T THINK IT'S THE SAME...
IT'S OUR BELOVED COMMANDER. **SOMETHING** HAPPENED IN THAT ENCOUNTER THAT SHE DIDN'T REPORT.
IT **HAS** TO EXPLAIN WHY SHE DOESN'T TRUST JINK! IT **HAS** TO!
"AND WHATEVER IT IS, SHE'S **GOT** TO TELL ME!"
ARE YOU SUGGESTING MY REPORT WAS **INCOMPLETE**, KULLYN KENN?
WELLLL... YES.
RESPECTFULLY.
MA'AM.
IF I DON'T FIND JINK, I GET SENT ON A SUICIDE RUN. I NEED **ALL** THE INFO I CAN GET.
THERE IS SOME **REASON** YOU MISTRUST THIS **JINK**.
I SUGGEST YOU **OWE** ME YOUR FULL STORY, COMMANDER... RESPECTFULLY.

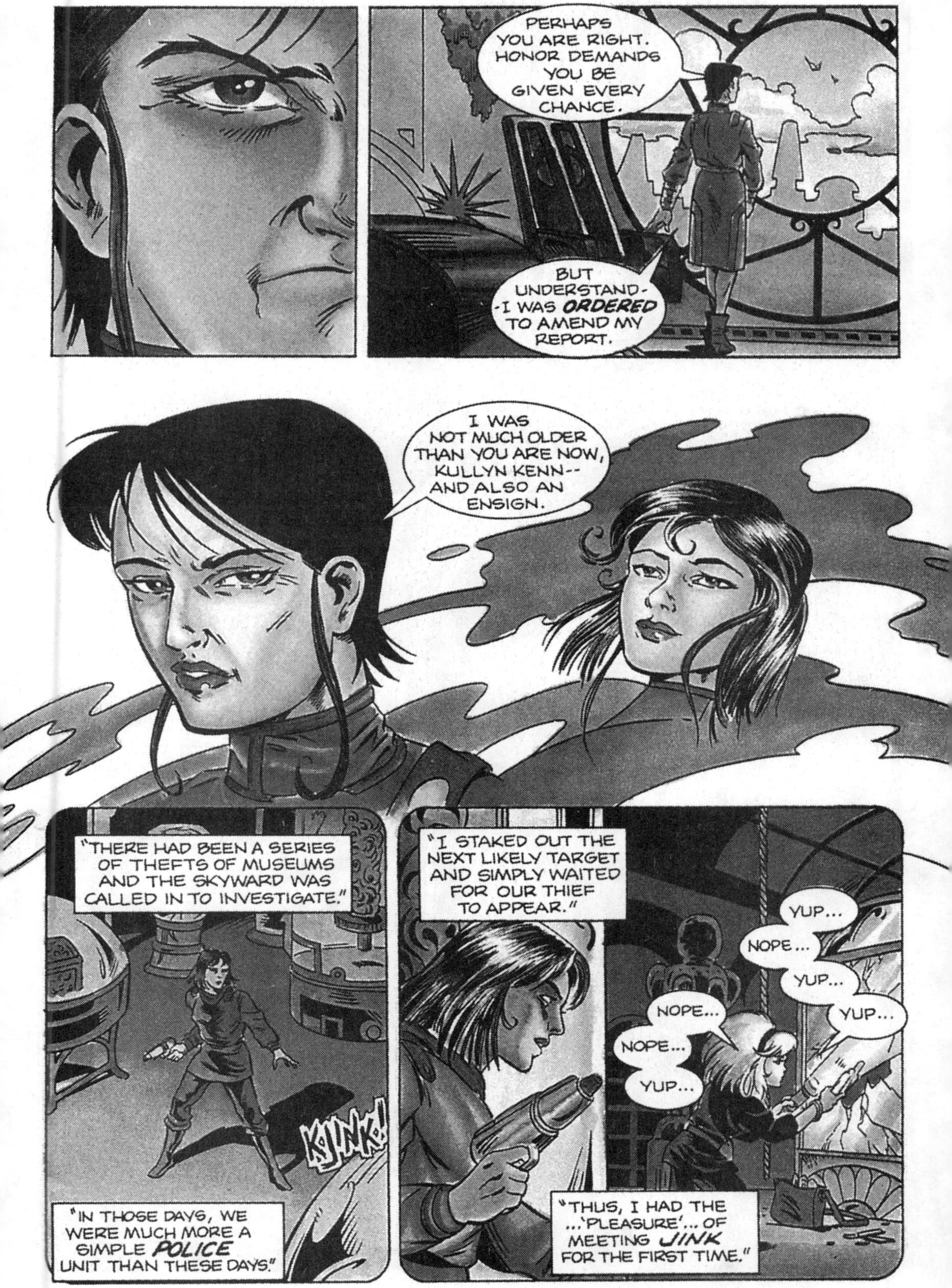
PERHAPS YOU ARE RIGHT. HONOR DEMANDS YOU BE GIVEN EVERY CHANCE.
BUT UNDERSTAND- -I WAS ORDERED TO AMEND MY REPORT.
I WAS NOT MUCH OLDER THAN YOU ARE NOW, KULLYN KENN-- AND ALSO AN ENSIGN.
"THERE HAD BEEN A SERIES OF THEFTS OF MUSEUMS AND THE SKYWARD WAS CALLED IN TO INVESTIGATE."
KSJINK!
"IN THOSE DAYS, WE WERE MUCH MORE A SIMPLE POLICE UNIT THAN THESE DAYS."
"I STAKED OUT THE NEXT LIKELY TARGET AND SIMPLY WAITED FOR OUR THIEF TO APPEAR."
YUP...
NOPE...
YUP...
YUP...
NOPE...
NOPE...
YUP...
"THUS, I HAD THE ...'PLEASURE'... OF MEETING JINK FOR THE FIRST TIME."

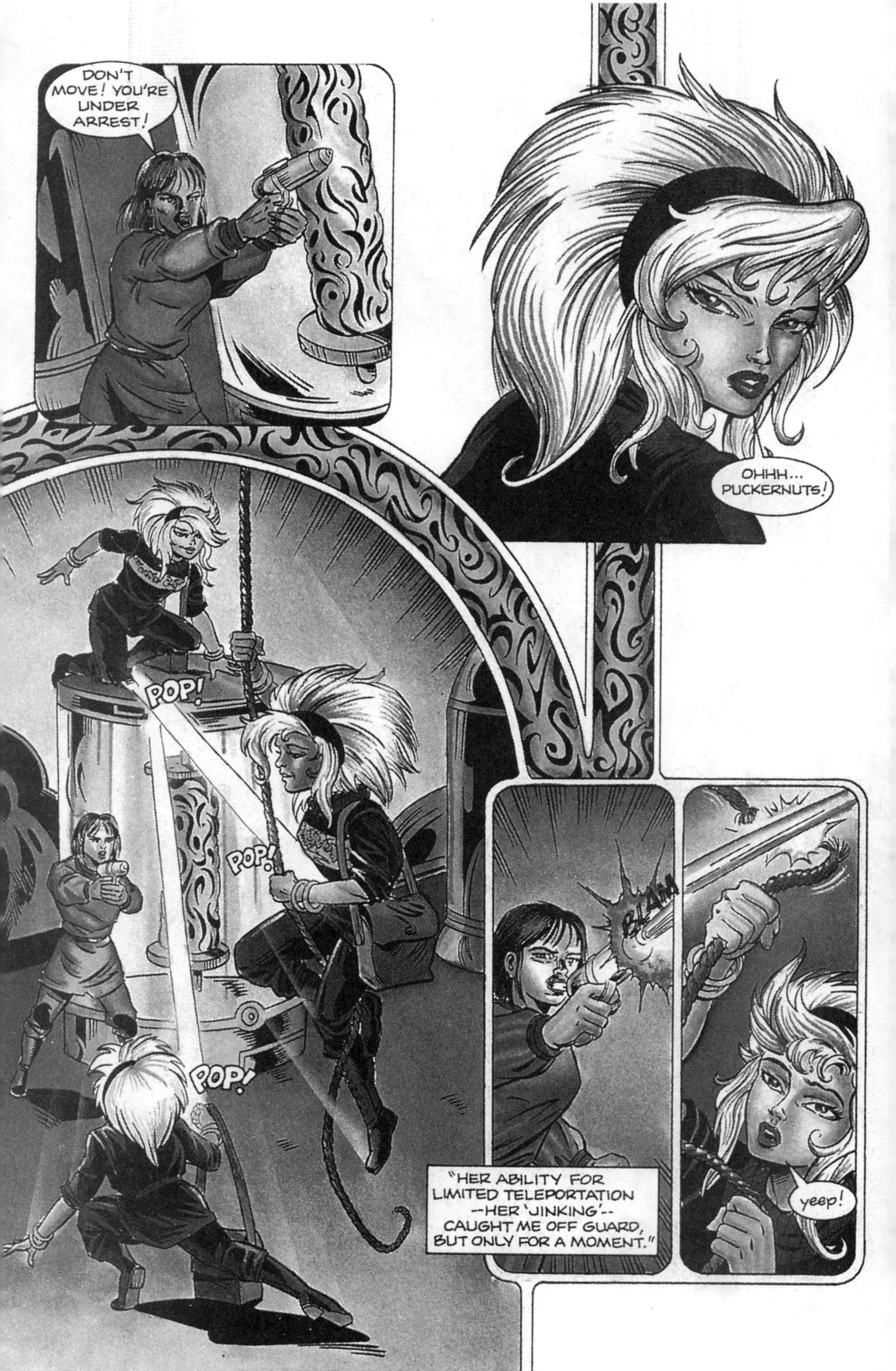
DON'T MOVE! YOU'RE UNDER ARREST!
OHHH... PUCKERNUTS!
POP!
POP!
POP!
BLAM
"HER ABILITY FOR LIMITED TELEPORTATION --HER 'JINKING'-- CAUGHT ME OFF GUARD, BUT ONLY FOR A MOMENT."
yeep!

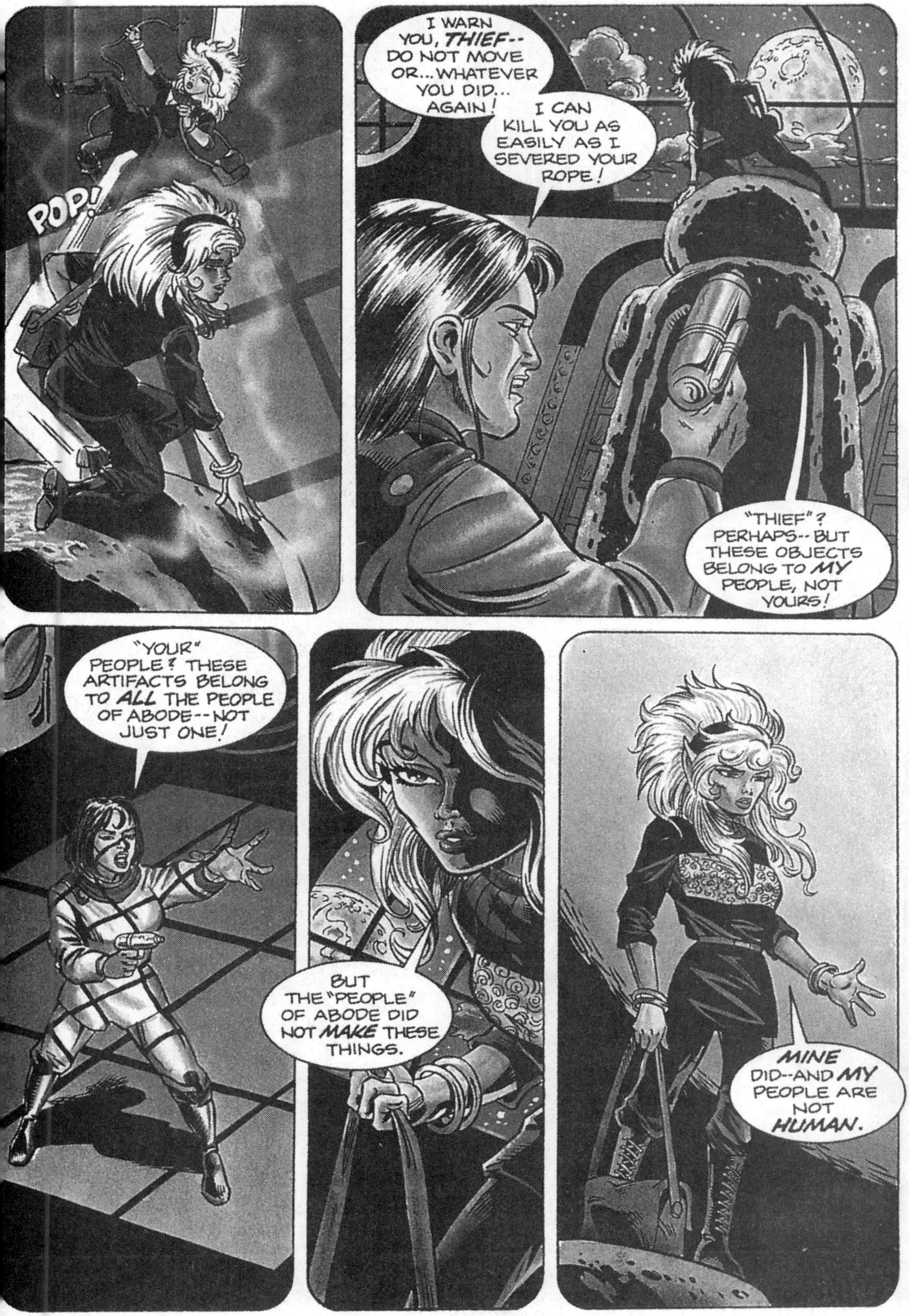
POP!
I WARN YOU, THIEF-- DO NOT MOVE OR... WHATEVER YOU DID... AGAIN!
I CAN KILL YOU AS EASILY AS I SEVERED YOUR ROPE!
"THIEF"? PERHAPS-- BUT THESE OBJECTS BELONG TO MY PEOPLE, NOT YOURS!
"YOUR" PEOPLE? THESE ARTIFACTS BELONG TO ALL THE PEOPLE OF ABODE--NOT JUST ONE!
BUT THE "PEOPLE" OF ABODE DID NOT MAKE THESE THINGS.
MINE DID--AND MY PEOPLE ARE NOT HUMAN.

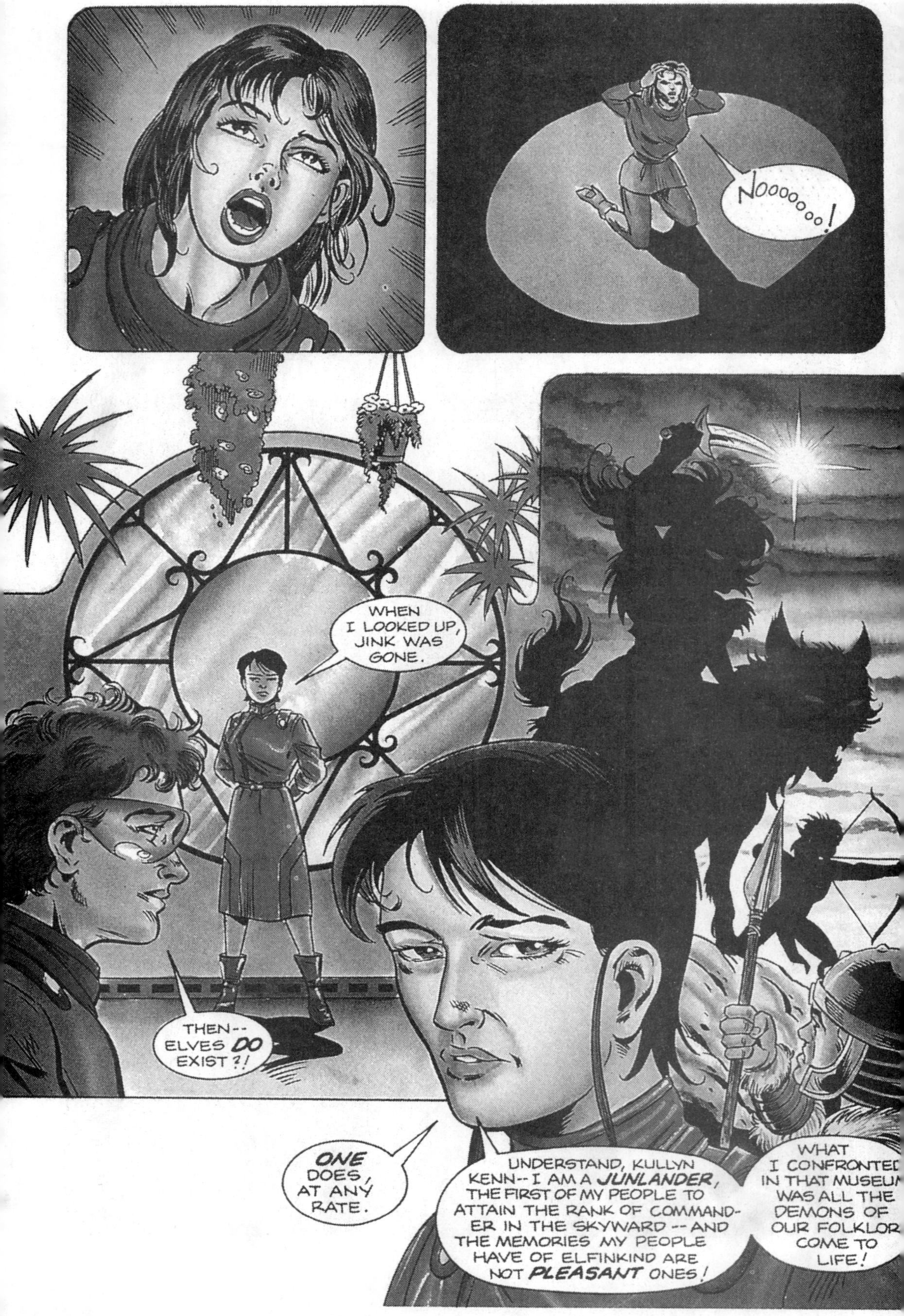
NOOOOOOO!
WHEN I LOOKED UP, JINK WAS GONE.
THEN-- ELVES DO EXIST ?!
ONE DOES, AT ANY RATE.
UNDERSTAND, KULLYN KENN-- I AM A JUNLANDER, THE FIRST OF MY PEOPLE TO ATTAIN THE RANK OF COMMANDER IN THE SKYWARD -- AND THE MEMORIES MY PEOPLE HAVE OF ELFINKIND ARE NOT PLEASANT ONES!
WHAT I CONFRONTED IN THAT MUSEUM WAS ALL THE DEMONS OF OUR FOLKLORE COME TO LIFE!

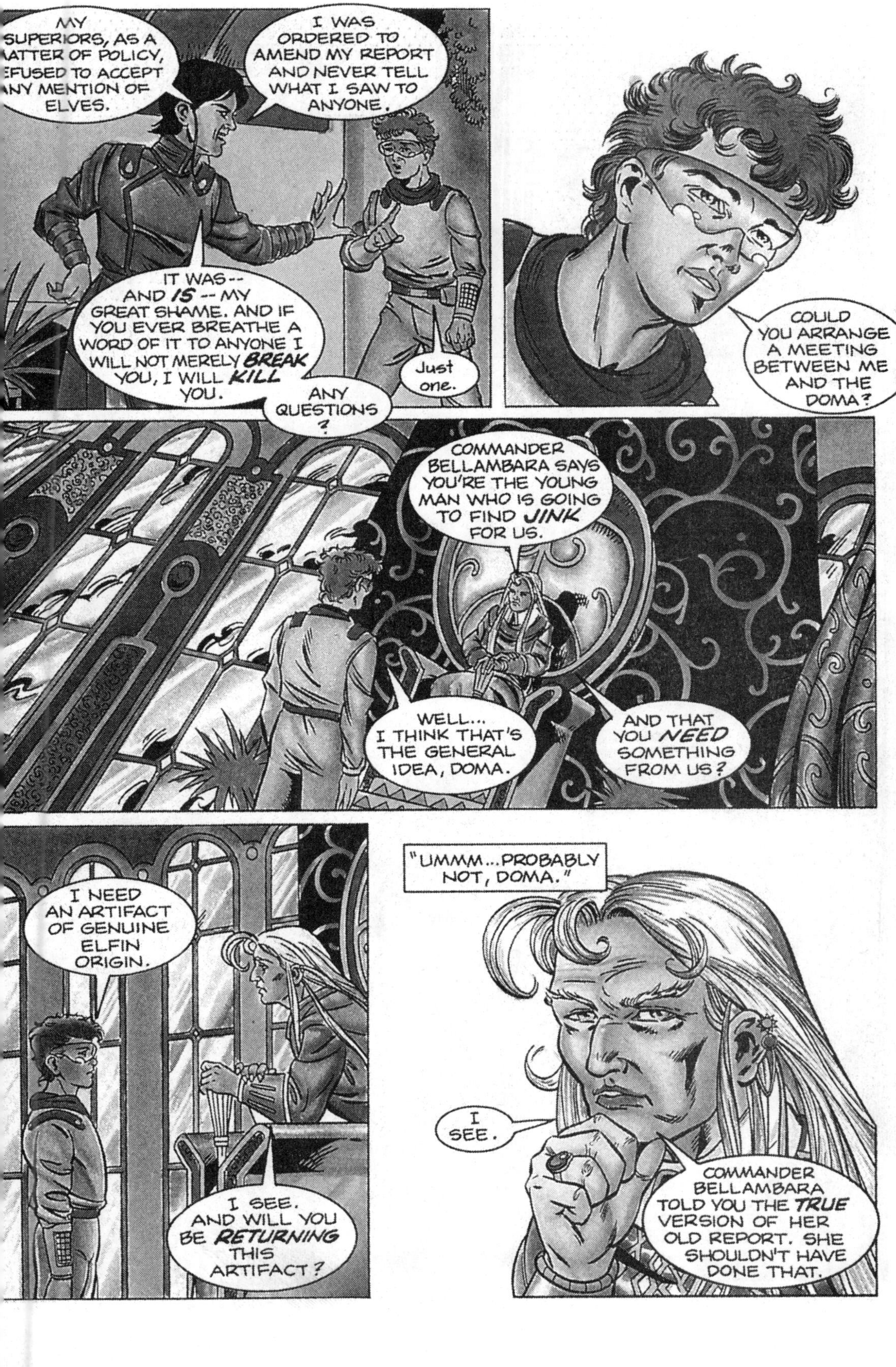
MY SUPERIORS, AS A ATTER OF POLICY, EFUSED TO ACCEPT NY MENTION OF ELVES.
I WAS ORDERED TO AMEND MY REPORT AND NEVER TELL WHAT I SAW TO ANYONE.
IT WAS-- AND *IS* -- MY GREAT SHAME. AND IF YOU EVER BREATHE A WORD OF IT TO ANYONE I WILL NOT MERELY *BREAK* YOU, I WILL *KILL* YOU.
ANY QUESTIONS ?
Just one.
COULD YOU ARRANGE A MEETING BETWEEN ME AND THE DOMA ?
COMMANDER BELLAMBARA SAYS YOU'RE THE YOUNG MAN WHO IS GOING TO FIND *JINK* FOR US.
WELL... I THINK THAT'S THE GENERAL IDEA, DOMA.
AND THAT YOU *NEED* SOMETHING FROM US ?
I NEED AN ARTIFACT OF GENUINE ELFIN ORIGIN.
I SEE. AND WILL YOU BE *RETURNING* THIS ARTIFACT ?
"UMMM... PROBABLY NOT, DOMA."
I SEE.
COMMANDER BELLAMBARA TOLD YOU THE *TRUE* VERSION OF HER OLD REPORT. SHE SHOULDN'T HAVE DONE THAT.

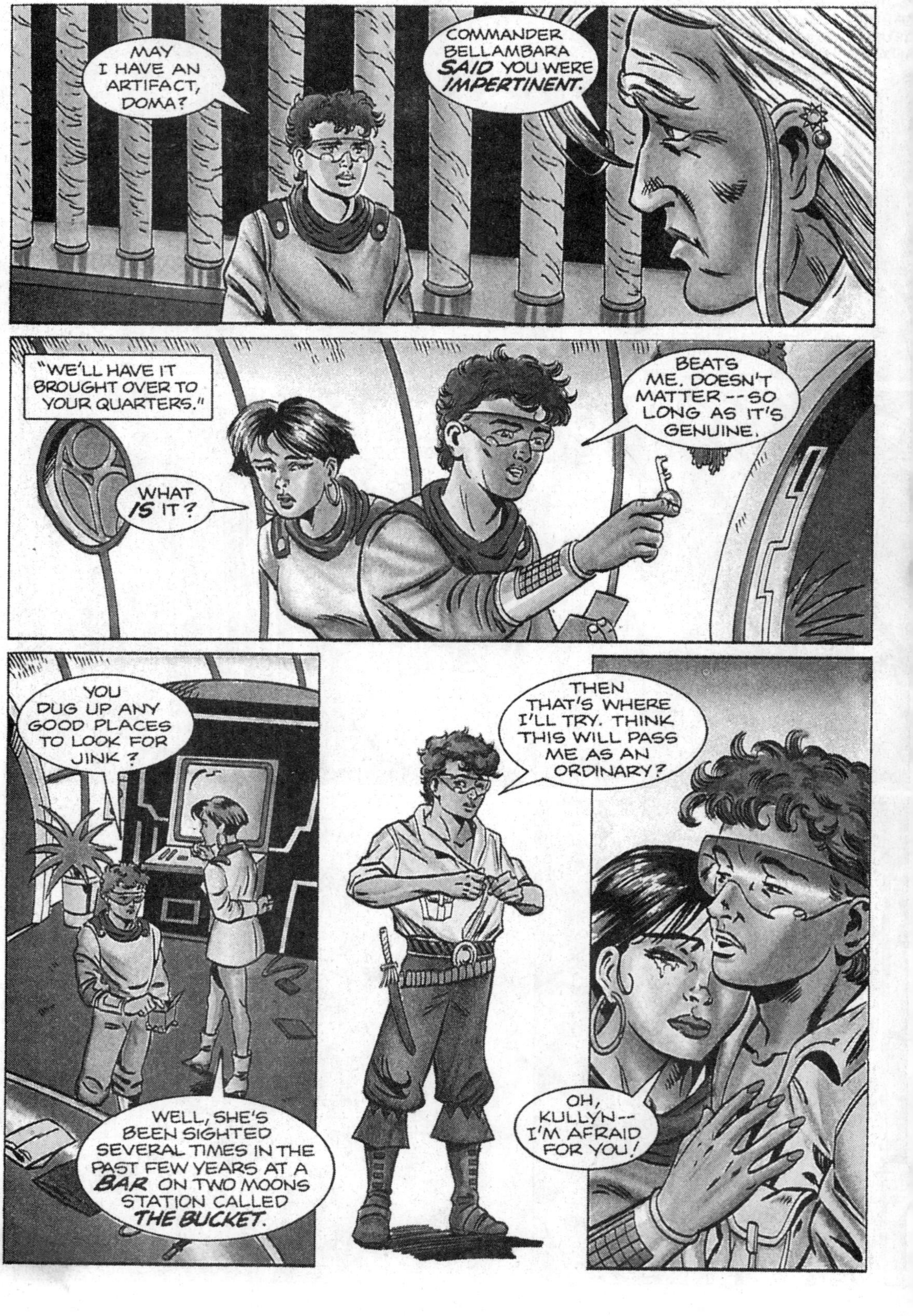
MAY I HAVE AN ARTIFACT, DOMA?
COMMANDER BELLAMBARA *SAID* YOU WERE *IMPERTINENT.*
"WE'LL HAVE IT BROUGHT OVER TO YOUR QUARTERS."
WHAT *IS* IT?
BEATS ME. DOESN'T MATTER -- SO LONG AS IT'S GENUINE.
YOU DUG UP ANY GOOD PLACES TO LOOK FOR JINK?
WELL, SHE'S BEEN SIGHTED SEVERAL TIMES IN THE PAST FEW YEARS AT A *BAR* ON TWO MOONS STATION CALLED *THE BUCKET*.
THEN THAT'S WHERE I'LL TRY. THINK THIS WILL PASS ME AS AN ORDINARY?
OH, KULLYN-- I'M AFRAID FOR YOU!

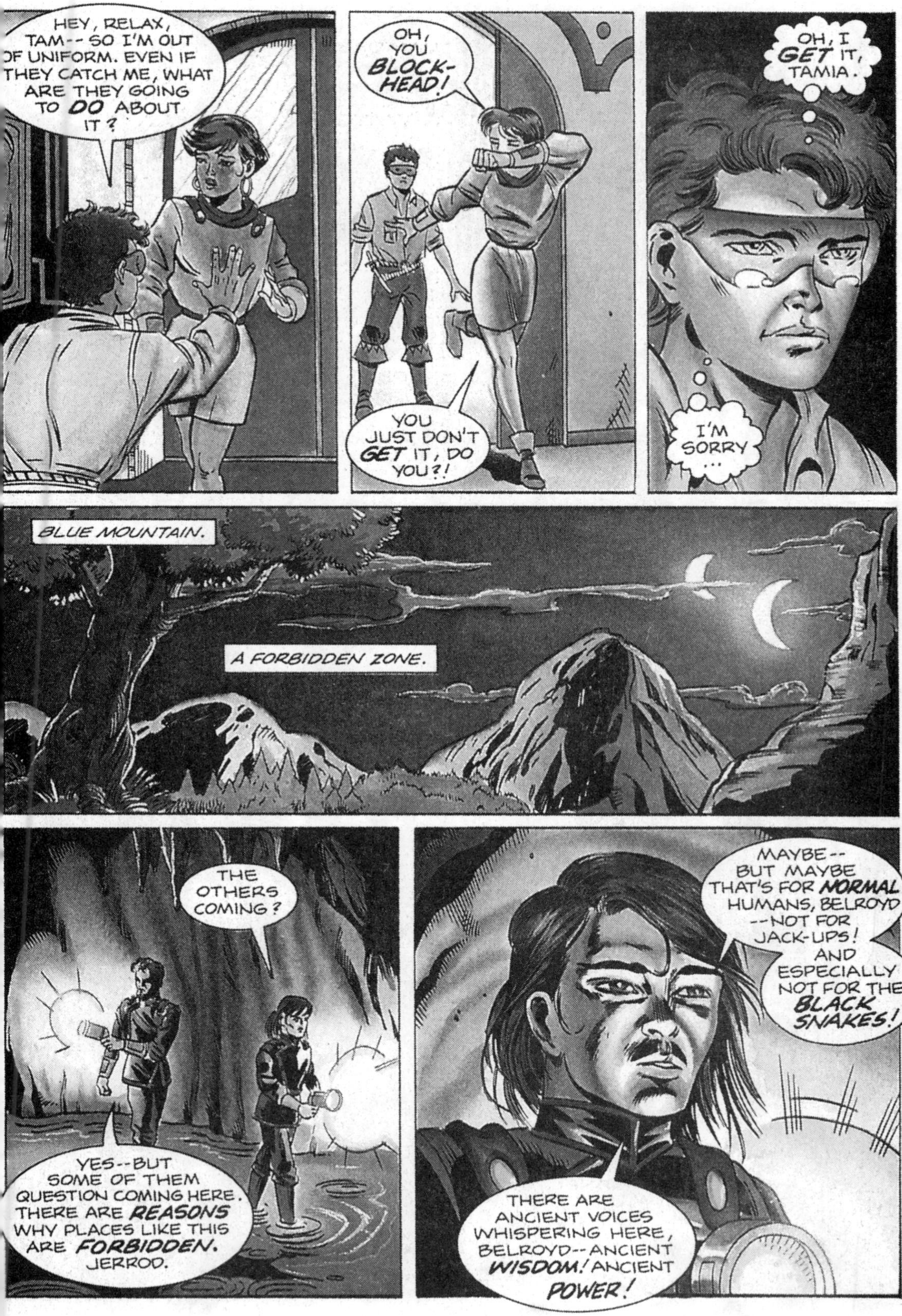

HEY, RELAX, TAM-- SO I'M OUT OF UNIFORM. EVEN IF THEY CATCH ME, WHAT ARE THEY GOING TO DO ABOUT IT?
OH, YOU BLOCK-HEAD!
YOU JUST DON'T GET IT, DO YOU?!
OH, I GET IT, TAMIA.
I'M SORRY...
BLUE MOUNTAIN.
A FORBIDDEN ZONE.
THE OTHERS COMING?
YES--BUT SOME OF THEM QUESTION COMING HERE. THERE ARE REASONS WHY PLACES LIKE THIS ARE FORBIDDEN. JERROD.
MAYBE-- BUT MAYBE THAT'S FOR NORMAL HUMANS, BELROYD --NOT FOR JACK-UPS!
AND ESPECIALLY NOT FOR THE BLACK SNAKES!
THERE ARE ANCIENT VOICES WHISPERING HERE, BELROYD--ANCIENT WISDOM! ANCIENT POWER!

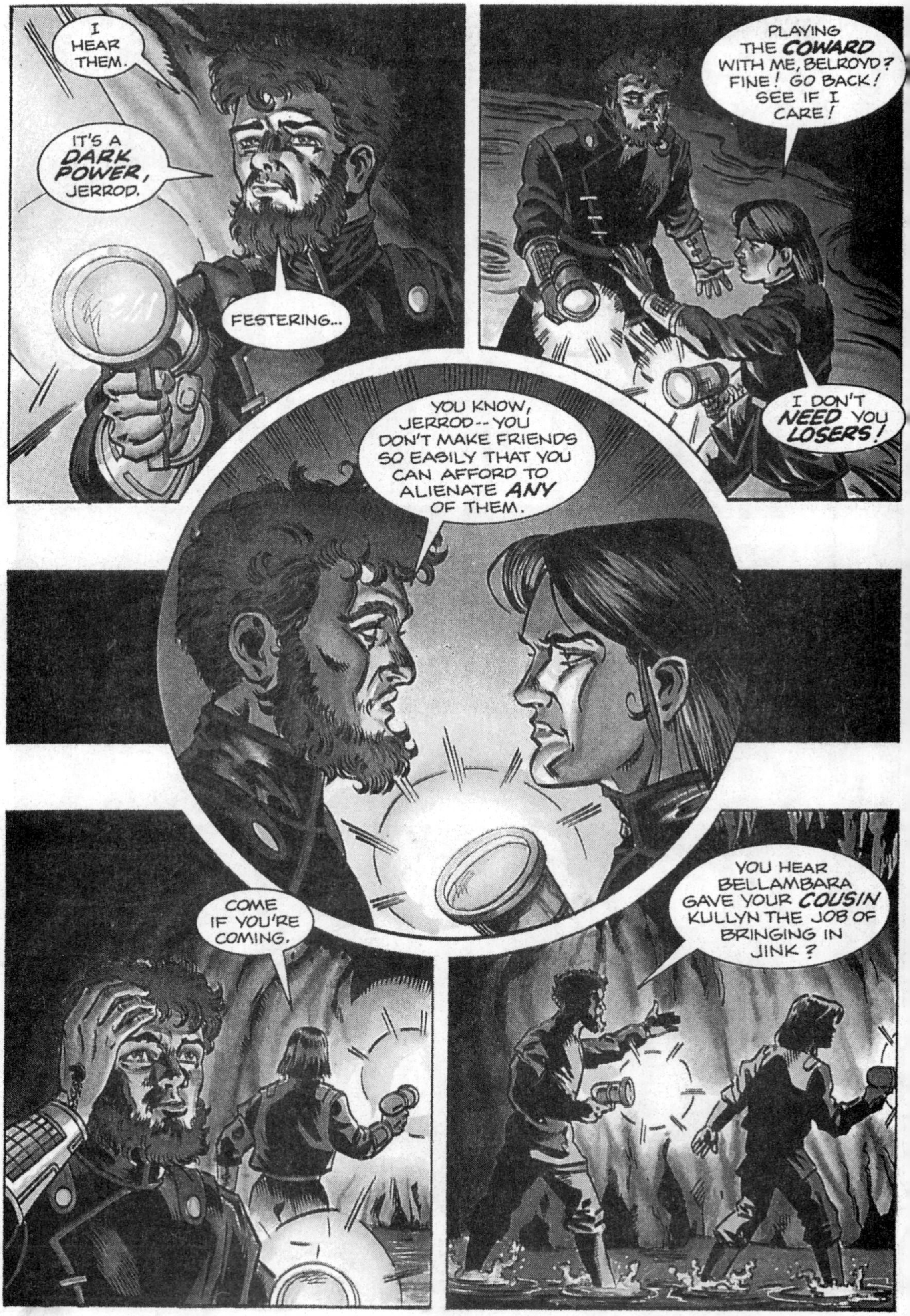
I HEAR THEM.
IT'S A DARK POWER, JERROD.
FESTERING...
PLAYING THE COWARD WITH ME, BELROYD? FINE! GO BACK! SEE IF I CARE!
I DON'T NEED YOU LOSERS!
YOU KNOW, JERROD-- YOU DON'T MAKE FRIENDS SO EASILY THAT YOU CAN AFFORD TO ALIENATE ANY OF THEM.
COME IF YOU'RE COMING.
YOU HEAR BELLAMBARA GAVE YOUR COUSIN KULLYN THE JOB OF BRINGING IN JINK?

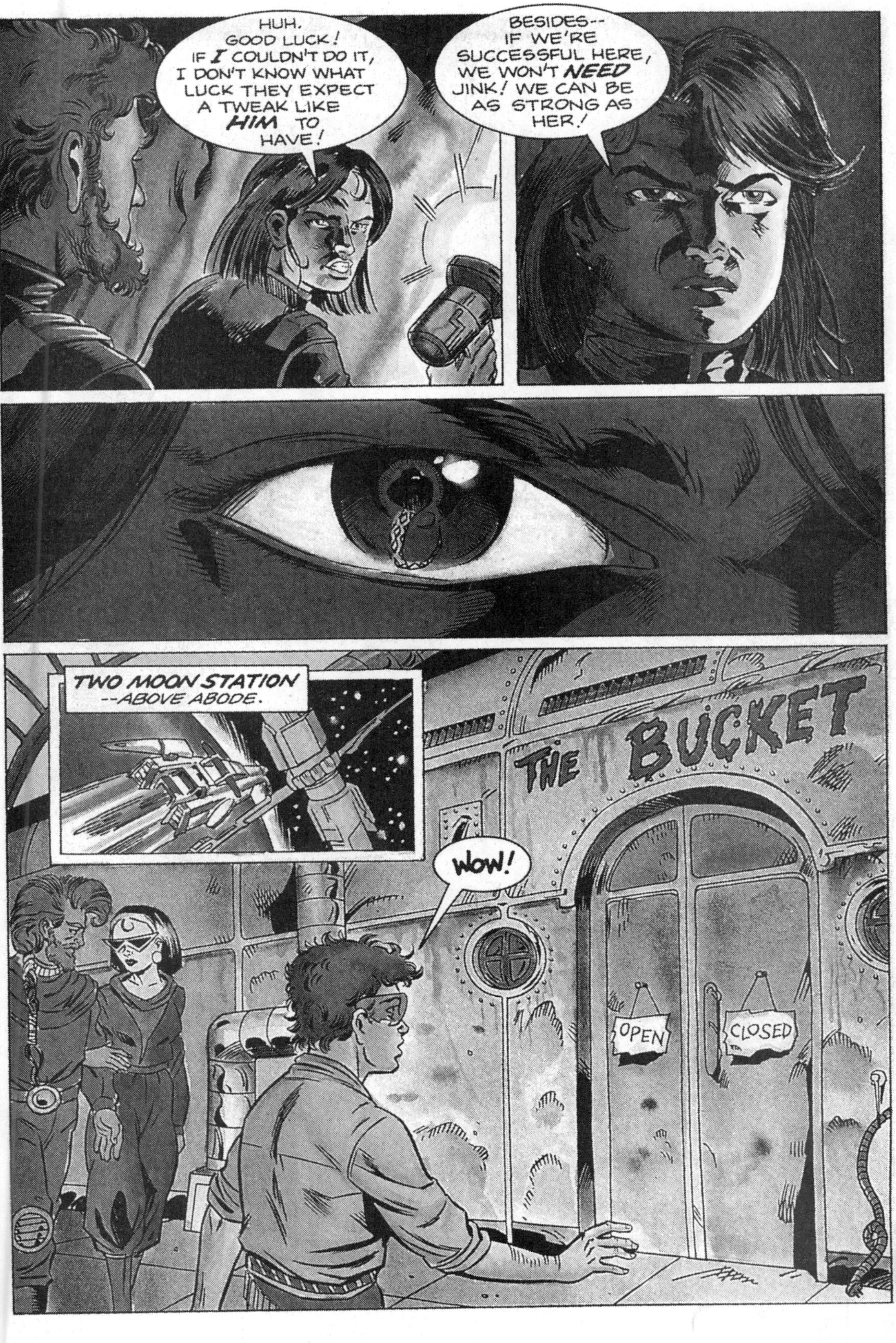
HUH. GOOD LUCK! IF I COULDN'T DO IT, I DON'T KNOW WHAT LUCK THEY EXPECT A TWEAK LIKE HIM TO HAVE!
BESIDES-- IF WE'RE SUCCESSFUL HERE, WE WON'T NEED JINK! WE CAN BE AS STRONG AS HER!
TWO MOON STATION --ABOVE ABODE.
THE BUCKET
WOW!
OPEN
CLOSED

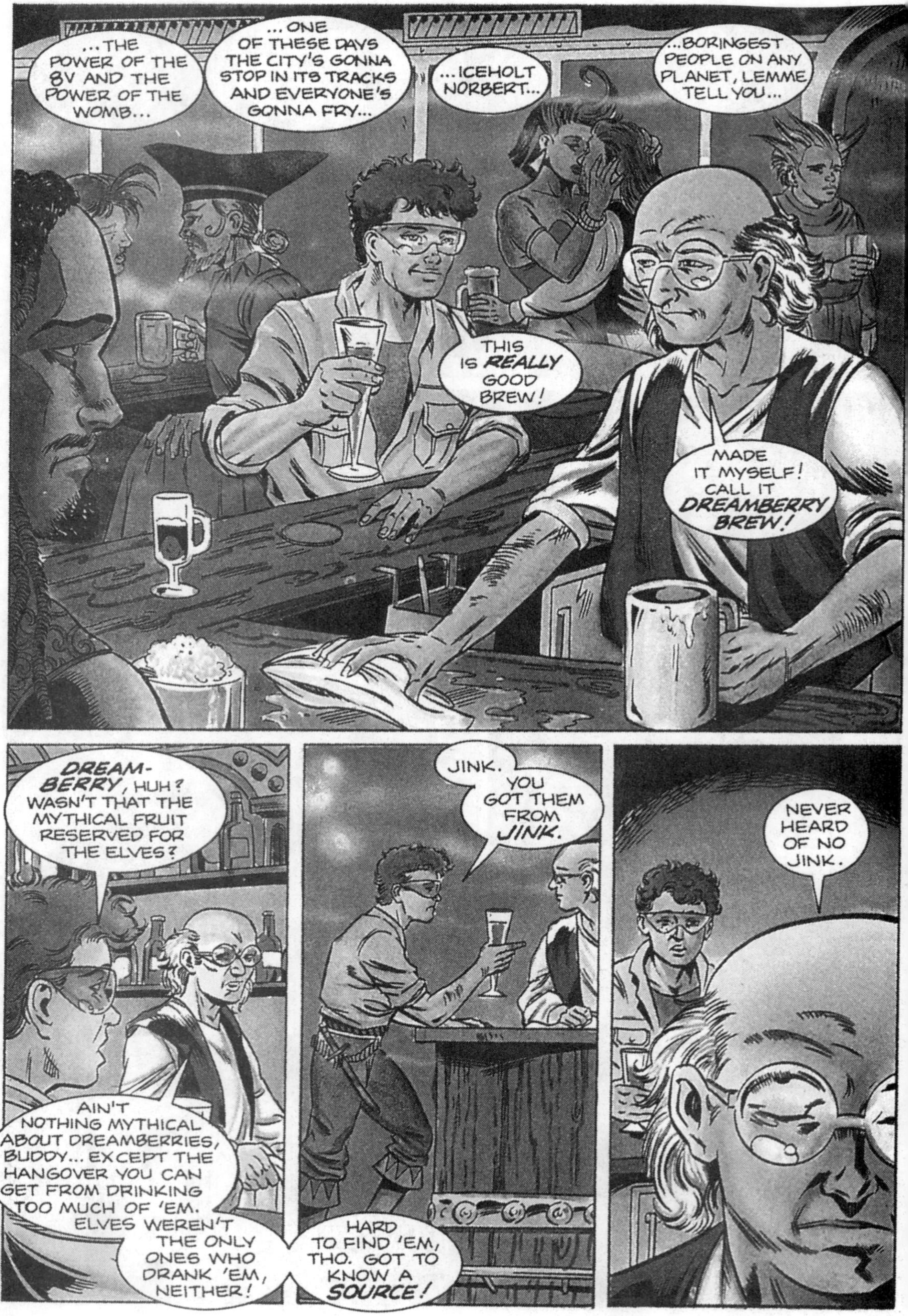
...THE POWER OF THE 8V AND THE POWER OF THE WOMB...
...ONE OF THESE DAYS THE CITY'S GONNA STOP IN ITS TRACKS AND EVERYONE'S GONNA FRY...
...ICEHOLT NORBERT...
...BORINGEST PEOPLE ON ANY PLANET, LEMME TELL YOU...
THIS IS REALLY GOOD BREW!
MADE IT MYSELF! CALL IT DREAMBERRY BREW!
DREAMBERRY, HUH? WASN'T THAT THE MYTHICAL FRUIT RESERVED FOR THE ELVES?
AIN'T NOTHING MYTHICAL ABOUT DREAMBERRIES, BUDDY... EXCEPT THE HANGOVER YOU CAN GET FROM DRINKING TOO MUCH OF 'EM. ELVES WEREN'T THE ONLY ONES WHO DRANK 'EM, NEITHER!
HARD TO FIND 'EM, THO. GOT TO KNOW A SOURCE!
JINK. YOU GOT THEM FROM JINK.
NEVER HEARD OF NO JINK.

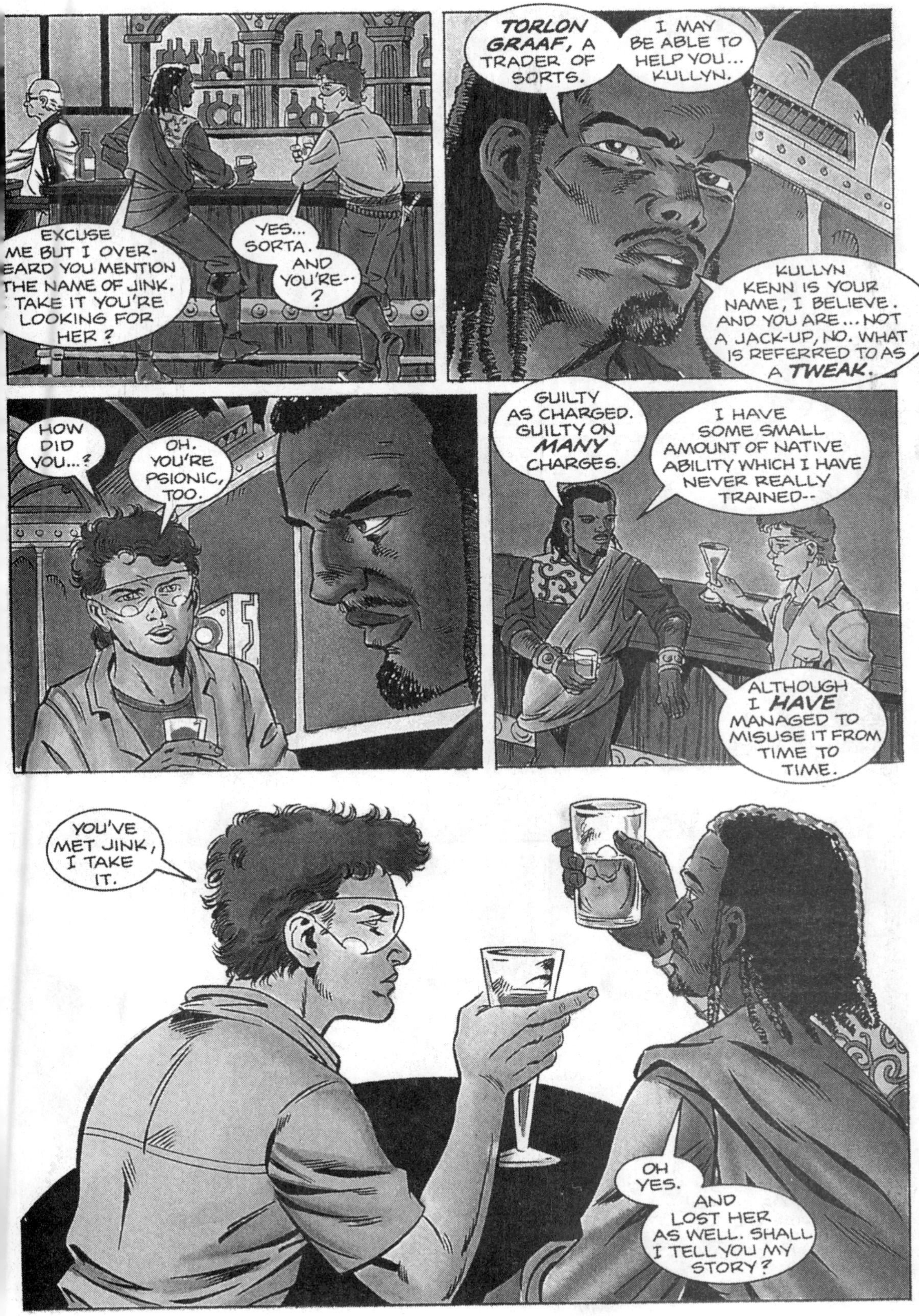
EXCUSE ME BUT I OVER-EARD YOU MENTION THE NAME OF JINK. TAKE IT YOU'RE LOOKING FOR HER?
YES... SORTA.
AND YOU'RE--?
TORLON GRAAF, A TRADER OF SORTS.
I MAY BE ABLE TO HELP YOU... KULLYN.
KULLYN KENN IS YOUR NAME, I BELIEVE. AND YOU ARE... NOT A JACK-UP, NO. WHAT IS REFERRED TO AS A TWEAK.
HOW DID YOU...?
OH. YOU'RE PSIONIC, TOO.
GUILTY AS CHARGED. GUILTY ON MANY CHARGES.
I HAVE SOME SMALL AMOUNT OF NATIVE ABILITY WHICH I HAVE NEVER REALLY TRAINED--
ALTHOUGH I HAVE MANAGED TO MISUSE IT FROM TIME TO TIME.
YOU'VE MET JINK, I TAKE IT.
OH YES.
AND LOST HER AS WELL. SHALL I TELL YOU MY STORY?

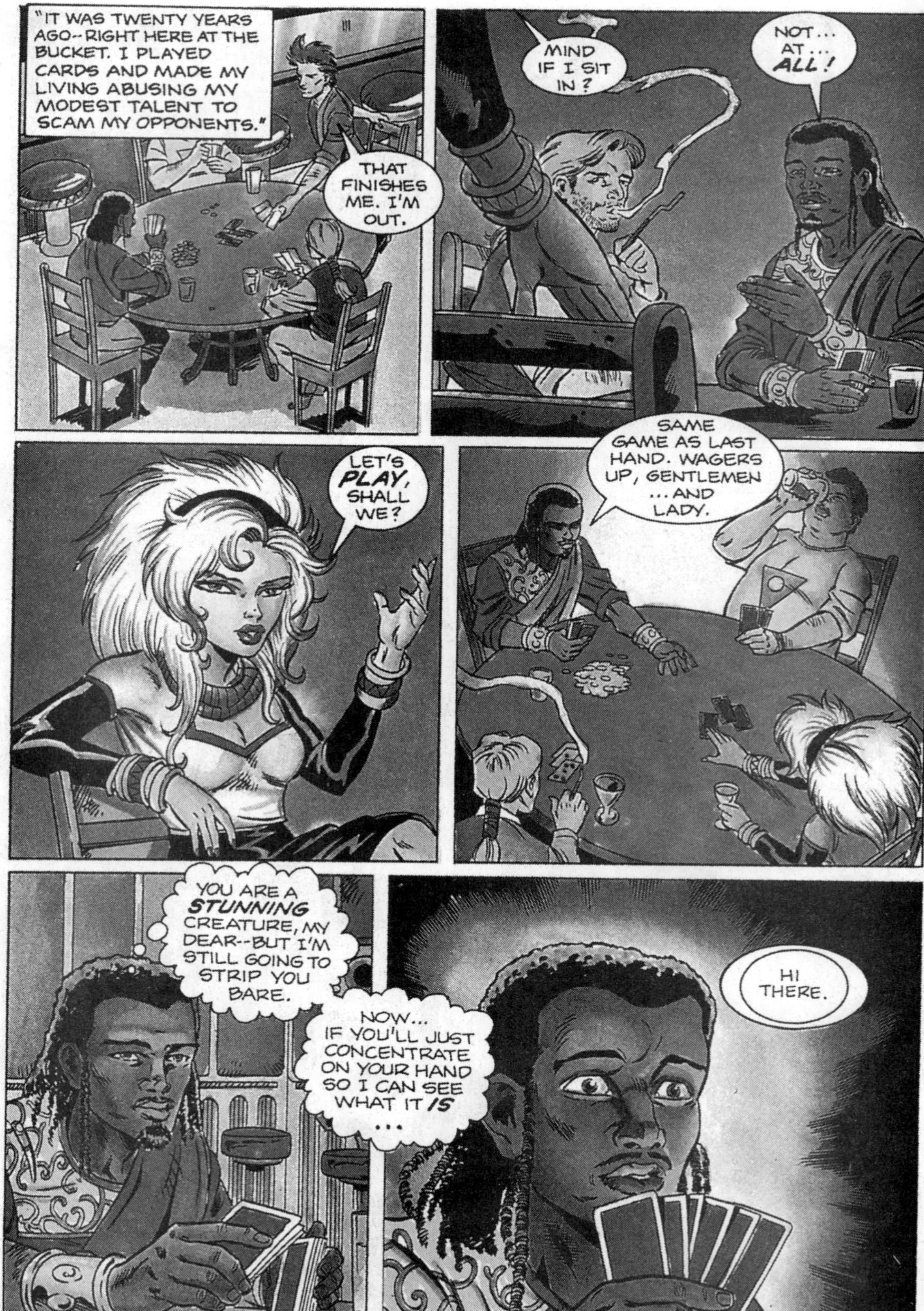
"IT WAS TWENTY YEARS AGO--RIGHT HERE AT THE BUCKET. I PLAYED CARDS AND MADE MY LIVING ABUSING MY MODEST TALENT TO SCAM MY OPPONENTS."
THAT FINISHES ME. I'M OUT.
MIND IF I SIT IN?
NOT... AT... ALL!
LET'S PLAY, SHALL WE?
SAME GAME AS LAST HAND. WAGERS UP, GENTLEMEN ...AND LADY.
YOU ARE A STUNNING CREATURE, MY DEAR--BUT I'M STILL GOING TO STRIP YOU BARE.
NOW... IF YOU'LL JUST CONCENTRATE ON YOUR HAND SO I CAN SEE WHAT IT IS ...
HI THERE.

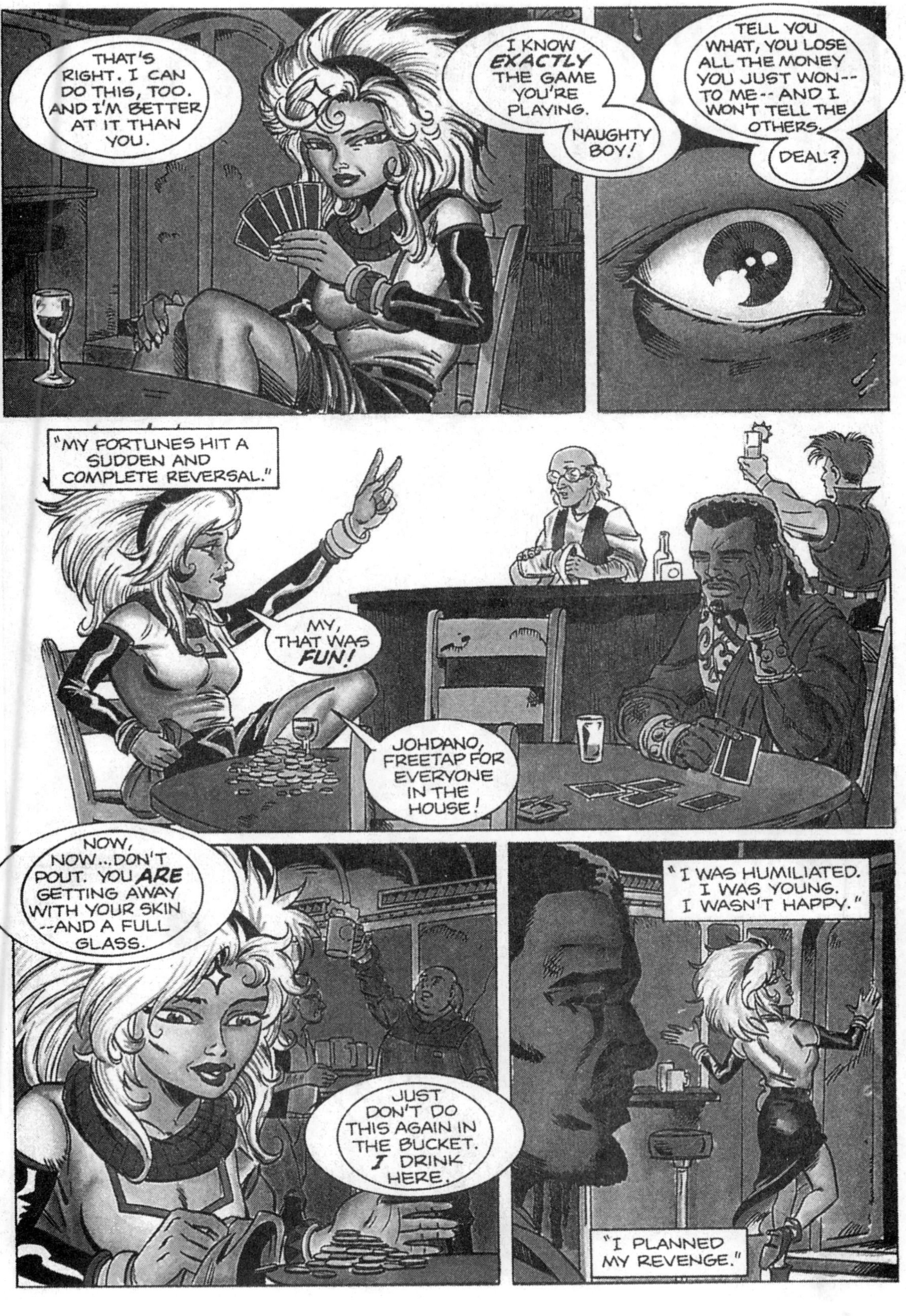
THAT'S RIGHT. I CAN DO THIS, TOO. AND I'M BETTER AT IT THAN YOU.
I KNOW EXACTLY THE GAME YOU'RE PLAYING.
NAUGHTY BOY!
TELL YOU WHAT, YOU LOSE ALL THE MONEY YOU JUST WON-- TO ME-- AND I WON'T TELL THE OTHERS.
DEAL?
"MY FORTUNES HIT A SUDDEN AND COMPLETE REVERSAL."
MY, THAT WAS FUN!
JOHDANO, FREETAP FOR EVERYONE IN THE HOUSE!
NOW, NOW...DON'T POUT. YOU ARE GETTING AWAY WITH YOUR SKIN --AND A FULL GLASS.
JUST DON'T DO THIS AGAIN IN THE BUCKET. I DRINK HERE.
"I WAS HUMILIATED. I WAS YOUNG. I WASN'T HAPPY."
"I PLANNED MY REVENGE."

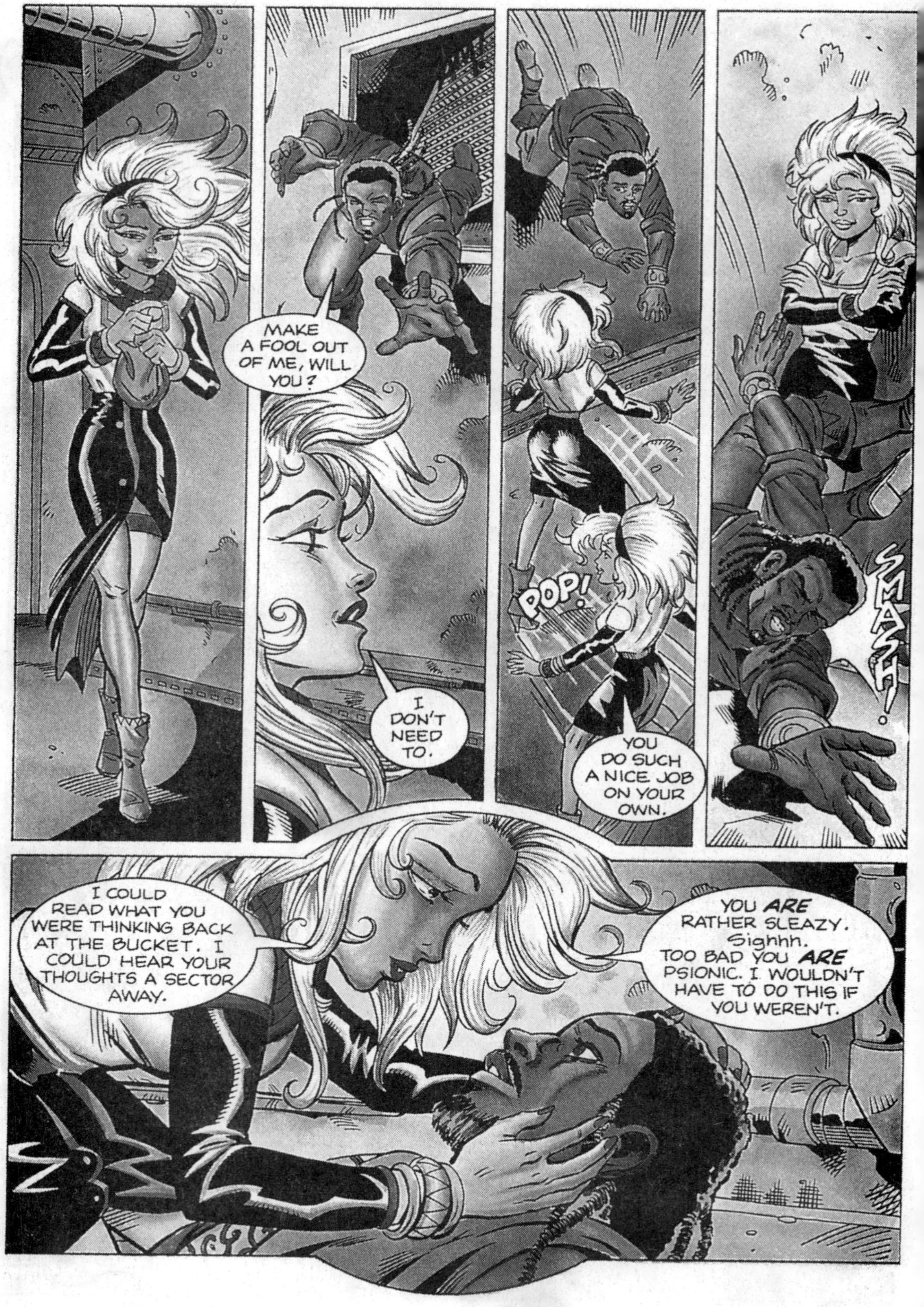
MAKE A FOOL OUT OF ME, WILL YOU?
I DON'T NEED TO.
POP!
YOU DO SUCH A NICE JOB ON YOUR OWN.
SMASH!
I COULD READ WHAT YOU WERE THINKING BACK AT THE BUCKET. I COULD HEAR YOUR THOUGHTS A SECTOR AWAY.
YOU ARE RATHER SLEAZY. Sighhh. TOO BAD YOU ARE PSIONIC. I WOULDN'T HAVE TO DO THIS IF YOU WEREN'T.

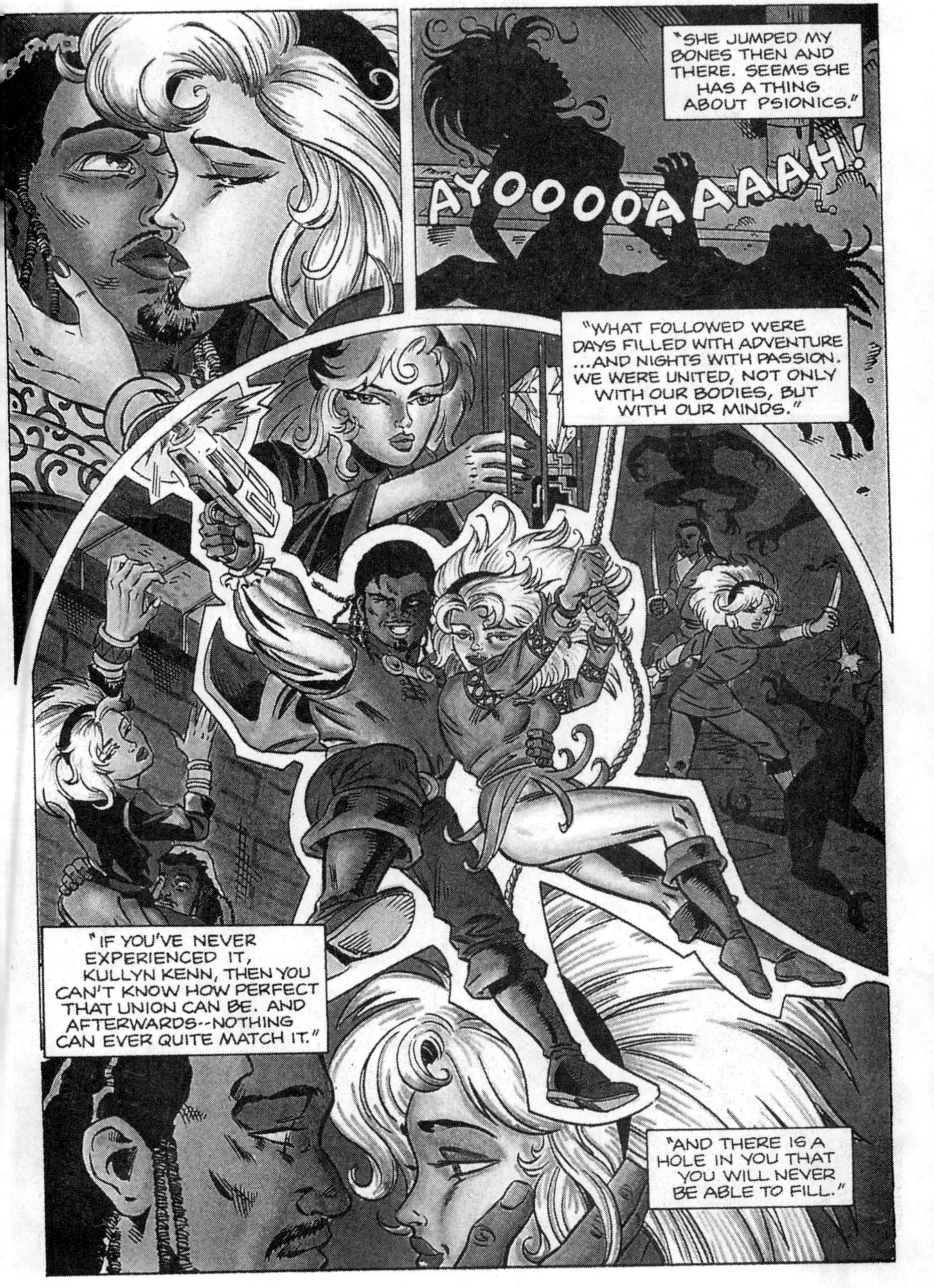
"SHE JUMPED MY BONES THEN AND THERE. SEEMS SHE HAS A THING ABOUT PSIONICS."
AYOOOOAAAAH!
"WHAT FOLLOWED WERE DAYS FILLED WITH ADVENTURE ...AND NIGHTS WITH PASSION. WE WERE UNITED, NOT ONLY WITH OUR BODIES, BUT WITH OUR MINDS."
"IF YOU'VE NEVER EXPERIENCED IT, KULLYN KENN, THEN YOU CAN'T KNOW HOW PERFECT THAT UNION CAN BE. AND AFTERWARDS--NOTHING CAN EVER QUITE MATCH IT."
"AND THERE IS A HOLE IN YOU THAT YOU WILL NEVER BE ABLE TO FILL."

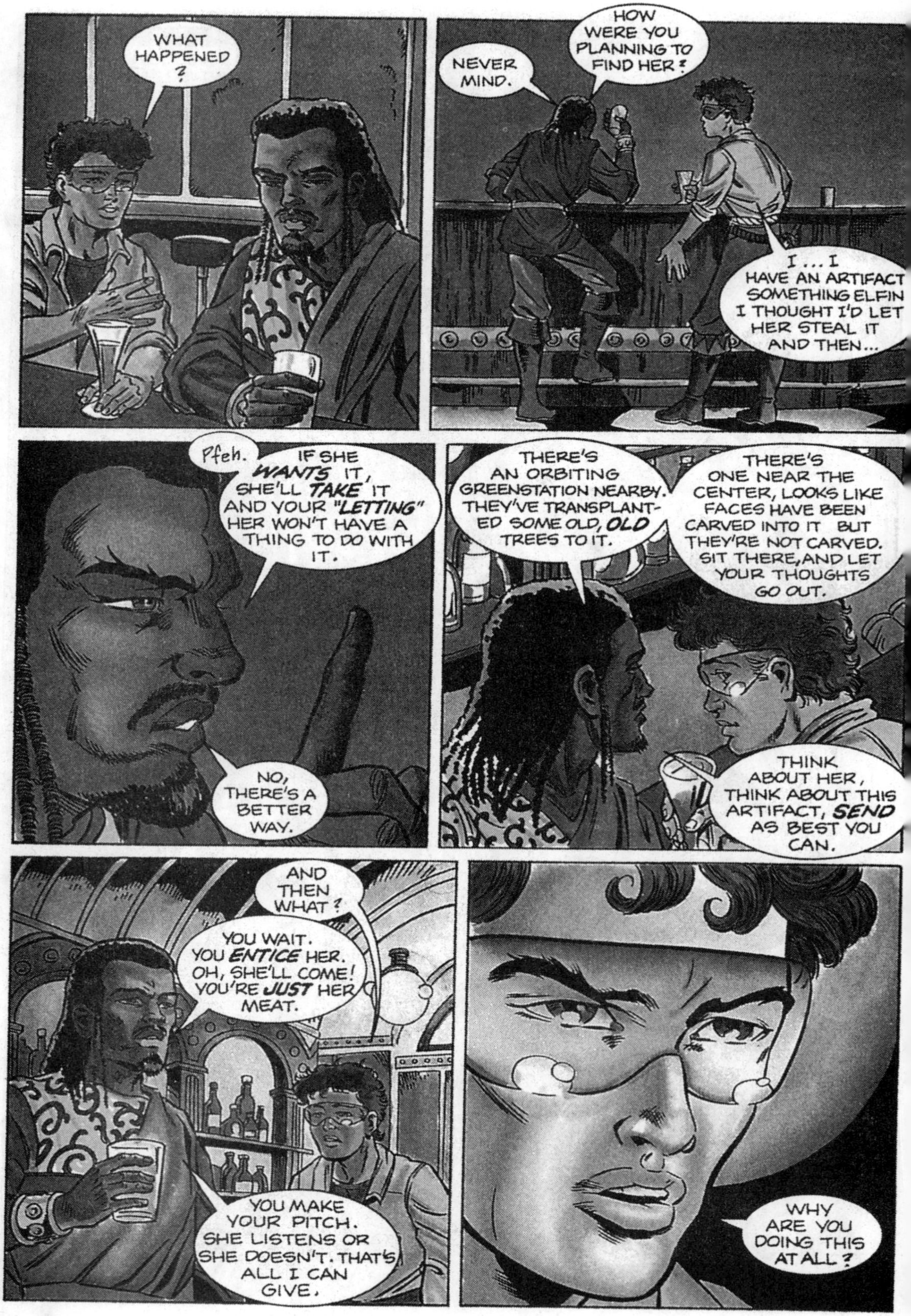
WHAT HAPPENED ?
NEVER MIND.
HOW WERE YOU PLANNING TO FIND HER ?
I ... I HAVE AN ARTIFACT SOMETHING ELFIN I THOUGHT I'D LET HER STEAL IT AND THEN...
Pfeh.
IF SHE WANTS IT, SHE'LL TAKE IT AND YOUR "LETTING" HER WON'T HAVE A THING TO DO WITH IT.
NO, THERE'S A BETTER WAY.
THERE'S AN ORBITING GREENSTATION NEARBY. THEY'VE TRANSPLANT-ED SOME OLD, OLD TREES TO IT.
THERE'S ONE NEAR THE CENTER, LOOKS LIKE FACES HAVE BEEN CARVED INTO IT BUT THEY'RE NOT CARVED. SIT THERE, AND LET YOUR THOUGHTS GO OUT.
THINK ABOUT HER, THINK ABOUT THIS ARTIFACT, SEND AS BEST YOU CAN.
AND THEN WHAT ?
YOU WAIT. YOU ENTICE HER. OH, SHE'LL COME! YOU'RE JUST HER MEAT.
YOU MAKE YOUR PITCH. SHE LISTENS OR SHE DOESN'T. THAT'S ALL I CAN GIVE.
WHY ARE YOU DOING THIS AT ALL ?

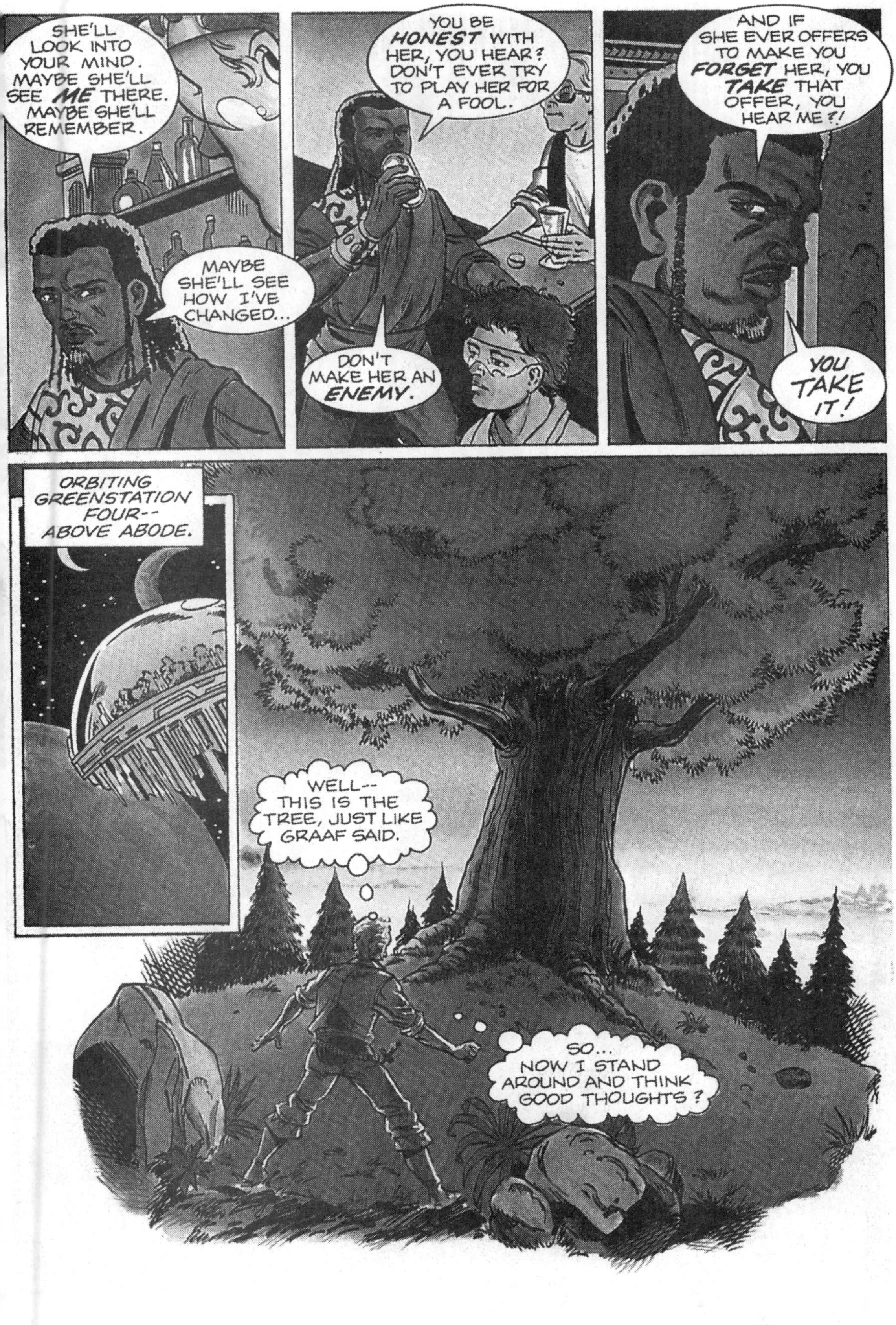
SHE'LL LOOK INTO YOUR MIND. MAYBE SHE'LL SEE ME THERE. MAYBE SHE'LL REMEMBER.
MAYBE SHE'LL SEE HOW I'VE CHANGED...
YOU BE HONEST WITH HER, YOU HEAR? DON'T EVER TRY TO PLAY HER FOR A FOOL.
DON'T MAKE HER AN ENEMY.
AND IF SHE EVER OFFERS TO MAKE YOU FORGET HER, YOU TAKE THAT OFFER, YOU HEAR ME?!
YOU TAKE IT!
ORBITING GREENSTATION FOUR-- ABOVE ABODE.
WELL-- THIS IS THE TREE, JUST LIKE GRAAF SAID.
SO... NOW I STAND AROUND AND THINK GOOD THOUGHTS?

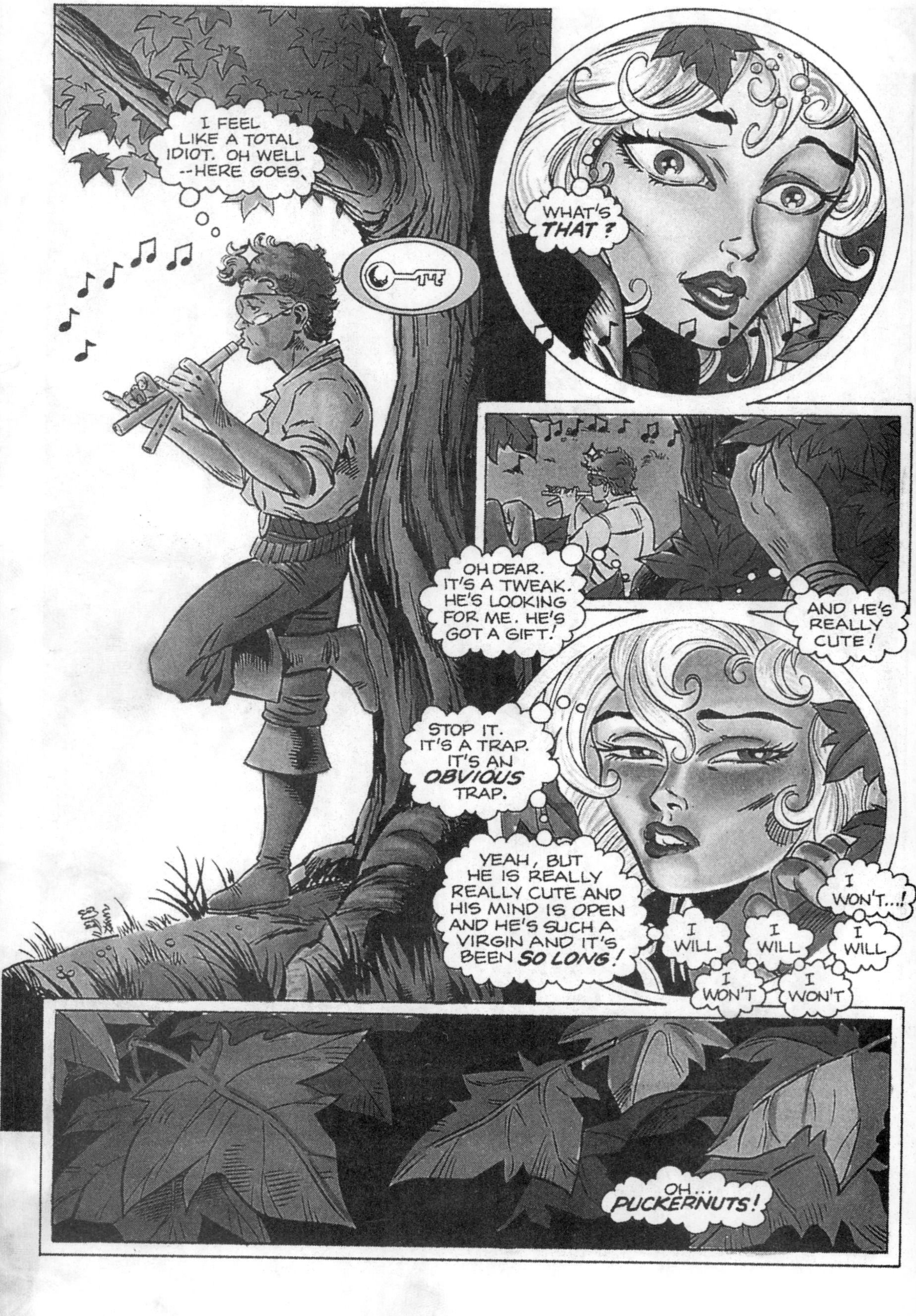

I FEEL LIKE A TOTAL IDIOT. OH WELL --HERE GOES.
WHAT'S THAT?
OH DEAR. IT'S A TWEAK. HE'S LOOKING FOR ME. HE'S GOT A GIFT!
AND HE'S REALLY CUTE!
STOP IT. IT'S A TRAP. IT'S AN OBVIOUS TRAP.
YEAH, BUT HE IS REALLY REALLY CUTE AND HIS MIND IS OPEN AND HE'S SUCH A VIRGIN AND IT'S BEEN SO LONG!
I WILL
I WON'T
I WILL
I WON'T
I WILL
I WON'T...!
OH... PUCKERNUTS!

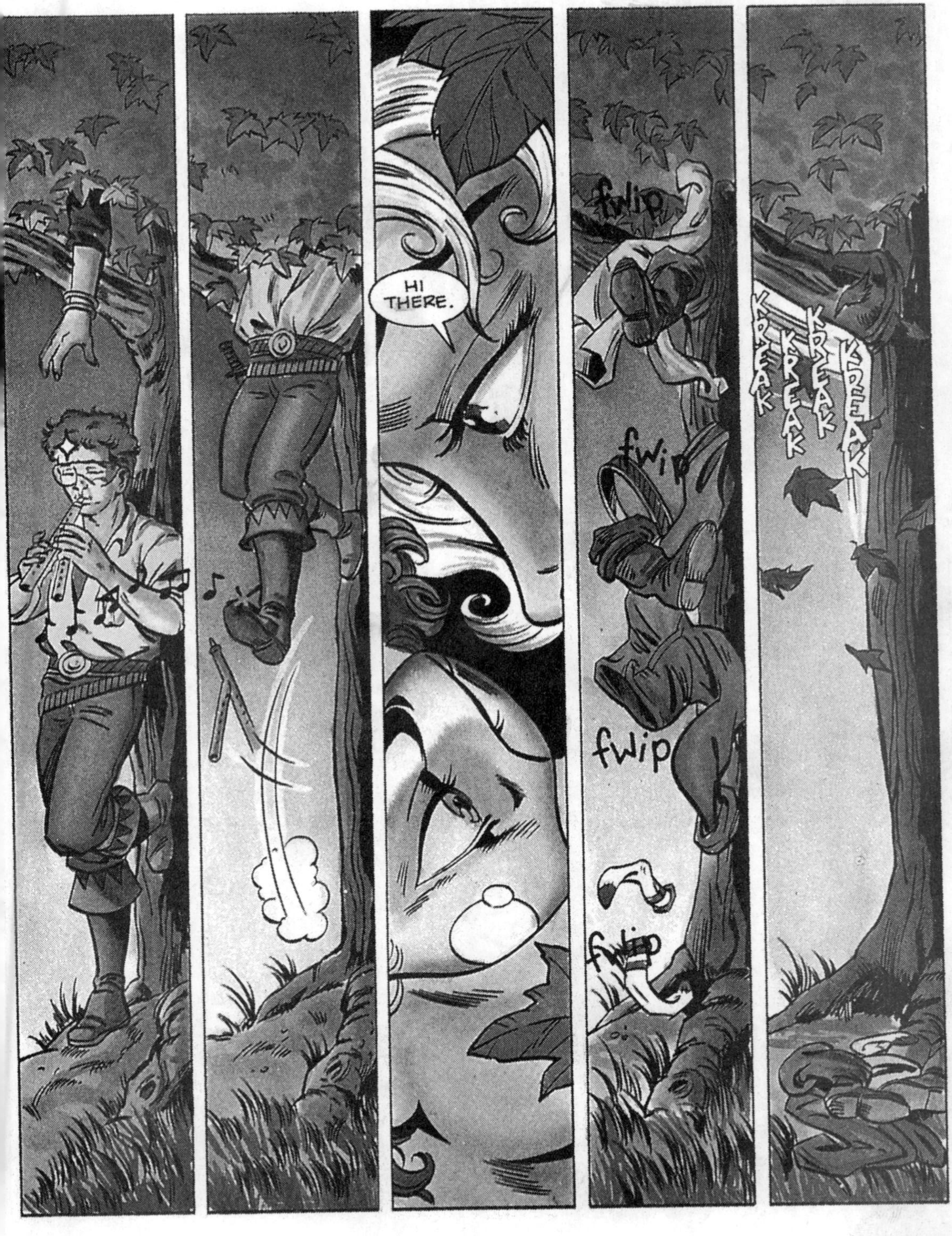

HI THERE.
fwip
fwip
fwip
fwip
KREAK
KREAK
KREAK
KREAK

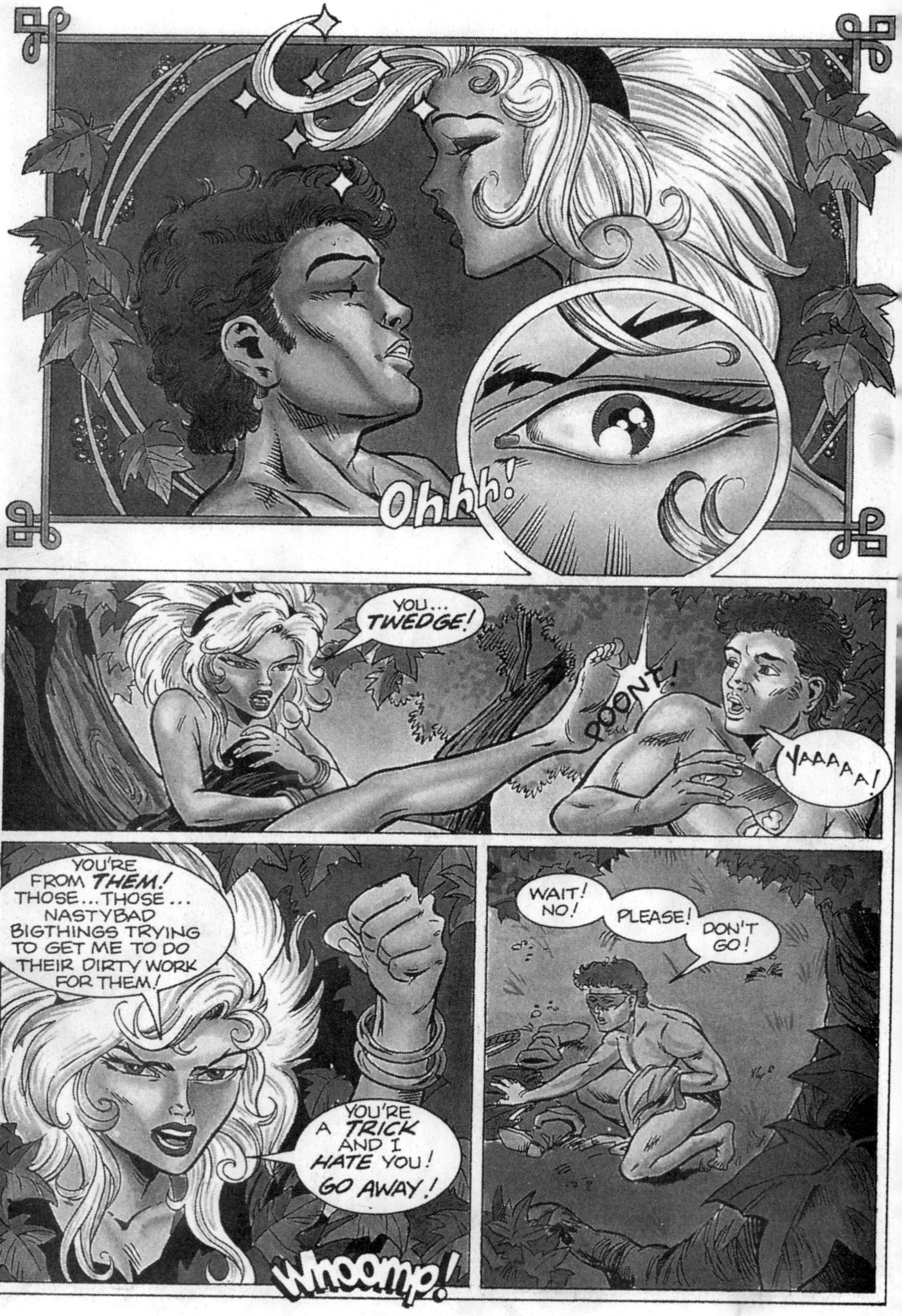

Ohhh!
YOU... TWEDGE!
POONT!
YAAAAA!
YOU'RE FROM THEM! THOSE... THOSE... NASTYBAD BIGTHINGS TRYING TO GET ME TO DO THEIR DIRTY WORK FOR THEM!
YOU'RE A TRICK AND I HATE YOU! GO AWAY!
Whoomp!
WAIT! NO!
PLEASE!
DON'T GO!

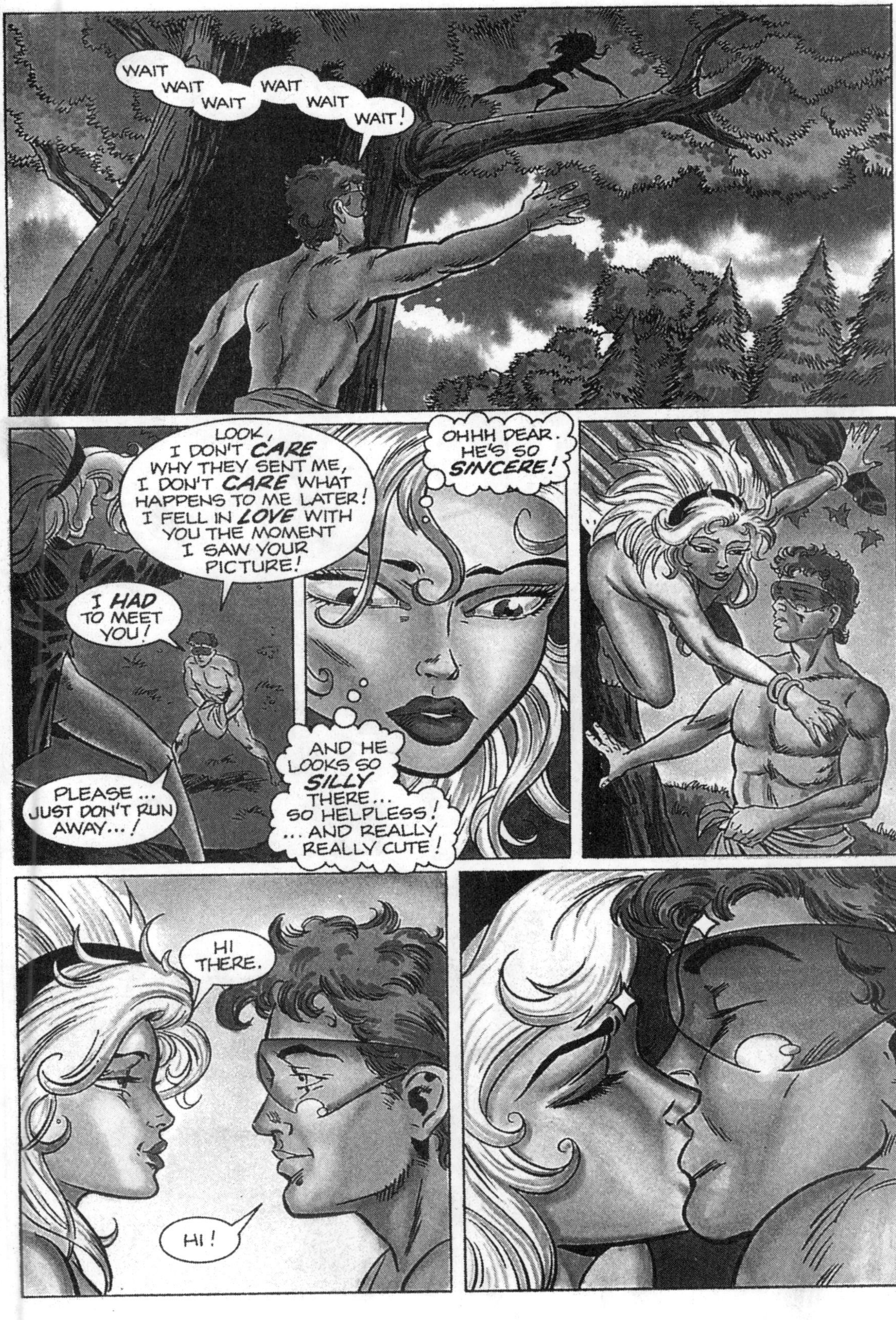
WAIT WAIT WAIT WAIT WAIT WAIT!
LOOK, I DON'T CARE WHY THEY SENT ME, I DON'T CARE WHAT HAPPENS TO ME LATER! I FELL IN LOVE WITH YOU THE MOMENT I SAW YOUR PICTURE!
I HAD TO MEET YOU!
PLEASE ... JUST DON'T RUN AWAY...!
OHHH DEAR. HE'S SO SINCERE!
AND HE LOOKS SO SILLY THERE... SO HELPLESS! ...AND REALLY REALLY CUTE!
HI THERE.
HI!

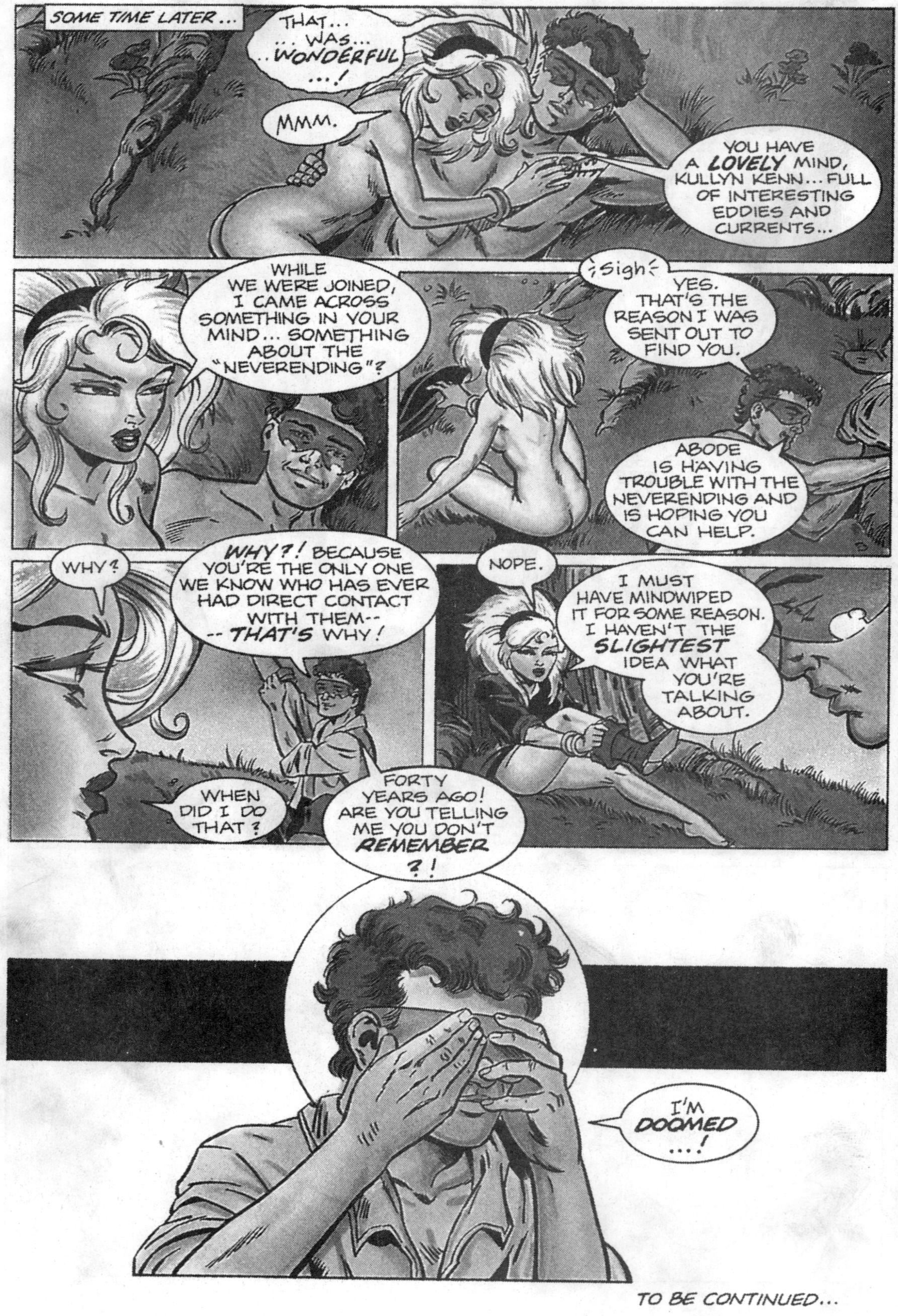
SOME TIME LATER...
THAT... ...WAS... ...WONDERFUL ...!
MMM.
YOU HAVE A LOVELY MIND, KULLYN KENN... FULL OF INTERESTING EDDIES AND CURRENTS...
WHILE WE WERE JOINED, I CAME ACROSS SOMETHING IN YOUR MIND... SOMETHING ABOUT THE "NEVERENDING"?
Sigh
YES. THAT'S THE REASON I WAS SENT OUT TO FIND YOU.
ABODE IS HAVING TROUBLE WITH THE NEVERENDING AND IS HOPING YOU CAN HELP.
WHY?
WHY?! BECAUSE YOU'RE THE ONLY ONE WE KNOW WHO HAS EVER HAD DIRECT CONTACT WITH THEM-- --THAT'S WHY!
WHEN DID I DO THAT?
FORTY YEARS AGO! ARE YOU TELLING ME YOU DON'T REMEMBER?!
NOPE.
I MUST HAVE MINDWIPED IT FOR SOME REASON. I HAVEN'T THE SLIGHTEST IDEA WHAT YOU'RE TALKING ABOUT.
I'M DOOMED...!

TO BE CONTINUED...

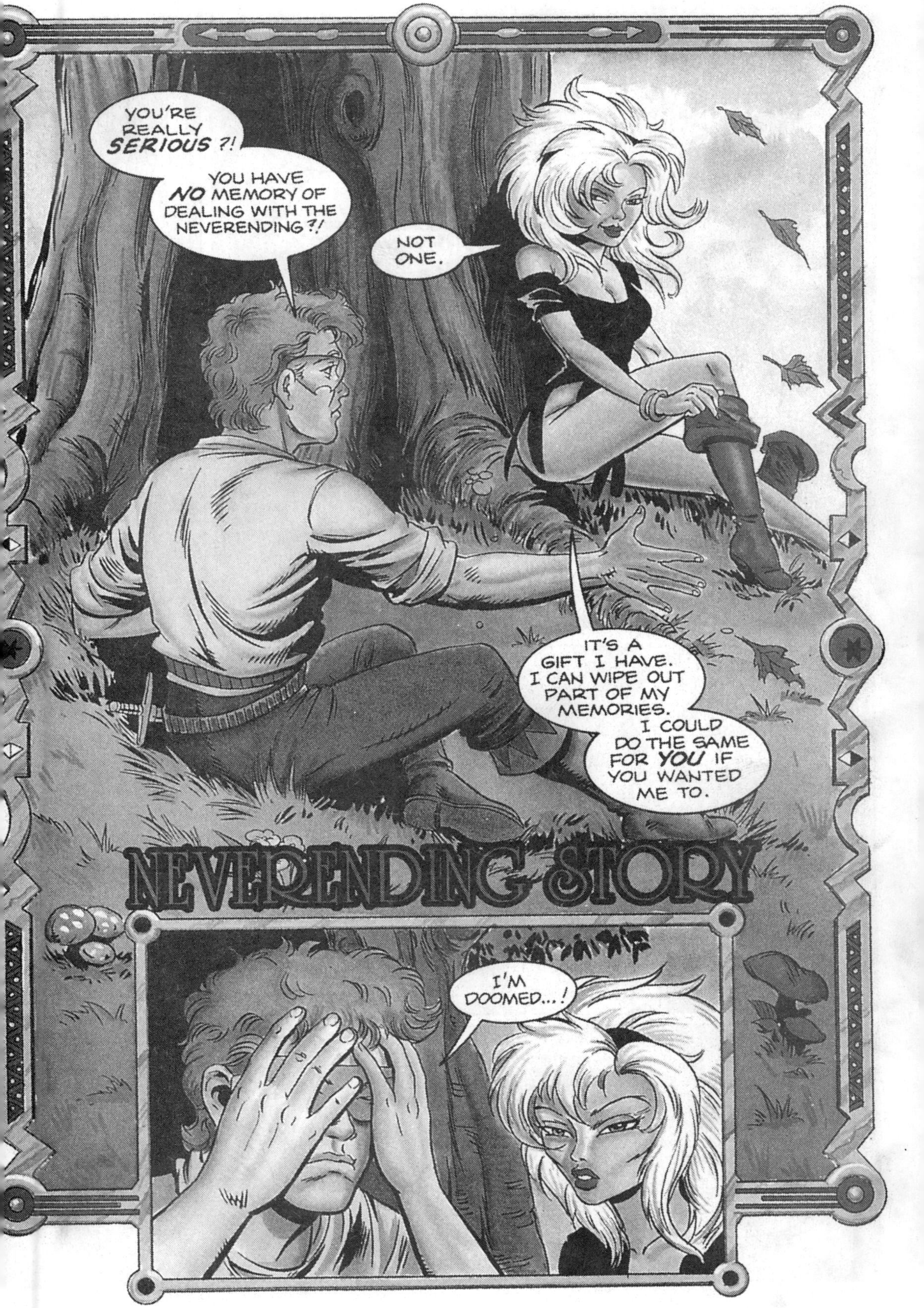
YOU'RE REALLY SERIOUS ?!
YOU HAVE NO MEMORY OF DEALING WITH THE NEVERENDING ?!
NOT ONE.
IT'S A GIFT I HAVE. I CAN WIPE OUT PART OF MY MEMORIES.
I COULD DO THE SAME FOR YOU IF YOU WANTED ME TO.
NEVERENDING STORY
I'M DOOMED...!

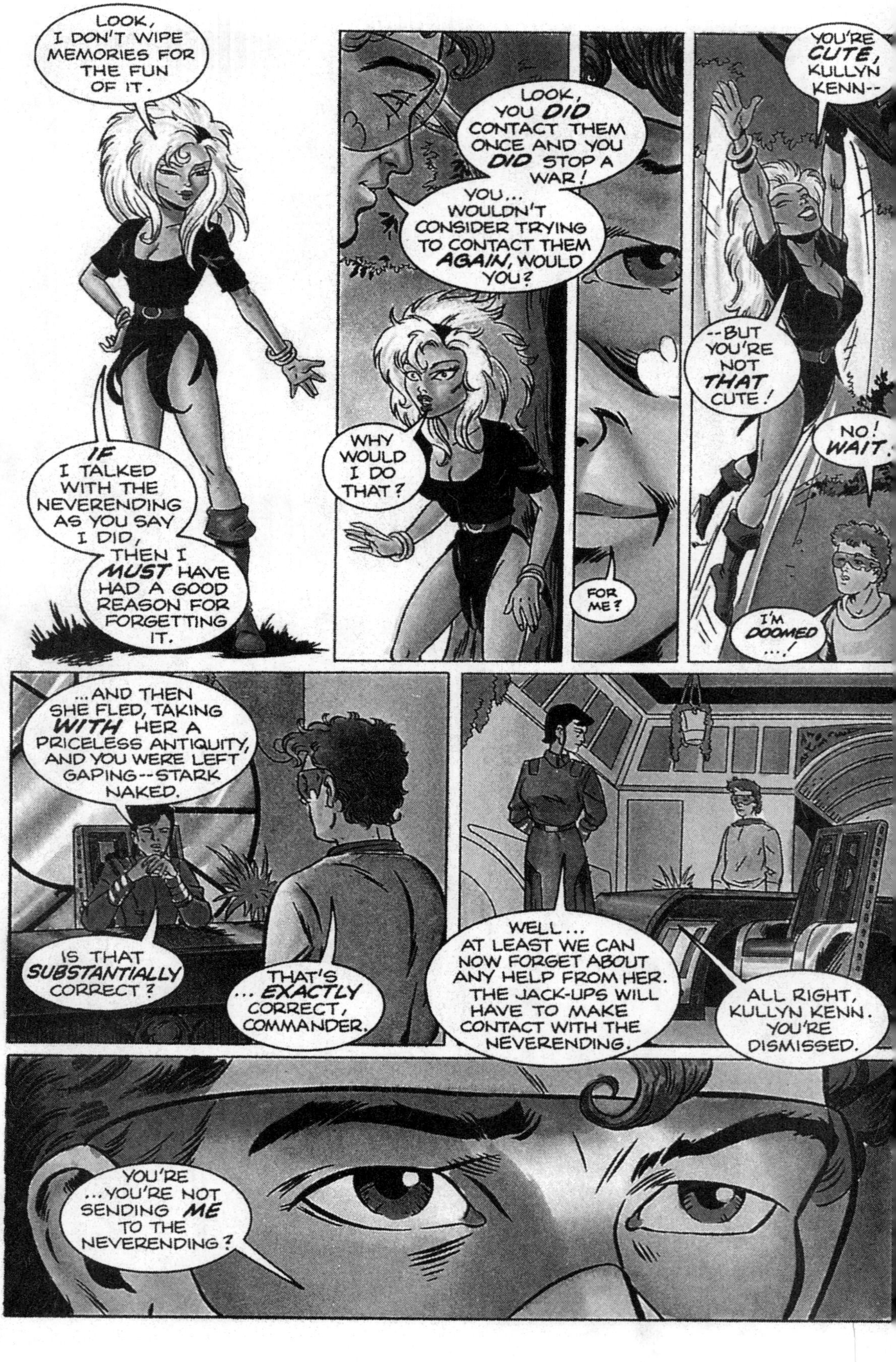
LOOK, I DON'T WIPE MEMORIES FOR THE FUN OF IT.
IF I TALKED WITH THE NEVERENDING AS YOU SAY I DID,
THEN I MUST HAVE HAD A GOOD REASON FOR FORGETTING IT.
LOOK, YOU DID CONTACT THEM ONCE AND YOU DID STOP A WAR!
YOU... WOULDN'T CONSIDER TRYING TO CONTACT THEM AGAIN, WOULD YOU?
WHY WOULD I DO THAT?
FOR ME?
YOU'RE CUTE, KULLYN KENN--
--BUT YOU'RE NOT THAT CUTE!
NO! WAIT.
I'M DOOMED...!
...AND THEN SHE FLED, TAKING WITH HER A PRICELESS ANTIQUITY, AND YOU WERE LEFT GAPING--STARK NAKED.
IS THAT SUBSTANTIALLY CORRECT?
THAT'S ...EXACTLY CORRECT, COMMANDER.
WELL... AT LEAST WE CAN NOW FORGET ABOUT ANY HELP FROM HER. THE JACK-UPS WILL HAVE TO MAKE CONTACT WITH THE NEVERENDING.
ALL RIGHT, KULLYN KENN. YOU'RE DISMISSED.
YOU'RE ...YOU'RE NOT SENDING ME TO THE NEVERENDING?

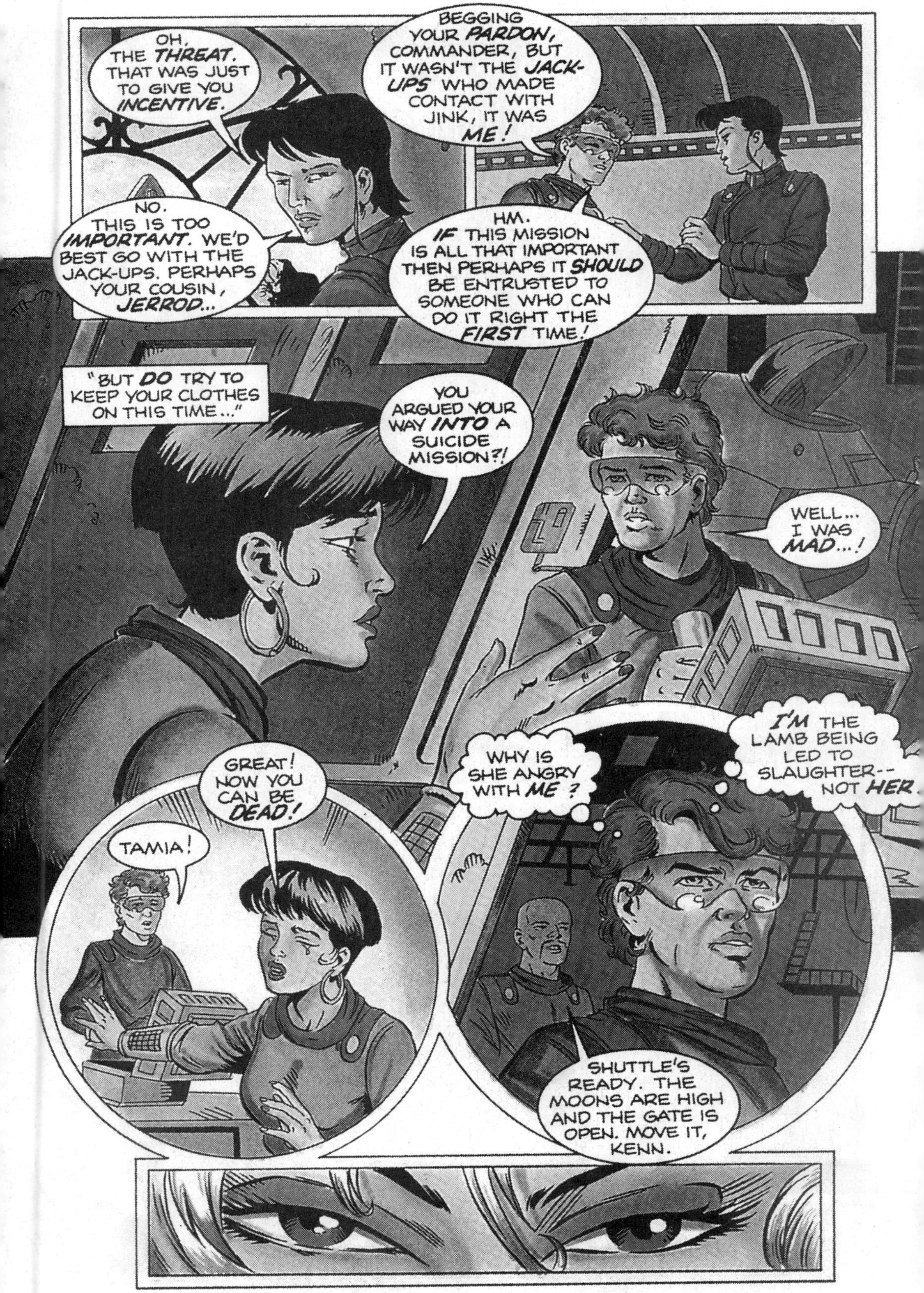
OH, THE THREAT. THAT WAS JUST TO GIVE YOU INCENTIVE.
BEGGING YOUR PARDON, COMMANDER, BUT IT WASN'T THE JACK-UPS WHO MADE CONTACT WITH JINK, IT WAS ME!
NO. THIS IS TOO IMPORTANT. WE'D BEST GO WITH THE JACK-UPS. PERHAPS YOUR COUSIN, JERROD...
HM. IF THIS MISSION IS ALL THAT IMPORTANT THEN PERHAPS IT SHOULD BE ENTRUSTED TO SOMEONE WHO CAN DO IT RIGHT THE FIRST TIME!
"BUT DO TRY TO KEEP YOUR CLOTHES ON THIS TIME..."
YOU ARGUED YOUR WAY INTO A SUICIDE MISSION?!
WELL... I WAS MAD...!
GREAT! NOW YOU CAN BE DEAD!
TAMIA!
WHY IS SHE ANGRY WITH ME?
I'M THE LAMB BEING LED TO SLAUGHTER--NOT HER.
SHUTTLE'S READY. THE MOONS ARE HIGH AND THE GATE IS OPEN. MOVE IT, KENN.

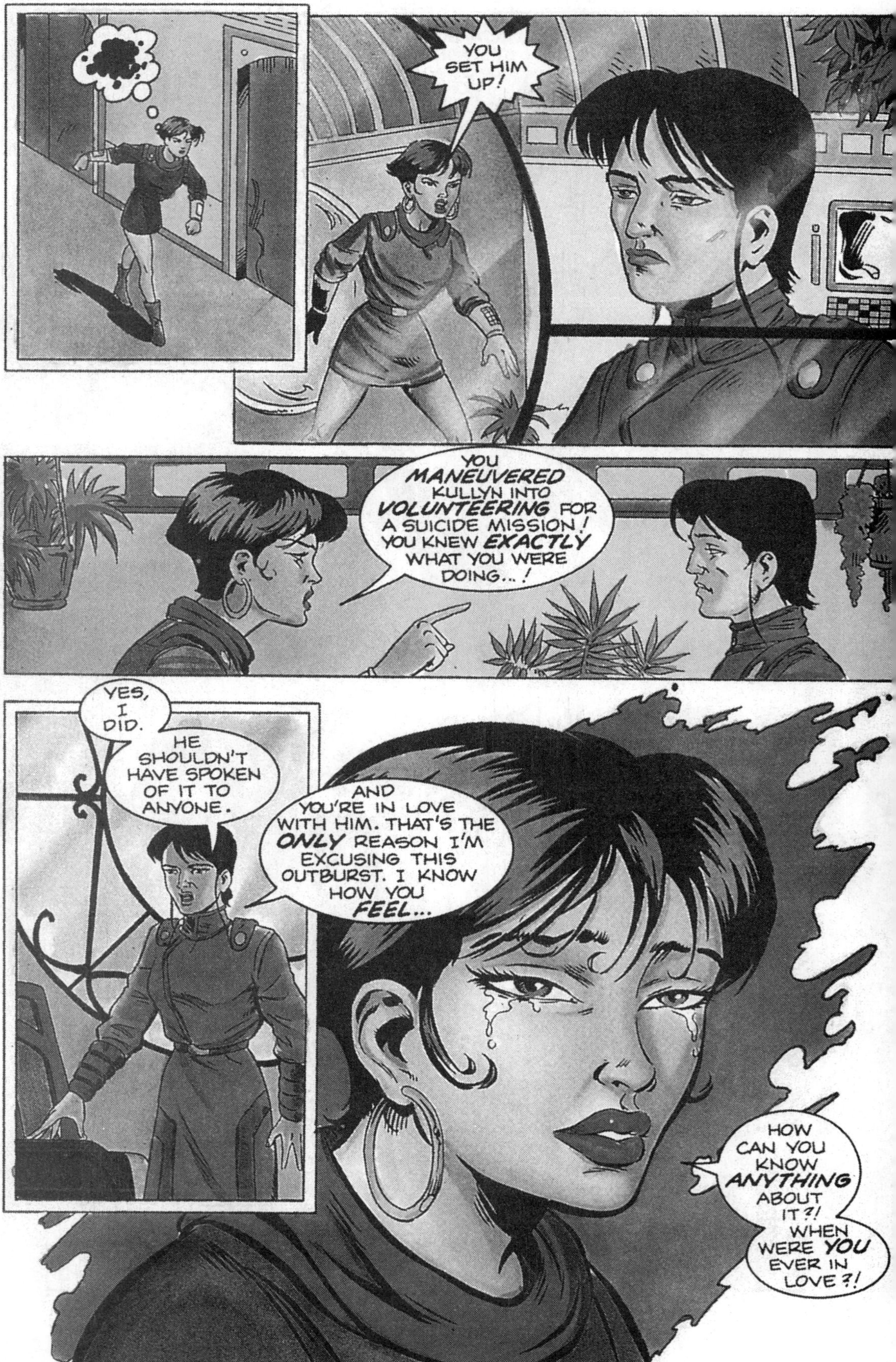
YOU SET HIM UP!
YOU MANEUVERED KULLYN INTO VOLUNTEERING FOR A SUICIDE MISSION! YOU KNEW EXACTLY WHAT YOU WERE DOING...!
YES, I DID.
HE SHOULDN'T HAVE SPOKEN OF IT TO ANYONE.
AND YOU'RE IN LOVE WITH HIM. THAT'S THE ONLY REASON I'M EXCUSING THIS OUTBURST. I KNOW HOW YOU FEEL...
HOW CAN YOU KNOW ANYTHING ABOUT IT?! WHEN WERE YOU EVER IN LOVE?!

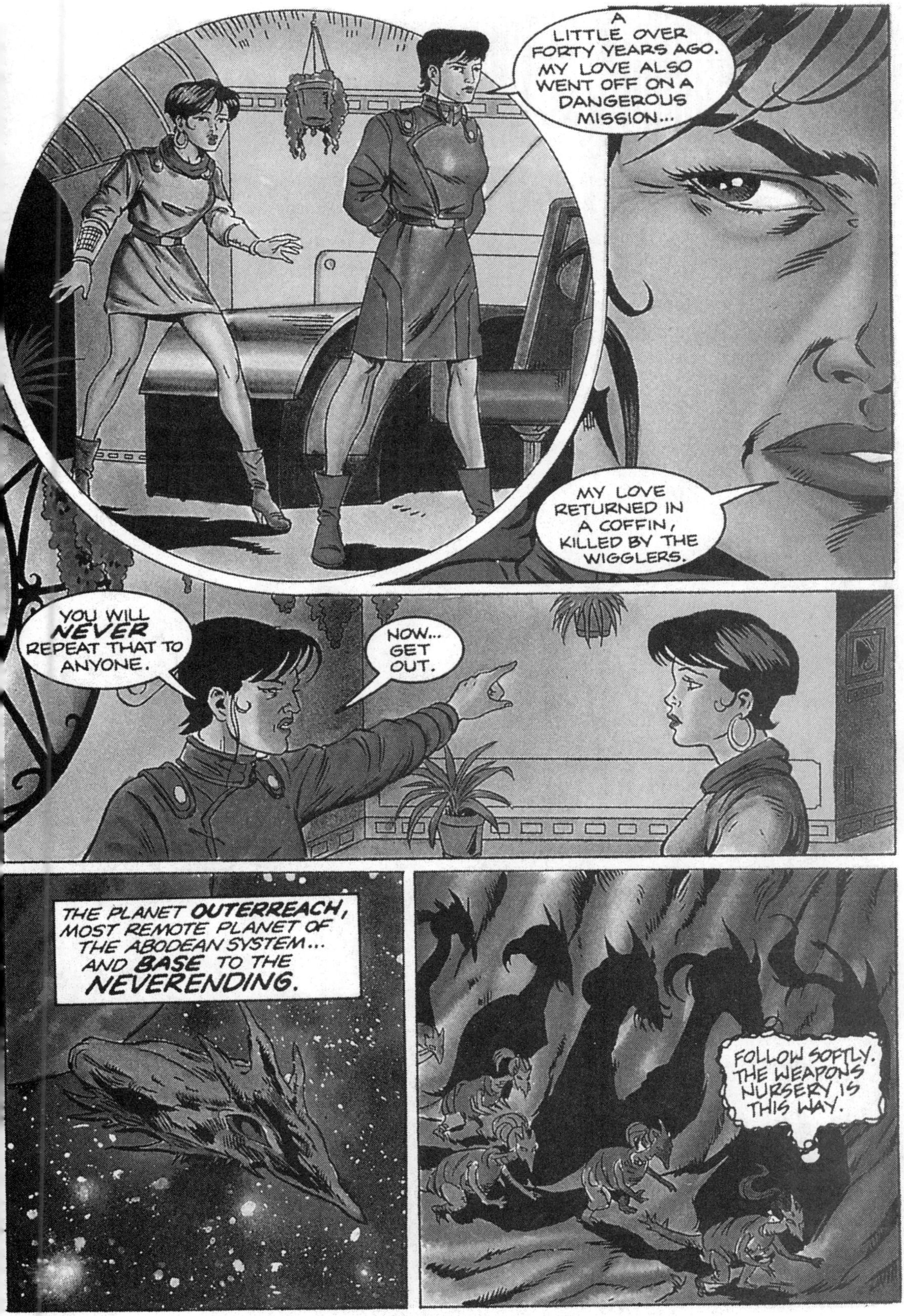
A LITTLE OVER FORTY YEARS AGO. MY LOVE ALSO WENT OFF ON A DANGEROUS MISSION...
MY LOVE RETURNED IN A COFFIN, KILLED BY THE WIGGLERS.
YOU WILL NEVER REPEAT THAT TO ANYONE.
NOW... GET OUT.
THE PLANET OUTERREACH, MOST REMOTE PLANET OF THE ABODEAN SYSTEM... AND BASE TO THE NEVERENDING.
FOLLOW SOFTLY. THE WEAPONS NURSERY IS THIS WAY.

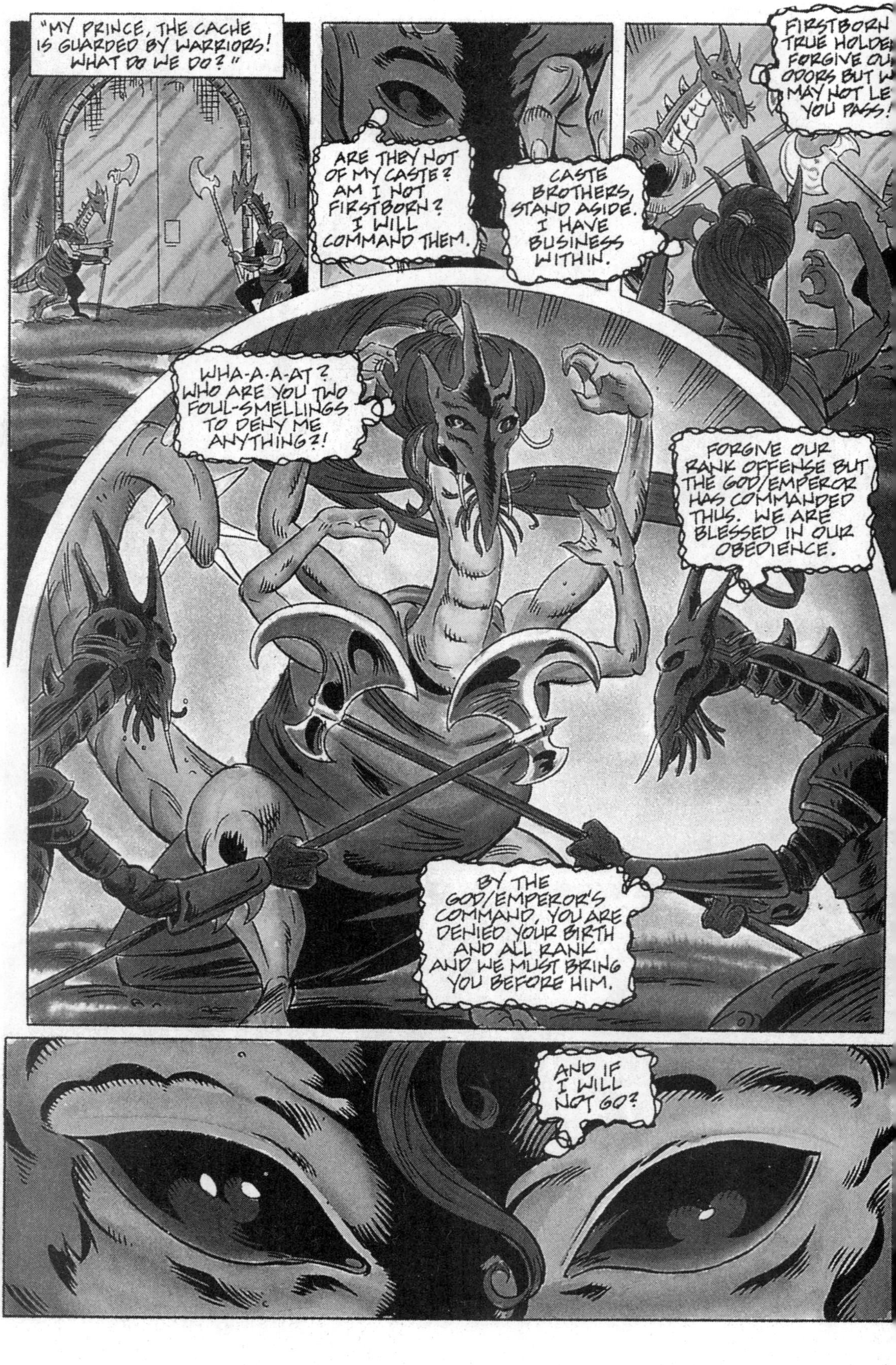
"MY PRINCE, THE CACHE IS GUARDED BY WARRIORS! WHAT DO WE DO?"
ARE THEY NOT OF MY CASTE? AM I NOT FIRSTBORN? I WILL COMMAND THEM.
CASTE BROTHERS, STAND ASIDE. I HAVE BUSINESS WITHIN.
WHA-A-A-AT? WHO ARE YOU TWO FOUL-SMELLINGS TO DENY ME ANYTHING?!
FORGIVE OUR RANK OFFENSE BUT THE GOD/EMPEROR HAS COMMANDED THUS. WE ARE BLESSED IN OUR OBEDIENCE.
BY THE GOD/EMPEROR'S COMMAND, YOU ARE DENIED YOUR BIRTH AND ALL RANK AND WE MUST BRING YOU BEFORE HIM.
AND IF I WILL NOT GO?

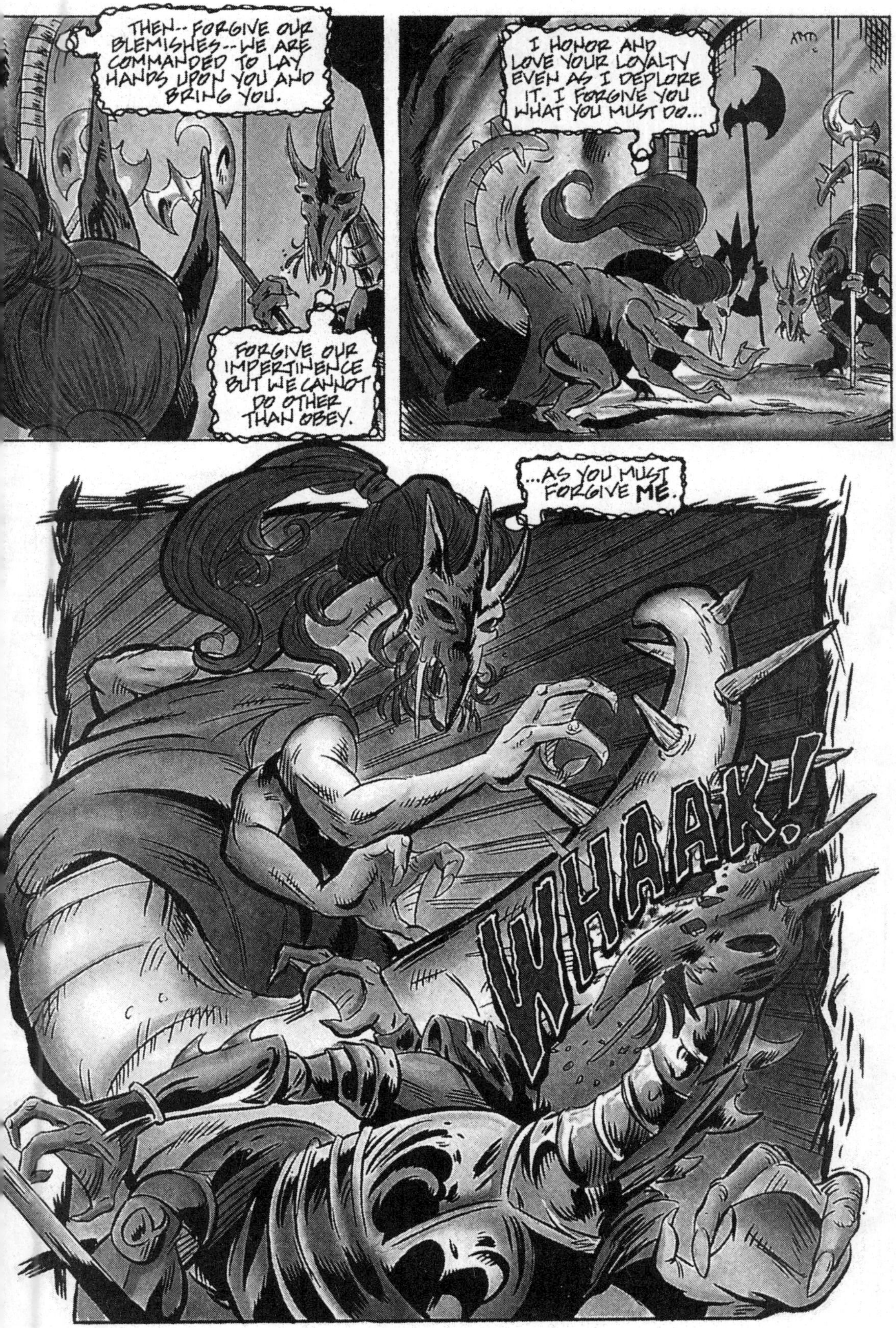
THEN.. FORGIVE OUR BLEMISHES--WE ARE COMMANDED TO LAY HANDS UPON YOU AND BRING YOU.
FORGIVE OUR IMPERTINENCE BUT WE CANNOT DO OTHER THAN OBEY.
I HONOR AND LOVE YOUR LOYALTY EVEN AS I DEPLORE IT. I FORGIVE YOU WHAT YOU MUST DO...
...AS YOU MUST FORGIVE ME.
WHAAK!

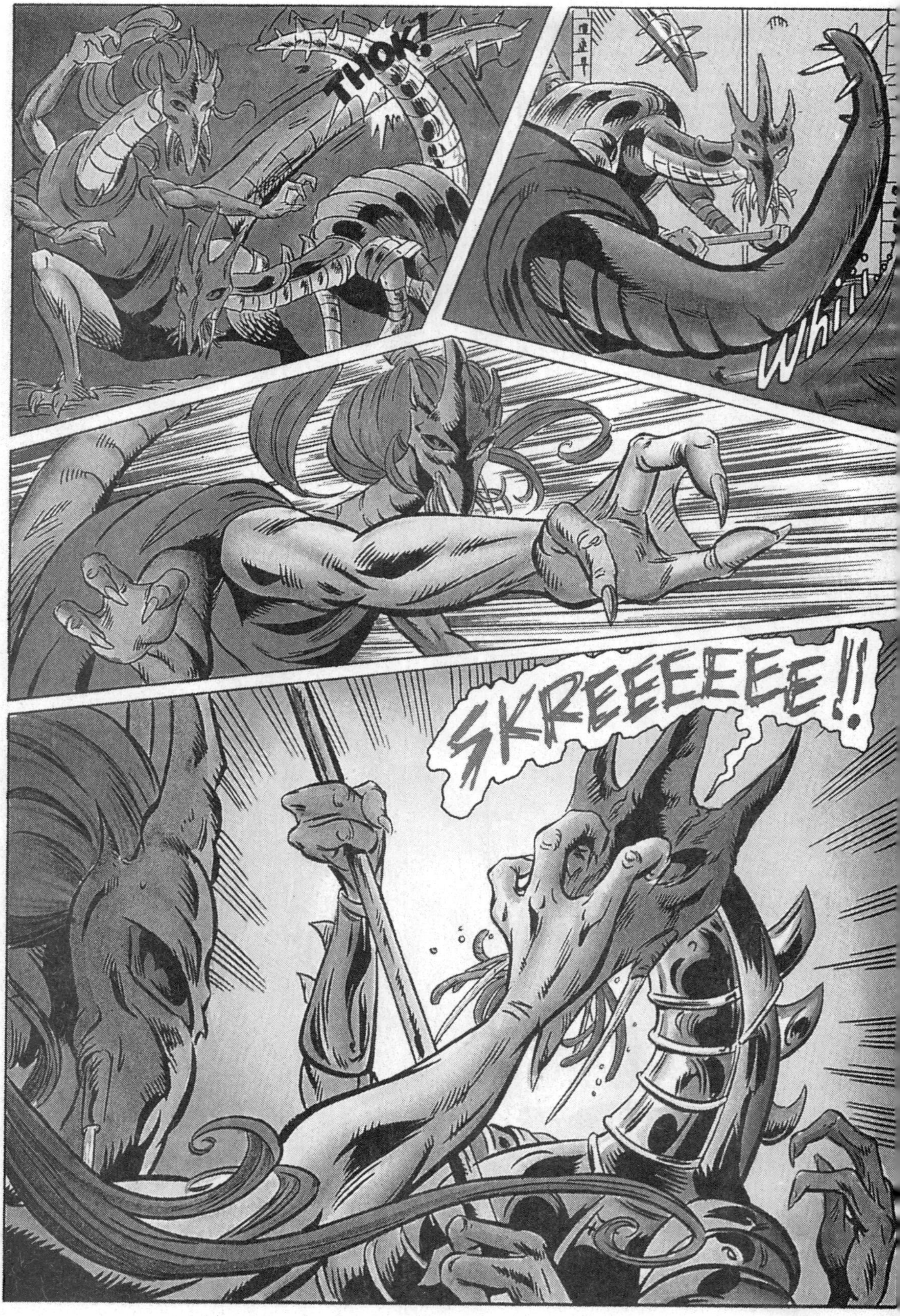
THOK!
Whiii
SKREEEEEEE!!

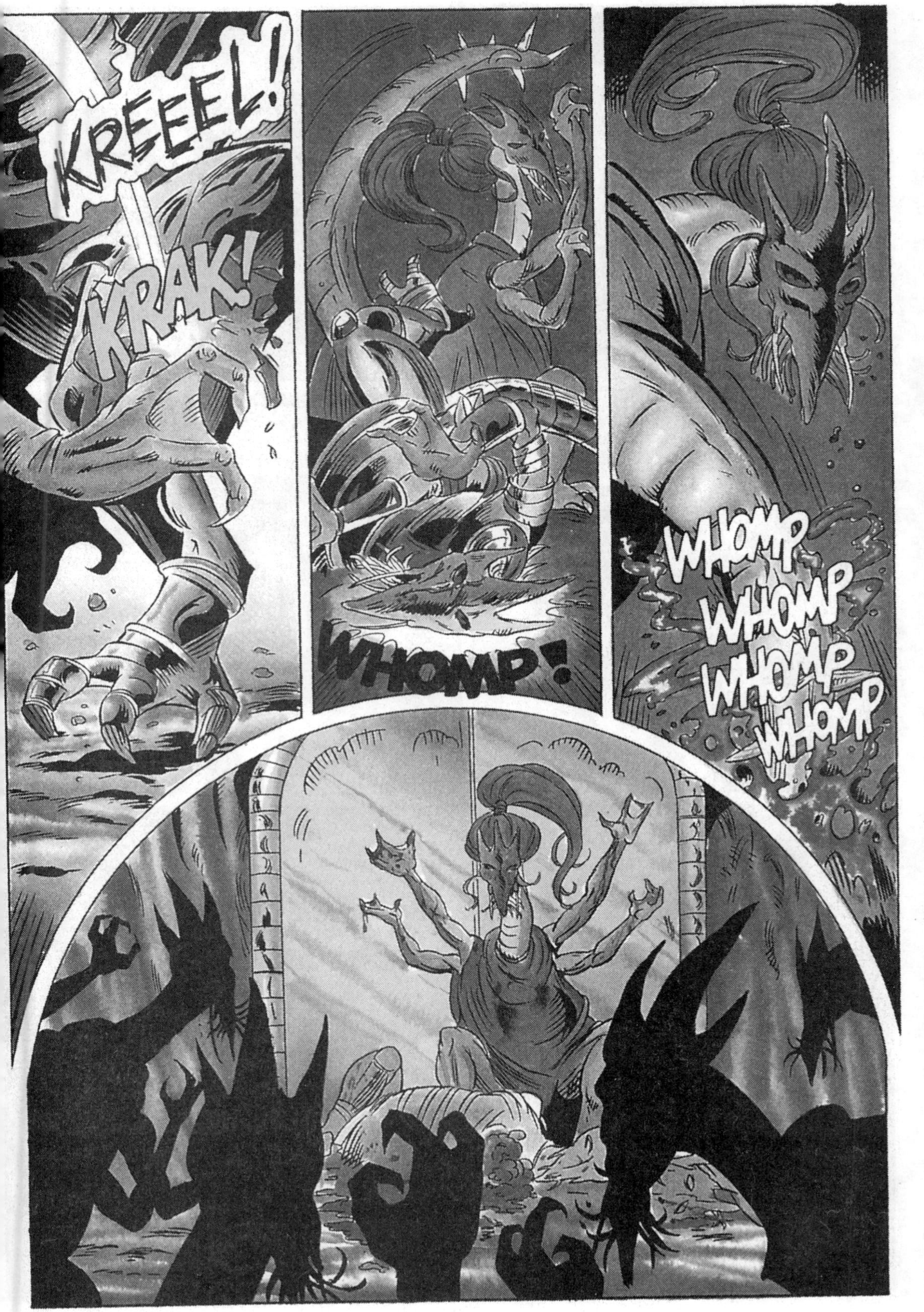

KREEEL!
KRAK!
WHOMP!
WHOMP
WHOMP
WHOMP
WHOMP

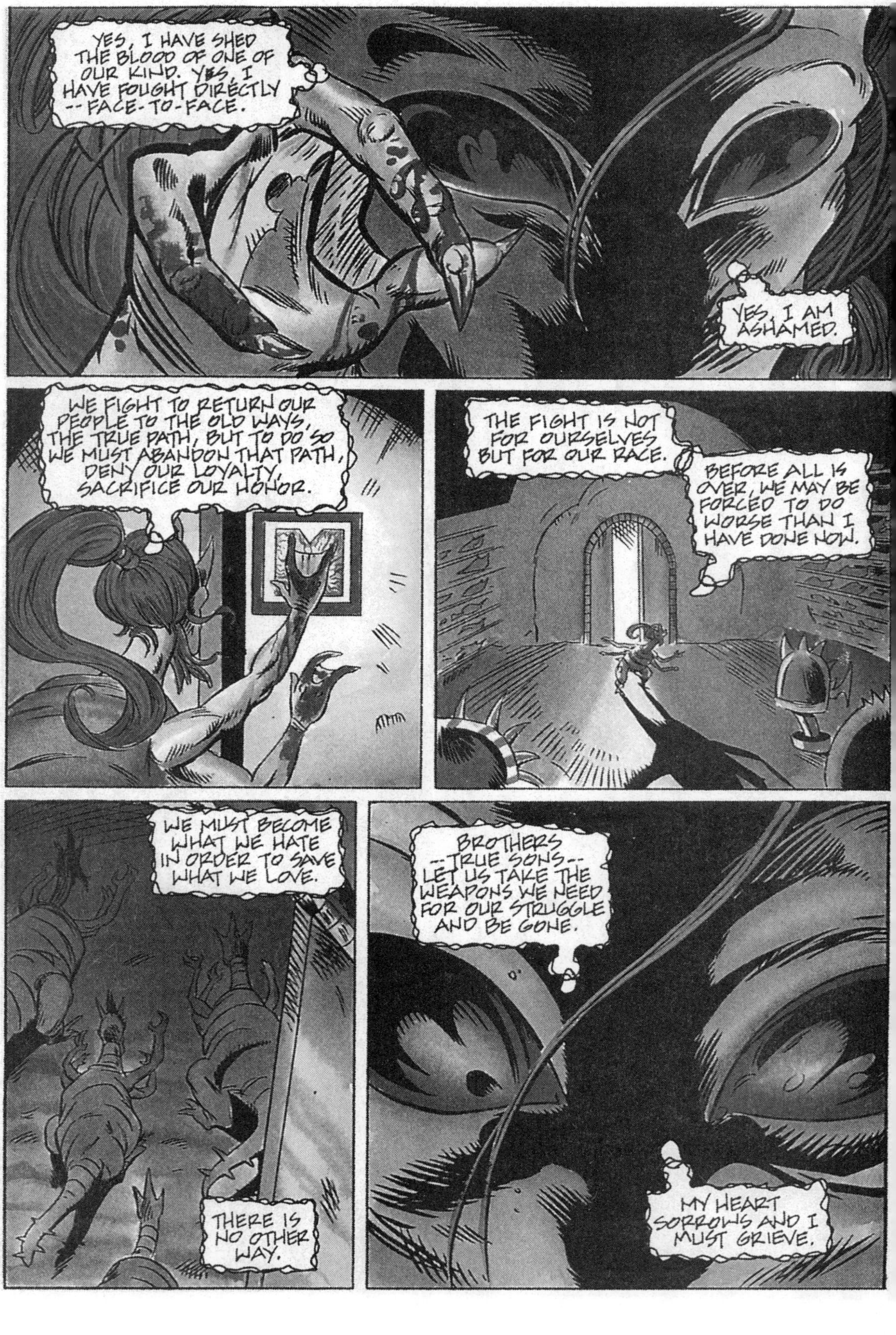
YES, I HAVE SHED THE BLOOD OF ONE OF OUR KIND. YES, I HAVE FOUGHT DIRECTLY --FACE-TO-FACE.
YES, I AM ASHAMED.
WE FIGHT TO RETURN OUR PEOPLE TO THE OLD WAYS, THE TRUE PATH, BUT TO DO SO WE MUST ABANDON THAT PATH, DENY OUR LOYALTY, SACRIFICE OUR HONOR.
THE FIGHT IS NOT FOR OURSELVES BUT FOR OUR RACE.
BEFORE ALL IS OVER, WE MAY BE FORCED TO DO WORSE THAN I HAVE DONE NOW.
WE MUST BECOME WHAT WE HATE IN ORDER TO SAVE WHAT WE LOVE.
THERE IS NO OTHER WAY.
BROTHERS --TRUE SONS-- LET US TAKE THE WEAPONS WE NEED FOR OUR STRUGGLE AND BE GONE.
MY HEART SORROWS AND I MUST GRIEVE.

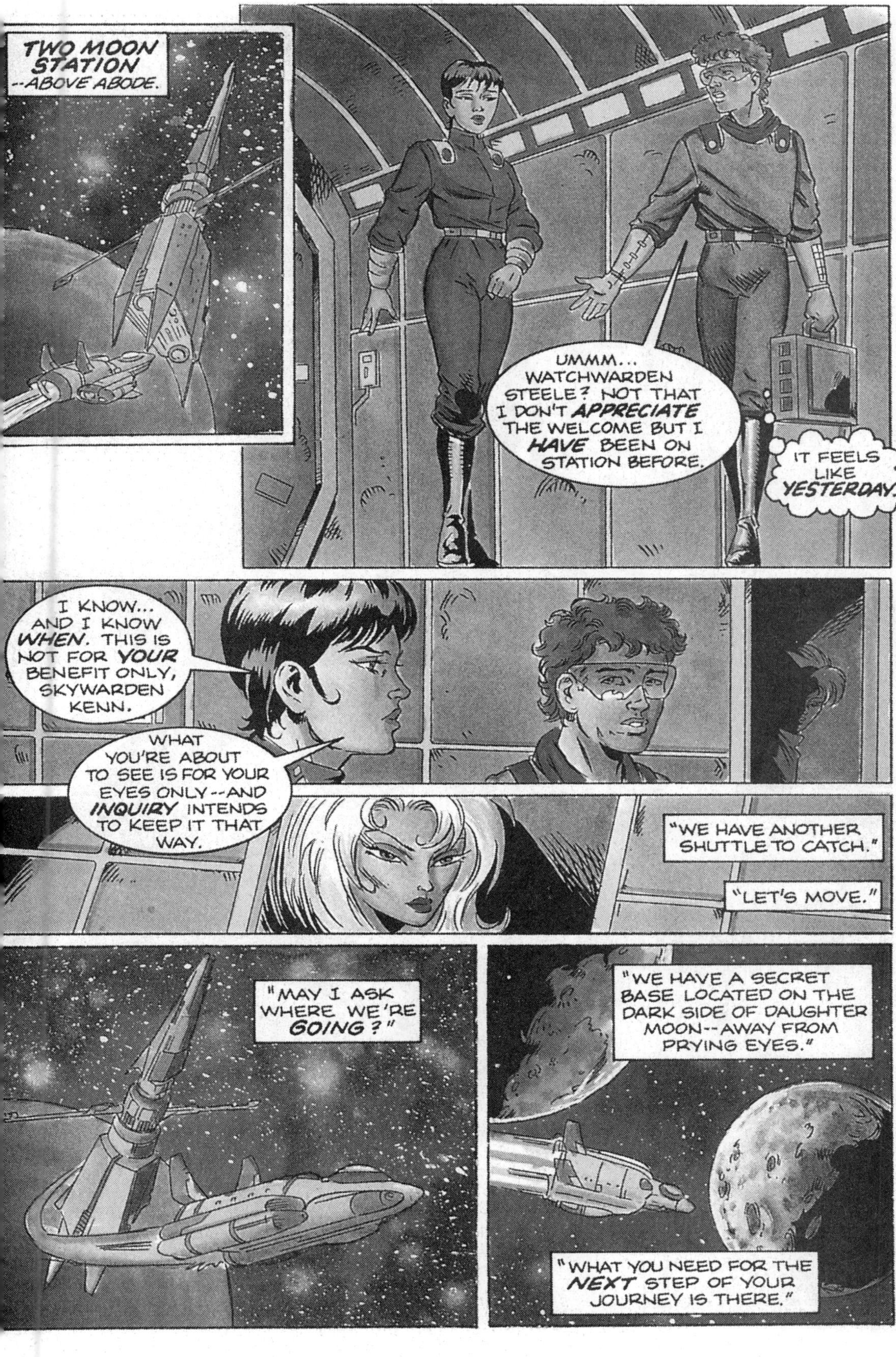
TWO MOON STATION --ABOVE ABODE.
UMMM... WATCHWARDEN STEELE? NOT THAT I DON'T APPRECIATE THE WELCOME BUT I HAVE BEEN ON STATION BEFORE.
IT FEELS LIKE YESTERDAY.
I KNOW... AND I KNOW WHEN. THIS IS NOT FOR YOUR BENEFIT ONLY, SKYWARDEN KENN.
WHAT YOU'RE ABOUT TO SEE IS FOR YOUR EYES ONLY--AND INQUIRY INTENDS TO KEEP IT THAT WAY.
"WE HAVE ANOTHER SHUTTLE TO CATCH."
"LET'S MOVE."
"MAY I ASK WHERE WE'RE GOING?"
"WE HAVE A SECRET BASE LOCATED ON THE DARK SIDE OF DAUGHTER MOON--AWAY FROM PRYING EYES."
"WHAT YOU NEED FOR THE NEXT STEP OF YOUR JOURNEY IS THERE."

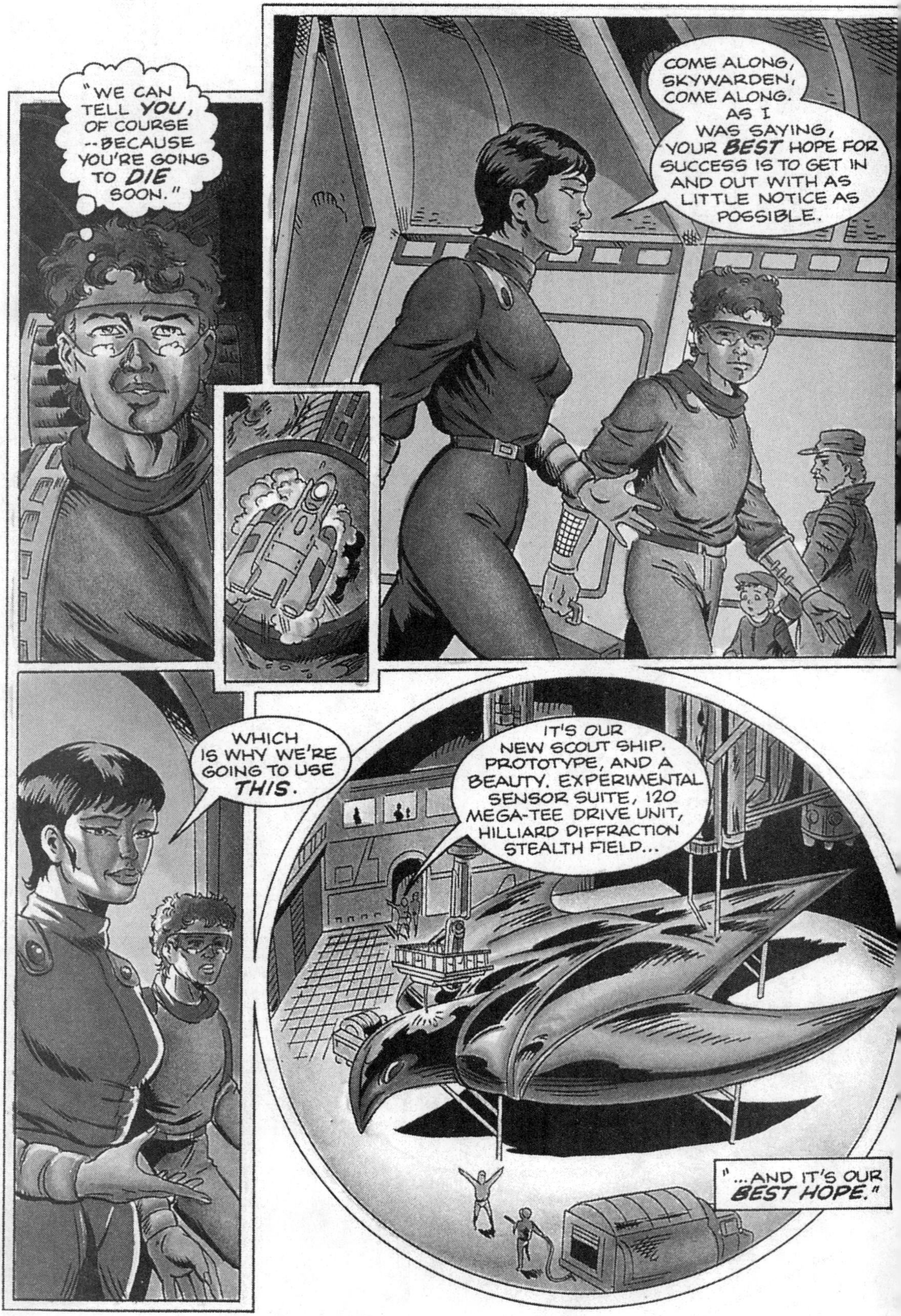
"WE CAN TELL YOU, OF COURSE --BECAUSE YOU'RE GOING TO DIE SOON."
COME ALONG, SKYWARDEN, COME ALONG. AS I WAS SAYING, YOUR BEST HOPE FOR SUCCESS IS TO GET IN AND OUT WITH AS LITTLE NOTICE AS POSSIBLE.
WHICH IS WHY WE'RE GOING TO USE THIS.
IT'S OUR NEW SCOUT SHIP. PROTOTYPE, AND A BEAUTY. EXPERIMENTAL SENSOR SUITE, 120 MEGA-TEE DRIVE UNIT, HILLIARD DIFFRACTION STEALTH FIELD...
"...AND IT'S OUR BEST HOPE."

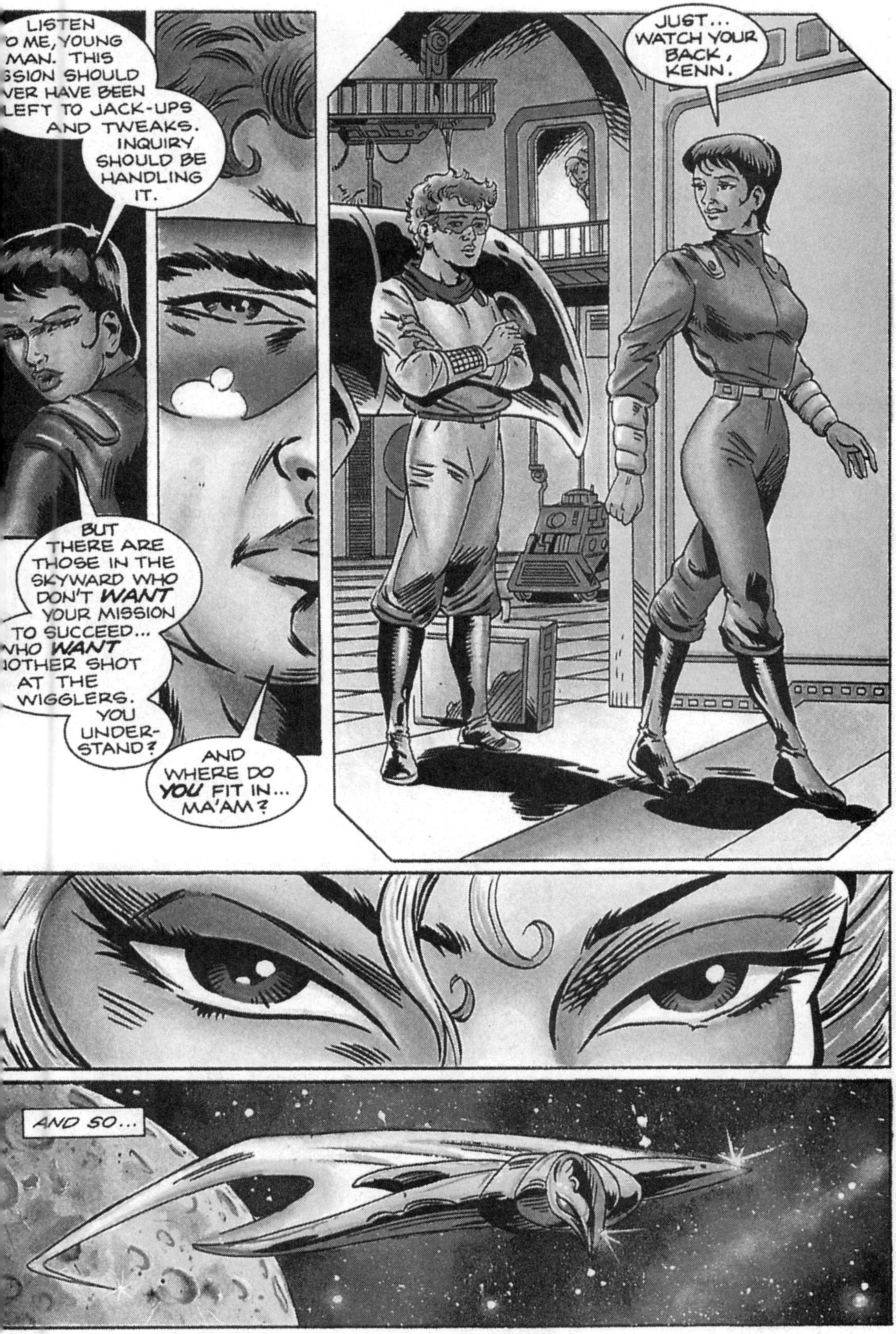
LISTEN TO ME, YOUNG MAN. THIS MISSION SHOULD NEVER HAVE BEEN LEFT TO JACK-UPS AND TWEAKS. INQUIRY SHOULD BE HANDLING IT.
BUT THERE ARE THOSE IN THE SKYWARD WHO DON'T WANT YOUR MISSION TO SUCCEED... WHO WANT ANOTHER SHOT AT THE WIGGLERS. YOU UNDERSTAND?
AND WHERE DO YOU FIT IN... MA'AM?
JUST... WATCH YOUR BACK, KENN.
AND SO...

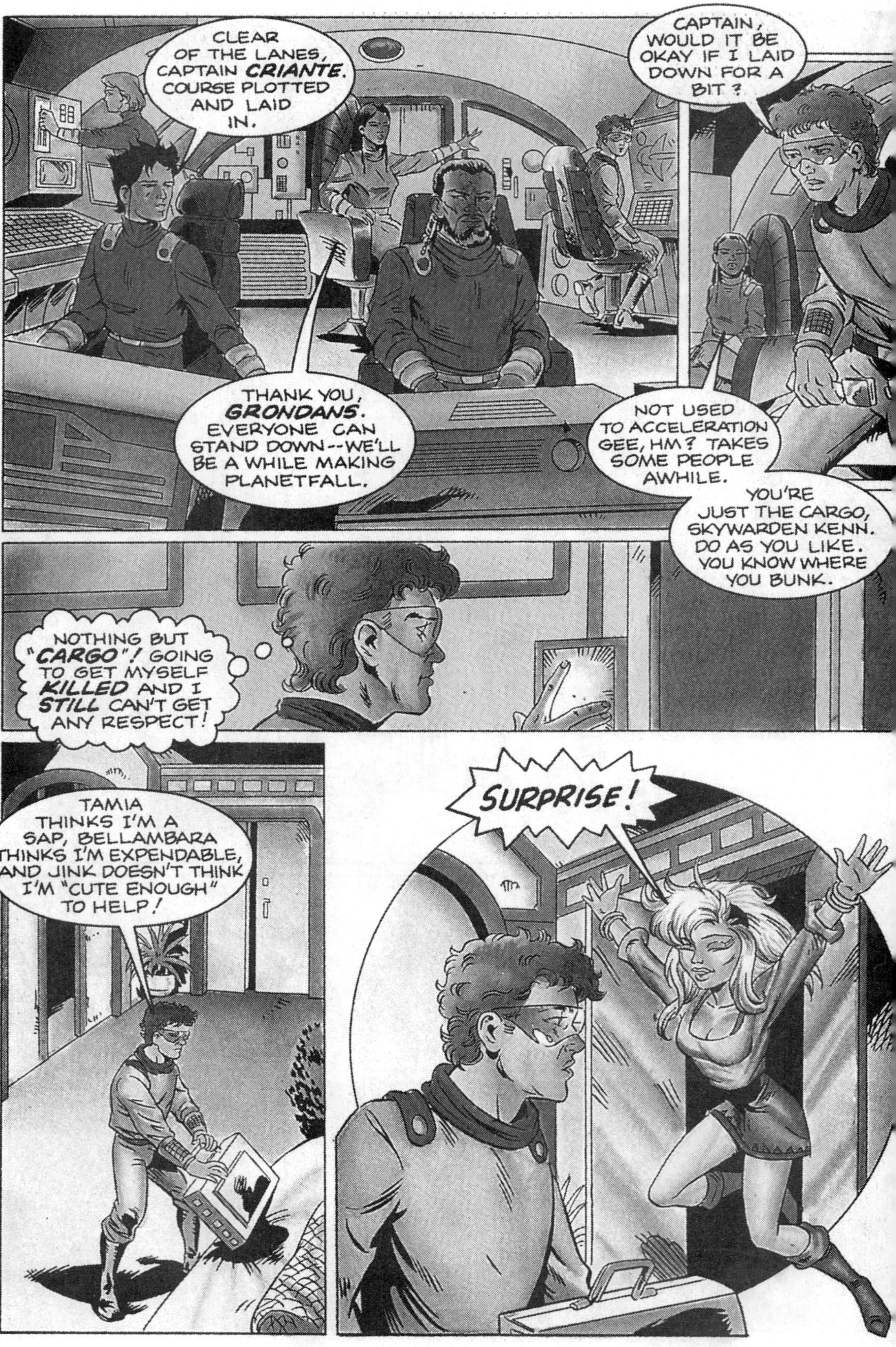
CLEAR OF THE LANES, CAPTAIN CRIANTE. COURSE PLOTTED AND LAID IN.
THANK YOU, GRONDANS. EVERYONE CAN STAND DOWN--WE'LL BE A WHILE MAKING PLANETFALL.
CAPTAIN, WOULD IT BE OKAY IF I LAID DOWN FOR A BIT?
NOT USED TO ACCELERATION GEE, HM? TAKES SOME PEOPLE AWHILE.
YOU'RE JUST THE CARGO, SKYWARDEN KENN. DO AS YOU LIKE. YOU KNOW WHERE YOU BUNK.
NOTHING BUT "CARGO"! GOING TO GET MYSELF KILLED AND I STILL CAN'T GET ANY RESPECT!
TAMIA THINKS I'M A SAP, BELLAMBARA THINKS I'M EXPENDABLE, AND JINK DOESN'T THINK I'M "CUTE ENOUGH" TO HELP!
SURPRISE!

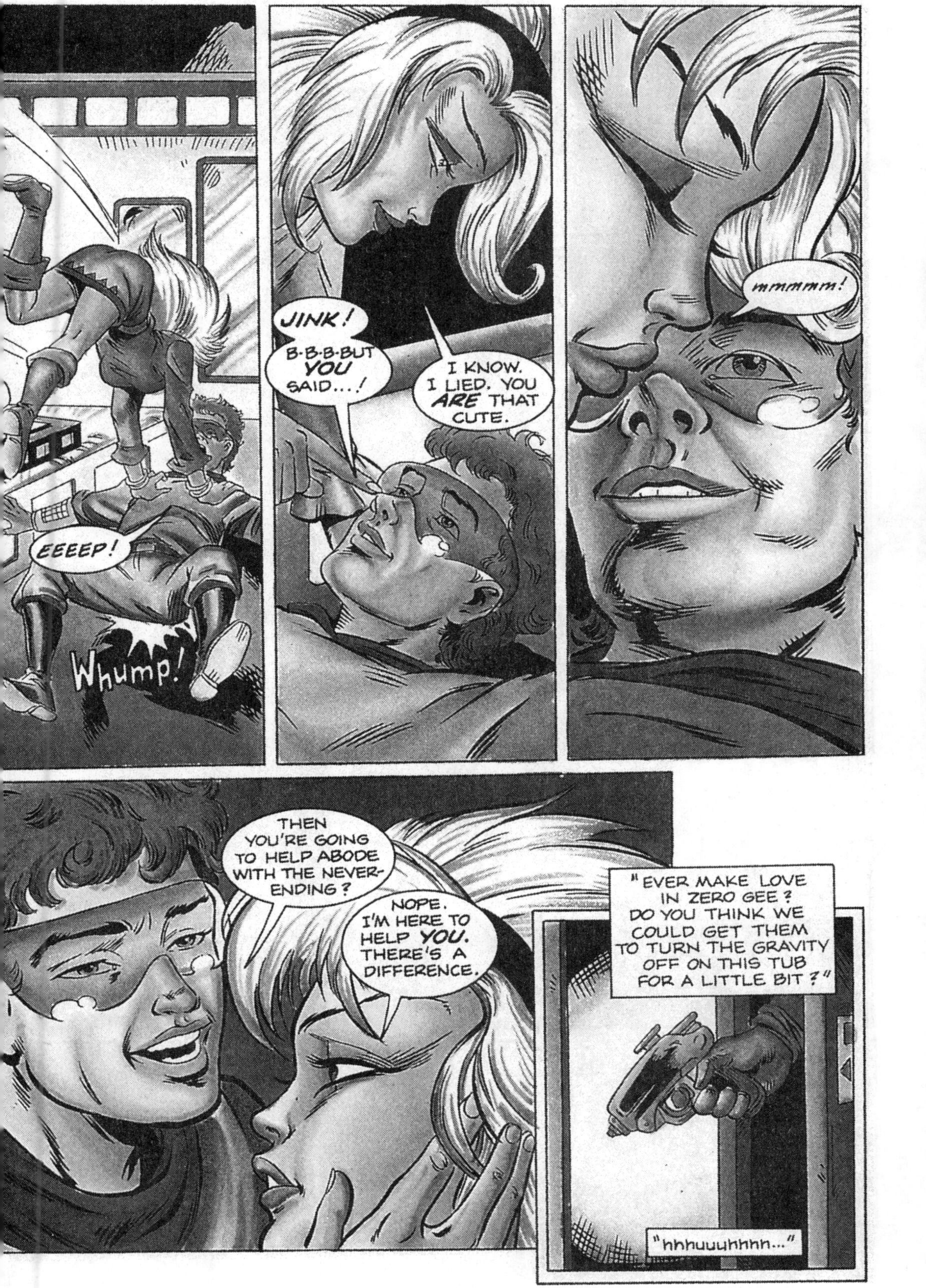
EEEEP!
Whump!
JINK!
B-B-B-BUT YOU SAID...!
I KNOW. I LIED. YOU ARE THAT CUTE.
mmmmmm!
THEN YOU'RE GOING TO HELP ABODE WITH THE NEVER-ENDING?
NOPE. I'M HERE TO HELP YOU. THERE'S A DIFFERENCE.
"EVER MAKE LOVE IN ZERO GEE? DO YOU THINK WE COULD GET THEM TO TURN THE GRAVITY OFF ON THIS TUB FOR A LITTLE BIT?"
"hhhuuuhhhn..."

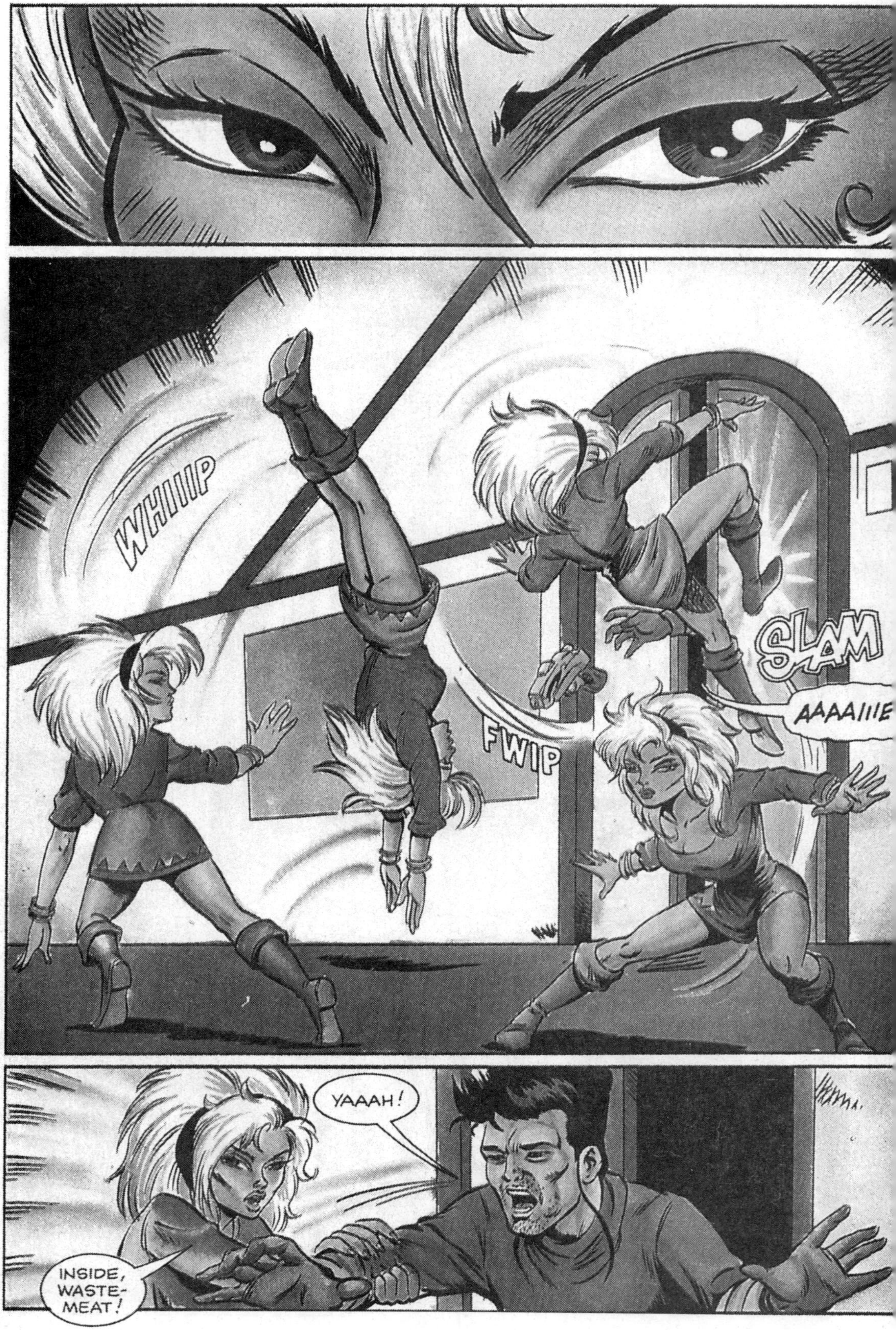
WHIIIP
SLAM
FWIP
AAAAIIIE
YAAAH!
INSIDE, WASTE-MEAT!

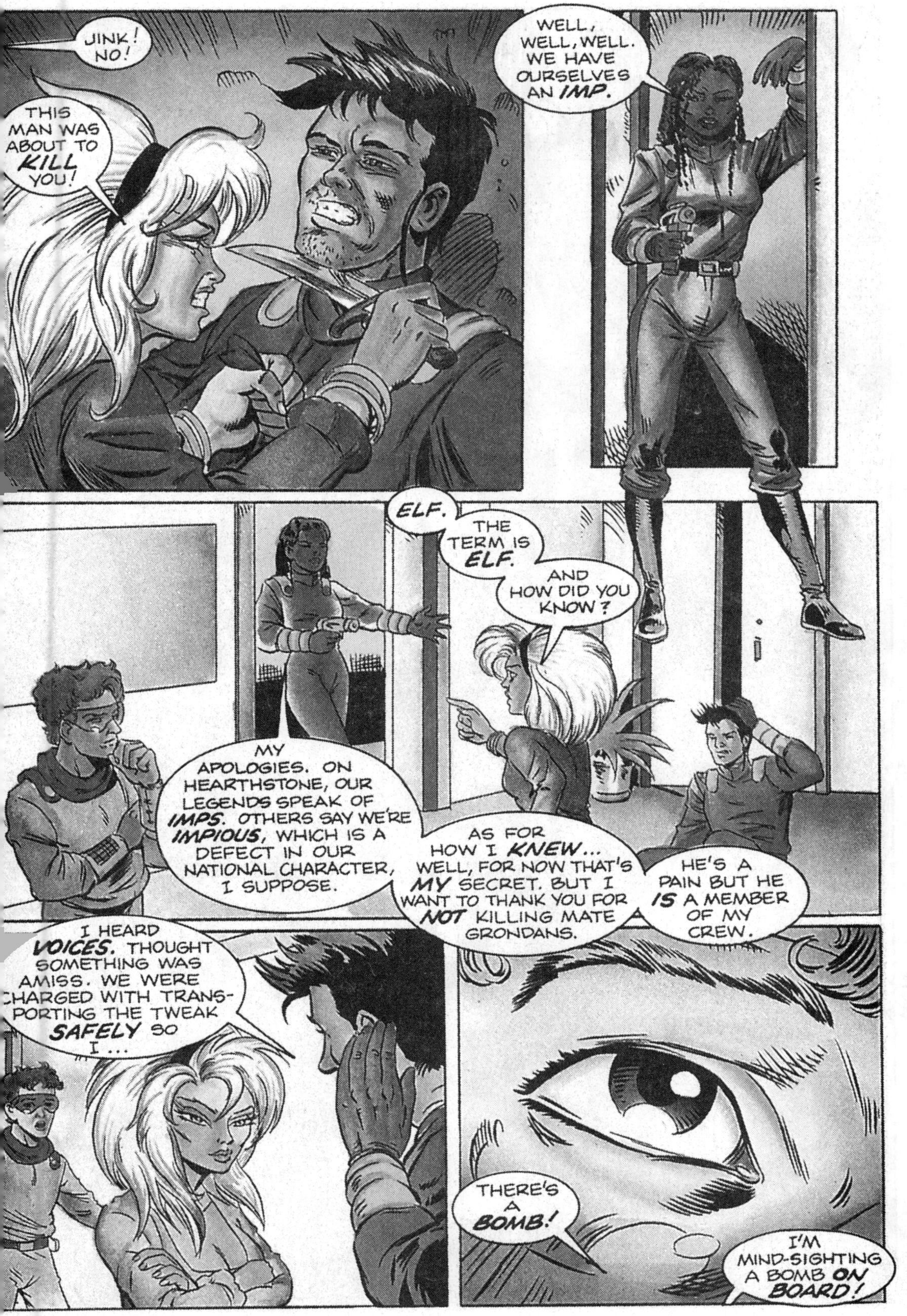
JINK! NO!
THIS MAN WAS ABOUT TO KILL YOU!
WELL, WELL, WELL. WE HAVE OURSELVES AN IMP.
ELF.
THE TERM IS ELF.
AND HOW DID YOU KNOW?
MY APOLOGIES. ON HEARTHSTONE, OUR LEGENDS SPEAK OF IMPS. OTHERS SAY WE'RE IMPIOUS, WHICH IS A DEFECT IN OUR NATIONAL CHARACTER, I SUPPOSE.
AS FOR HOW I KNEW... WELL, FOR NOW THAT'S MY SECRET. BUT I WANT TO THANK YOU FOR NOT KILLING MATE GRONDANS.
HE'S A PAIN BUT HE IS A MEMBER OF MY CREW.
I HEARD VOICES. THOUGHT SOMETHING WAS AMISS. WE WERE CHARGED WITH TRANS-PORTING THE TWEAK SAFELY SO I...
THERE'S A BOMB!
I'M MIND-SIGHTING A BOMB ON BOARD!

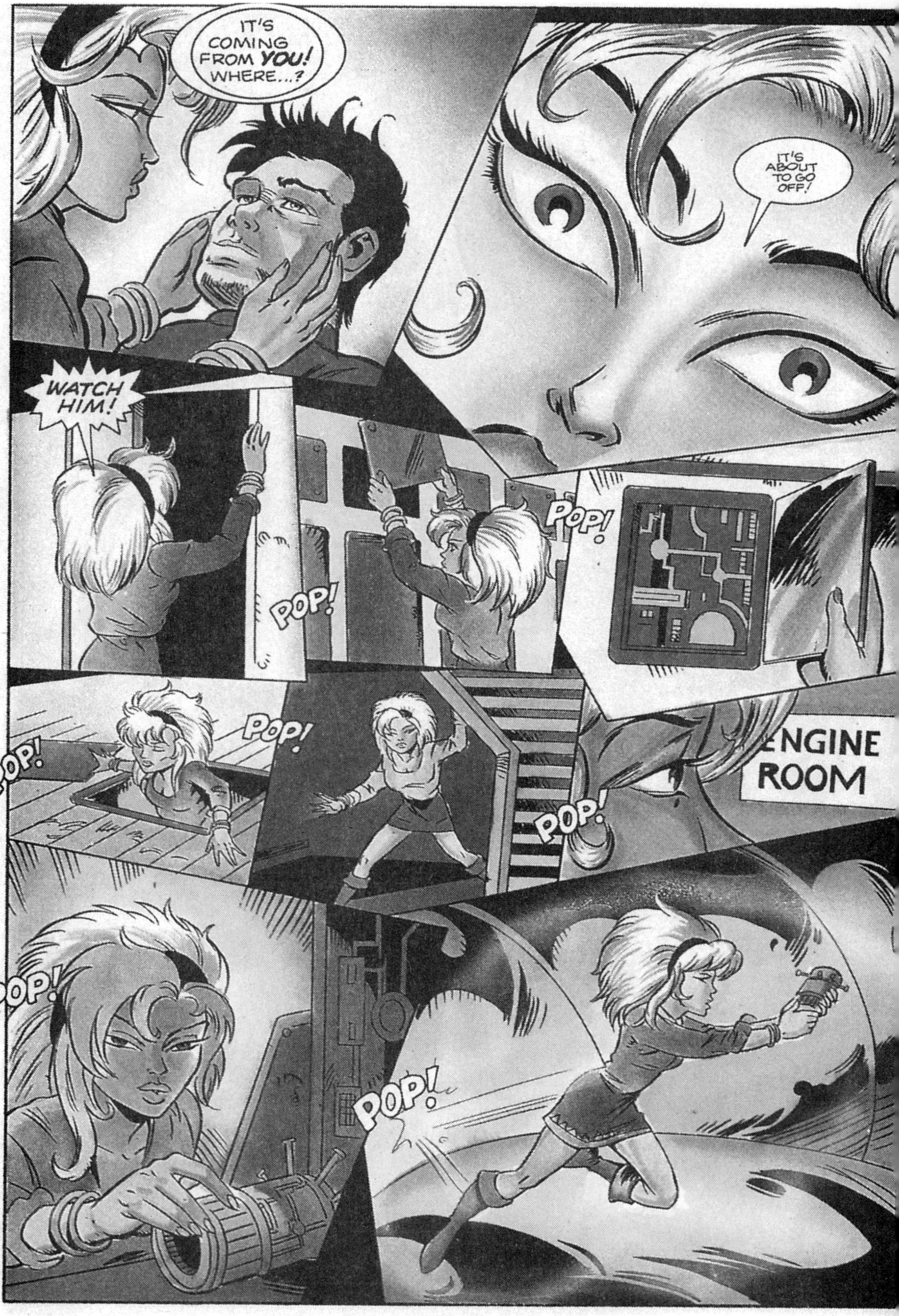
IT'S COMING FROM YOU! WHERE...?
IT'S ABOUT TO GO OFF!
WATCH HIM!
POP!
POP!
POP!
POP!
ENGINE ROOM
POP!
POP!
POP!

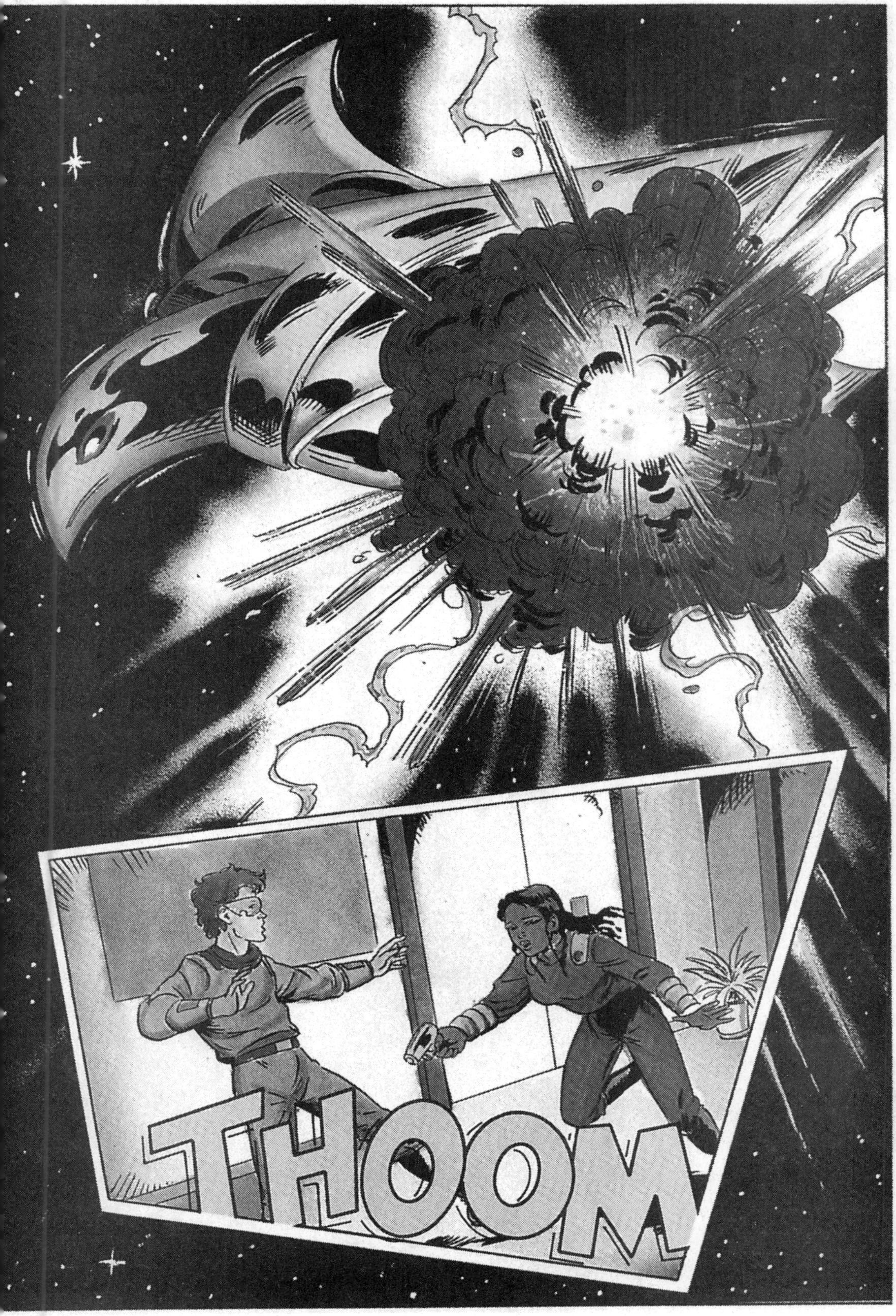
THOOM

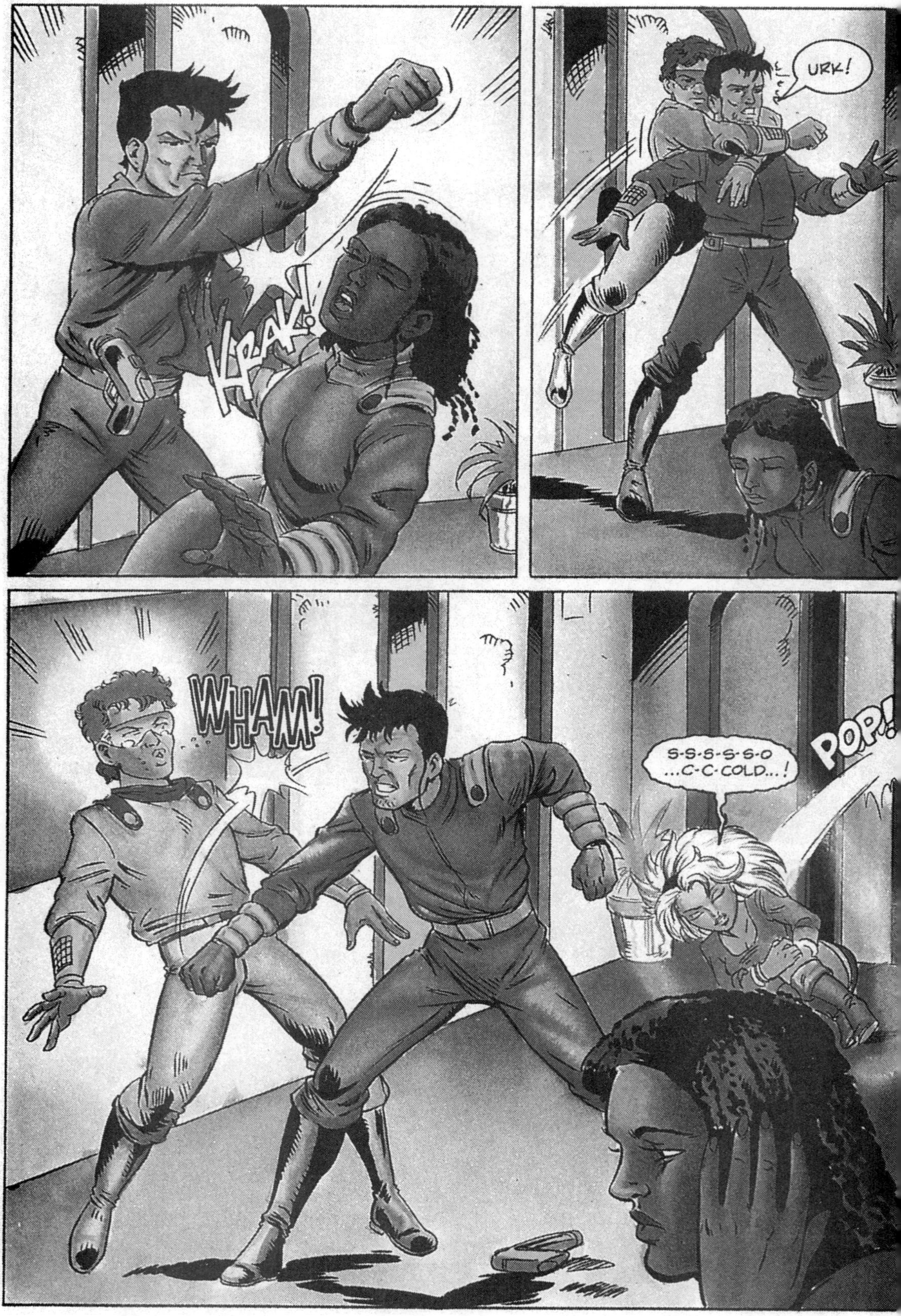
KRAK!
URK!
WHAM!
S-S-S-S-S-O ...C-C-COLD...!
POP!

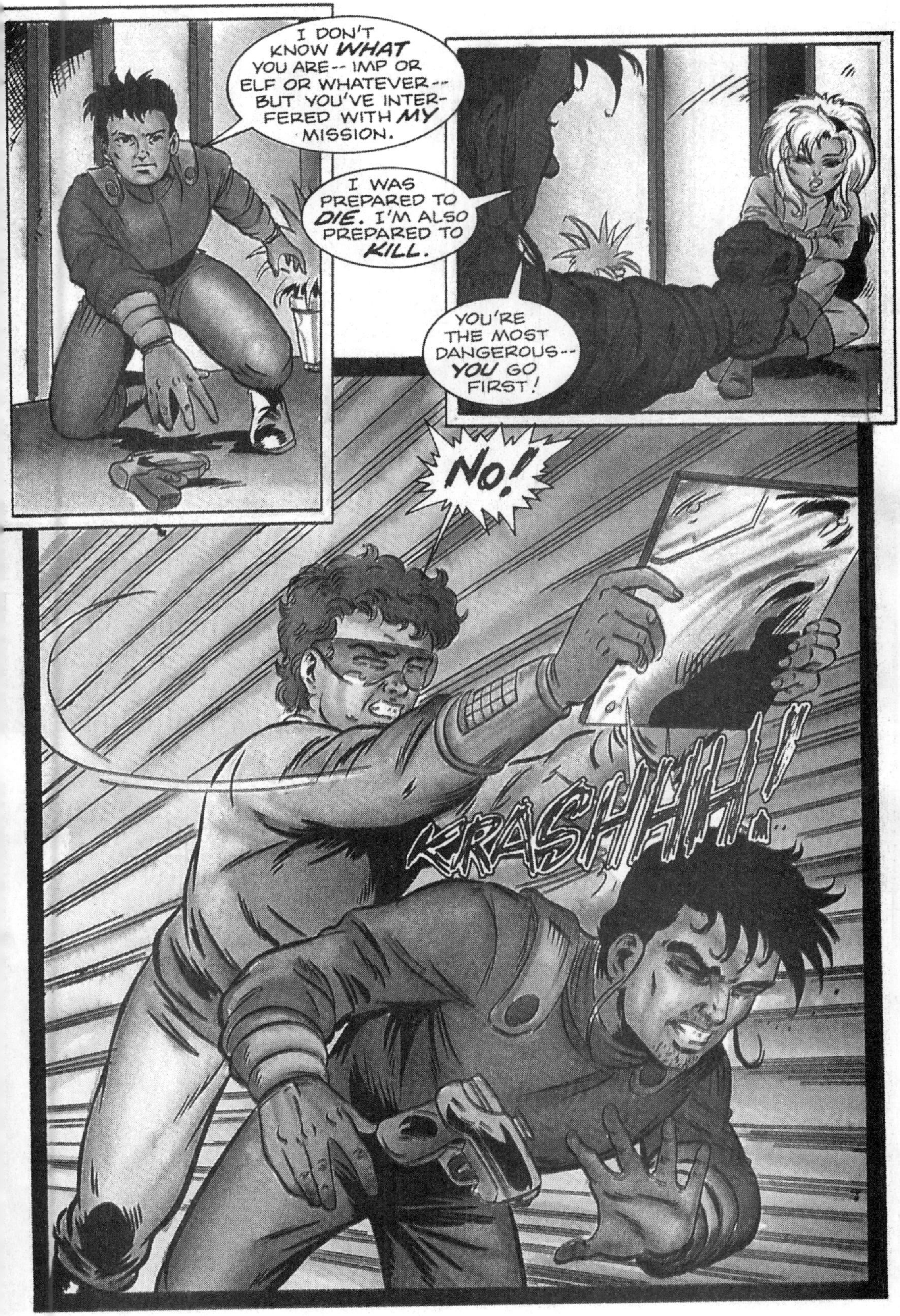
I DON'T KNOW WHAT YOU ARE-- IMP OR ELF OR WHATEVER-- BUT YOU'VE INTERFERED WITH MY MISSION.
I WAS PREPARED TO DIE. I'M ALSO PREPARED TO KILL.
YOU'RE THE MOST DANGEROUS-- YOU GO FIRST!
NO!
KRASHHH!

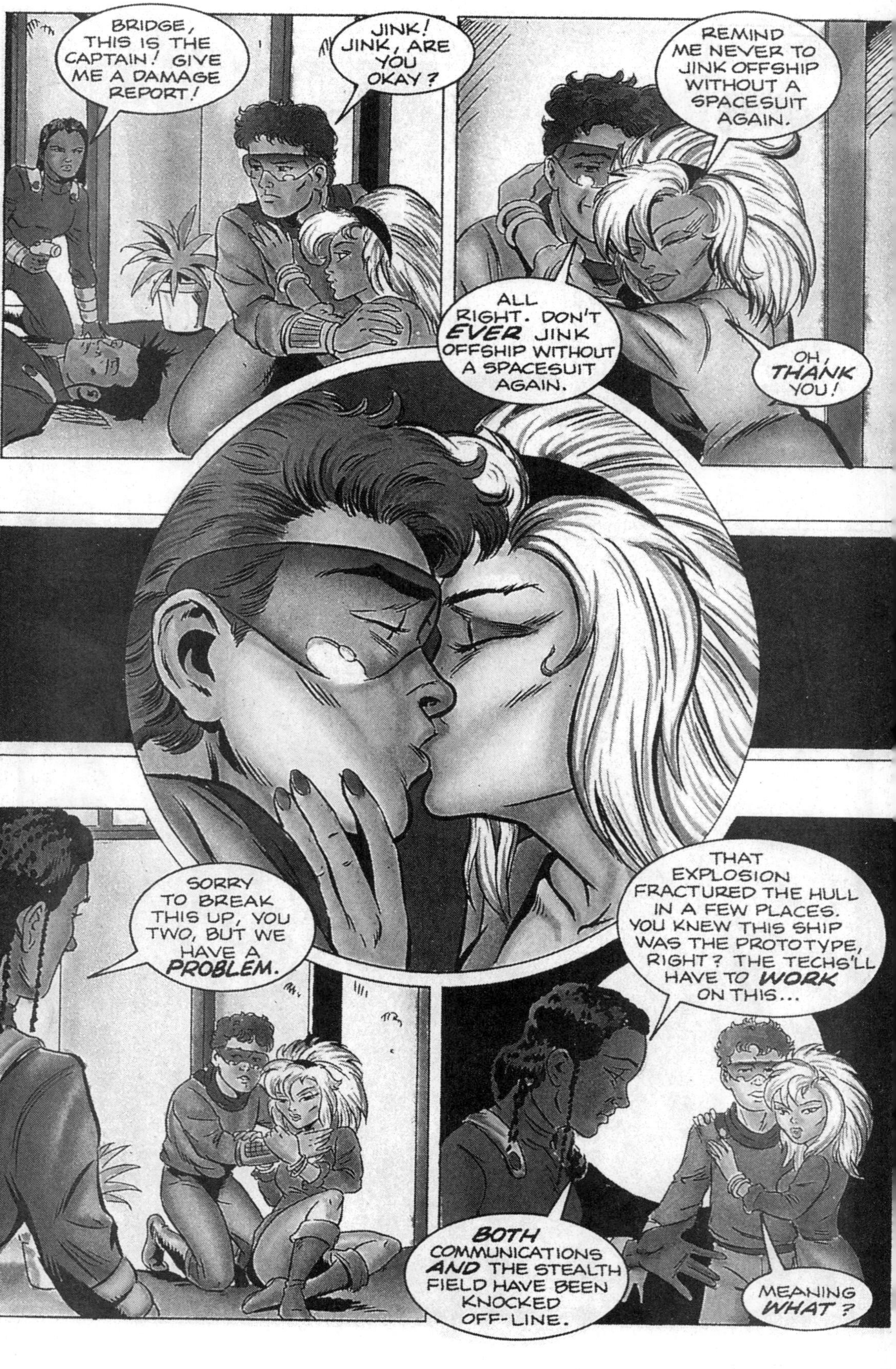

BRIDGE, THIS IS THE CAPTAIN! GIVE ME A DAMAGE REPORT!
JINK! JINK, ARE YOU OKAY?
REMIND ME NEVER TO JINK OFFSHIP WITHOUT A SPACESUIT AGAIN.
ALL RIGHT. DON'T EVER JINK OFFSHIP WITHOUT A SPACESUIT AGAIN.
OH, THANK YOU!
SORRY TO BREAK THIS UP, YOU TWO, BUT WE HAVE A PROBLEM.
THAT EXPLOSION FRACTURED THE HULL IN A FEW PLACES. YOU KNEW THIS SHIP WAS THE PROTOTYPE, RIGHT? THE TECHS'LL HAVE TO WORK ON THIS...
BOTH COMMUNICATIONS AND THE STEALTH FIELD HAVE BEEN KNOCKED OFF-LINE.
MEANING WHAT?

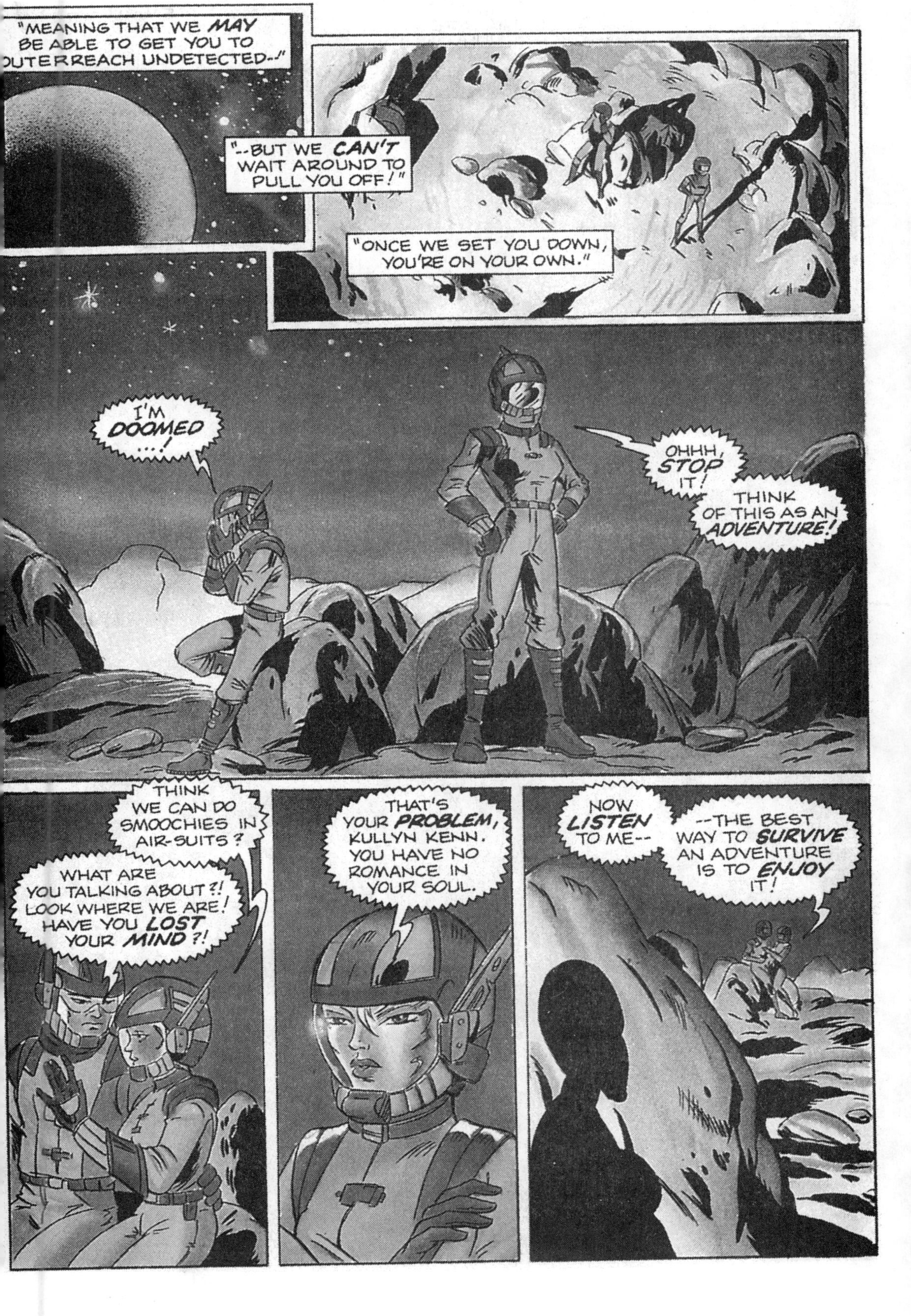
"MEANING THAT WE MAY BE ABLE TO GET YOU TO OUTERREACH UNDETECTED--"
"--BUT WE CAN'T WAIT AROUND TO PULL YOU OFF!"
"ONCE WE SET YOU DOWN, YOU'RE ON YOUR OWN."
I'M DOOMED...!
OHHH, STOP IT!
THINK OF THIS AS AN ADVENTURE!
THINK WE CAN DO SMOOCHIES IN AIR-SUITS?
WHAT ARE YOU TALKING ABOUT?! LOOK WHERE WE ARE! HAVE YOU LOST YOUR MIND?!
THAT'S YOUR PROBLEM, KULLYN KENN. YOU HAVE NO ROMANCE IN YOUR SOUL.
NOW LISTEN TO ME--
--THE BEST WAY TO SURVIVE AN ADVENTURE IS TO ENJOY IT!

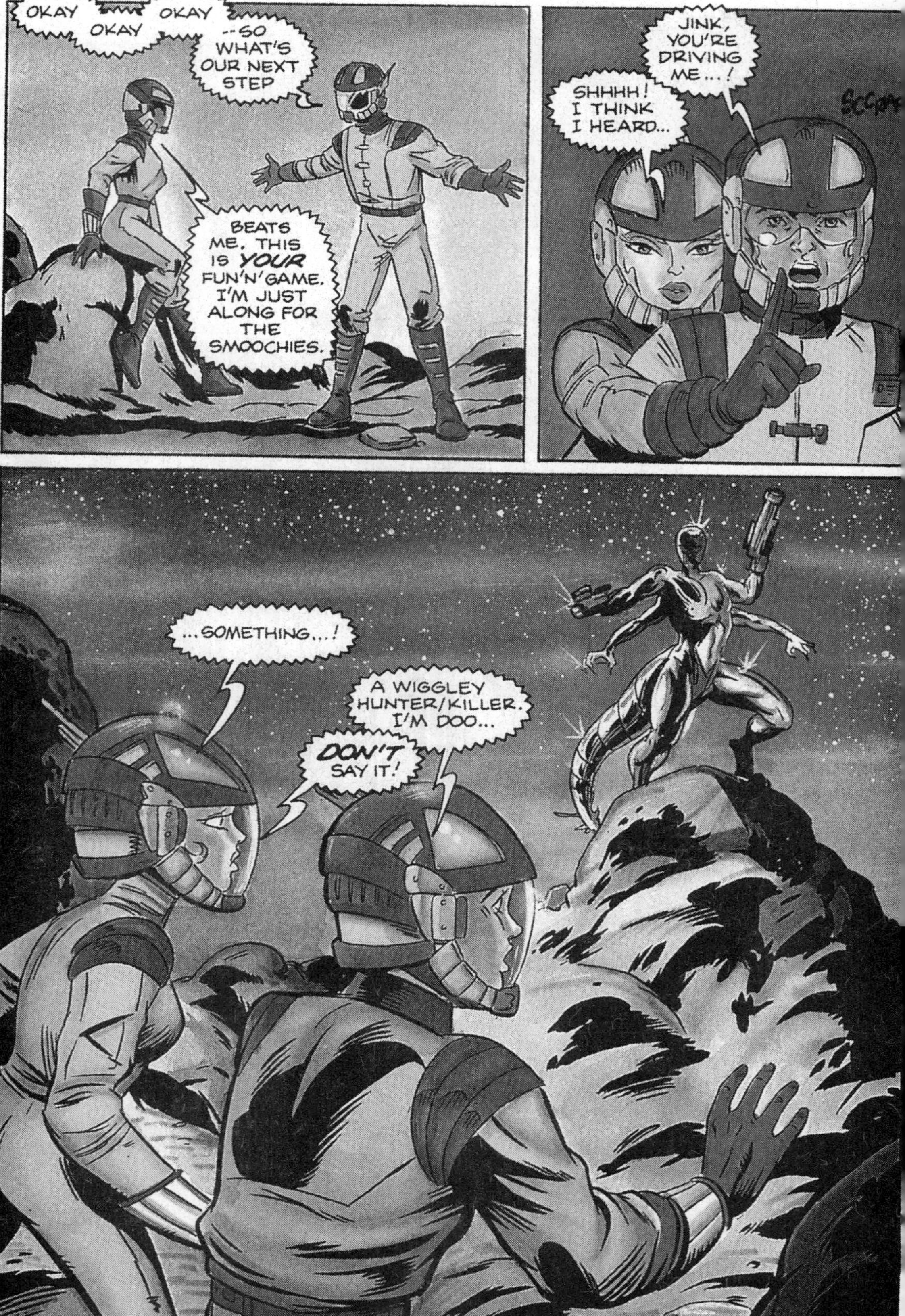
OKAY OKAY OKAY
--SO WHAT'S OUR NEXT STEP
BEATS ME. THIS IS YOUR FUN'N'GAME. I'M JUST ALONG FOR THE SMOOCHIES.
JINK, YOU'RE DRIVING ME...!
SHHHH! I THINK I HEARD...
...SOMETHING...!
A WIGGLEY HUNTER/KILLER. I'M DOO...
DON'T SAY IT!

TO BE CONTINUED...

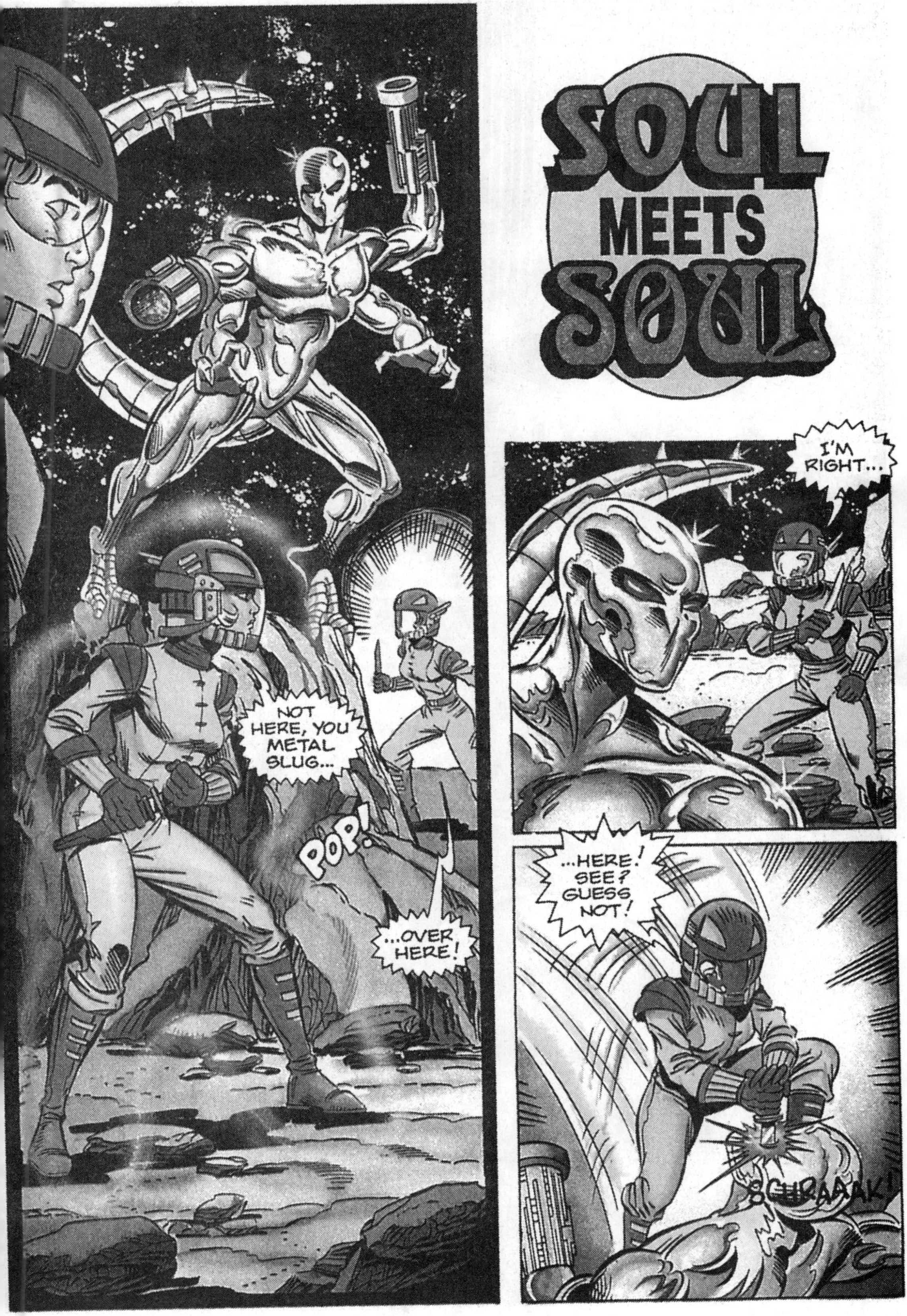
SOUL MEETS SOUL
NOT HERE, YOU METAL SLUG...
POP!
...OVER HERE!
I'M RIGHT...
...HERE! SEE? GUESS NOT!
SCHRAAAK!

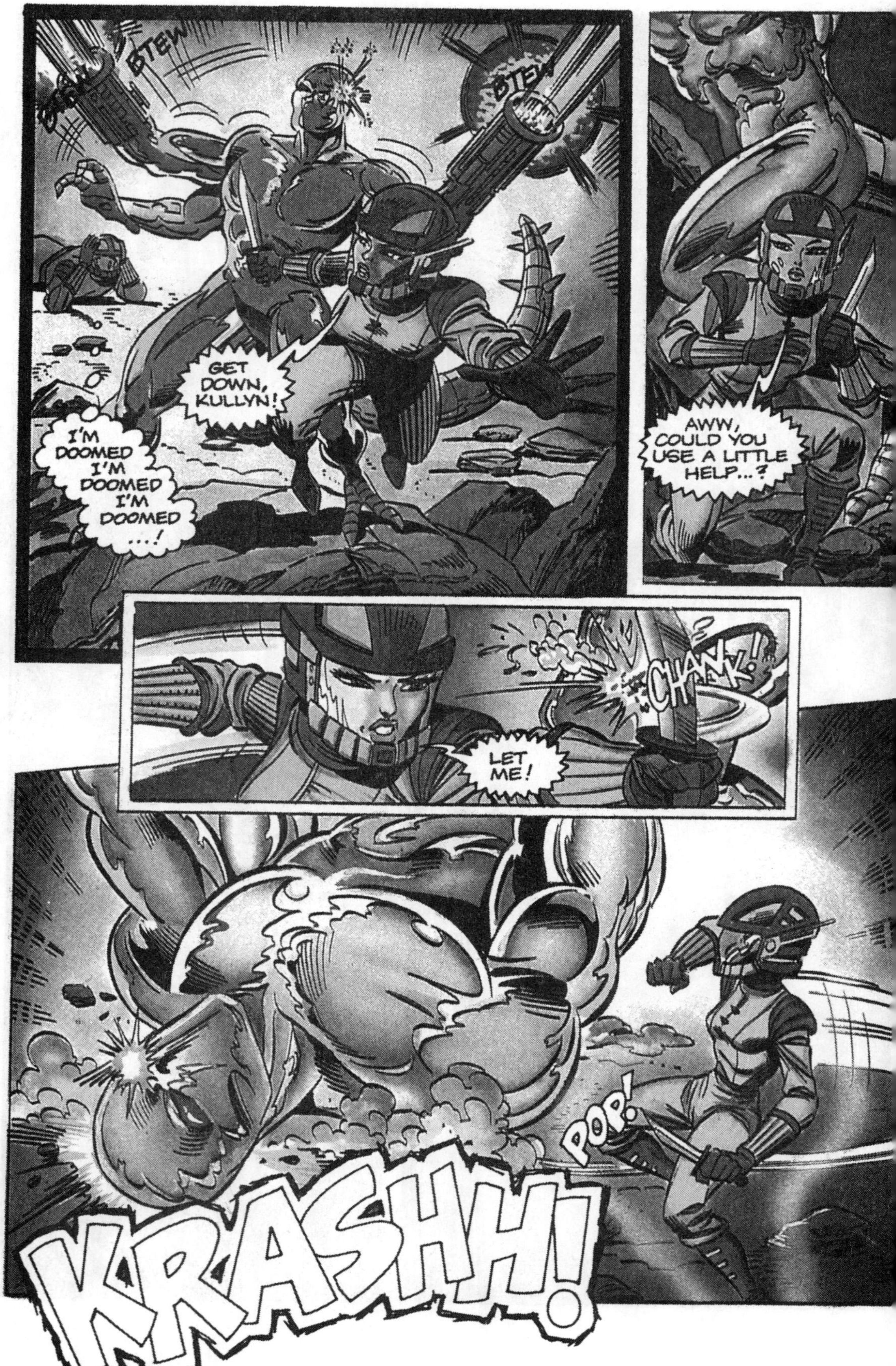

BTEW
BTEW
BTEW
GET DOWN, KULLYN!
I'M DOOMED I'M DOOMED I'M DOOMED ...!
AWW, COULD YOU USE A LITTLE HELP...?
CHANK!
LET ME!
POP!
KRASHH!

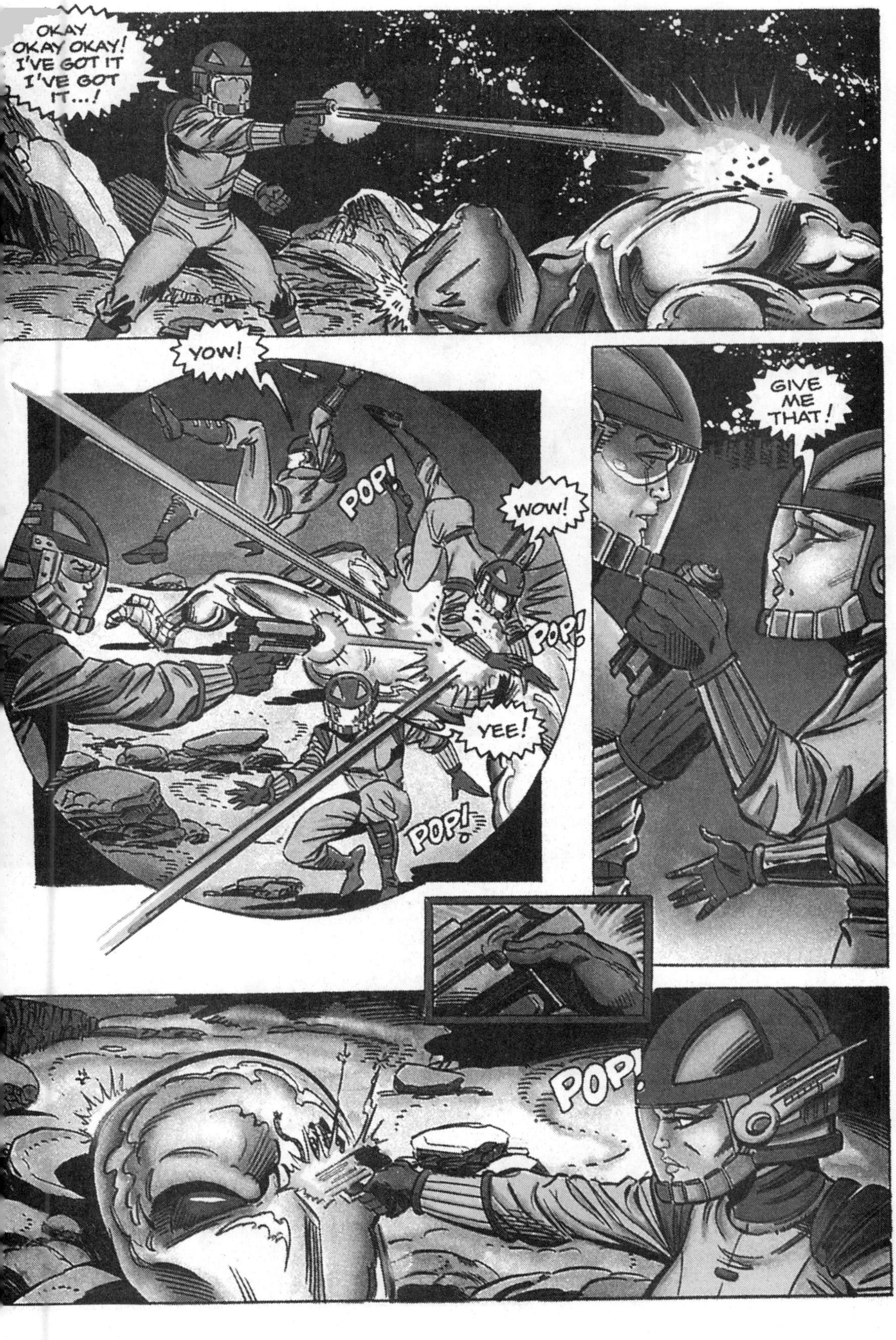

OKAY OKAY OKAY! I'VE GOT IT I'VE GOT IT...!
YOW!
POP!
WOW!
POP!
YEE!
POP!
GIVE ME THAT!
POP!

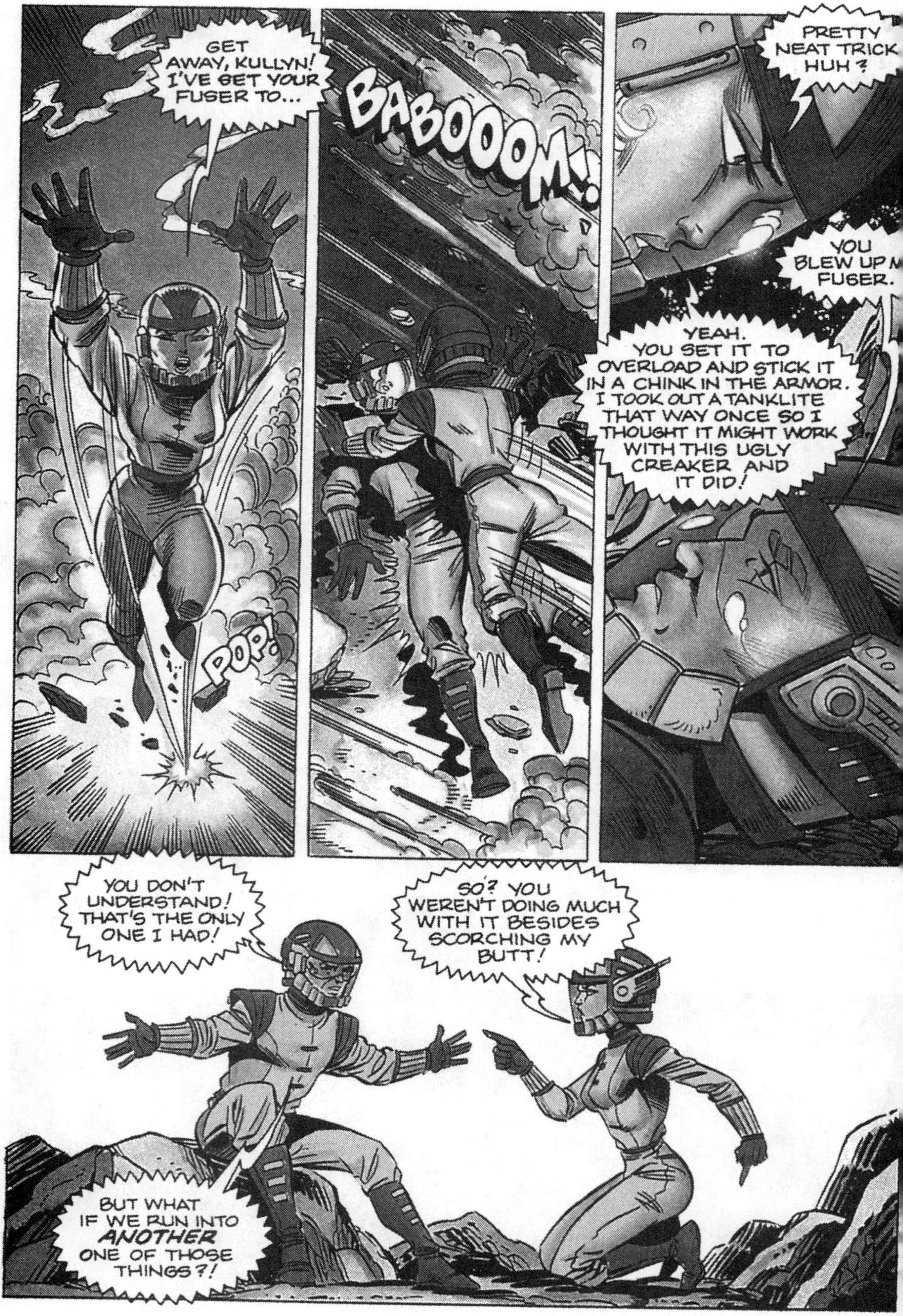
GET AWAY, KULLYN! I'VE SET YOUR FUSER TO...
POP!
BABOOOM!
PRETTY NEAT TRICK HUH?
YOU BLEW UP M
FUSER.
YEAH. YOU SET IT TO OVERLOAD AND STICK IT IN A CHINK IN THE ARMOR. I TOOK OUT A TANKLITE THAT WAY ONCE SO I THOUGHT IT MIGHT WORK WITH THIS UGLY CREAKER AND IT DID!
YOU DON'T UNDERSTAND! THAT'S THE ONLY ONE I HAD!
SO? YOU WEREN'T DOING MUCH WITH IT BESIDES SCORCHING MY BUTT!
BUT WHAT IF WE RUN INTO ***ANOTHER*** ONE OF THOSE THINGS?!

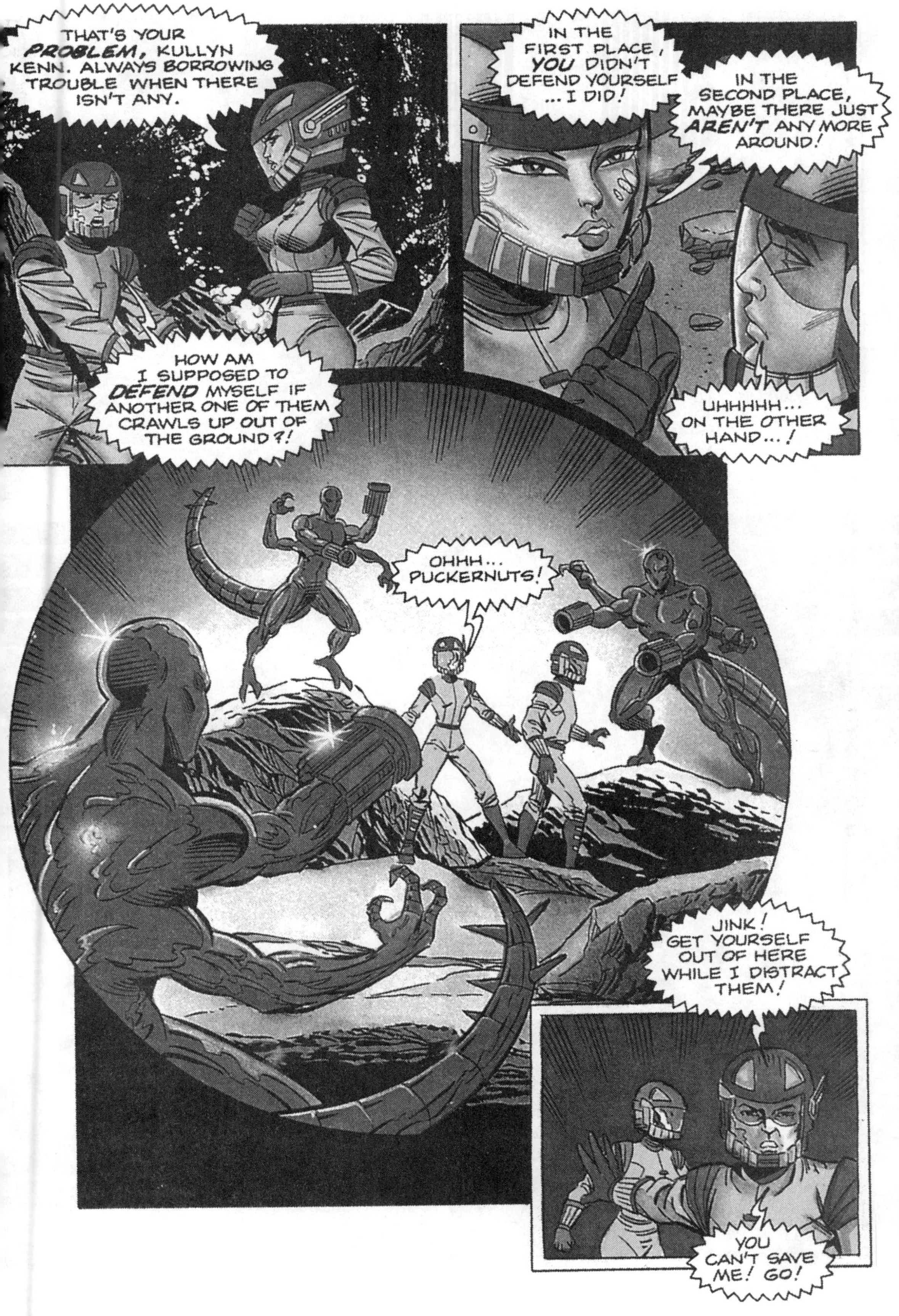
THAT'S YOUR PROBLEM, KULLYN KENN. ALWAYS BORROWING TROUBLE WHEN THERE ISN'T ANY.
HOW AM I SUPPOSED TO DEFEND MYSELF IF ANOTHER ONE OF THEM CRAWLS UP OUT OF THE GROUND?!
IN THE FIRST PLACE, YOU DIDN'T DEFEND YOURSELF ... I DID!
IN THE SECOND PLACE, MAYBE THERE JUST AREN'T ANY MORE AROUND!
UHHHHH... ON THE OTHER HAND...!
OHHH... PUCKERNUTS!
JINK! GET YOURSELF OUT OF HERE WHILE I DISTRACT THEM!
YOU CAN'T SAVE ME! GO!

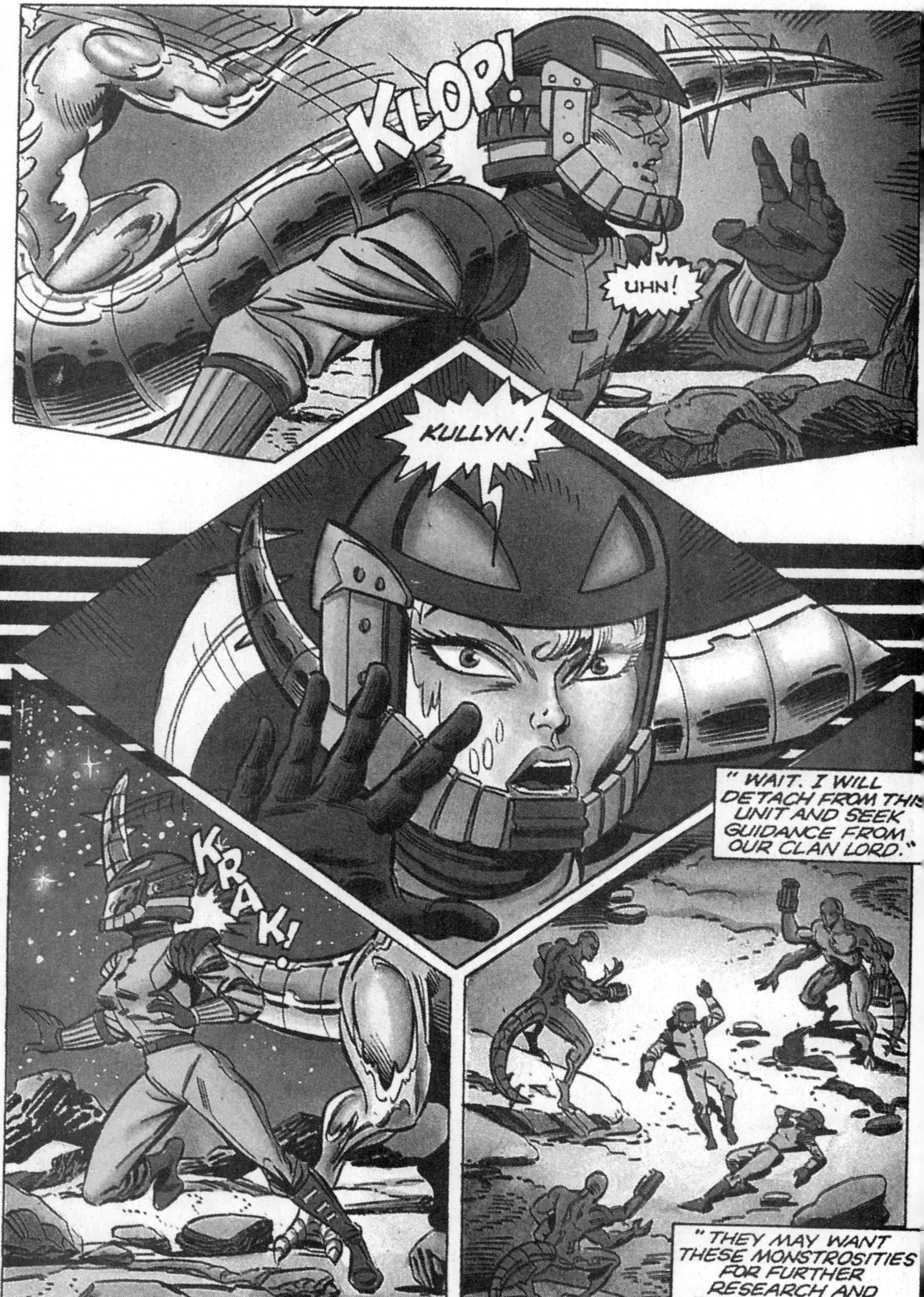
KLOP!
UHN!
KULLYN!
"WAIT. I WILL DETACH FROM THIS UNIT AND SEEK GUIDANCE FROM OUR CLAN LORD."
KRAK!
"THEY MAY WANT THESE MONSTROSITIES FOR FURTHER RESEARCH AND EXPERIMENTATION."

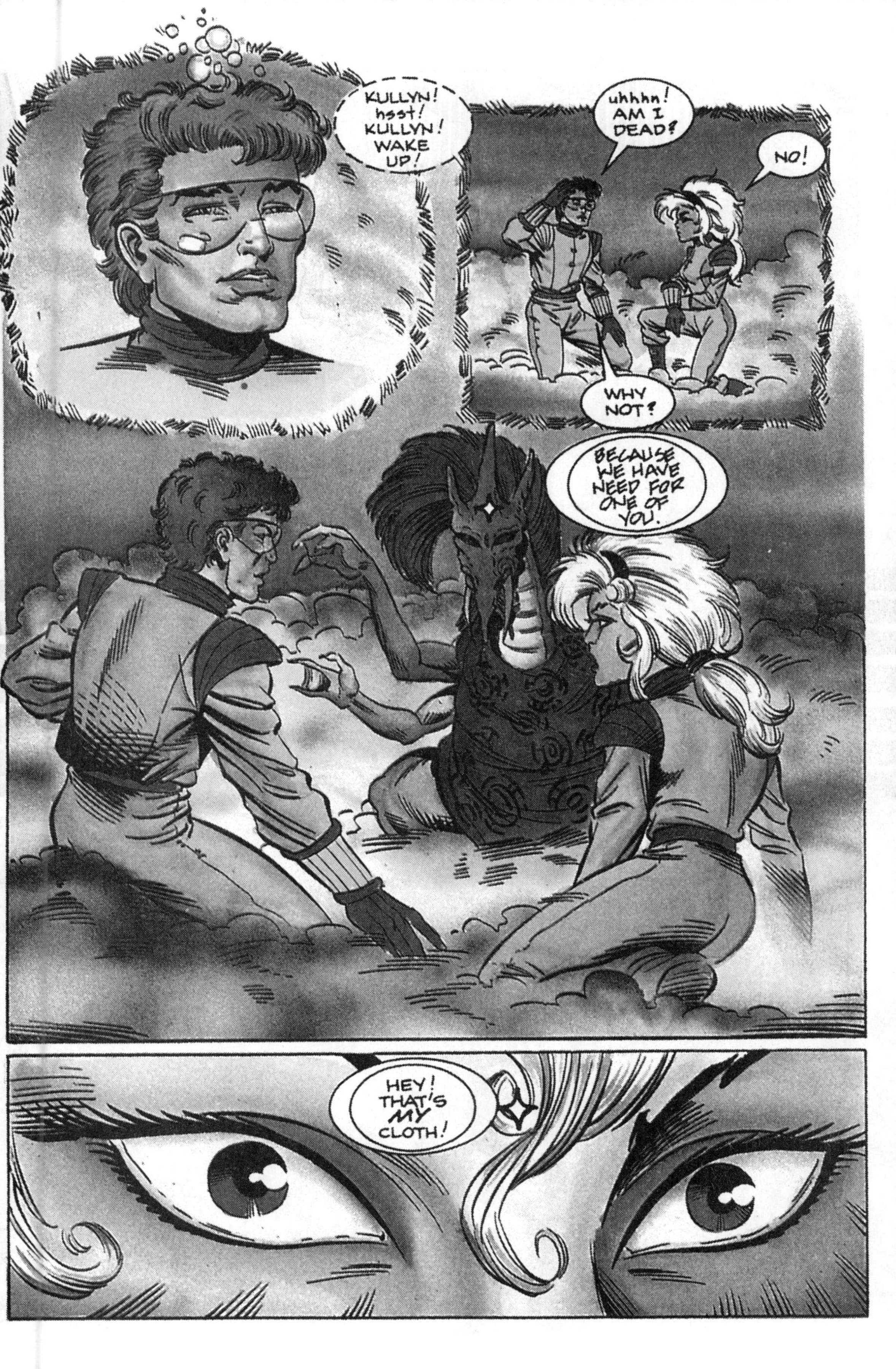
KULLYN! hsst! KULLYN! WAKE UP!
uhhhn! AM I DEAD?
NO!
WHY NOT?
BECAUSE WE HAVE NEED FOR ONE OF YOU.
HEY! THAT'S MY CLOTH!

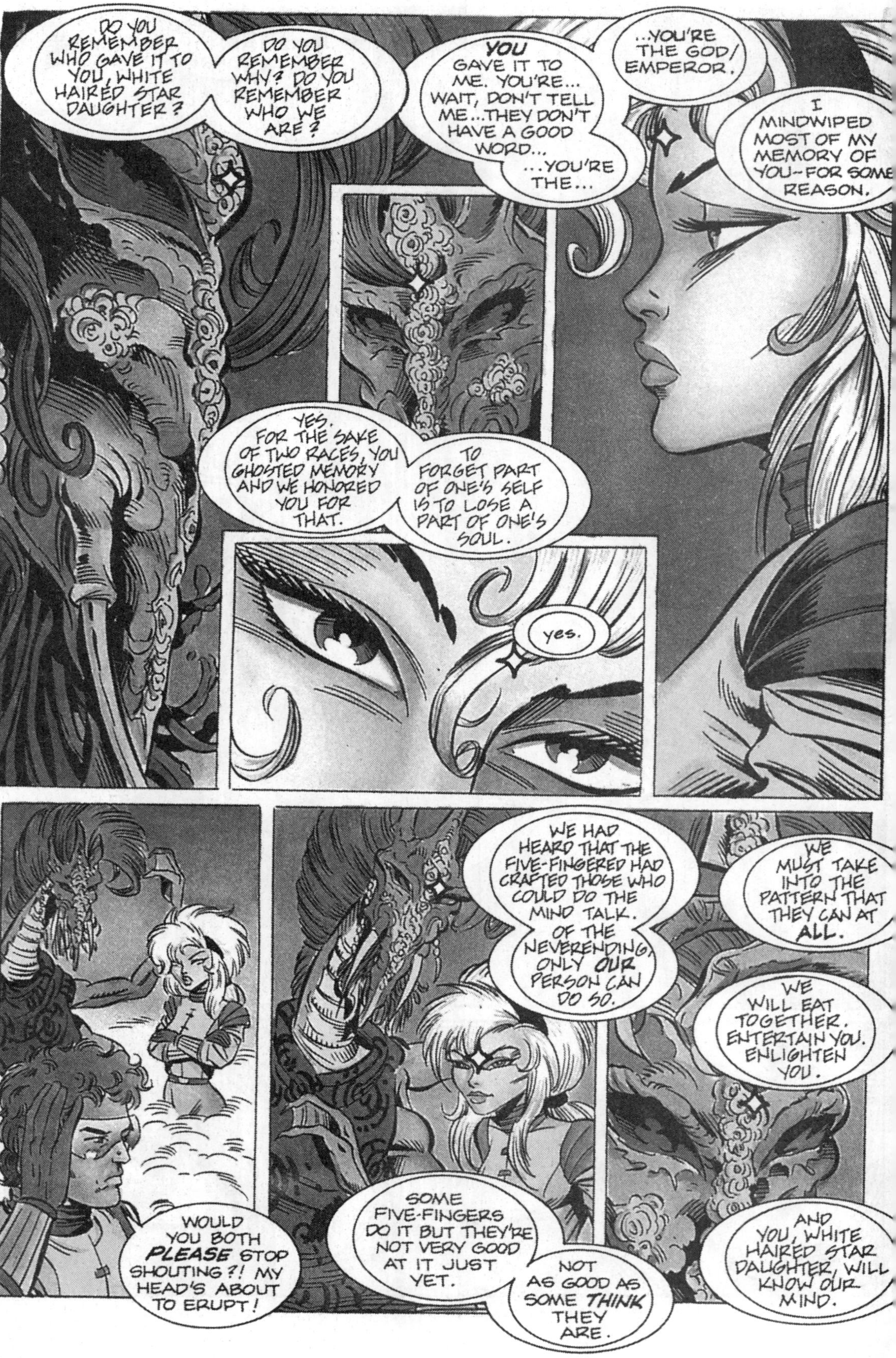
DO YOU REMEMBER WHO GAVE IT TO YOU, WHITE HAIRED STAR DAUGHTER?
DO YOU REMEMBER WHY? DO YOU REMEMBER WHO WE ARE?
YOU GAVE IT TO ME. YOU'RE... WAIT, DON'T TELL ME...THEY DON'T HAVE A GOOD WORD...
...YOU'RE THE...
...YOU'RE THE GOD/ EMPEROR.
I MINDWIPED MOST OF MY MEMORY OF YOU--FOR SOME REASON.
YES. FOR THE SAKE OF TWO RACES, YOU GHOSTED MEMORY AND WE HONORED YOU FOR THAT.
TO FORGET PART OF ONE'S SELF IS TO LOSE A PART OF ONE'S SOUL.
yes.
WE HAD HEARD THAT THE FIVE-FINGERED HAD CRAFTED THOSE WHO COULD DO THE MIND TALK.
OF THE NEVERENDING, ONLY OUR PERSON CAN DO SO.
WE MUST TAKE INTO THE PATTERN THAT THEY CAN AT ALL.
WE WILL EAT TOGETHER. ENTERTAIN YOU. ENLIGHTEN YOU.
WOULD YOU BOTH PLEASE STOP SHOUTING?! MY HEAD'S ABOUT TO ERUPT!
SOME FIVE-FINGERS DO IT BUT THEY'RE NOT VERY GOOD AT IT JUST YET.
NOT AS GOOD AS SOME THINK THEY ARE.
AND YOU, WHITE HAIRED STAR DAUGHTER, WILL KNOW OUR MIND.

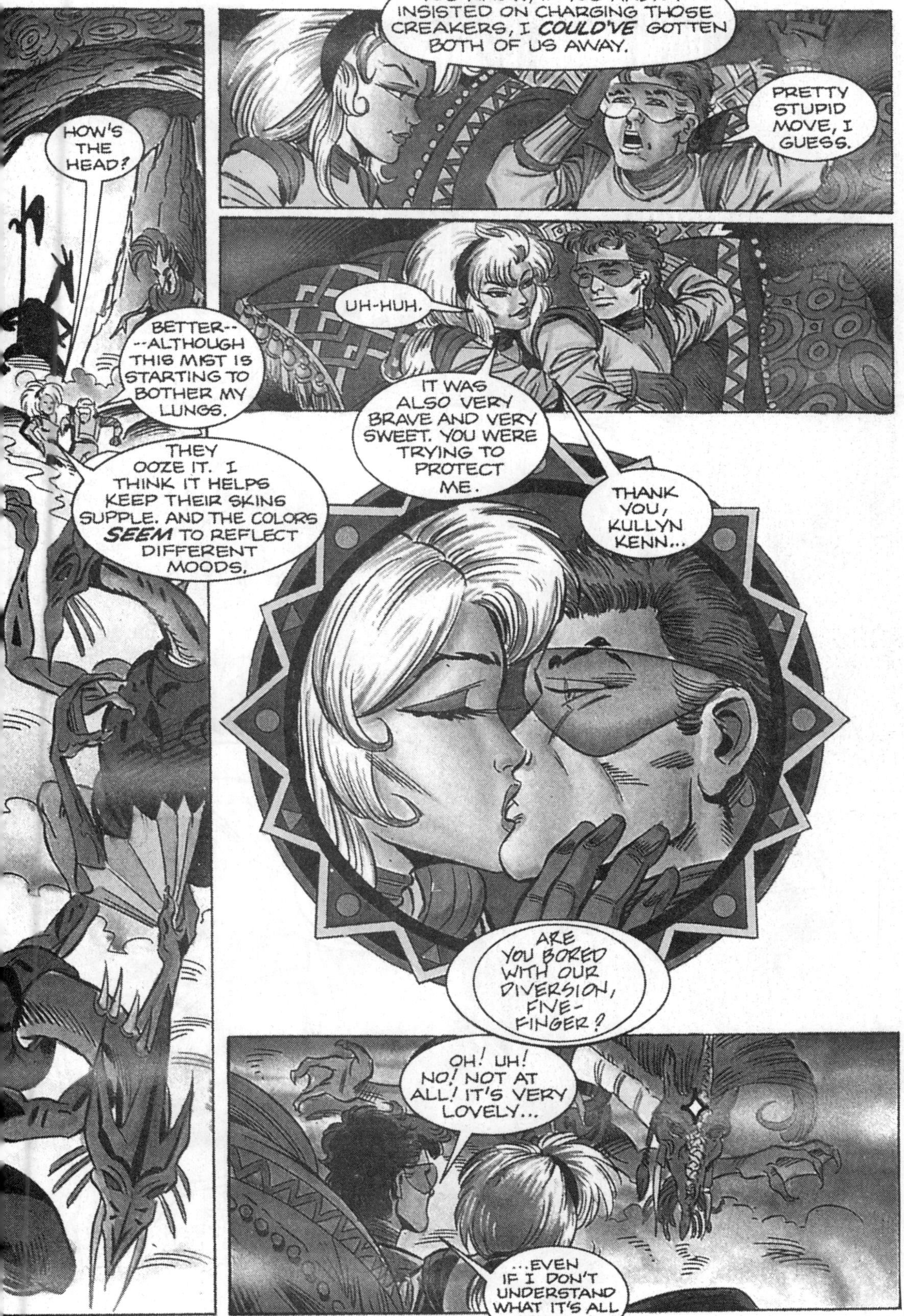
HOW'S THE HEAD?
YOU KNOW, IF YOU HADN'T INSISTED ON CHARGING THOSE CREAKERS, I COULD'VE GOTTEN BOTH OF US AWAY.
PRETTY STUPID MOVE, I GUESS.
UH-HUH.
BETTER-- --ALTHOUGH THIS MIST IS STARTING TO BOTHER MY LUNGS.
IT WAS ALSO VERY BRAVE AND VERY SWEET. YOU WERE TRYING TO PROTECT ME.
THEY OOZE IT. I THINK IT HELPS KEEP THEIR SKINS SUPPLE. AND THE COLORS SEEM TO REFLECT DIFFERENT MOODS.
THANK YOU, KULLYN KENN...
ARE YOU BORED WITH OUR DIVERSION, FIVE-FINGER?
OH! UH! NO! NOT AT ALL! IT'S VERY LOVELY...
...EVEN IF I DON'T UNDERSTAND WHAT IT'S ALL ABOUT...!

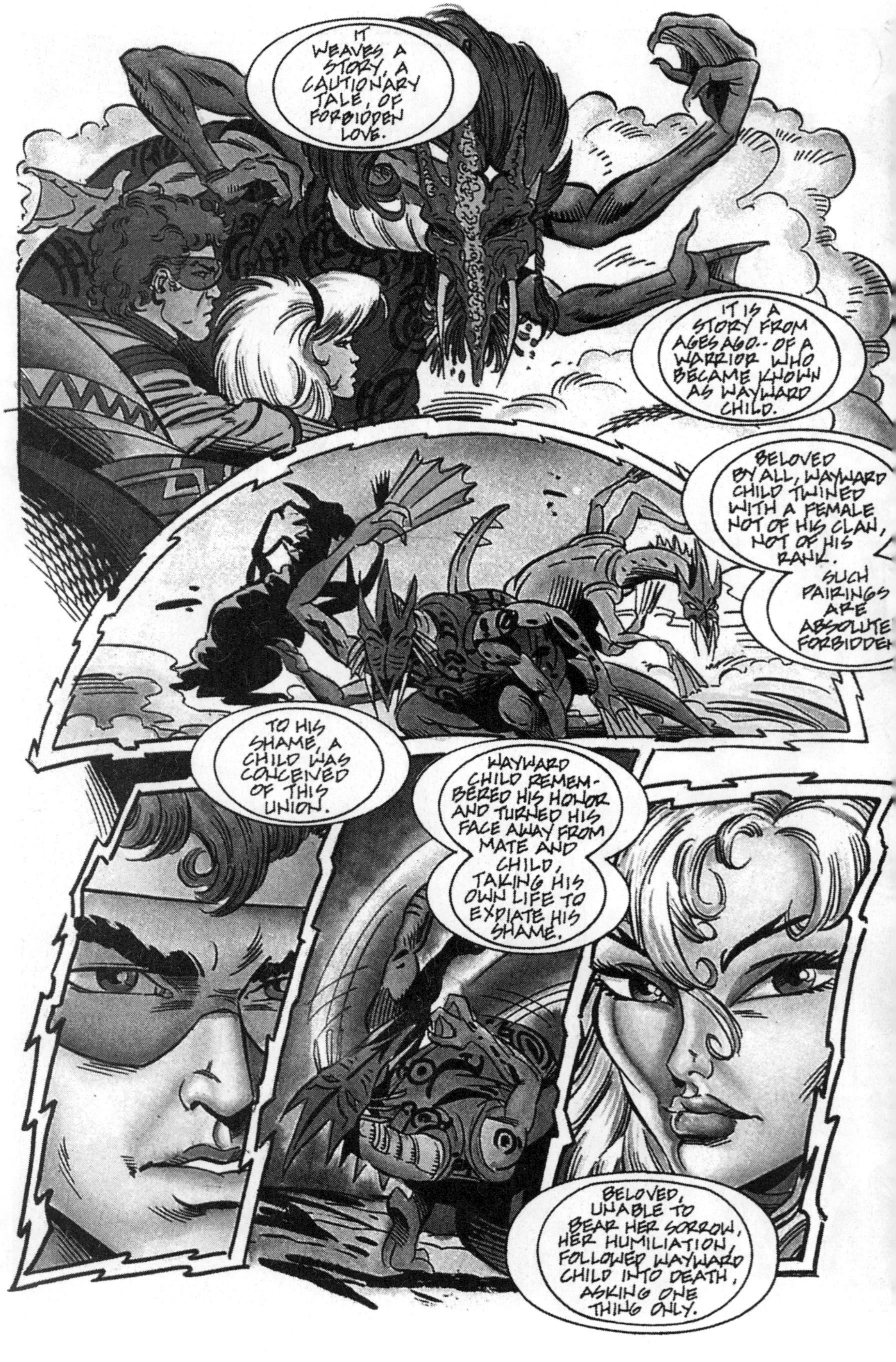
IT WEAVES A STORY, A CAUTIONARY TALE, OF FORBIDDEN LOVE.
IT IS A STORY FROM AGES AGO-- OF A WARRIOR WHO BECAME KNOWN AS WAYWARD CHILD.
BELOVED BY ALL, WAYWARD CHILD TWINED WITH A FEMALE NOT OF HIS CLAN, NOT OF HIS RANK.
SUCH PAIRINGS ARE ABSOLUTE FORBIDDE
TO HIS SHAME, A CHILD WAS CONCEIVED OF THIS UNION.
WAYWARD CHILD REMEMBERED HIS HONOR AND TURNED HIS FACE AWAY FROM MATE AND CHILD, TAKING HIS OWN LIFE TO EXPIATE HIS SHAME.
BELOVED, UNABLE TO BEAR HER SORROW, HER HUMILIATION, FOLLOWED WAYWARD CHILD INTO DEATH, ASKING ONE THING ONLY.

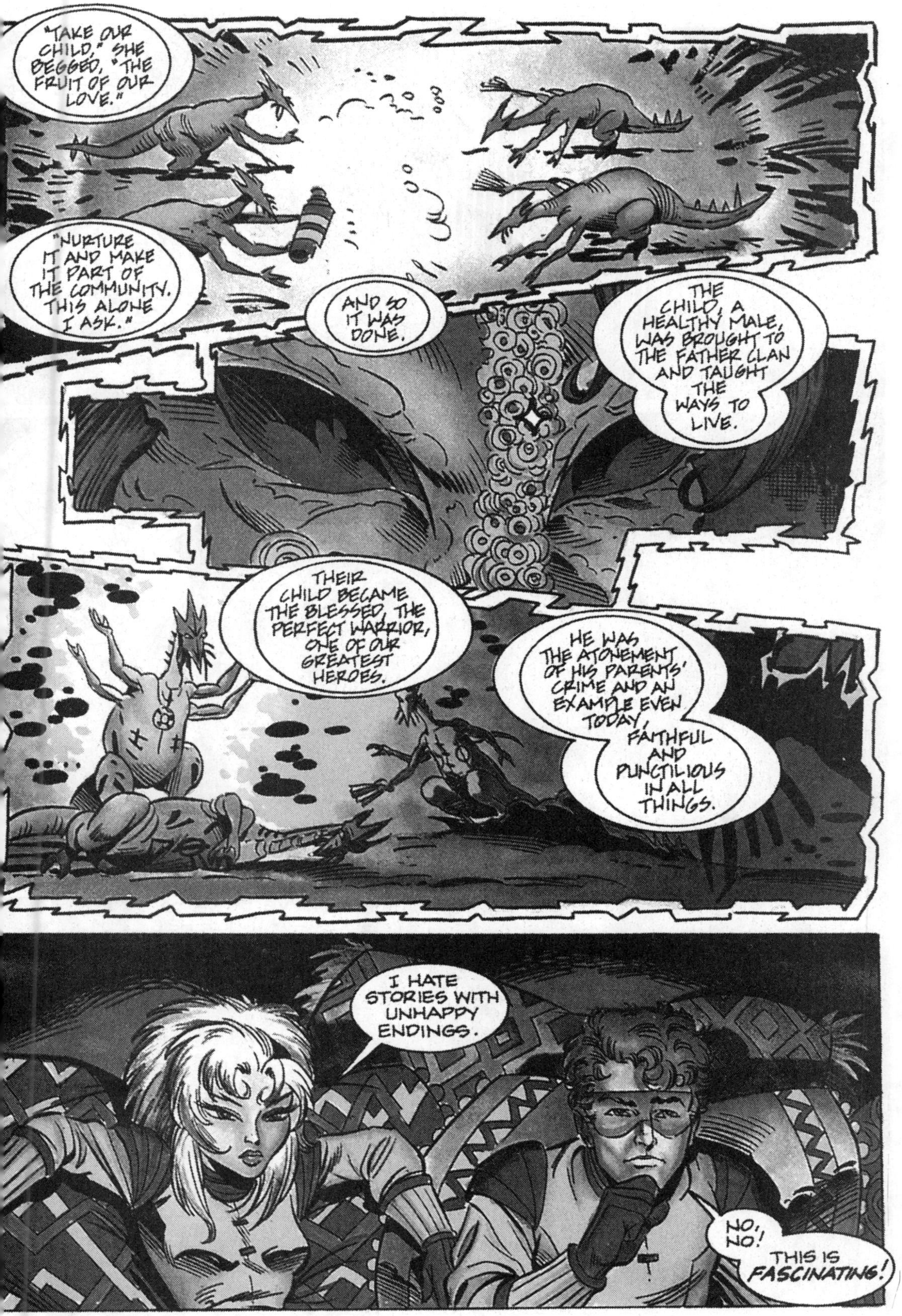
"TAKE OUR CHILD," SHE BEGGED, "THE FRUIT OF OUR LOVE."
"NURTURE IT AND MAKE IT PART OF THE COMMUNITY. THIS ALONE I ASK."
AND SO IT WAS DONE.
THE CHILD, A HEALTHY MALE, WAS BROUGHT TO THE FATHER CLAN AND TAUGHT THE WAYS TO LIVE.
THEIR CHILD BECAME THE BLESSED, THE PERFECT WARRIOR, ONE OF OUR GREATEST HEROES.
HE WAS THE ATONEMENT OF HIS PARENTS' CRIME AND AN EXAMPLE EVEN TODAY, FAITHFUL AND PUNCTILIOUS IN ALL THINGS.
I HATE STORIES WITH UNHAPPY ENDINGS.
NO, NO!
THIS IS FASCINATING!

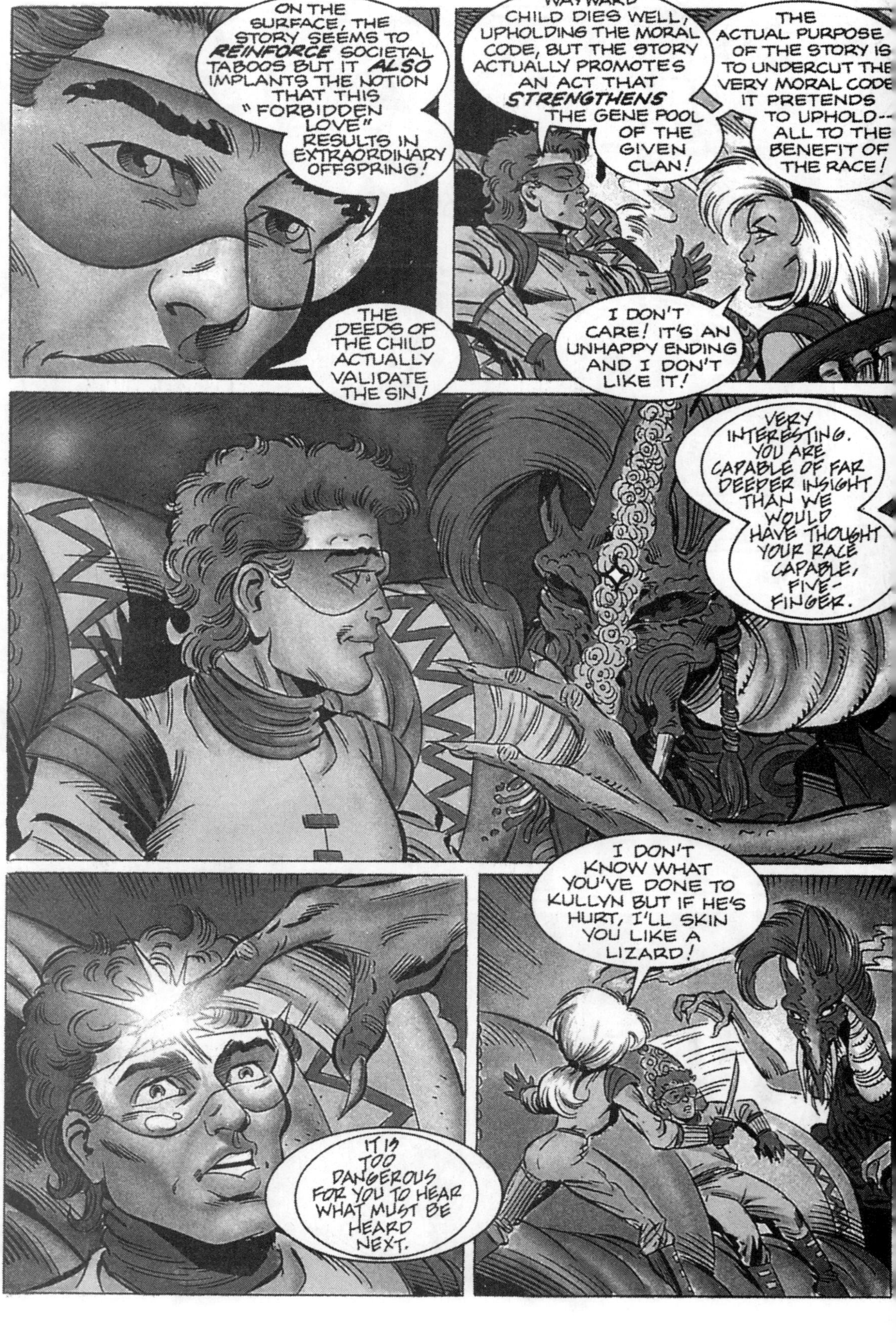
ON THE SURFACE, THE STORY SEEMS TO REINFORCE SOCIETAL TABOOS BUT IT ALSO IMPLANTS THE NOTION THAT THIS "FORBIDDEN LOVE" RESULTS IN EXTRAORDINARY OFFSPRING!
THE DEEDS OF THE CHILD ACTUALLY VALIDATE THE SIN!
WAYWARD CHILD DIES WELL, UPHOLDING THE MORAL CODE, BUT THE STORY ACTUALLY PROMOTES AN ACT THAT STRENGTHENS THE GENE POOL OF THE GIVEN CLAN!
THE ACTUAL PURPOSE OF THE STORY IS TO UNDERCUT THE VERY MORAL CODE IT PRETENDS TO UPHOLD-- ALL TO THE BENEFIT OF THE RACE!
I DON'T CARE! IT'S AN UNHAPPY ENDING AND I DON'T LIKE IT!
VERY INTERESTING. YOU ARE CAPABLE OF FAR DEEPER INSIGHT THAN WE WOULD HAVE THOUGHT YOUR RACE CAPABLE, FIVE-FINGER.
IT IS TOO DANGEROUS FOR YOU TO HEAR WHAT MUST BE HEARD NEXT.
I DON'T KNOW WHAT YOU'VE DONE TO KULLYN BUT IF HE'S HURT, I'LL SKIN YOU LIKE A LIZARD!

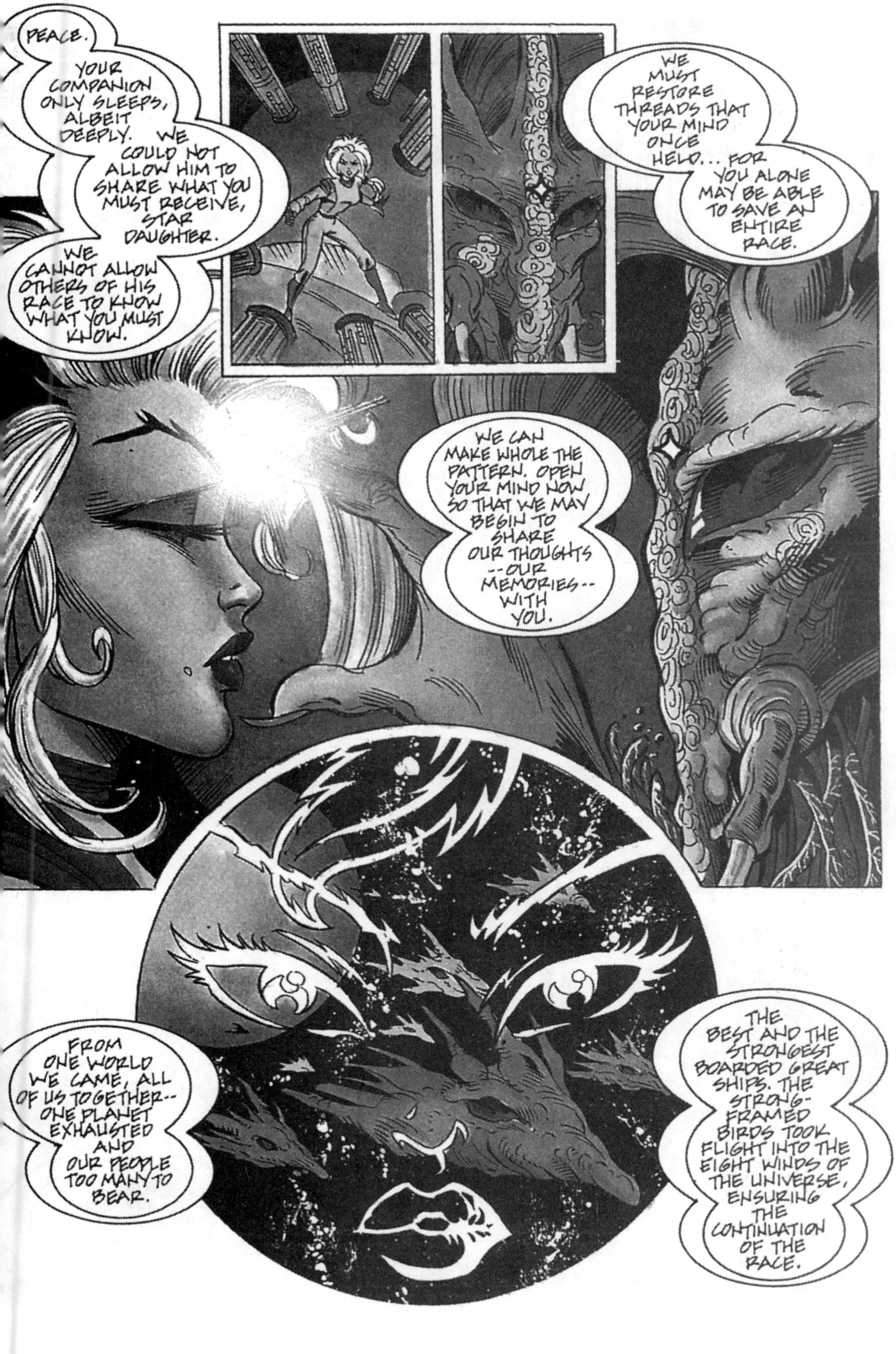
PEACE.
YOUR COMPANION ONLY SLEEPS, ALBEIT DEEPLY. WE COULD NOT ALLOW HIM TO SHARE WHAT YOU MUST RECEIVE, STAR DAUGHTER.
WE CANNOT ALLOW OTHERS OF HIS RACE TO KNOW WHAT YOU MUST KNOW.
WE MUST RESTORE THREADS THAT YOUR MIND ONCE HELD... FOR YOU ALONE MAY BE ABLE TO SAVE AN ENTIRE RACE.
WE CAN MAKE WHOLE THE PATTERN. OPEN YOUR MIND NOW SO THAT WE MAY BEGIN TO SHARE OUR THOUGHTS --OUR MEMORIES-- WITH YOU.
FROM ONE WORLD WE CAME, ALL OF US TOGETHER-- ONE PLANET EXHAUSTED AND OUR PEOPLE TOO MANY TO BEAR.
THE BEST AND THE STRONGEST BOARDED GREAT SHIPS. THE STRONG-FRAMED BIRDS TOOK FLIGHT INTO THE EIGHT WINDS OF THE UNIVERSE, ENSURING THE CONTINUATION OF THE RACE.

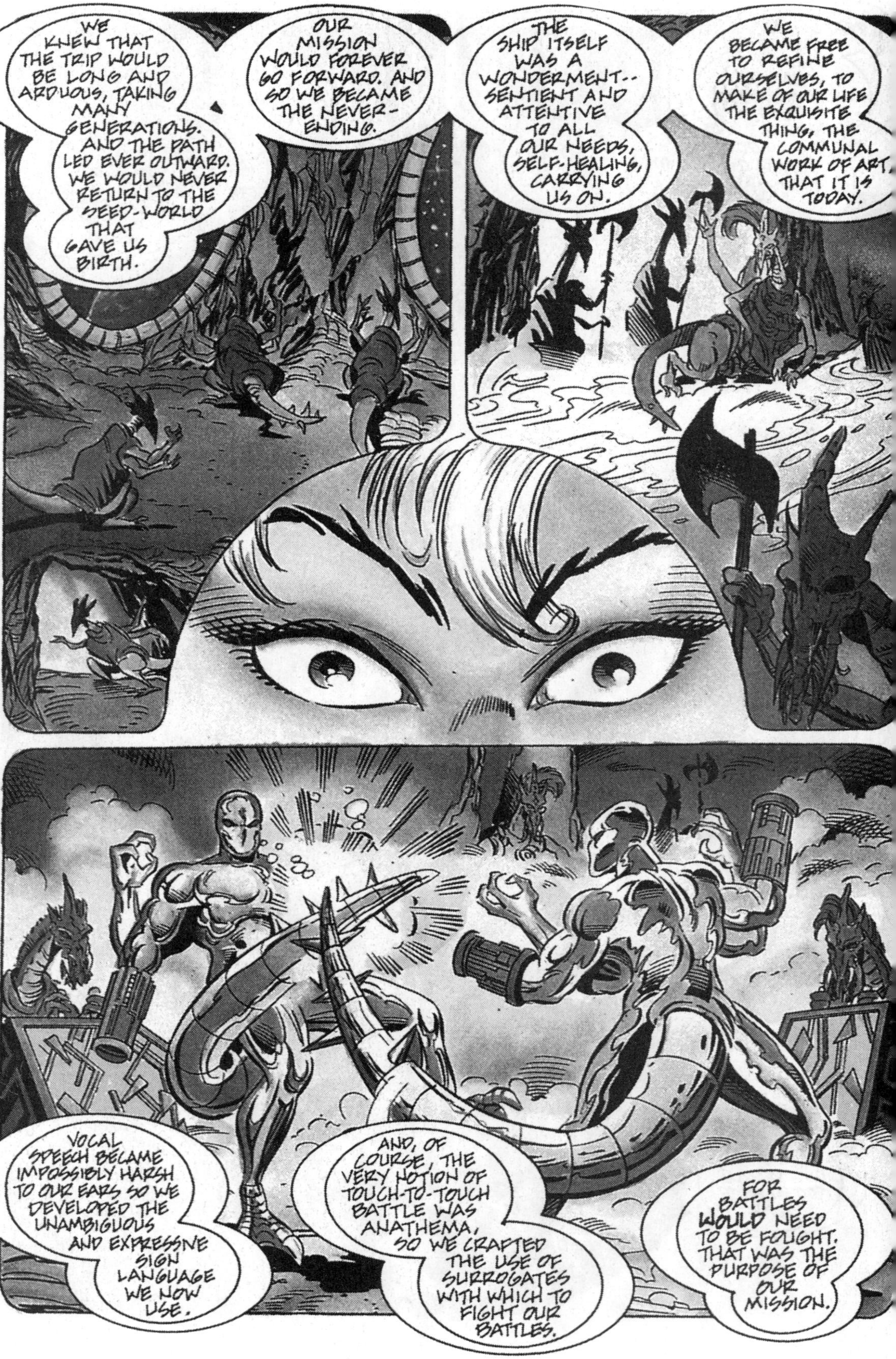
WE KNEW THAT THE TRIP WOULD BE LONG AND ARDUOUS, TAKING MANY GENERATIONS. AND THE PATH LED EVER OUTWARD. WE WOULD NEVER RETURN TO THE SEED-WORLD THAT GAVE US BIRTH.
OUR MISSION WOULD FOREVER GO FORWARD. AND SO WE BECAME THE NEVER-ENDING.
THE SHIP ITSELF WAS A WONDERMENT-- SENTIENT AND ATTENTIVE TO ALL OUR NEEDS, SELF-HEALING, CARRYING US ON.
WE BECAME FREE TO REFINE OURSELVES, TO MAKE OF OUR LIFE THE EXQUISITE THING, THE COMMUNAL WORK OF ART, THAT IT IS TODAY.
VOCAL SPEECH BECAME IMPOSSIBLY HARSH TO OUR EARS SO WE DEVELOPED THE UNAMBIGUOUS AND EXPRESSIVE SIGN LANGUAGE WE NOW USE.
AND, OF COURSE, THE VERY NOTION OF TOUCH-TO-TOUCH BATTLE WAS ANATHEMA, SO WE CRAFTED THE USE OF SURROGATES WITH WHICH TO FIGHT OUR BATTLES.
FOR BATTLES WOULD NEED TO BE FOUGHT. THAT WAS THE PURPOSE OF OUR MISSION.

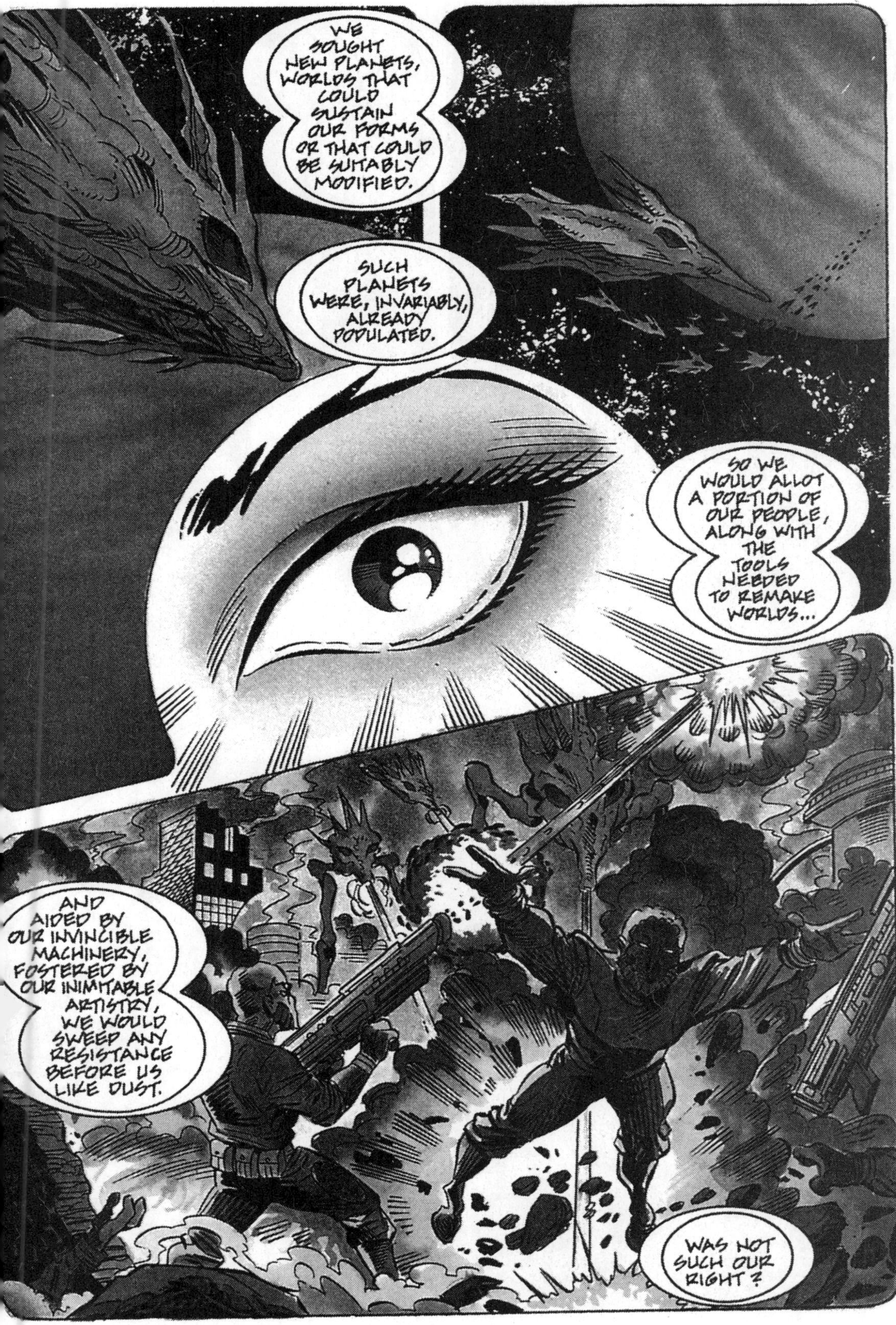
WE SOUGHT NEW PLANETS, WORLDS THAT COULD SUSTAIN OUR FORMS OR THAT COULD BE SUITABLY MODIFIED.
SUCH PLANETS WERE, INVARIABLY, ALREADY POPULATED.
SO WE WOULD ALLOT A PORTION OF OUR PEOPLE, ALONG WITH THE TOOLS NEEDED TO REMAKE WORLDS...
AND AIDED BY OUR INVINCIBLE MACHINERY, FOSTERED BY OUR INIMITABLE ARTISTRY, WE WOULD SWEEP ANY RESISTANCE BEFORE US LIKE DUST.
WAS NOT SUCH OUR RIGHT?

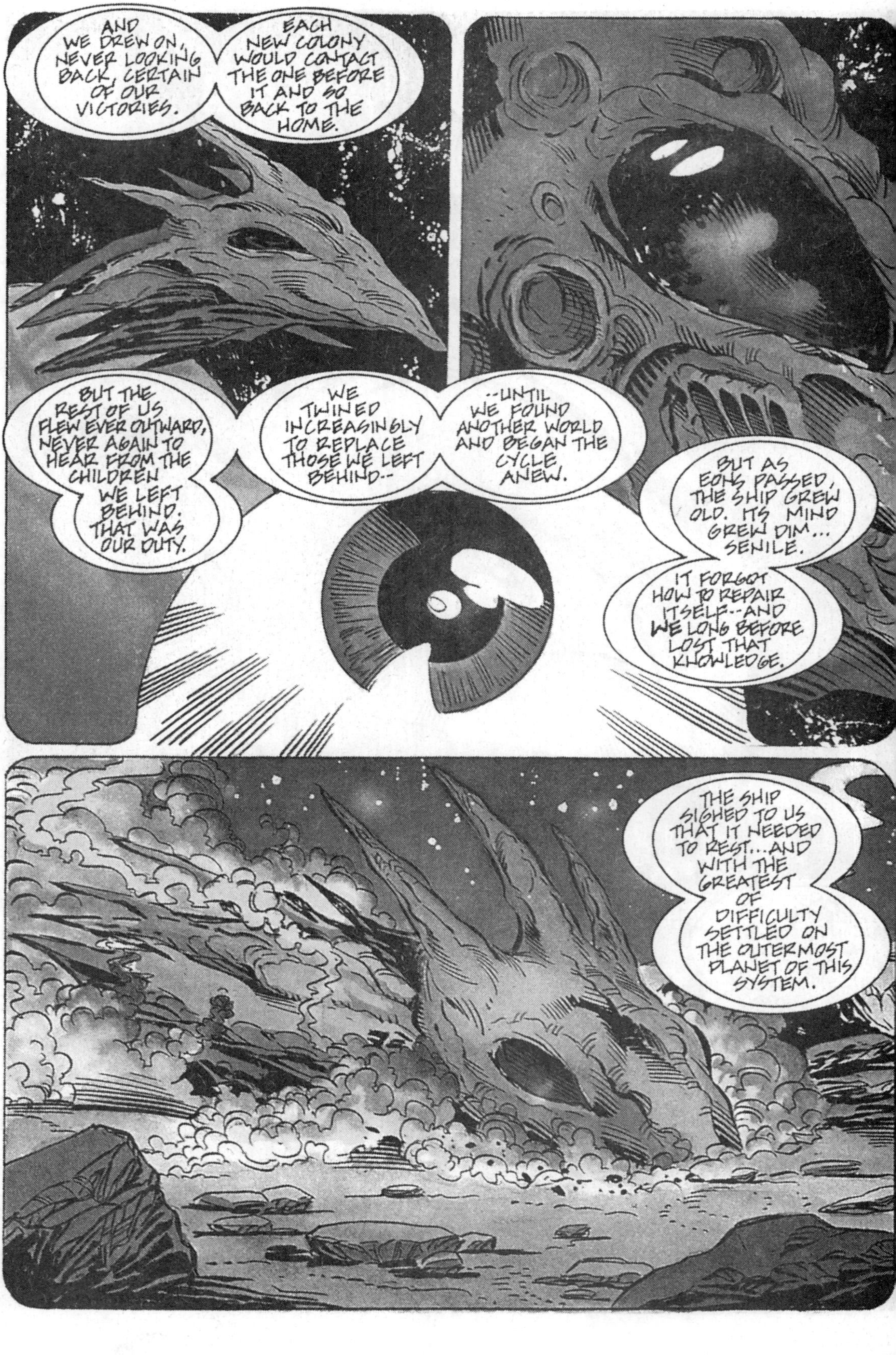
AND WE DREW ON, NEVER LOOKING BACK, CERTAIN OF OUR VICTORIES.
EACH NEW COLONY WOULD CONTACT THE ONE BEFORE IT AND SO BACK TO THE HOME.
BUT THE REST OF US FLEW EVER OUTWARD, NEVER AGAIN TO HEAR FROM THE CHILDREN WE LEFT BEHIND. THAT WAS OUR DUTY.
WE TWINED INCREASINGLY TO REPLACE THOSE WE LEFT BEHIND--
--UNTIL WE FOUND ANOTHER WORLD AND BEGAN THE CYCLE ANEW.
BUT AS EONS PASSED, THE SHIP GREW OLD. ITS MIND GREW DIM... SENILE.
IT FORGOT HOW TO REPAIR ITSELF--AND WE LONG BEFORE LOST THAT KNOWLEDGE.
THE SHIP SIGHED TO US THAT IT NEEDED TO REST...AND WITH THE GREATEST OF DIFFICULTY SETTLED ON THE OUTERMOST PLANET OF THIS SYSTEM.

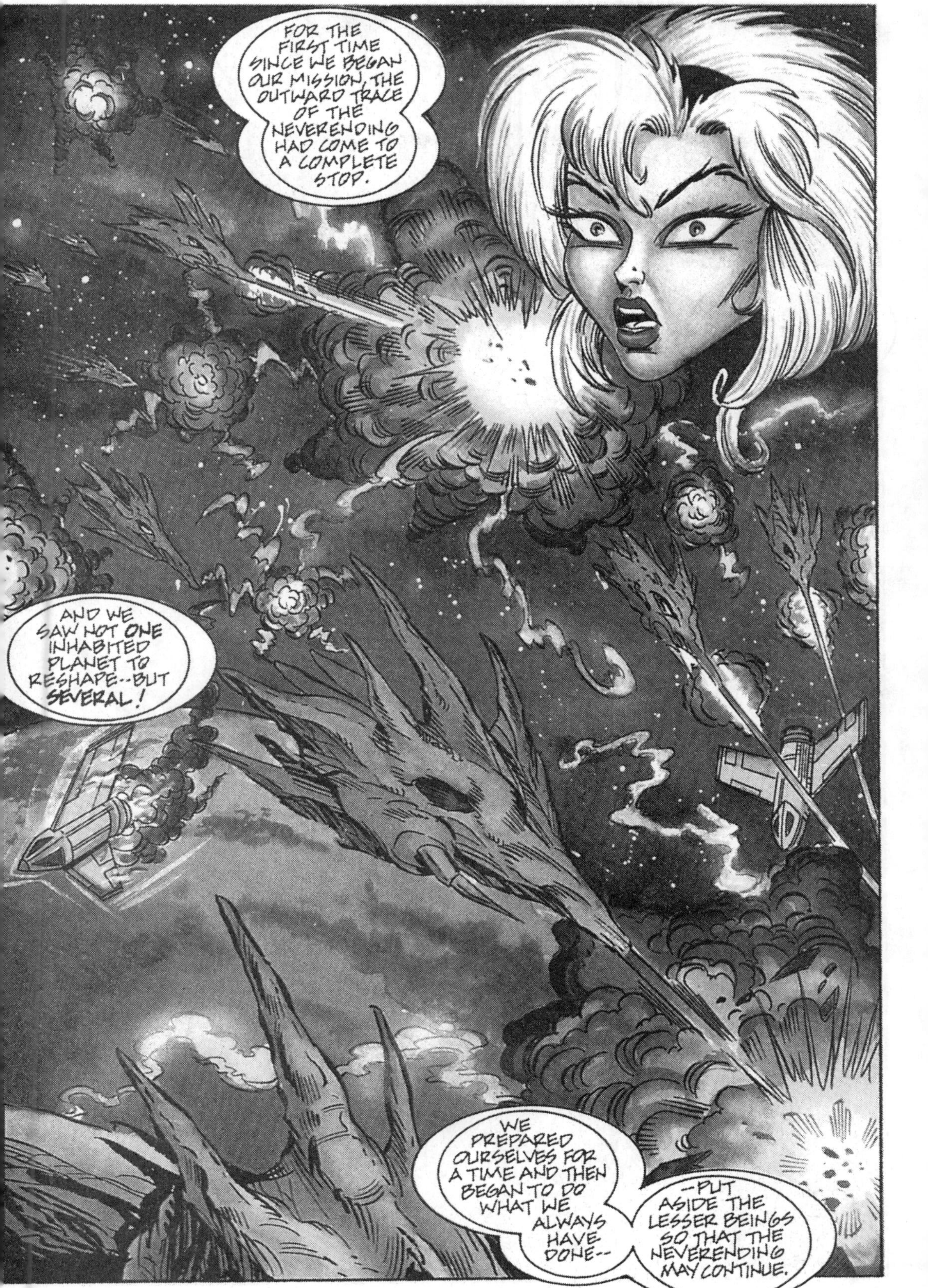
FOR THE FIRST TIME SINCE WE BEGAN OUR MISSION, THE OUTWARD TRACE OF THE NEVERENDING HAD COME TO A COMPLETE STOP.
AND WE SAW NOT ONE INHABITED PLANET TO RESHAPE--BUT SEVERAL!
WE PREPARED OURSELVES FOR A TIME AND THEN BEGAN TO DO WHAT WE ALWAYS HAVE DONE--
--PUT ASIDE THE LESSER BEINGS SO THAT THE NEVERENDING MAY CONTINUE.

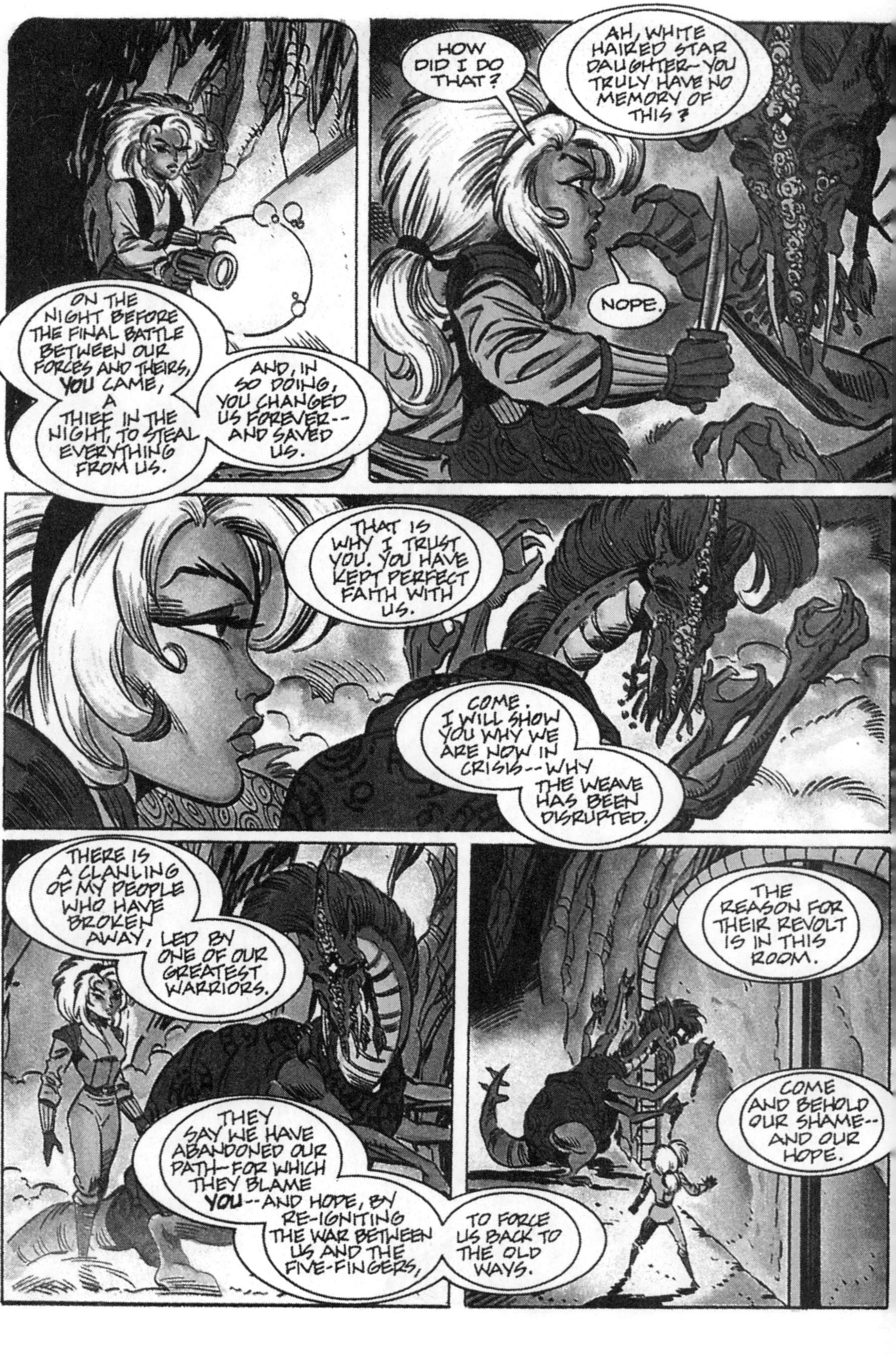
ON THE NIGHT BEFORE THE FINAL BATTLE BETWEEN OUR FORCES AND THEIRS, YOU CAME, A THIEF IN THE NIGHT, TO STEAL EVERYTHING FROM US.
AND, IN SO DOING, YOU CHANGED US FOREVER-- AND SAVED US.
HOW DID I DO THAT?
AH, WHITE HAIRED STAR DAUGHTER-- YOU TRULY HAVE NO MEMORY OF THIS?
NOPE.
THAT IS WHY I TRUST YOU. YOU HAVE KEPT PERFECT FAITH WITH US.
COME. I WILL SHOW YOU WHY WE ARE NOW IN CRISIS--WHY THE WEAVE HAS BEEN DISRUPTED.
THERE IS A CLANLING OF MY PEOPLE WHO HAVE BROKEN AWAY, LED BY ONE OF OUR GREATEST WARRIORS.
THEY SAY WE HAVE ABANDONED OUR PATH--FOR WHICH THEY BLAME YOU--AND HOPE, BY RE-IGNITING THE WAR BETWEEN US AND THE FIVE-FINGERS,
TO FORCE US BACK TO THE OLD WAYS.
THE REASON FOR THEIR REVOLT IS IN THIS ROOM.
COME AND BEHOLD OUR SHAME-- AND OUR HOPE.

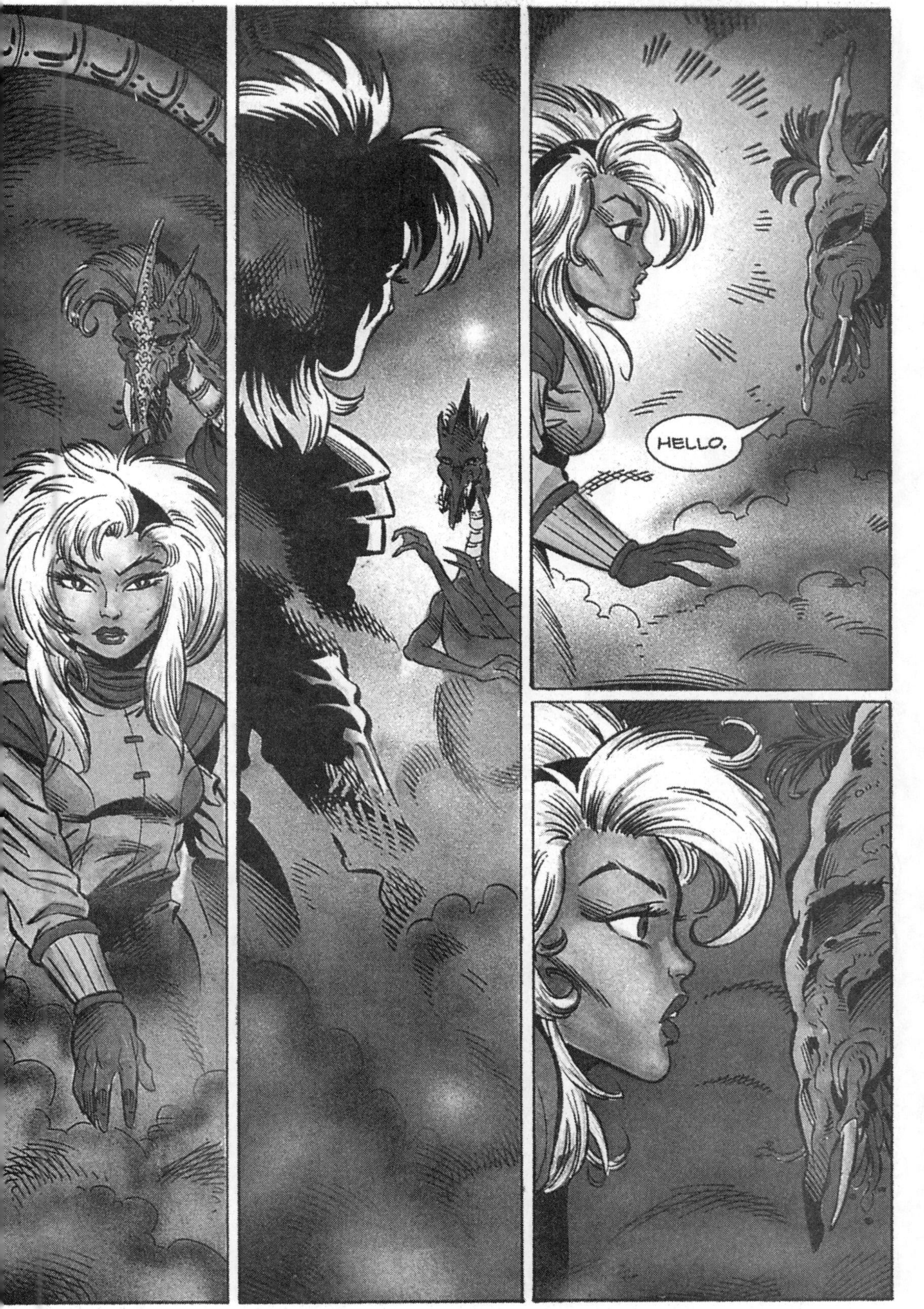
HELLO.

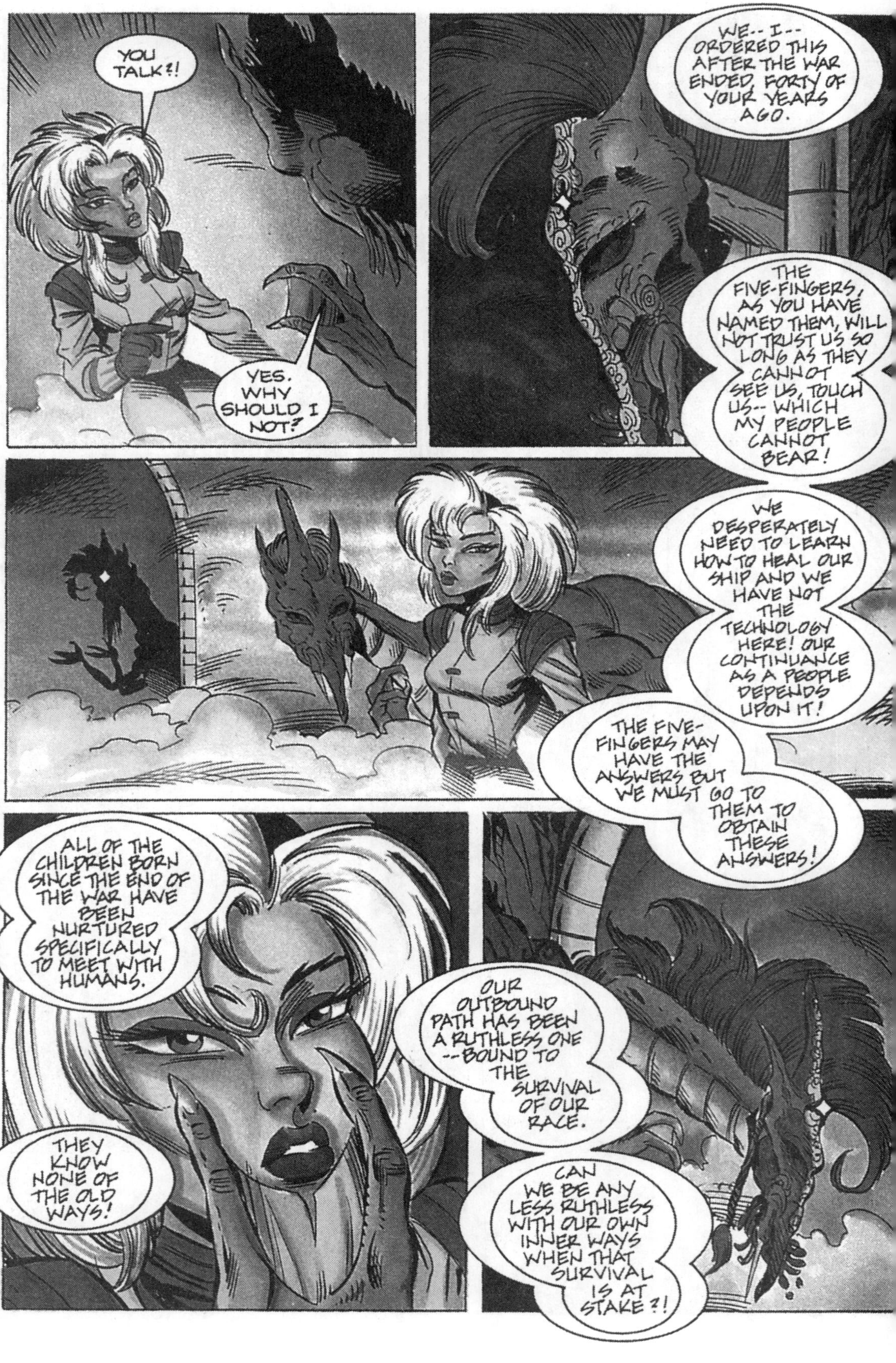
YOU TALK?!
YES. WHY SHOULD I NOT?
WE.. I-- ORDERED THIS AFTER THE WAR ENDED, FORTY OF YOUR YEARS AGO.
THE FIVE-FINGERS, AS YOU HAVE NAMED THEM, WILL NOT TRUST US SO LONG AS THEY CANNOT SEE US, TOUCH US-- WHICH MY PEOPLE CANNOT BEAR!
WE DESPERATELY NEED TO LEARN HOW TO HEAL OUR SHIP AND WE HAVE NOT THE TECHNOLOGY HERE! OUR CONTINUANCE AS A PEOPLE DEPENDS UPON IT!
THE FIVE-FINGERS MAY HAVE THE ANSWERS BUT WE MUST GO TO THEM TO OBTAIN THESE ANSWERS!
ALL OF THE CHILDREN BORN SINCE THE END OF THE WAR HAVE BEEN NURTURED SPECIFICALLY TO MEET WITH HUMANS.
THEY KNOW NONE OF THE OLD WAYS!
OUR OUTBOUND PATH HAS BEEN A RUTHLESS ONE --BOUND TO THE SURVIVAL OF OUR RACE.
CAN WE BE ANY LESS RUTHLESS WITH OUR OWN INNER WAYS WHEN THAT SURVIVAL IS AT STAKE?!

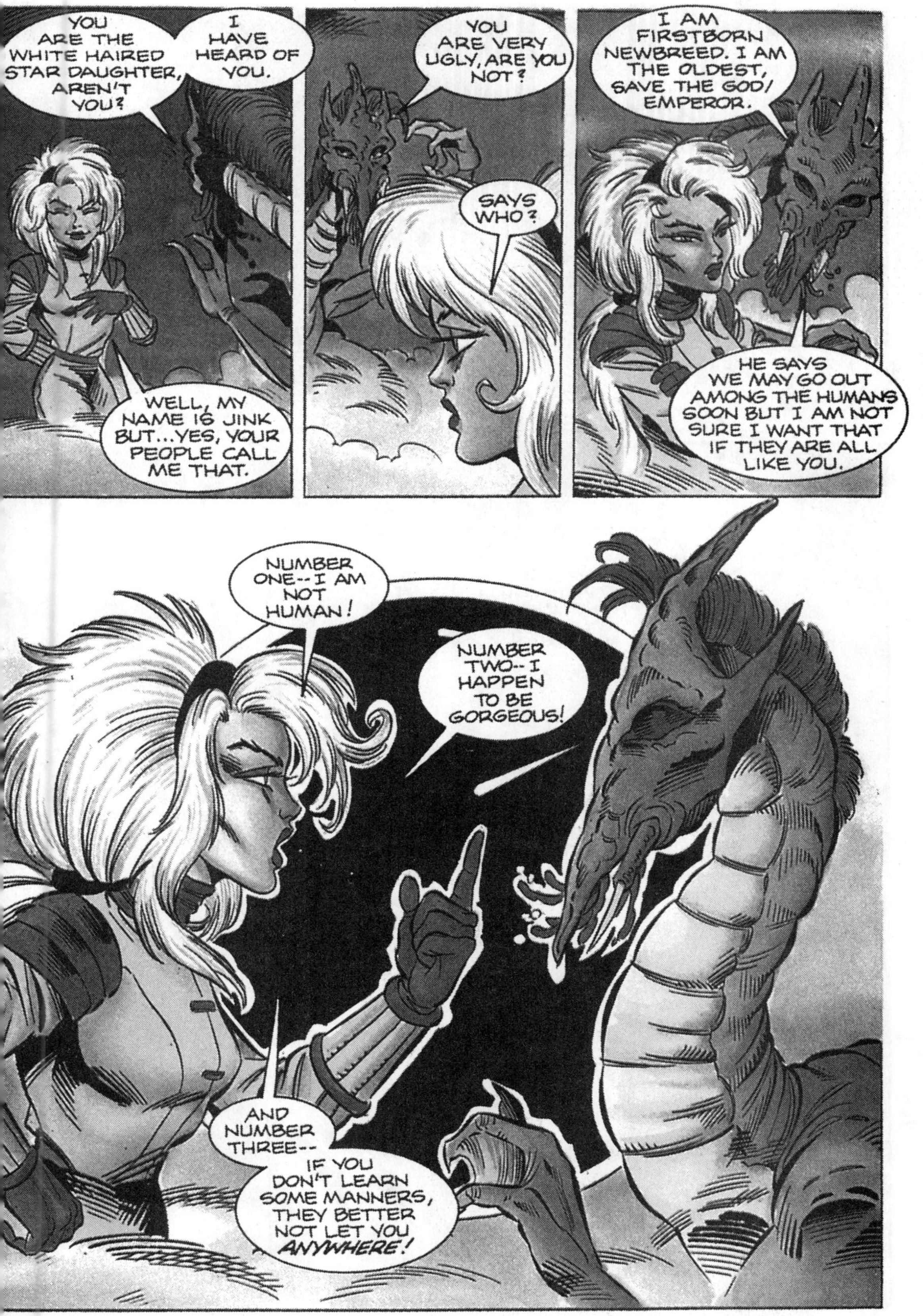
YOU ARE THE WHITE HAIRED STAR DAUGHTER, AREN'T YOU?
I HAVE HEARD OF YOU.
WELL, MY NAME IS JINK BUT...YES, YOUR PEOPLE CALL ME THAT.
YOU ARE VERY UGLY, ARE YOU NOT?
SAYS WHO?
I AM FIRSTBORN NEWBREED. I AM THE OLDEST, SAVE THE GOD/ EMPEROR.
HE SAYS WE MAY GO OUT AMONG THE HUMANS SOON BUT I AM NOT SURE I WANT THAT IF THEY ARE ALL LIKE YOU.
NUMBER ONE-- I AM NOT HUMAN!
NUMBER TWO-- I HAPPEN TO BE GORGEOUS!
AND NUMBER THREE--
IF YOU DON'T LEARN SOME MANNERS, THEY BETTER NOT LET YOU ANYWHERE!

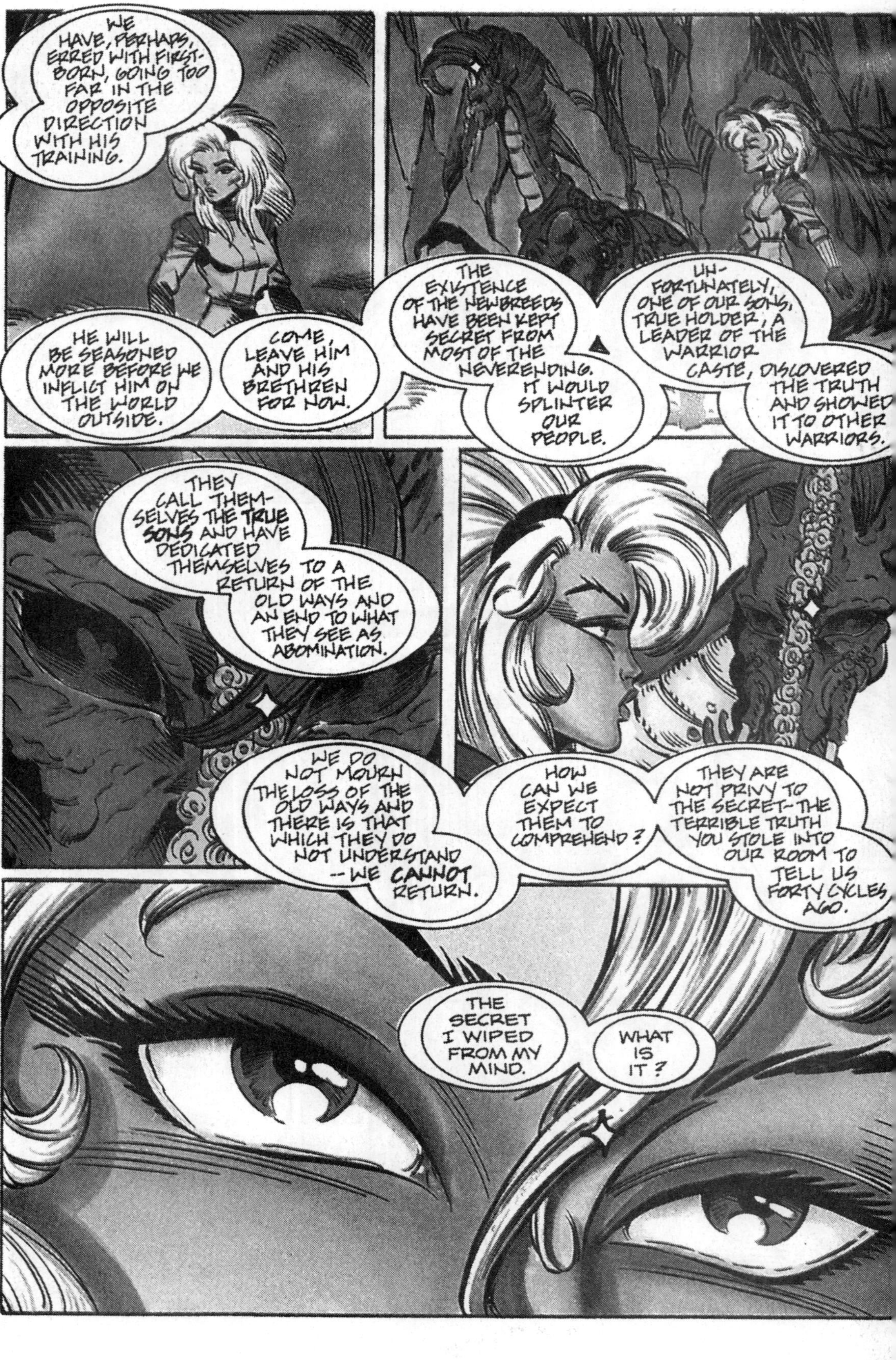
WE HAVE, PERHAPS, ERRED WITH FIRST-BORN, GOING TOO FAR IN THE OPPOSITE DIRECTION WITH HIS TRAINING.
HE WILL BE SEASONED MORE BEFORE WE INFLICT HIM ON THE WORLD OUTSIDE.
COME, LEAVE HIM AND HIS BRETHREN FOR NOW.
THE EXISTENCE OF THE NEWBREEDS HAVE BEEN KEPT SECRET FROM MOST OF THE NEVERENDING.
IT WOULD SPLINTER OUR PEOPLE.
UN-FORTUNATELY, ONE OF OUR SONS, TRUE HOLDER, A LEADER OF THE WARRIOR CASTE, DISCOVERED THE TRUTH AND SHOWED IT TO OTHER WARRIORS.
THEY CALL THEM-SELVES THE TRUE SONS AND HAVE DEDICATED THEMSELVES TO A RETURN OF THE OLD WAYS AND AN END TO WHAT THEY SEE AS ABOMINATION.
WE DO NOT MOURN THE LOSS OF THE OLD WAYS AND THERE IS THAT WHICH THEY DO NOT UNDERSTAND --WE CANNOT RETURN.
HOW CAN WE EXPECT THEM TO COMPREHEND?
THEY ARE NOT PRIVY TO THE SECRET-THE TERRIBLE TRUTH YOU STOLE INTO OUR ROOM TO TELL US FORTY CYCLES AGO.
THE SECRET I WIPED FROM MY MIND.
WHAT IS IT?

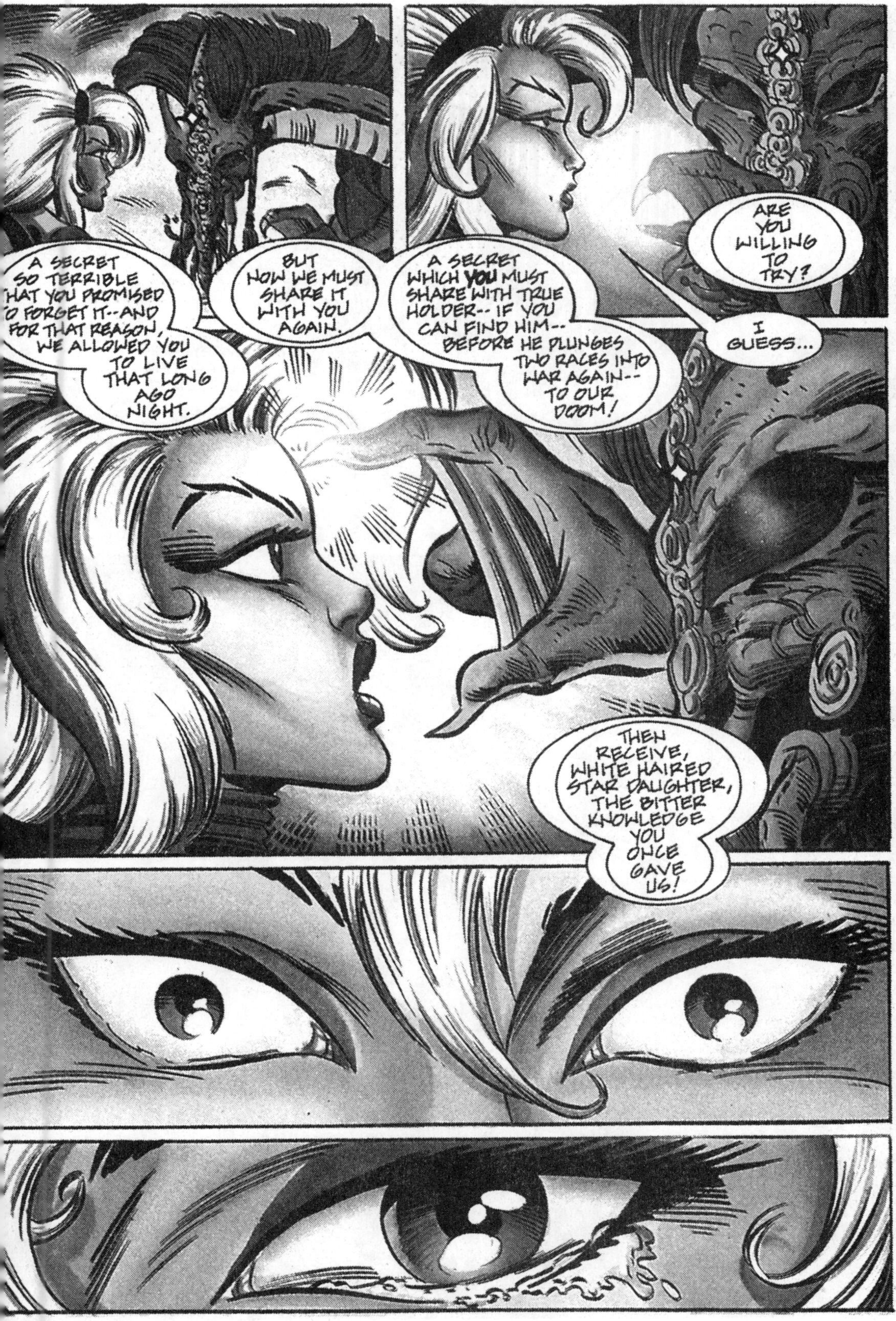
A SECRET SO TERRIBLE THAT YOU PROMISED TO FORGET IT--AND FOR THAT REASON, WE ALLOWED YOU TO LIVE THAT LONG AGO NIGHT.
BUT NOW WE MUST SHARE IT WITH YOU AGAIN.
A SECRET WHICH YOU MUST SHARE WITH TRUE HOLDER-- IF YOU CAN FIND HIM-- BEFORE HE PLUNGES TWO RACES INTO WAR AGAIN-- TO OUR DOOM!
ARE YOU WILLING TO TRY?
I GUESS...
THEN RECEIVE, WHITE HAIRED STAR DAUGHTER, THE BITTER KNOWLEDGE YOU ONCE GAVE US!

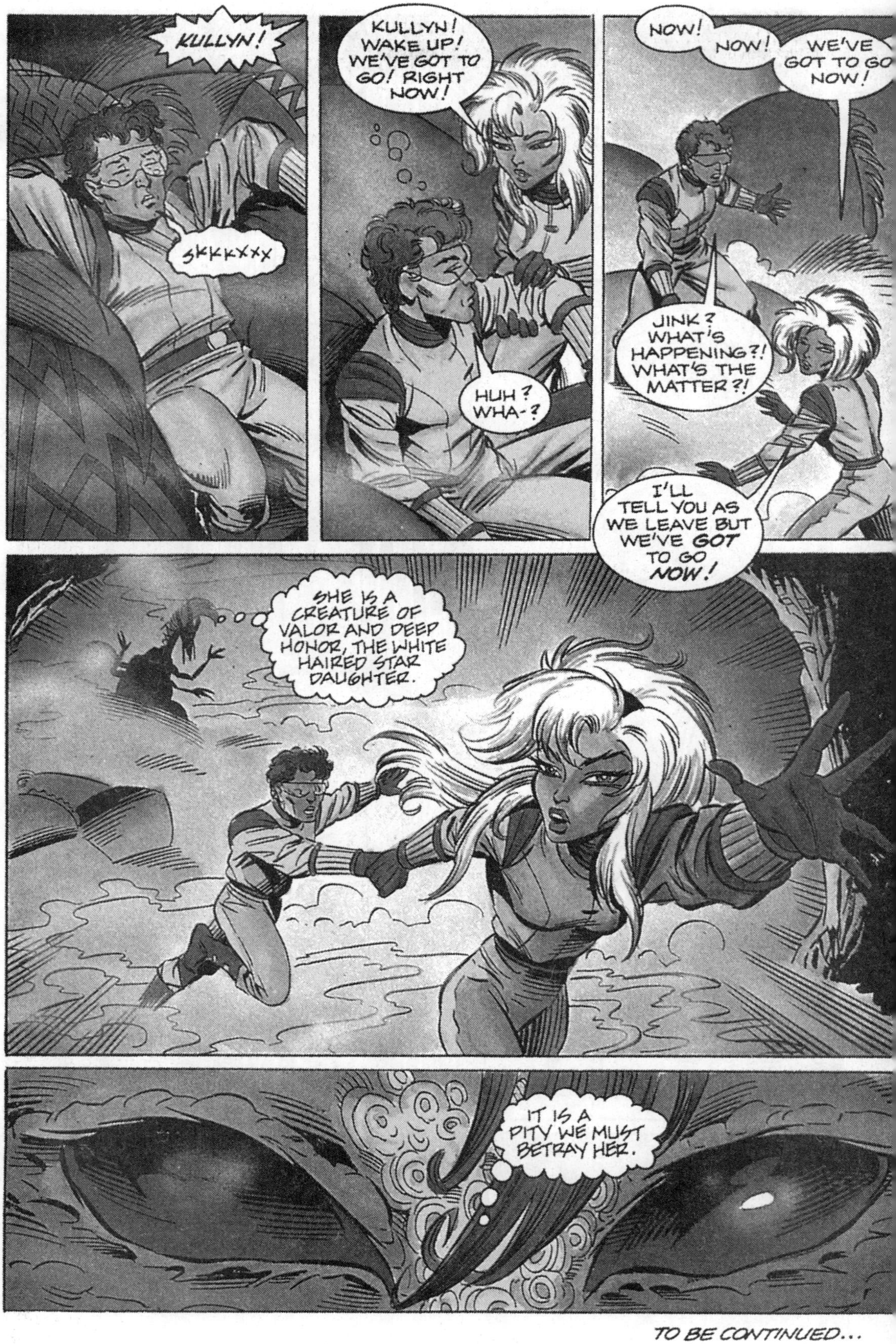
KULLYN!
SKKKXXX
KULLYN! WAKE UP! WE'VE GOT TO GO! RIGHT NOW!
HUH? WHA-?
NOW!
NOW!
WE'VE GOT TO GO NOW!
JINK? WHAT'S HAPPENING?! WHAT'S THE MATTER?!
I'LL TELL YOU AS WE LEAVE BUT WE'VE GOT TO GO NOW!
SHE IS A CREATURE OF VALOR AND DEEP HONOR, THE WHITE HAIRED STAR DAUGHTER.
IT IS A PITY WE MUST BETRAY HER.

TO BE CONTINUED...

CONVERGENCE
(Hide and Seek)
ABODE, THIS IS TWO-MOON STATION. YOU THERE, JONOST?
ONLINE, BERNHAR. WHAT'S UP?
WE'VE GOT ONE INCOMING NEVERENDING SHUTTLE--WANTS TO DOCK WITH US BEFORE HEADING YOUR WAY.
WELL, NOW, THAT'S FRANGING PECULIAR. WE'VE HAD NO ADVISORIES ON THEIR COMING. MAYBE SOME SORT OF WIGGLER ATTACK?

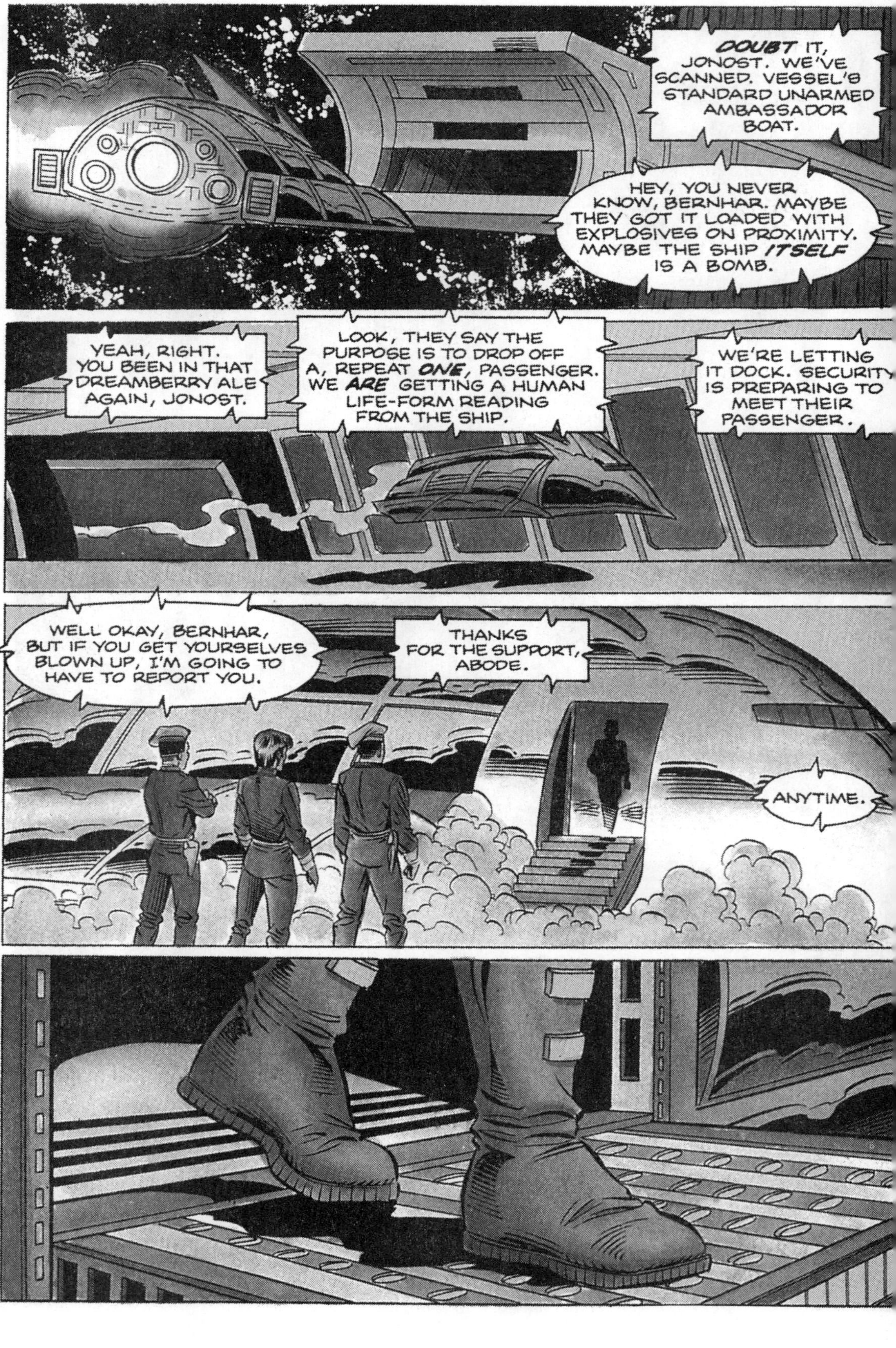
DOUBT IT, JONOST. WE'VE SCANNED. VESSEL'S STANDARD UNARMED AMBASSADOR BOAT.
HEY, YOU NEVER KNOW, BERNHAR. MAYBE THEY GOT IT LOADED WITH EXPLOSIVES ON PROXIMITY. MAYBE THE SHIP ITSELF IS A BOMB.
YEAH, RIGHT. YOU BEEN IN THAT DREAMBERRY ALE AGAIN, JONOST.
LOOK, THEY SAY THE PURPOSE IS TO DROP OFF A, REPEAT ONE, PASSENGER. WE ARE GETTING A HUMAN LIFE-FORM READING FROM THE SHIP.
WE'RE LETTING IT DOCK. SECURITY IS PREPARING TO MEET THEIR PASSENGER.
WELL OKAY, BERNHAR, BUT IF YOU GET YOURSELVES BLOWN UP, I'M GOING TO HAVE TO REPORT YOU.
THANKS FOR THE SUPPORT, ABODE.
ANYTIME.

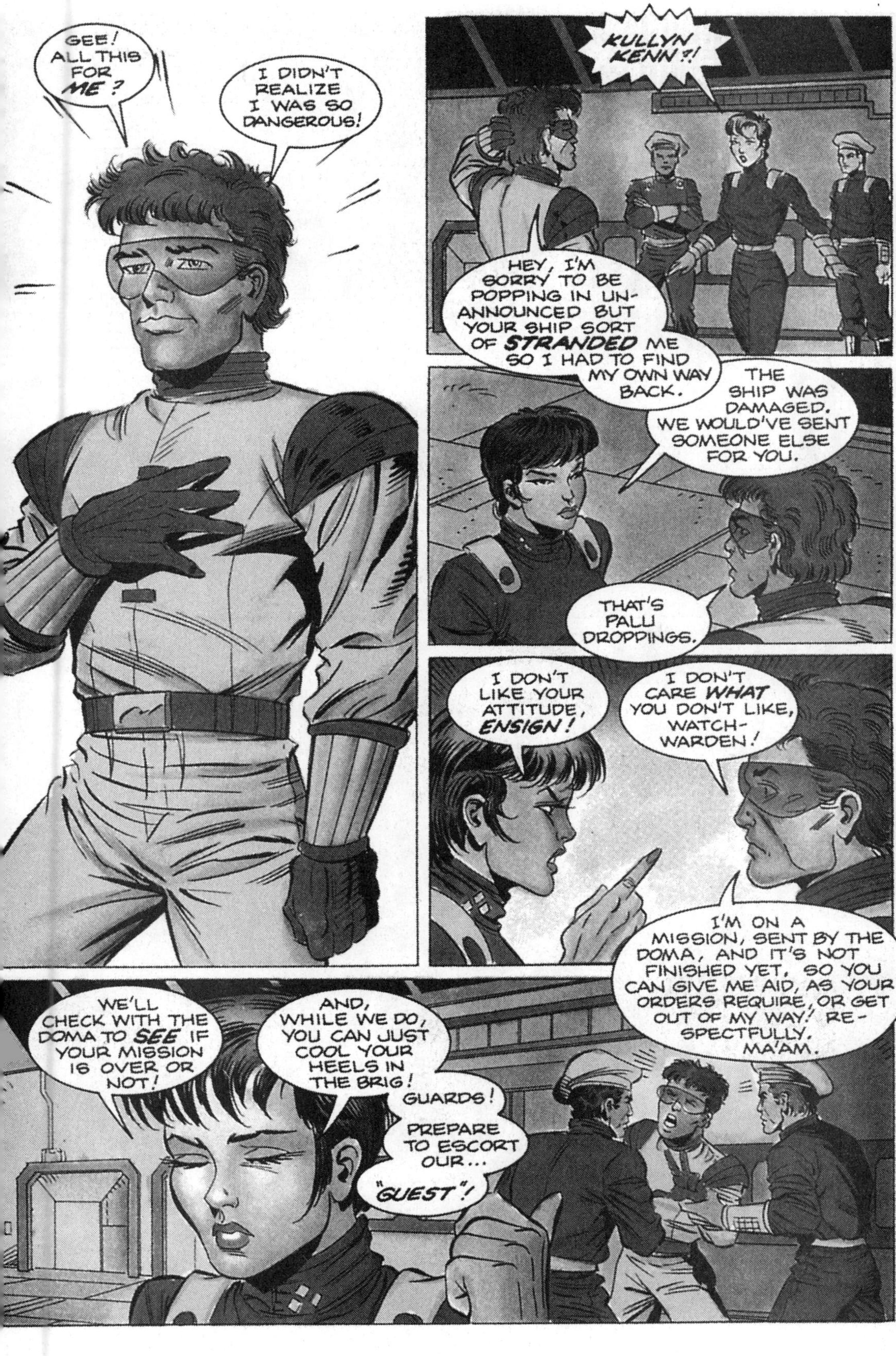
GEE! ALL THIS FOR ME?
I DIDN'T REALIZE I WAS SO DANGEROUS!
KULLYN KENN?!
HEY, I'M SORRY TO BE POPPING IN UN-ANNOUNCED BUT YOUR SHIP SORT OF STRANDED ME SO I HAD TO FIND MY OWN WAY BACK.
THE SHIP WAS DAMAGED. WE WOULD'VE SENT SOMEONE ELSE FOR YOU.
THAT'S PALU DROPPINGS.
I DON'T LIKE YOUR ATTITUDE, ENSIGN!
I DON'T CARE WHAT YOU DON'T LIKE, WATCH-WARDEN!
I'M ON A MISSION, SENT BY THE DOMA, AND IT'S NOT FINISHED YET, SO YOU CAN GIVE ME AID, AS YOUR ORDERS REQUIRE, OR GET OUT OF MY WAY! RE-SPECTFULLY. MA'AM.
WE'LL CHECK WITH THE DOMA TO SEE IF YOUR MISSION IS OVER OR NOT!
AND, WHILE WE DO, YOU CAN JUST COOL YOUR HEELS IN THE BRIG!
GUARDS!
PREPARE TO ESCORT OUR...
"GUEST"!

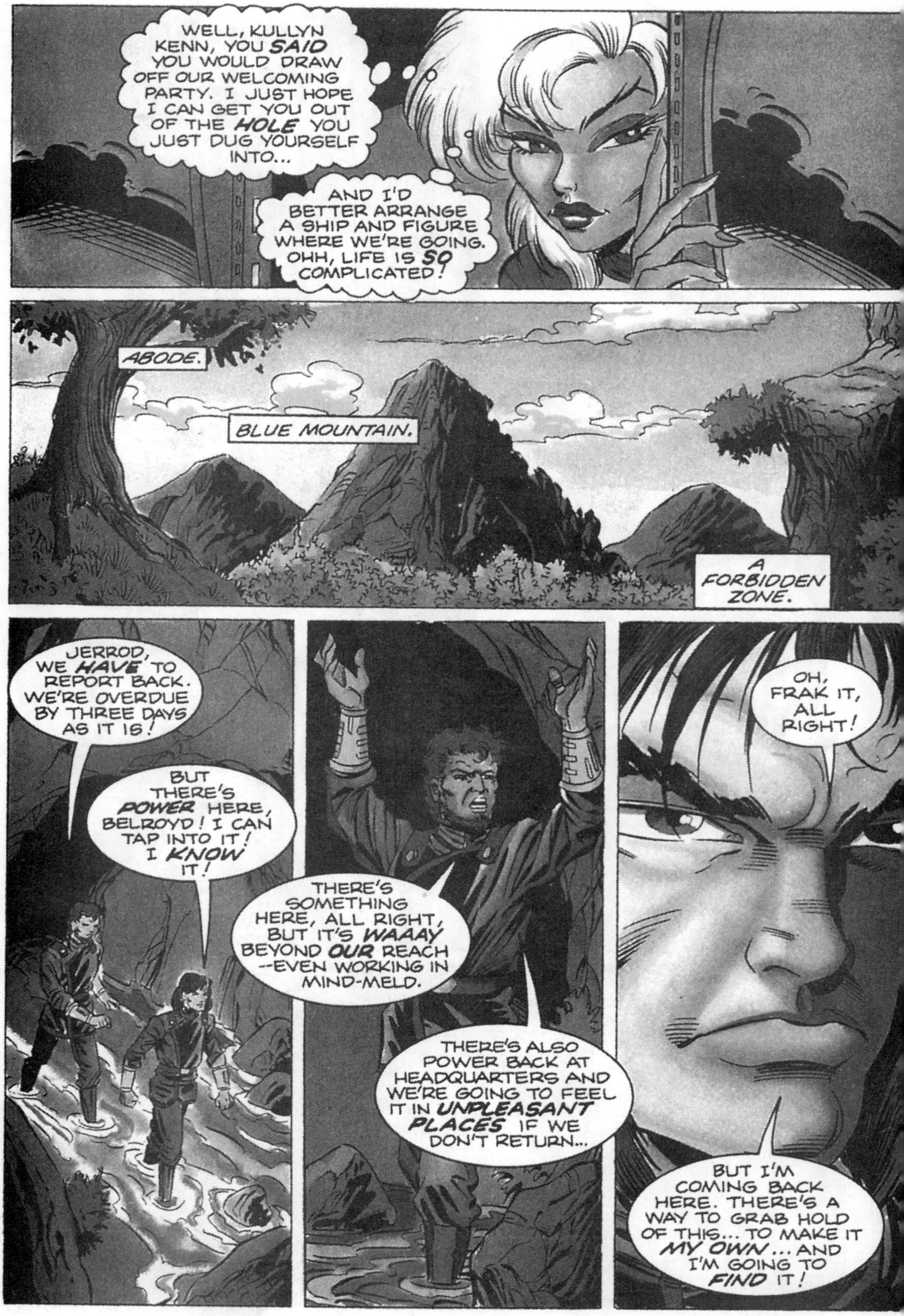
WELL, KULLYN KENN, YOU SAID YOU WOULD DRAW OFF OUR WELCOMING PARTY. I JUST HOPE I CAN GET YOU OUT OF THE HOLE YOU JUST DUG YOURSELF INTO...
AND I'D BETTER ARRANGE A SHIP AND FIGURE WHERE WE'RE GOING. OHH, LIFE IS SO COMPLICATED!
ABODE.
BLUE MOUNTAIN.
A FORBIDDEN ZONE.
JERROD, WE HAVE TO REPORT BACK. WE'RE OVERDUE BY THREE DAYS AS IT IS!
BUT THERE'S POWER HERE, BELROYD! I CAN TAP INTO IT! I KNOW IT!
THERE'S SOMETHING HERE, ALL RIGHT, BUT IT'S WAAAY BEYOND OUR REACH --EVEN WORKING IN MIND-MELD.
THERE'S ALSO POWER BACK AT HEADQUARTERS AND WE'RE GOING TO FEEL IT IN UNPLEASANT PLACES IF WE DON'T RETURN...
OH, FRAK IT, ALL RIGHT!
BUT I'M COMING BACK HERE. THERE'S A WAY TO GRAB HOLD OF THIS... TO MAKE IT MY OWN... AND I'M GOING TO FIND IT!

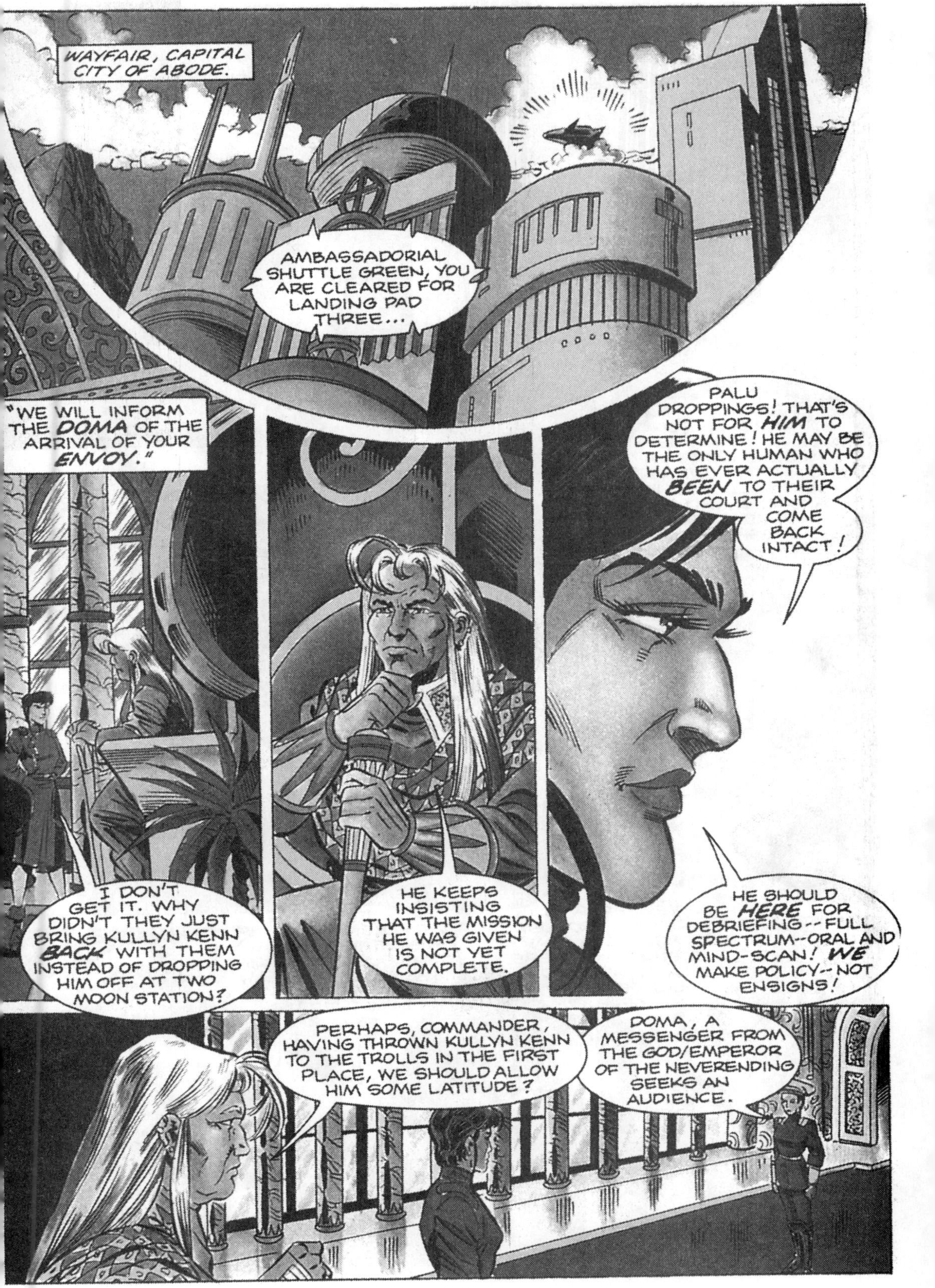
WAYFAIR, CAPITAL CITY OF ABODE.
AMBASSADORIAL SHUTTLE GREEN, YOU ARE CLEARED FOR LANDING PAD THREE...
"WE WILL INFORM THE DOMA OF THE ARRIVAL OF YOUR ENVOY."
I DON'T GET IT. WHY DIDN'T THEY JUST BRING KULLYN KENN BACK WITH THEM INSTEAD OF DROPPING HIM OFF AT TWO MOON STATION?
HE KEEPS INSISTING THAT THE MISSION HE WAS GIVEN IS NOT YET COMPLETE.
PALU DROPPINGS! THAT'S NOT FOR HIM TO DETERMINE! HE MAY BE THE ONLY HUMAN WHO HAS EVER ACTUALLY BEEN TO THEIR COURT AND COME BACK INTACT!
HE SHOULD BE HERE FOR DEBRIEFING--FULL SPECTRUM--ORAL AND MIND-SCAN! WE MAKE POLICY--NOT ENSIGNS!
PERHAPS, COMMANDER, HAVING THROWN KULLYN KENN TO THE TROLLS IN THE FIRST PLACE, WE SHOULD ALLOW HIM SOME LATITUDE?
DOMA, A MESSENGER FROM THE GOD/EMPEROR OF THE NEVERENDING SEEKS AN AUDIENCE.

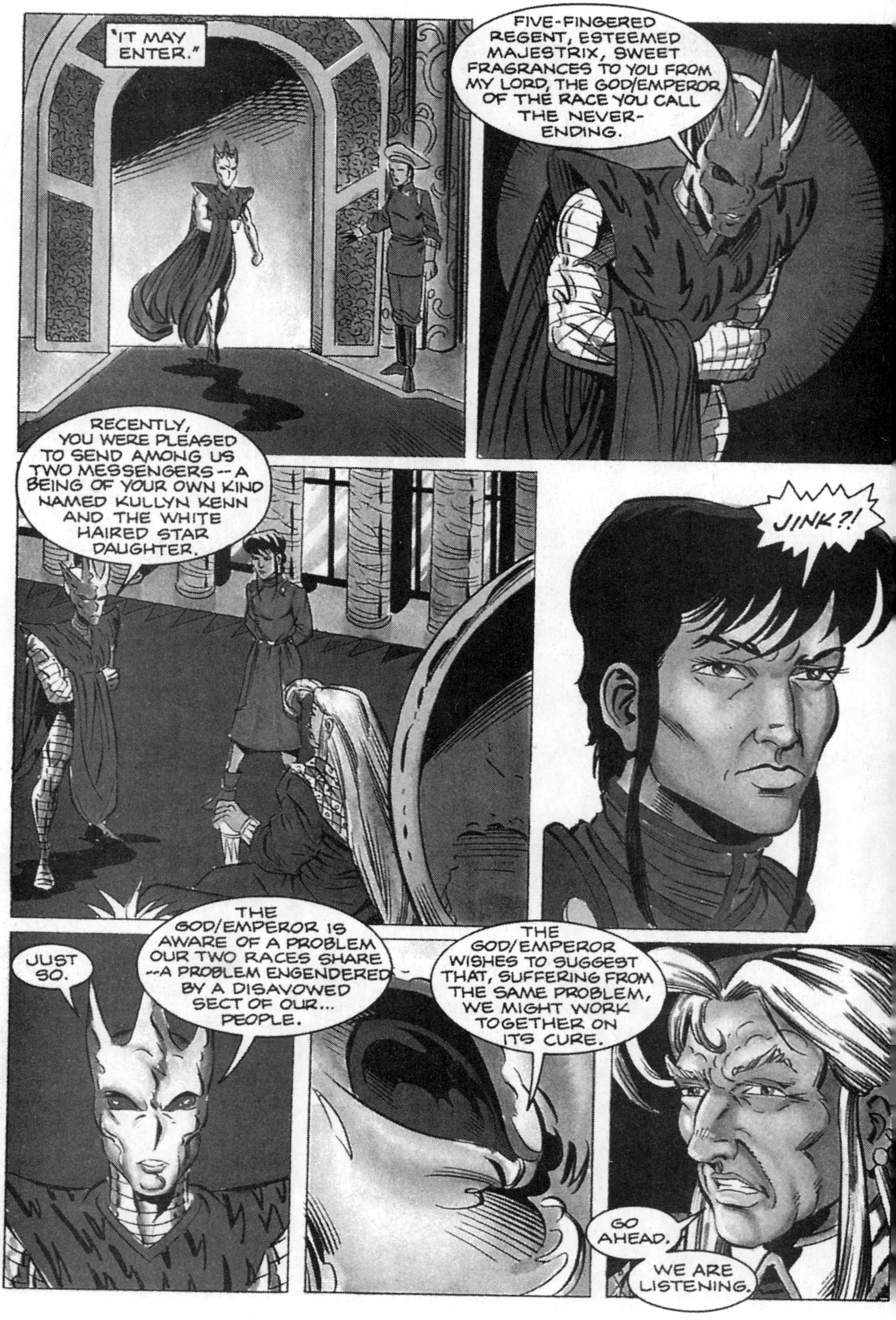
"IT MAY ENTER."
FIVE-FINGERED REGENT, ESTEEMED MAJESTRIX, SWEET FRAGRANCES TO YOU FROM MY LORD, THE GOD/EMPEROR OF THE RACE YOU CALL THE NEVER-ENDING.
RECENTLY, YOU WERE PLEASED TO SEND AMONG US TWO MESSENGERS--A BEING OF YOUR OWN KIND NAMED KULLYN KENN AND THE WHITE HAIRED STAR DAUGHTER.
JINK?!
JUST SO.
THE GOD/EMPEROR IS AWARE OF A PROBLEM OUR TWO RACES SHARE --A PROBLEM ENGENDERED BY A DISAVOWED SECT OF OUR... PEOPLE.
THE GOD/EMPEROR WISHES TO SUGGEST THAT, SUFFERING FROM THE SAME PROBLEM, WE MIGHT WORK TOGETHER ON ITS CURE.
GO AHEAD.
WE ARE LISTENING.

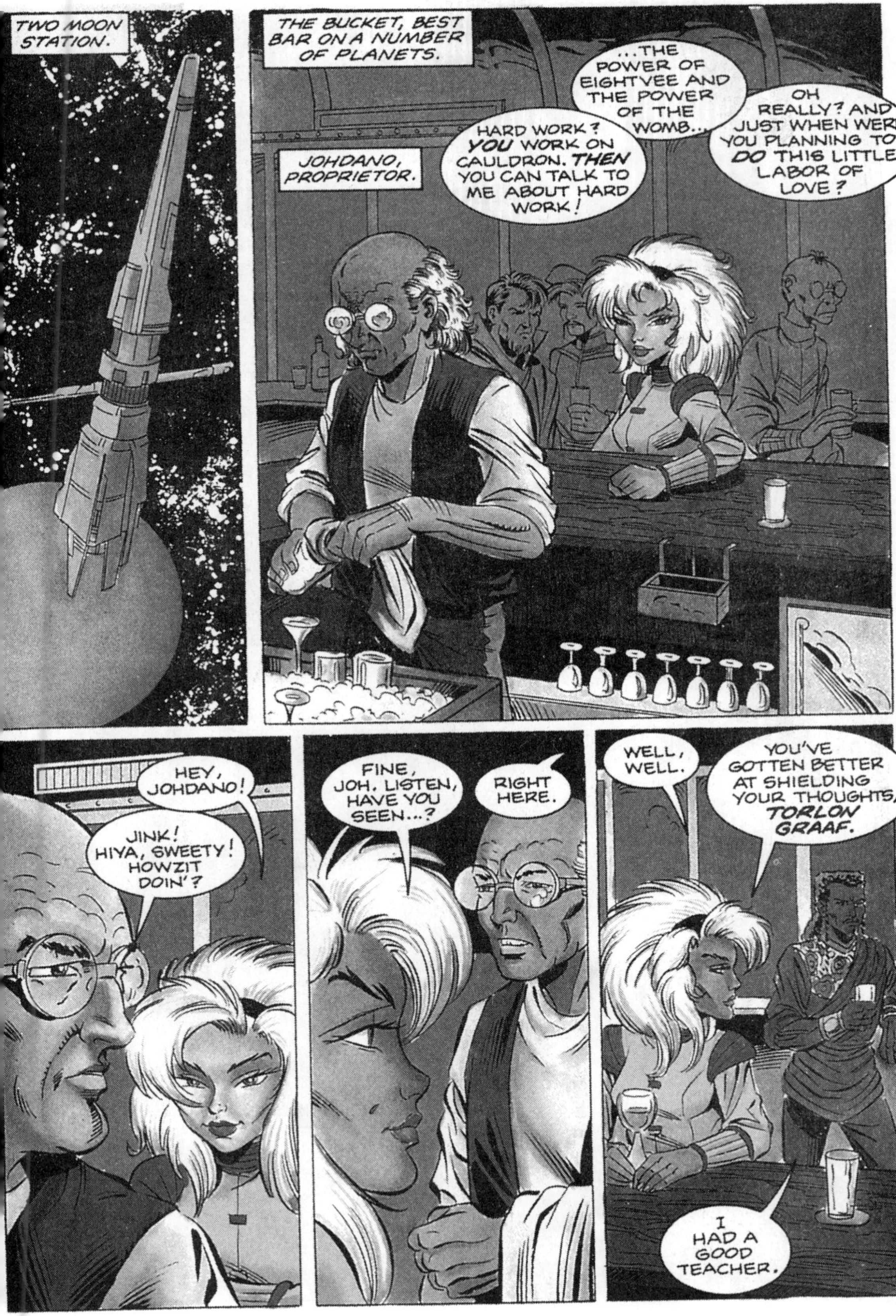
TWO MOON STATION.
THE BUCKET, BEST BAR ON A NUMBER OF PLANETS.
JOHDANO, PROPRIETOR.
...THE POWER OF EIGHTVEE AND THE POWER OF THE WOMB...
HARD WORK? YOU WORK ON CAULDRON. THEN YOU CAN TALK TO ME ABOUT HARD WORK!
OH REALLY? AND JUST WHEN WERE YOU PLANNING TO DO THIS LITTLE LABOR OF LOVE?
HEY, JOHDANO!
JINK! HIYA, SWEETY! HOWZIT DOIN'?
FINE, JOH. LISTEN, HAVE YOU SEEN...?
RIGHT HERE.
WELL, WELL.
YOU'VE GOTTEN BETTER AT SHIELDING YOUR THOUGHTS, TORLON GRAAF.
I HAD A GOOD TEACHER.

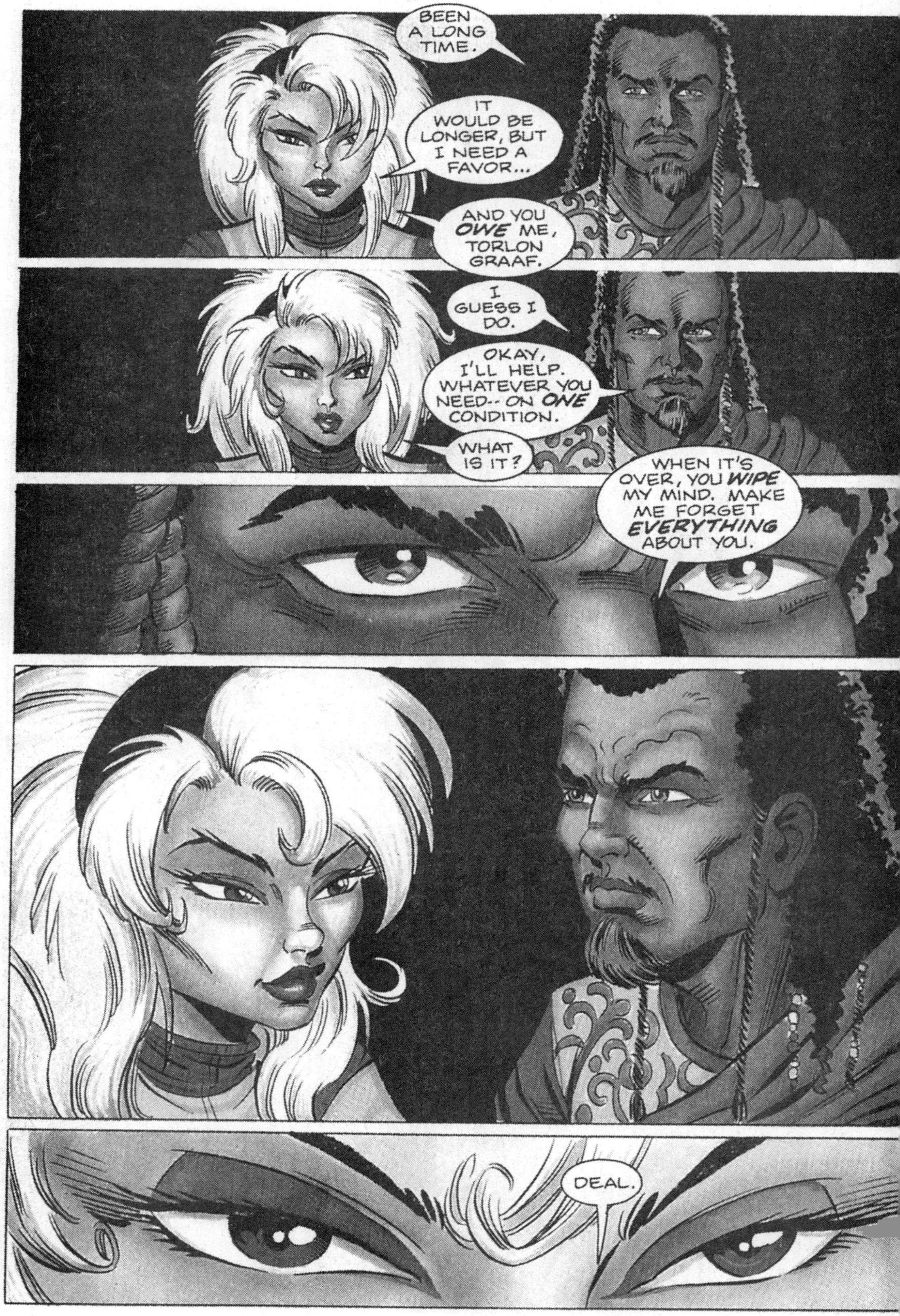
BEEN A LONG TIME.
IT WOULD BE LONGER, BUT I NEED A FAVOR...
AND YOU OWE ME, TORLON GRAAF.
I GUESS I DO.
OKAY, I'LL HELP. WHATEVER YOU NEED-- ON ONE CONDITION.
WHAT IS IT?
WHEN IT'S OVER, YOU WIPE MY MIND. MAKE ME FORGET EVERYTHING ABOUT YOU.
DEAL.

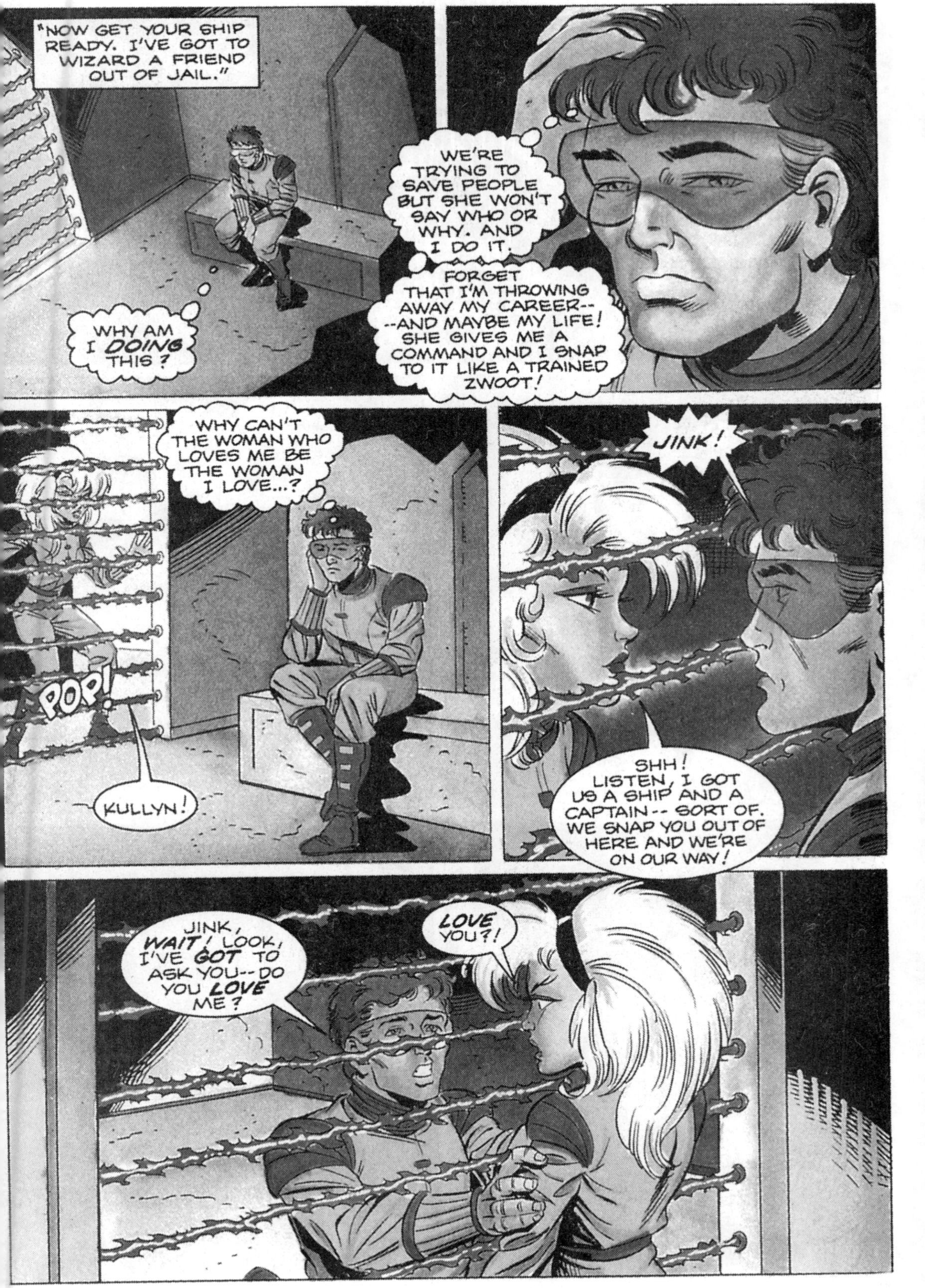
"NOW GET YOUR SHIP READY. I'VE GOT TO WIZARD A FRIEND OUT OF JAIL."
WHY AM I DOING THIS?
WE'RE TRYING TO SAVE PEOPLE BUT SHE WON'T SAY WHO OR WHY. AND I DO IT.
FORGET THAT I'M THROWING AWAY MY CAREER-- --AND MAYBE MY LIFE! SHE GIVES ME A COMMAND AND I SNAP TO IT LIKE A TRAINED ZWOOT!
WHY CAN'T THE WOMAN WHO LOVES ME BE THE WOMAN I LOVE...?
POP!
KULLYN!
JINK!
SHH! LISTEN, I GOT US A SHIP AND A CAPTAIN -- SORT OF. WE SNAP YOU OUT OF HERE AND WE'RE ON OUR WAY!
JINK, WAIT! LOOK, I'VE GOT TO ASK YOU-- DO YOU LOVE ME?
LOVE YOU?!

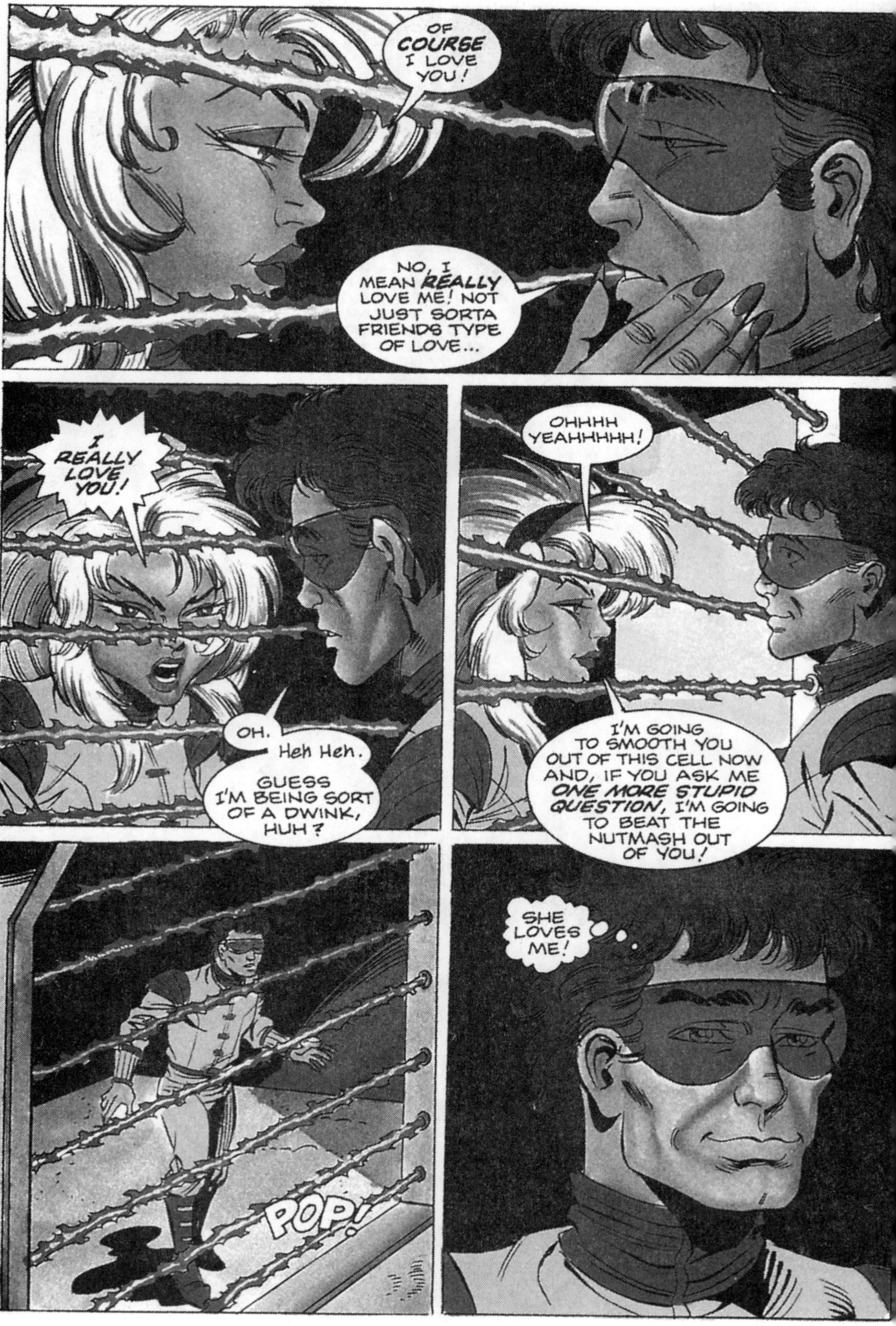

OF COURSE I LOVE YOU!
NO, I MEAN REALLY LOVE ME! NOT JUST SORTA FRIENDS TYPE OF LOVE...
I REALLY LOVE YOU!
OH. Heh Heh. GUESS I'M BEING SORT OF A DWINK, HUH?
OHHHH YEAHHHHH!
I'M GOING TO SMOOTH YOU OUT OF THIS CELL NOW AND, IF YOU ASK ME ONE MORE STUPID QUESTION, I'M GOING TO BEAT THE NUTMASH OUT OF YOU!
POP!
SHE LOVES ME!

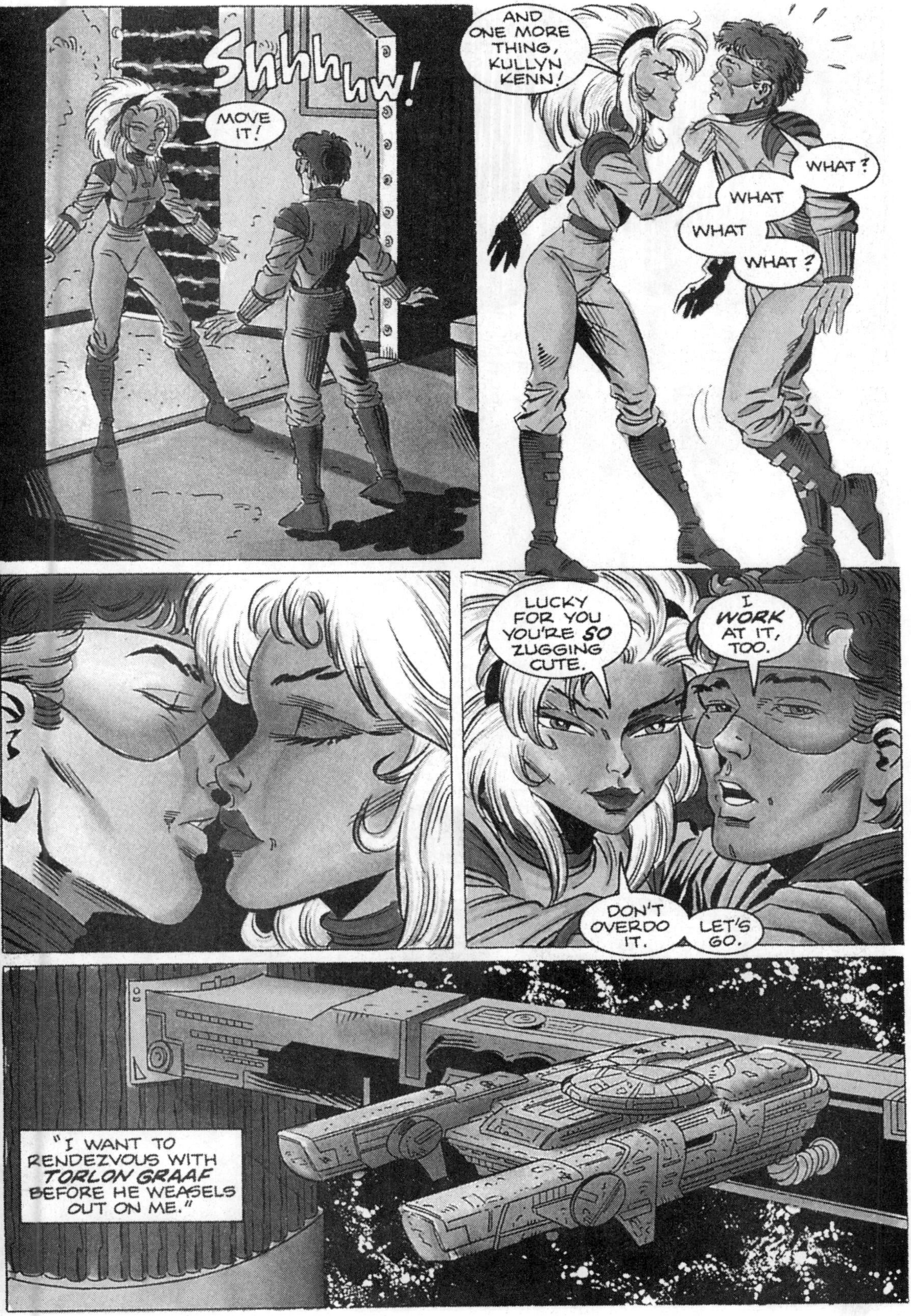
Shhhhw!
MOVE IT!
AND ONE MORE THING, KULLYN KENN!
WHAT?
WHAT
WHAT
WHAT?
LUCKY FOR YOU YOU'RE SO ZUGGING CUTE.
I WORK AT IT, TOO.
DON'T OVERDO IT.
LET'S GO.
"I WANT TO RENDEZVOUS WITH TORLON GRAAF BEFORE HE WEASELS OUT ON ME."

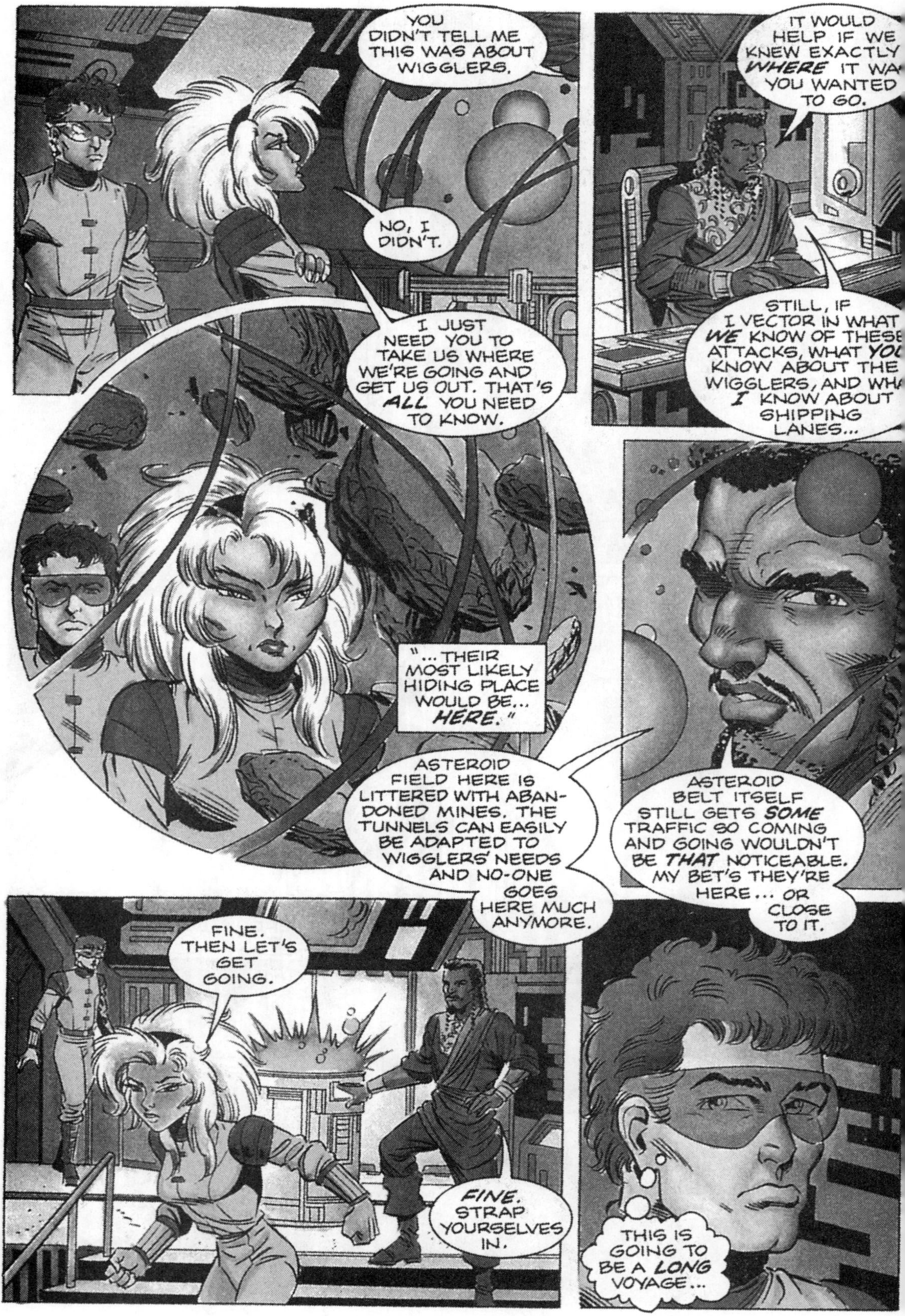
YOU DIDN'T TELL ME THIS WAS ABOUT WIGGLERS.
NO, I DIDN'T.
I JUST NEED YOU TO TAKE US WHERE WE'RE GOING AND GET US OUT. THAT'S ALL YOU NEED TO KNOW.
IT WOULD HELP IF WE KNEW EXACTLY WHERE IT WA YOU WANTED TO GO.
STILL, IF I VECTOR IN WHAT WE KNOW OF THESE ATTACKS, WHAT YOU KNOW ABOUT THE WIGGLERS, AND WHA I KNOW ABOUT SHIPPING LANES...
"...THEIR MOST LIKELY HIDING PLACE WOULD BE... HERE."
ASTEROID FIELD HERE IS LITTERED WITH ABAN-DONED MINES. THE TUNNELS CAN EASILY BE ADAPTED TO WIGGLERS' NEEDS AND NO-ONE GOES HERE MUCH ANYMORE.
ASTEROID BELT ITSELF STILL GETS SOME TRAFFIC SO COMING AND GOING WOULDN'T BE THAT NOTICEABLE. MY BET'S THEY'RE HERE... OR CLOSE TO IT.
FINE. THEN LET'S GET GOING.
FINE. STRAP YOURSELVES IN.
THIS IS GOING TO BE A LONG VOYAGE...

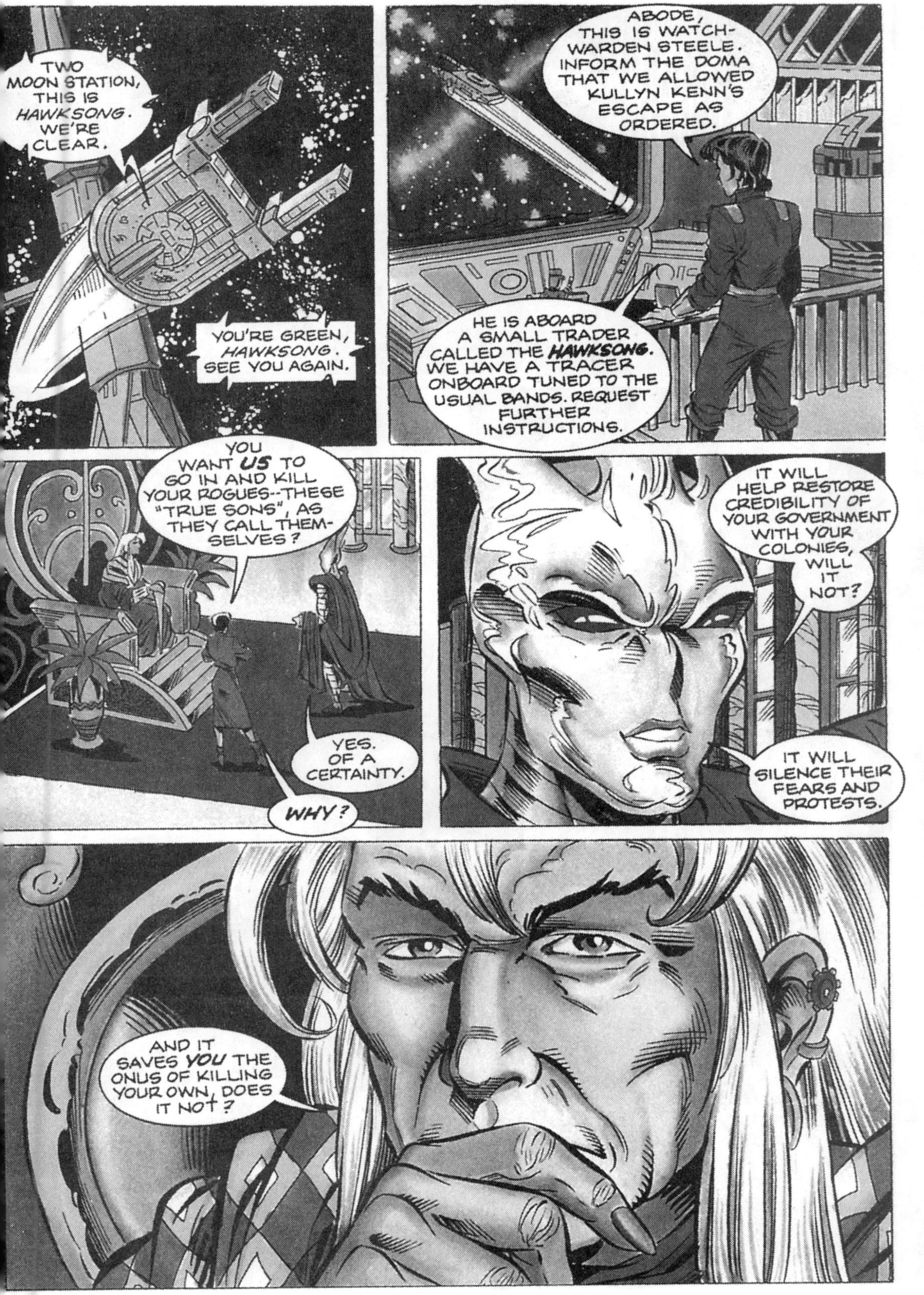
TWO MOON STATION, THIS IS HAWKSONG. WE'RE CLEAR.
YOU'RE GREEN, HAWKSONG. SEE YOU AGAIN.
ABODE, THIS IS WATCH-WARDEN STEELE. INFORM THE DOMA THAT WE ALLOWED KULLYN KENN'S ESCAPE AS ORDERED.
HE IS ABOARD A SMALL TRADER CALLED THE HAWKSONG. WE HAVE A TRACER ONBOARD TUNED TO THE USUAL BANDS. REQUEST FURTHER INSTRUCTIONS.
YOU WANT US TO GO IN AND KILL YOUR ROGUES--THESE "TRUE SONS", AS THEY CALL THEM-SELVES?
YES. OF A CERTAINTY.
WHY?
IT WILL HELP RESTORE CREDIBILITY OF YOUR GOVERNMENT WITH YOUR COLONIES, WILL IT NOT?
IT WILL SILENCE THEIR FEARS AND PROTESTS.
AND IT SAVES YOU THE ONUS OF KILLING YOUR OWN, DOES IT NOT?

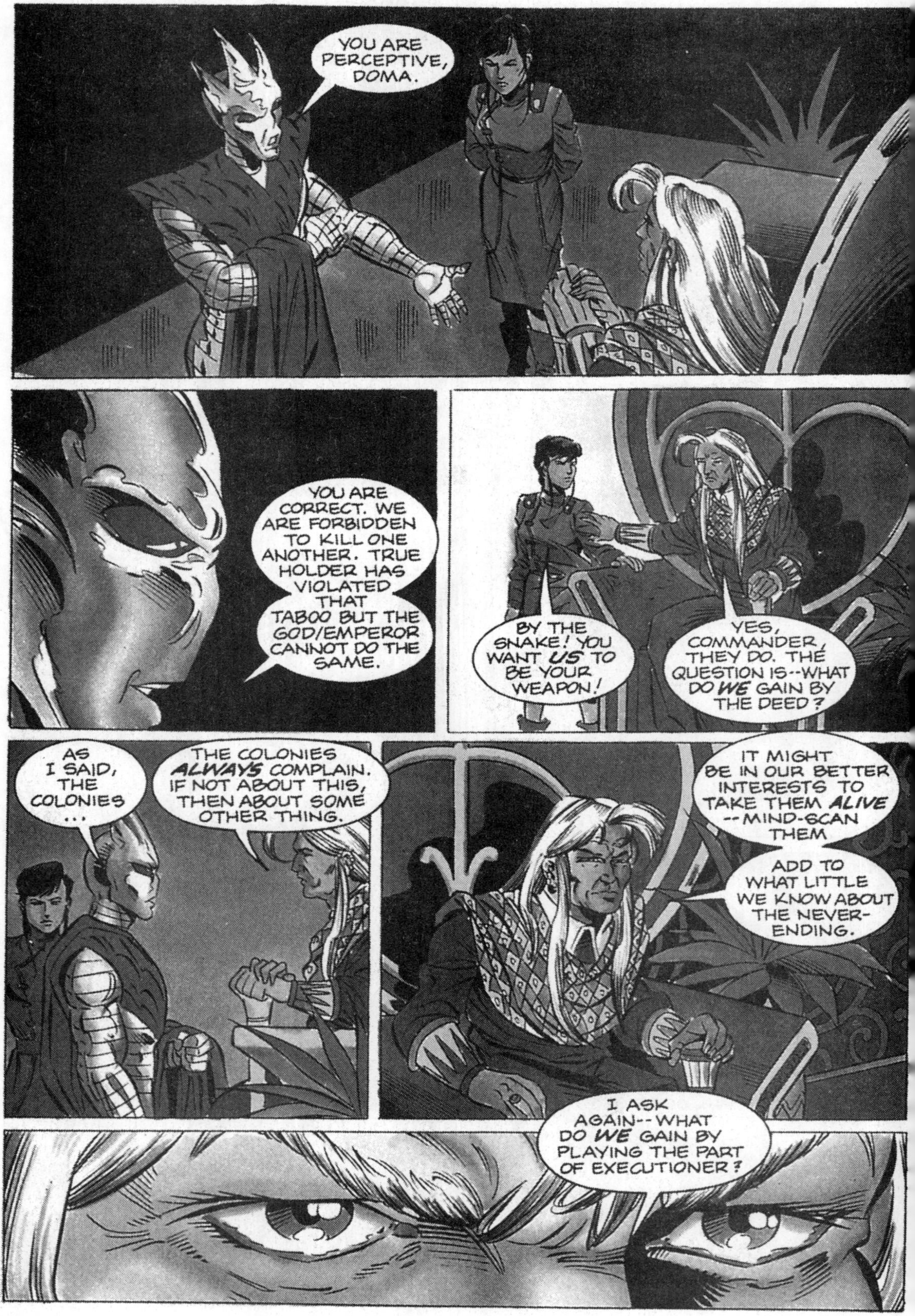
YOU ARE PERCEPTIVE, DOMA.
YOU ARE CORRECT. WE ARE FORBIDDEN TO KILL ONE ANOTHER. TRUE HOLDER HAS VIOLATED THAT TABOO BUT THE GOD/EMPEROR CANNOT DO THE SAME.
BY THE SNAKE! YOU WANT US TO BE YOUR WEAPON!
YES, COMMANDER, THEY DO. THE QUESTION IS--WHAT DO WE GAIN BY THE DEED?
AS I SAID, THE COLONIES ...
THE COLONIES ALWAYS COMPLAIN. IF NOT ABOUT THIS, THEN ABOUT SOME OTHER THING.
IT MIGHT BE IN OUR BETTER INTERESTS TO TAKE THEM ALIVE --MIND-SCAN THEM
ADD TO WHAT LITTLE WE KNOW ABOUT THE NEVER-ENDING.
I ASK AGAIN--WHAT DO WE GAIN BY PLAYING THE PART OF EXECUTIONER?

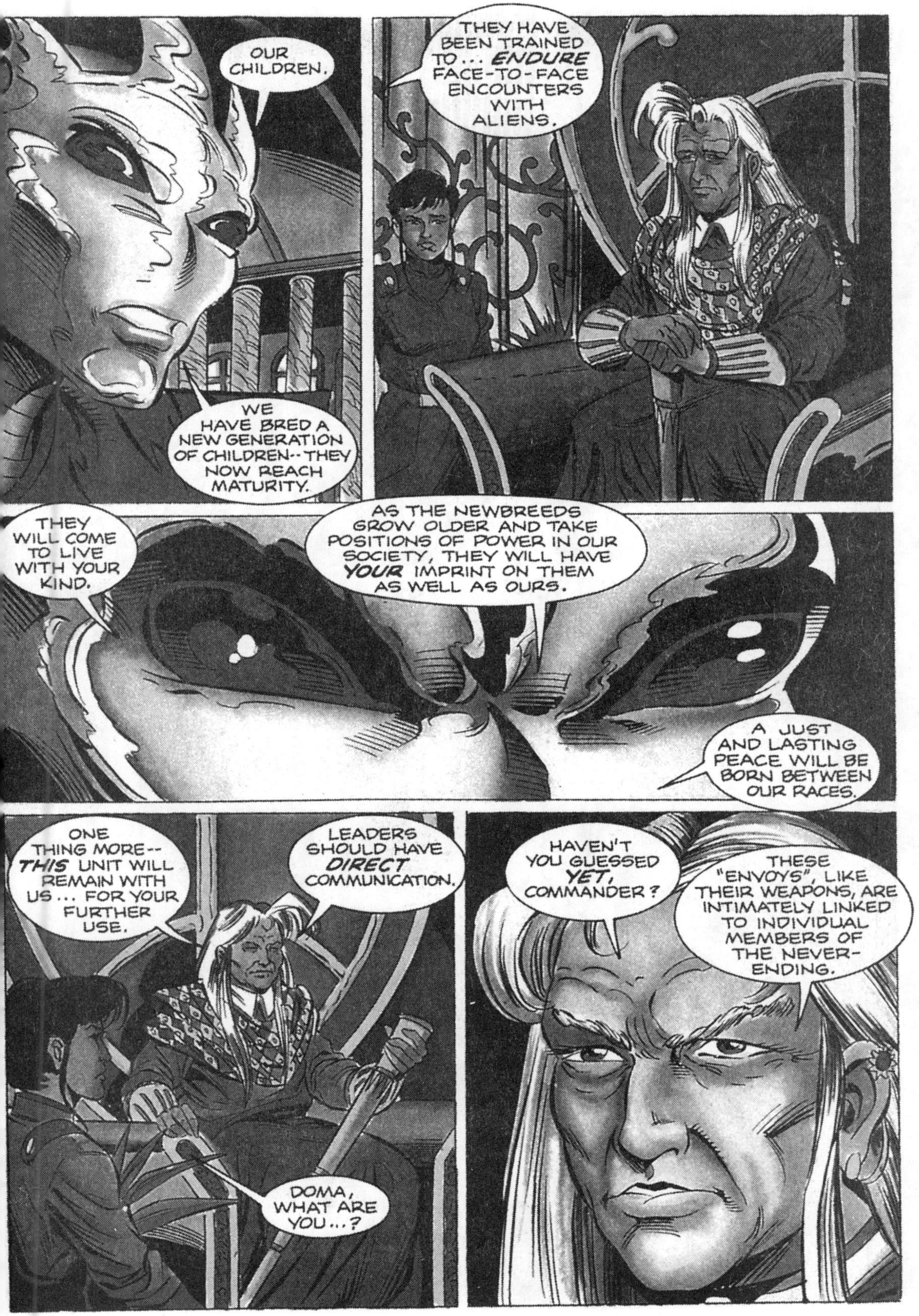
OUR CHILDREN.
WE HAVE BRED A NEW GENERATION OF CHILDREN-- THEY NOW REACH MATURITY.
THEY HAVE BEEN TRAINED TO... ENDURE FACE-TO-FACE ENCOUNTERS WITH ALIENS.
THEY WILL COME TO LIVE WITH YOUR KIND.
AS THE NEWBREEDS GROW OLDER AND TAKE POSITIONS OF POWER IN OUR SOCIETY, THEY WILL HAVE YOUR IMPRINT ON THEM AS WELL AS OURS.
A JUST AND LASTING PEACE WILL BE BORN BETWEEN OUR RACES.
ONE THING MORE-- THIS UNIT WILL REMAIN WITH US... FOR YOUR FURTHER USE.
LEADERS SHOULD HAVE DIRECT COMMUNICATION.
DOMA, WHAT ARE YOU...?
HAVEN'T YOU GUESSED YET, COMMANDER?
THESE "ENVOYS", LIKE THEIR WEAPONS, ARE INTIMATELY LINKED TO INDIVIDUAL MEMBERS OF THE NEVER-ENDING.

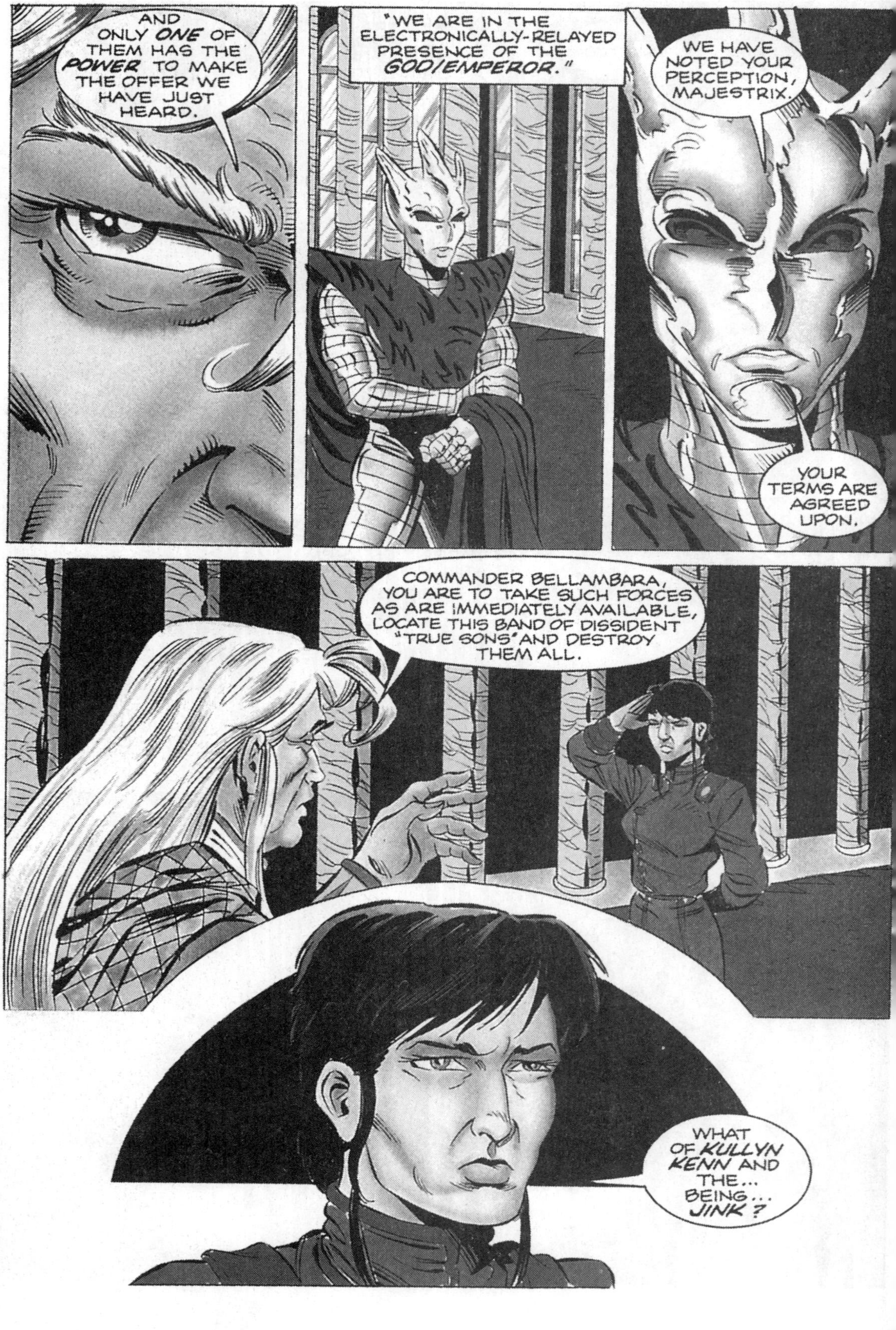
AND ONLY ONE OF THEM HAS THE POWER TO MAKE THE OFFER WE HAVE JUST HEARD.
"WE ARE IN THE ELECTRONICALLY-RELAYED PRESENCE OF THE GOD/EMPEROR."
WE HAVE NOTED YOUR PERCEPTION, MAJESTRIX.
YOUR TERMS ARE AGREED UPON.
COMMANDER BELLAMBARA, YOU ARE TO TAKE SUCH FORCES AS ARE IMMEDIATELY AVAILABLE, LOCATE THIS BAND OF DISSIDENT "TRUE SONS" AND DESTROY THEM ALL.
WHAT OF KULLYN KENN AND THE... BEING... JINK?

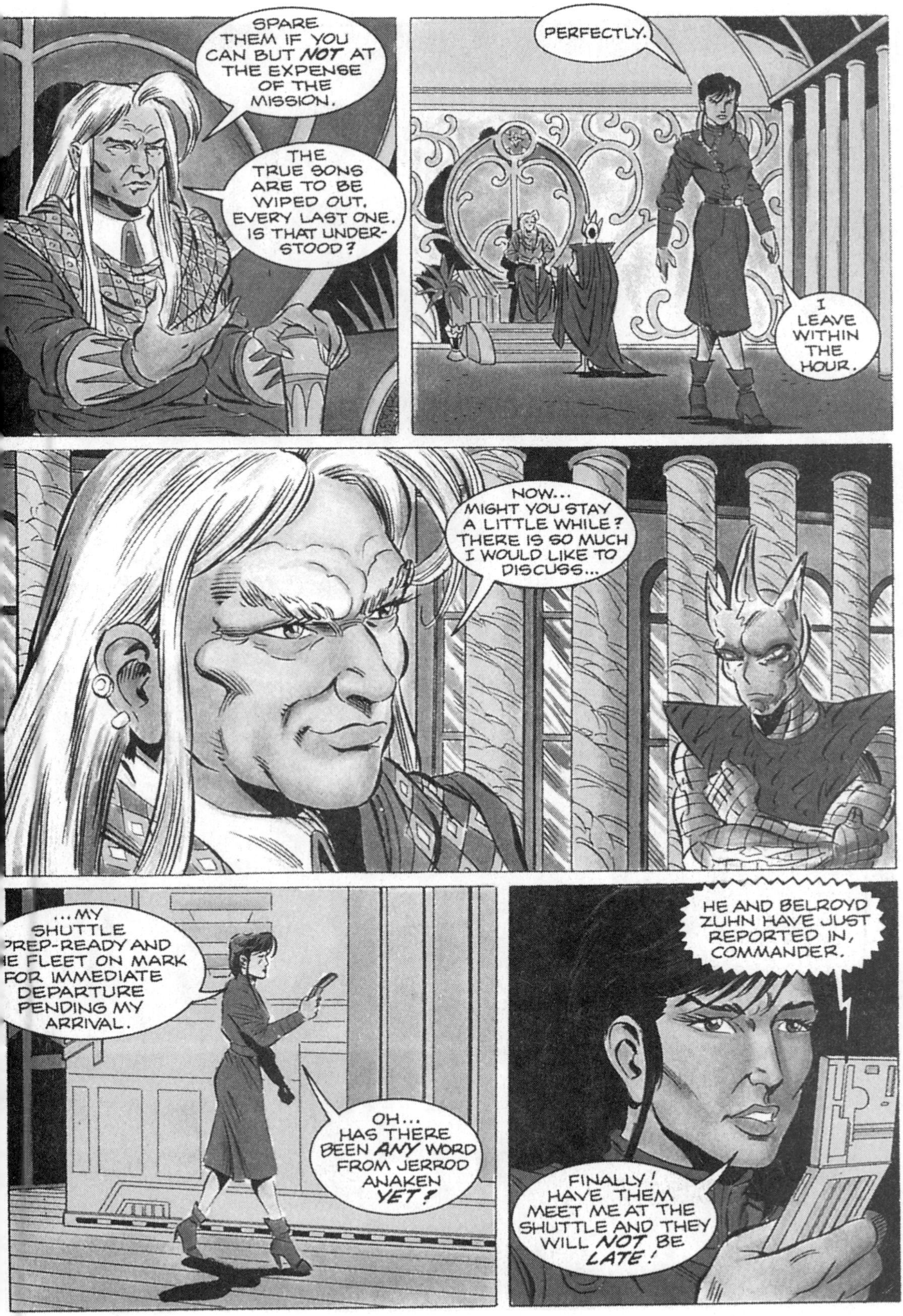
SPARE THEM IF YOU CAN BUT *NOT* AT THE EXPENSE OF THE MISSION.
THE TRUE SONS ARE TO BE WIPED OUT. EVERY LAST ONE. IS THAT UNDER-STOOD?
PERFECTLY.
I LEAVE WITHIN THE HOUR.
NOW... MIGHT YOU STAY A LITTLE WHILE? THERE IS SO MUCH I WOULD LIKE TO DISCUSS...
...MY SHUTTLE PREP-READY AND HE FLEET ON MARK FOR IMMEDIATE DEPARTURE PENDING MY ARRIVAL.
OH... HAS THERE BEEN *ANY* WORD FROM JERROD ANAKEN *YET?*
HE AND BELROYD ZUHN HAVE JUST REPORTED IN, COMMANDER.
FINALLY! HAVE THEM MEET ME AT THE SHUTTLE AND THEY WILL *NOT* BE *LATE!*

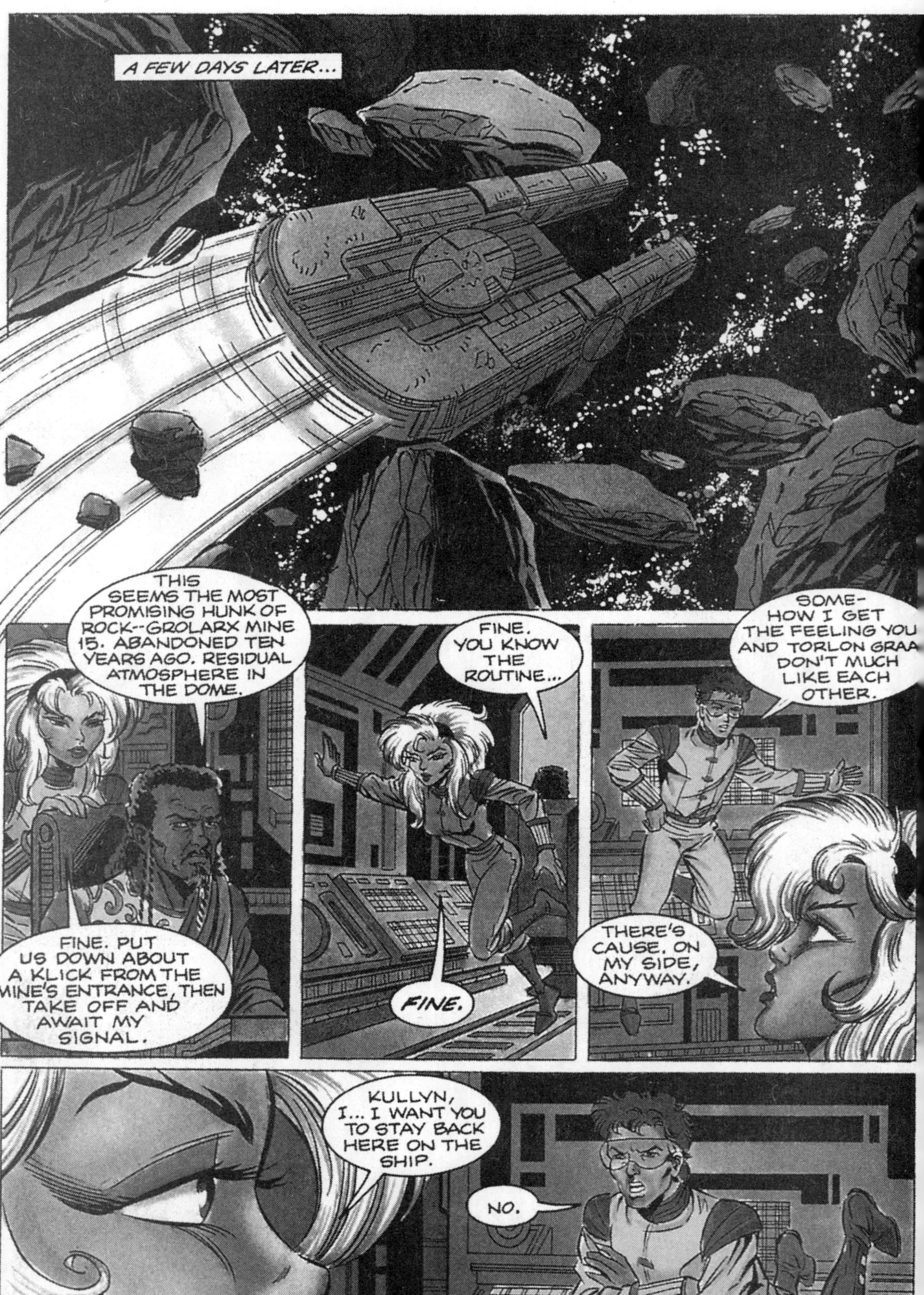
A FEW DAYS LATER...
THIS SEEMS THE MOST PROMISING HUNK OF ROCK--GROLARX MINE 15. ABANDONED TEN YEARS AGO. RESIDUAL ATMOSPHERE IN THE DOME.
FINE. PUT US DOWN ABOUT A KLICK FROM THE MINE'S ENTRANCE, THEN TAKE OFF AND AWAIT MY SIGNAL.
FINE. YOU KNOW THE ROUTINE...
FINE.
SOME-HOW I GET THE FEELING YOU AND TORLON GRAA DON'T MUCH LIKE EACH OTHER.
THERE'S CAUSE. ON MY SIDE, ANYWAY.
KULLYN, I... I WANT YOU TO STAY BACK HERE ON THE SHIP.
NO.

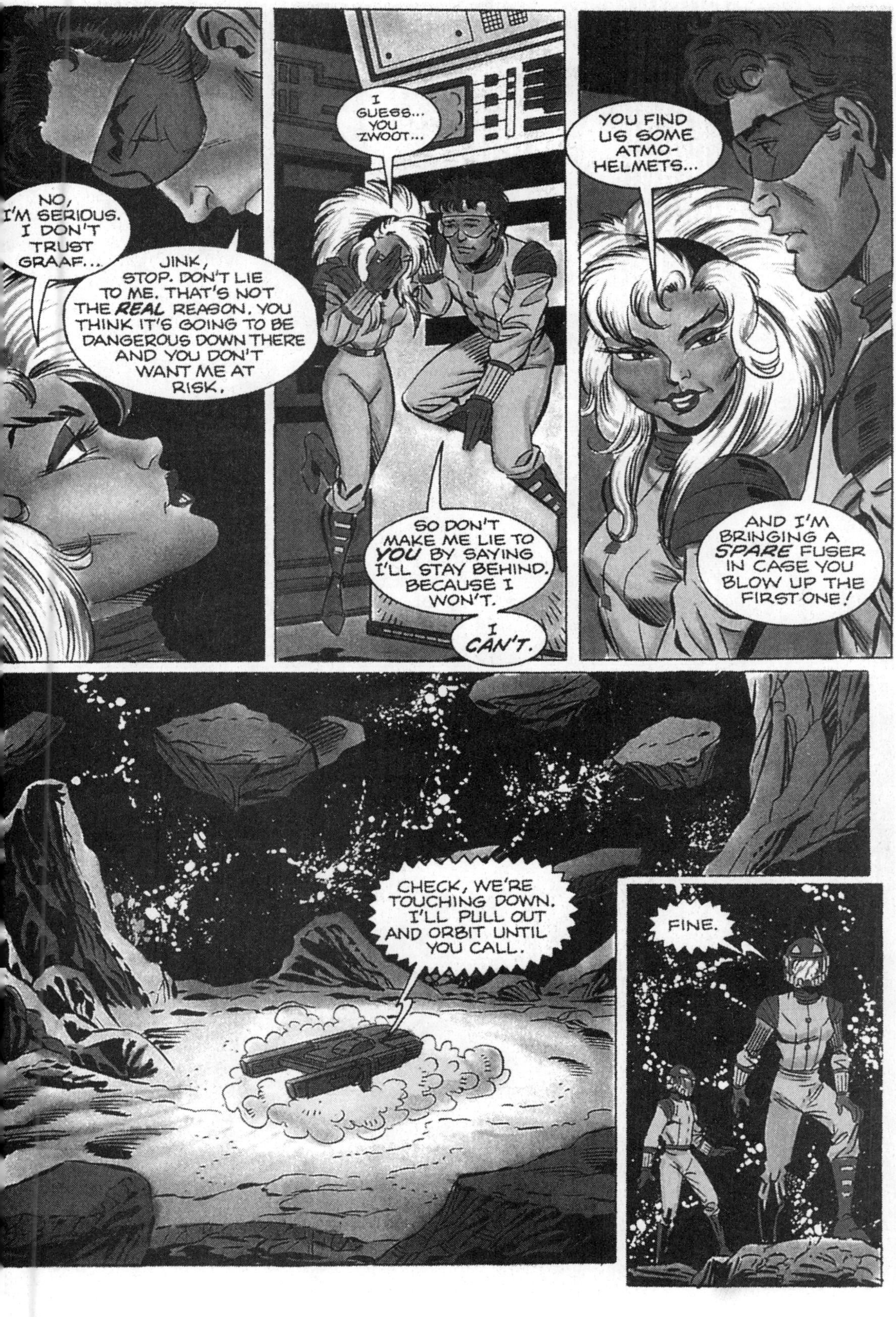
NO, I'M SERIOUS. I DON'T TRUST GRAAF...
JINK, STOP. DON'T LIE TO ME. THAT'S NOT THE REAL REASON. YOU THINK IT'S GOING TO BE DANGEROUS DOWN THERE AND YOU DON'T WANT ME AT RISK.
I GUESS... YOU ZWOOT...
SO DON'T MAKE ME LIE TO YOU BY SAYING I'LL STAY BEHIND. BECAUSE I WON'T.
I CAN'T.
YOU FIND US SOME ATMO-HELMETS...
AND I'M BRINGING A SPARE FUSER IN CASE YOU BLOW UP THE FIRST ONE!
CHECK, WE'RE TOUCHING DOWN. I'LL PULL OUT AND ORBIT UNTIL YOU CALL.
FINE.

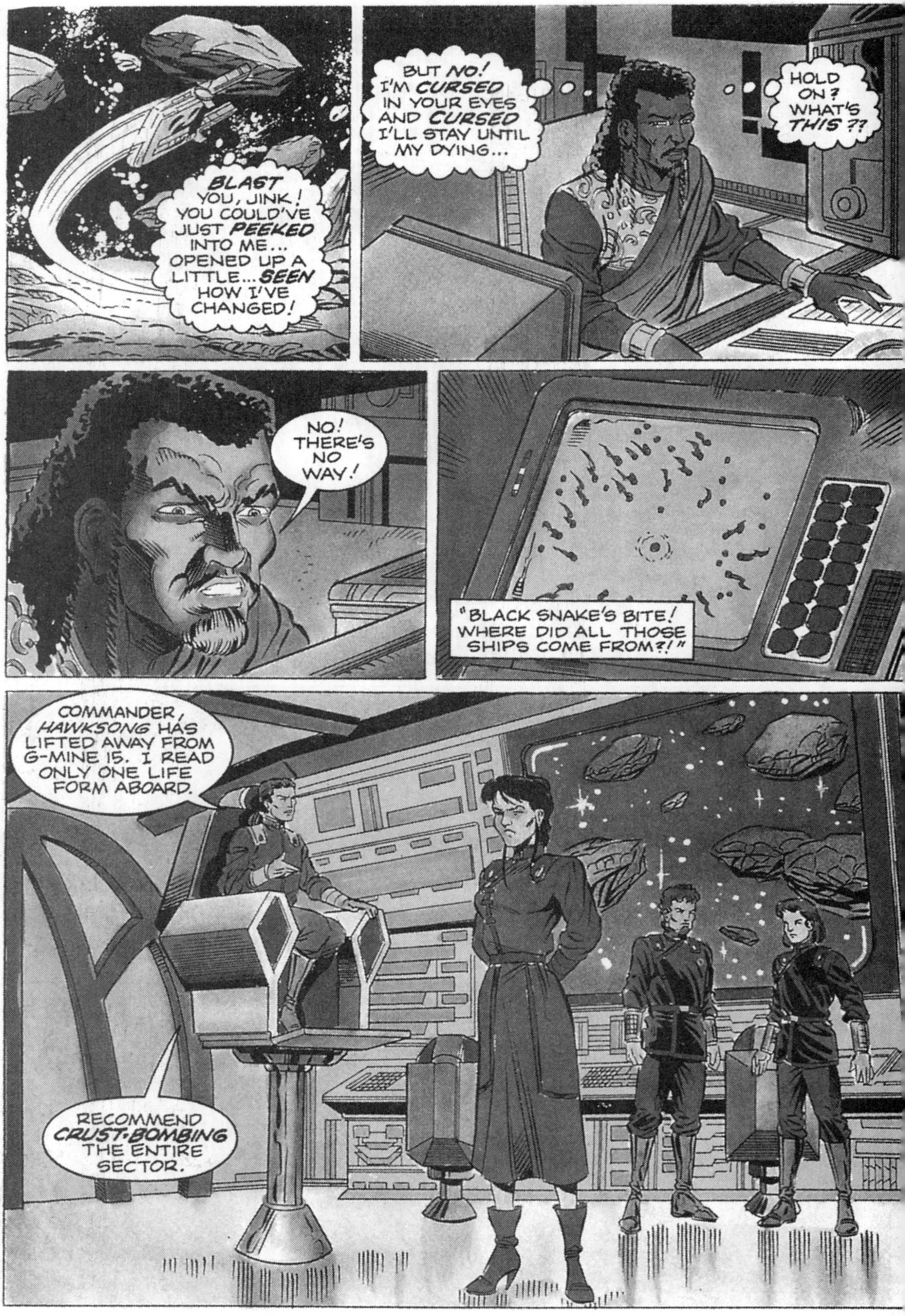
BLAST YOU, JINK! YOU COULD'VE JUST PEEKED INTO ME... OPENED UP A LITTLE... SEEN HOW I'VE CHANGED!
BUT NO! I'M CURSED IN YOUR EYES AND CURSED I'LL STAY UNTIL MY DYING...
HOLD ON? WHAT'S THIS??
NO! THERE'S NO WAY!
"BLACK SNAKE'S BITE! WHERE DID ALL THOSE SHIPS COME FROM?!"
COMMANDER, HAWKSONG HAS LIFTED AWAY FROM G-MINE 15. I READ ONLY ONE LIFE FORM ABOARD.
RECOMMEND CRUST-BOMBING THE ENTIRE SECTOR.

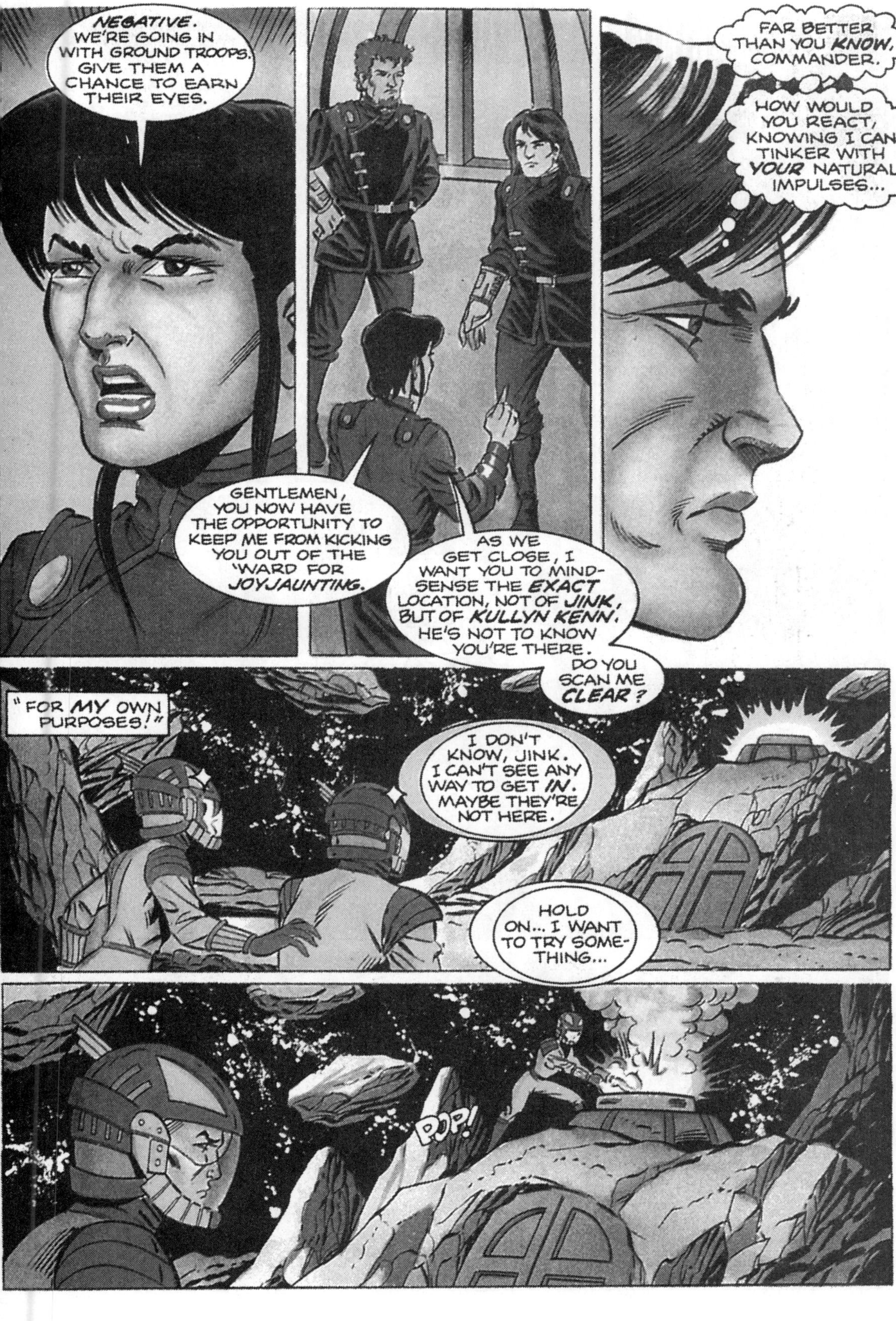
NEGATIVE. WE'RE GOING IN WITH GROUND TROOPS. GIVE THEM A CHANCE TO EARN THEIR EYES.
GENTLEMEN, YOU NOW HAVE THE OPPORTUNITY TO KEEP ME FROM KICKING YOU OUT OF THE 'WARD FOR JOYJAUNTING.
AS WE GET CLOSE, I WANT YOU TO MIND-SENSE THE EXACT LOCATION, NOT OF JINK, BUT OF KULLYN KENN. HE'S NOT TO KNOW YOU'RE THERE.
DO YOU SCAN ME CLEAR?
FAR BETTER THAN YOU KNOW, COMMANDER.
HOW WOULD YOU REACT, KNOWING I CAN TINKER WITH YOUR NATURAL IMPULSES...
"FOR MY OWN PURPOSES!"
I DON'T KNOW, JINK. I CAN'T SEE ANY WAY TO GET IN. MAYBE THEY'RE NOT HERE.
HOLD ON... I WANT TO TRY SOME-THING...
POP!

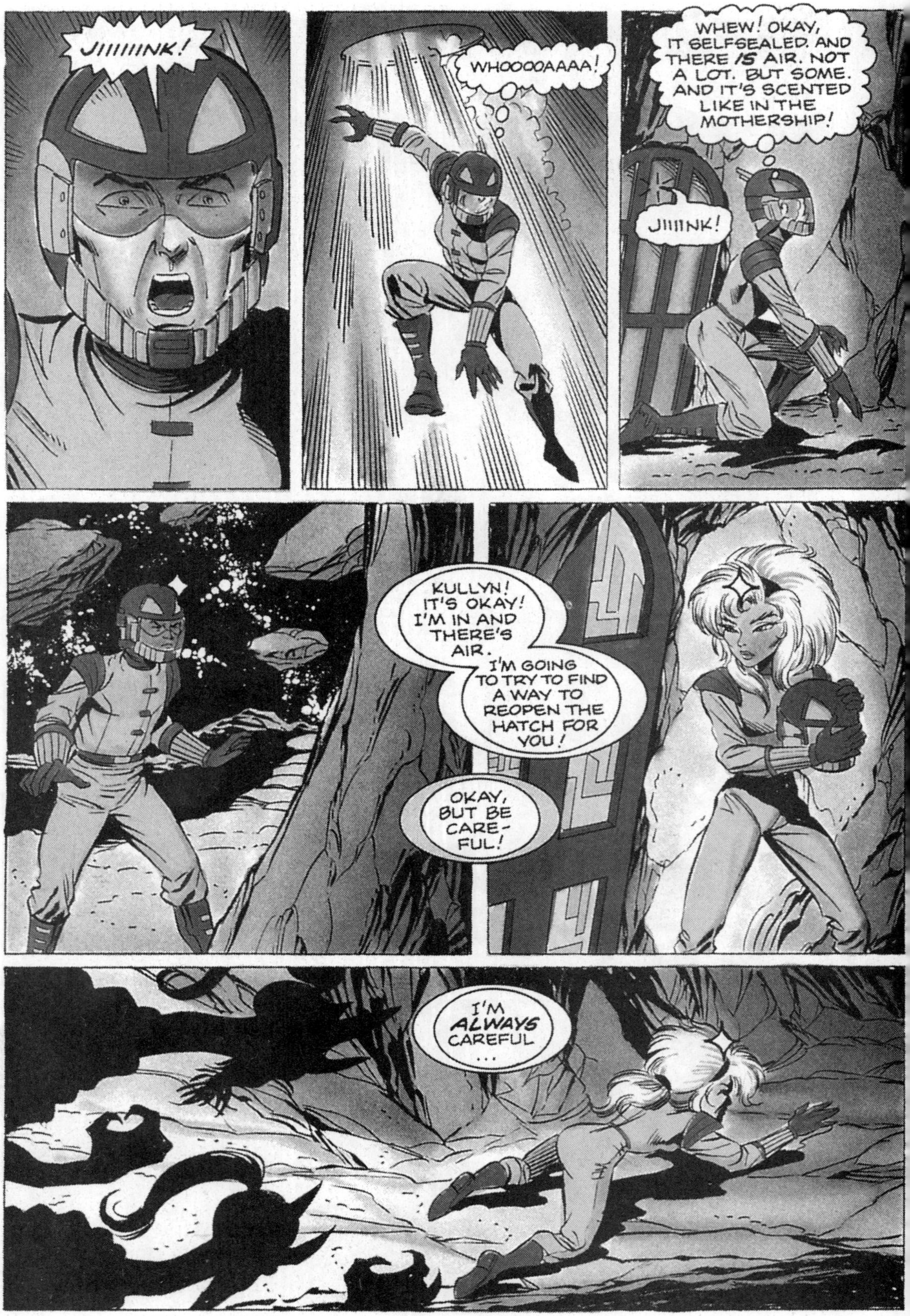
JIIIIIINK!
WHOOOOAAAA!
WHEW! OKAY, IT SELFSEALED. AND THERE IS AIR. NOT A LOT. BUT SOME. AND IT'S SCENTED LIKE IN THE MOTHERSHIP!
JIIIINK!
KULLYN! IT'S OKAY! I'M IN AND THERE'S AIR.
I'M GOING TO TRY TO FIND A WAY TO REOPEN THE HATCH FOR YOU!
OKAY, BUT BE CARE-FUL!
I'M ALWAYS CAREFUL ...

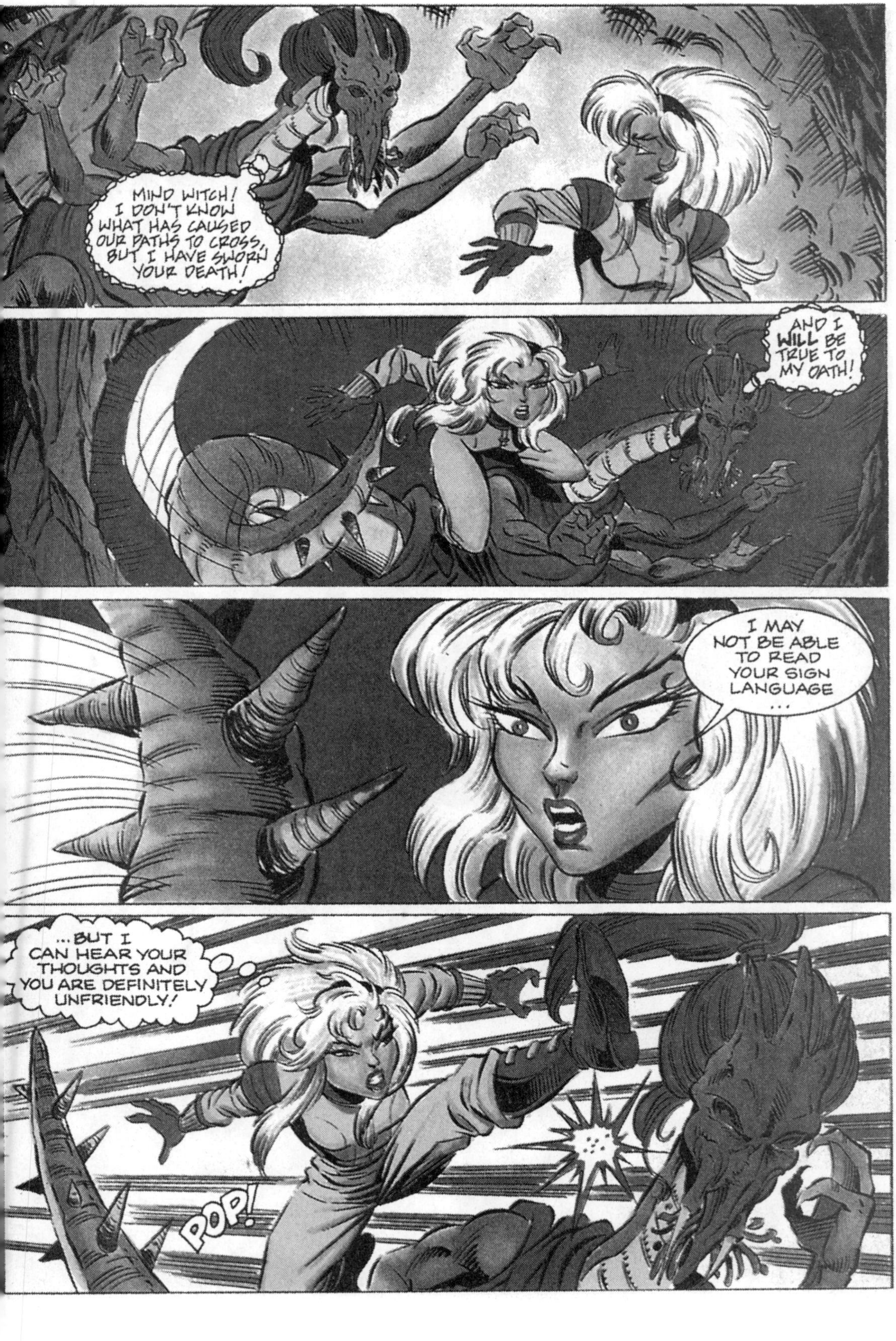
MIND WITCH! I DON'T KNOW WHAT HAS CAUSED OUR PATHS TO CROSS, BUT I HAVE SWORN YOUR DEATH!
AND I **WILL** BE TRUE TO MY OATH!
I MAY NOT BE ABLE TO READ YOUR SIGN LANGUAGE ...
... BUT I CAN HEAR YOUR THOUGHTS AND YOU ARE DEFINITELY UNFRIENDLY!
POP!

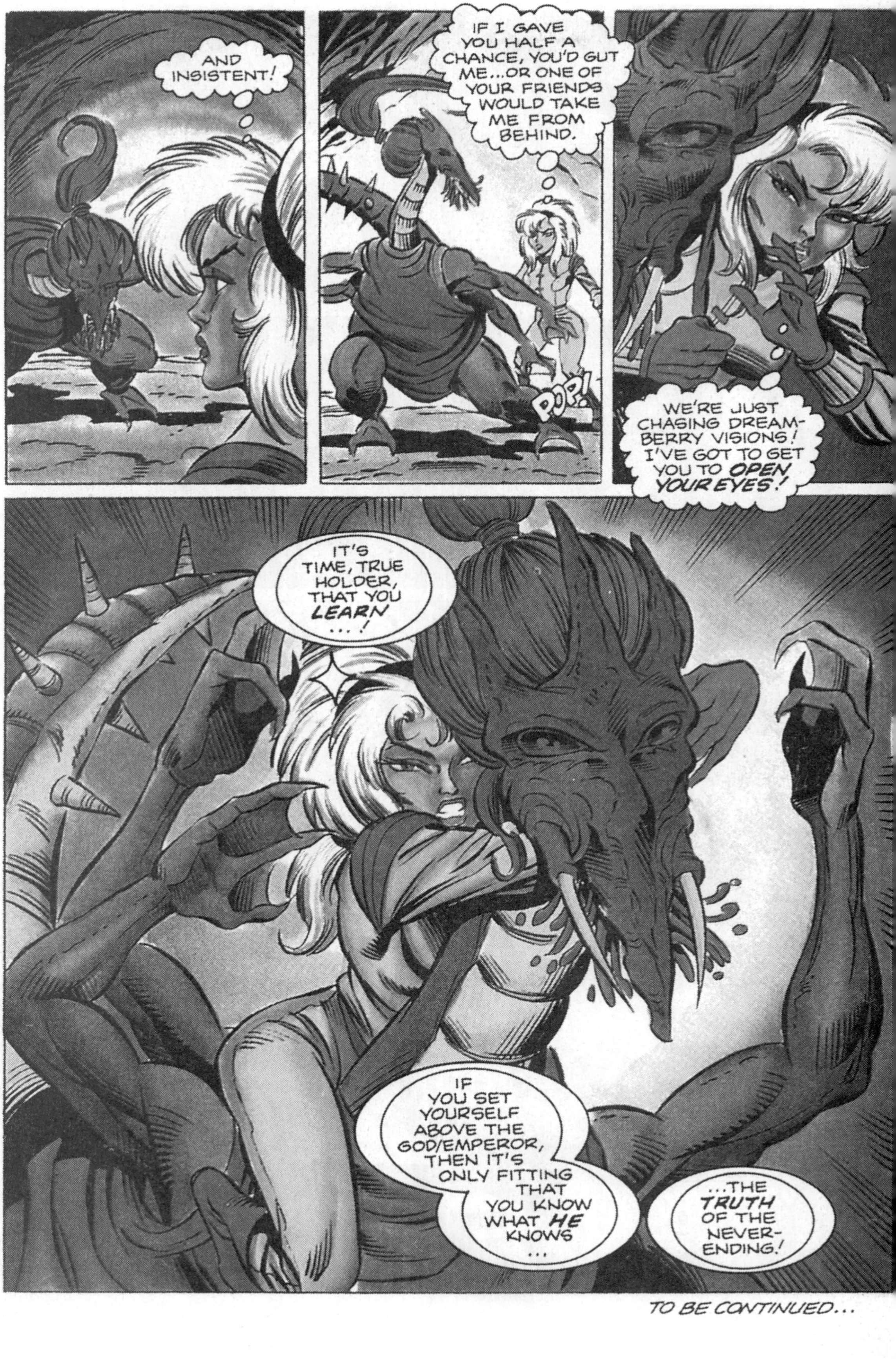
AND INSISTENT!
IF I GAVE YOU HALF A CHANCE, YOU'D GUT ME...OR ONE OF YOUR FRIENDS WOULD TAKE ME FROM BEHIND.
POP!
WE'RE JUST CHASING DREAM-BERRY VISIONS! I'VE GOT TO GET YOU TO OPEN YOUR EYES!
IT'S TIME, TRUE HOLDER, THAT YOU LEARN...!
IF YOU SET YOURSELF ABOVE THE GOD/EMPEROR, THEN IT'S ONLY FITTING THAT YOU KNOW WHAT HE KNOWS...
...THE TRUTH OF THE NEVER-ENDING!

TO BE CONTINUED...

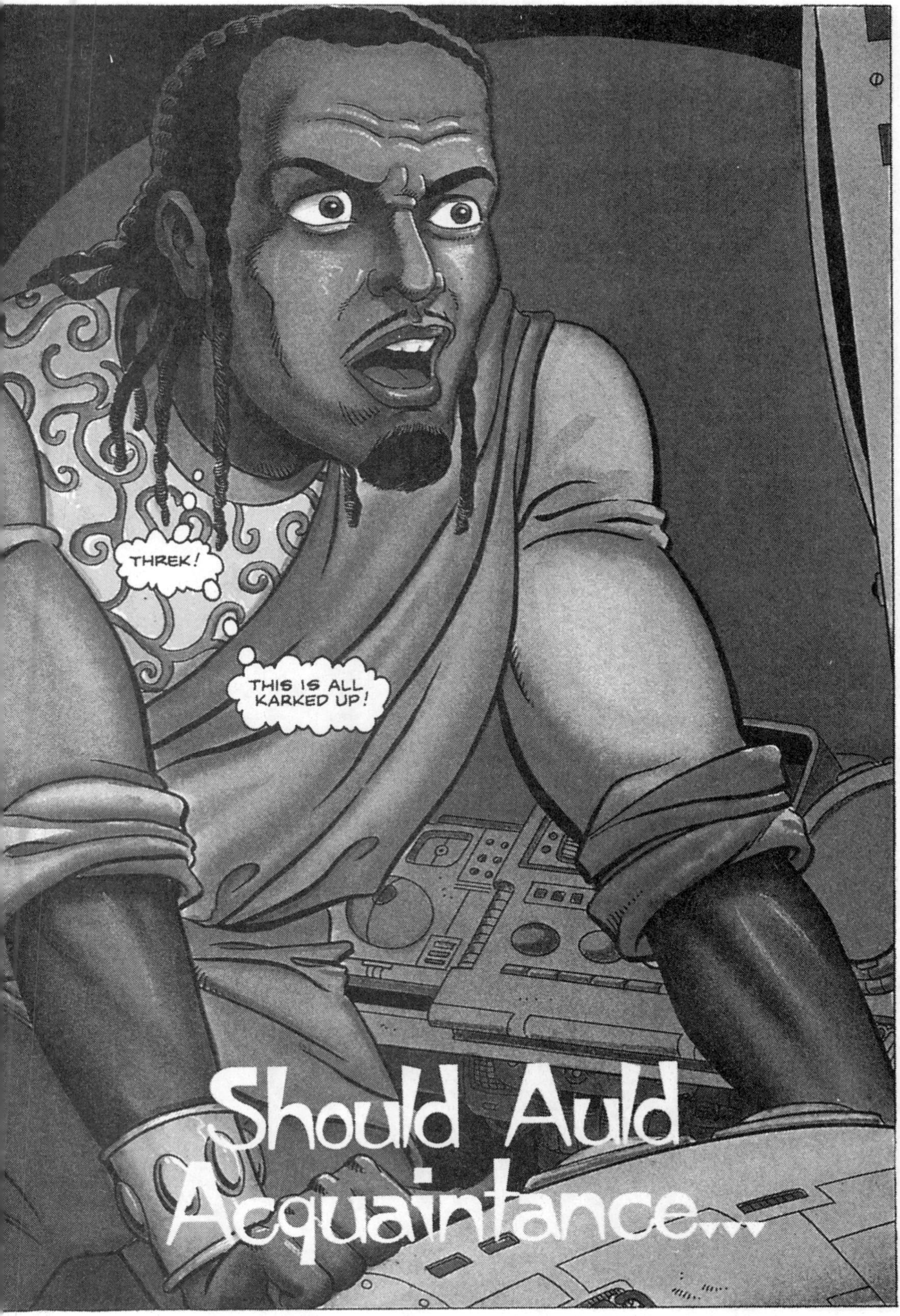
THREK!
THIS IS ALL KARKED UP!
Should Auld Acquaintance...

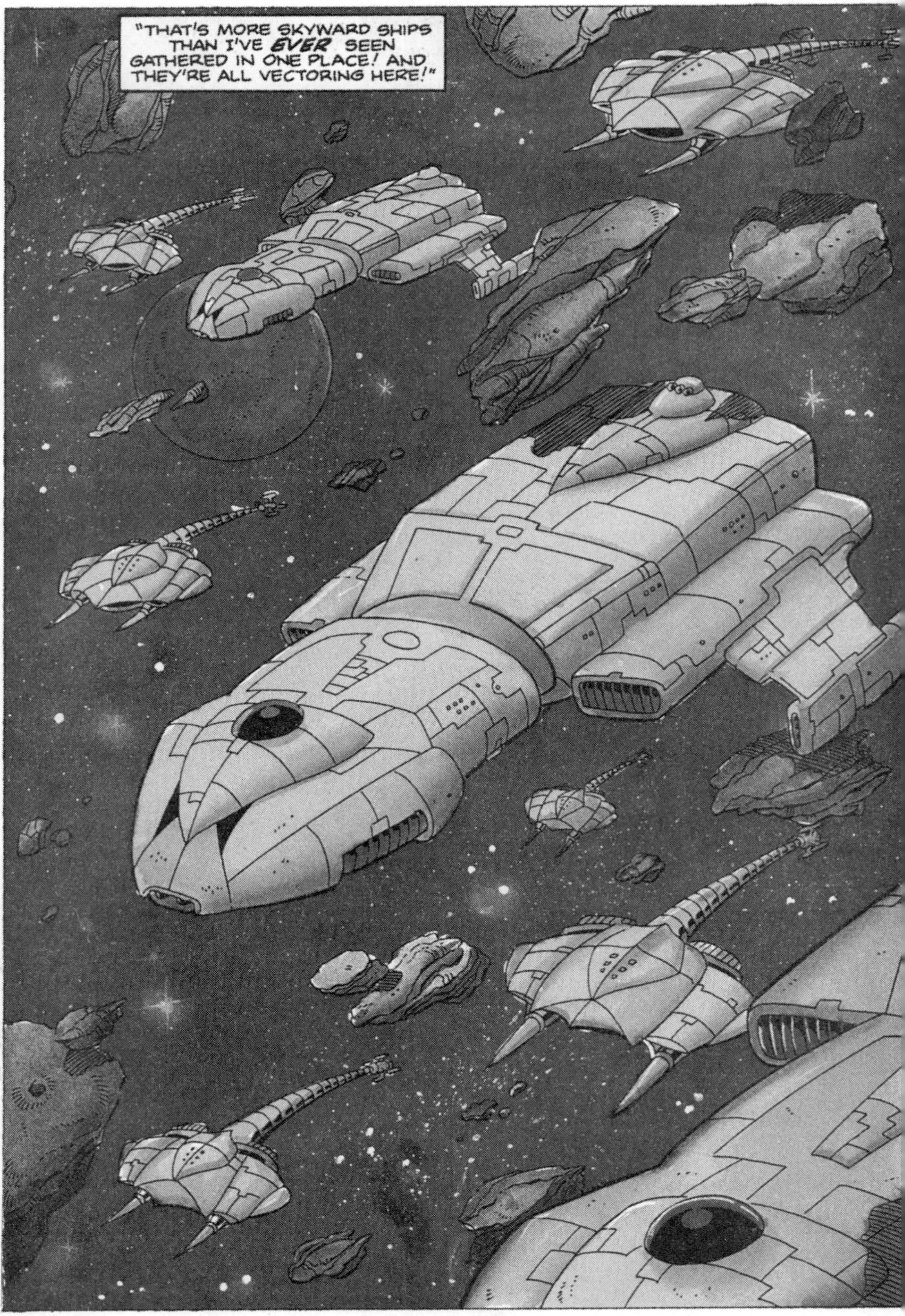
"THAT'S MORE SKYWARD SHIPS THAN I'VE EVER SEEN GATHERED IN ONE PLACE! AND THEY'RE ALL VECTORING HERE!"

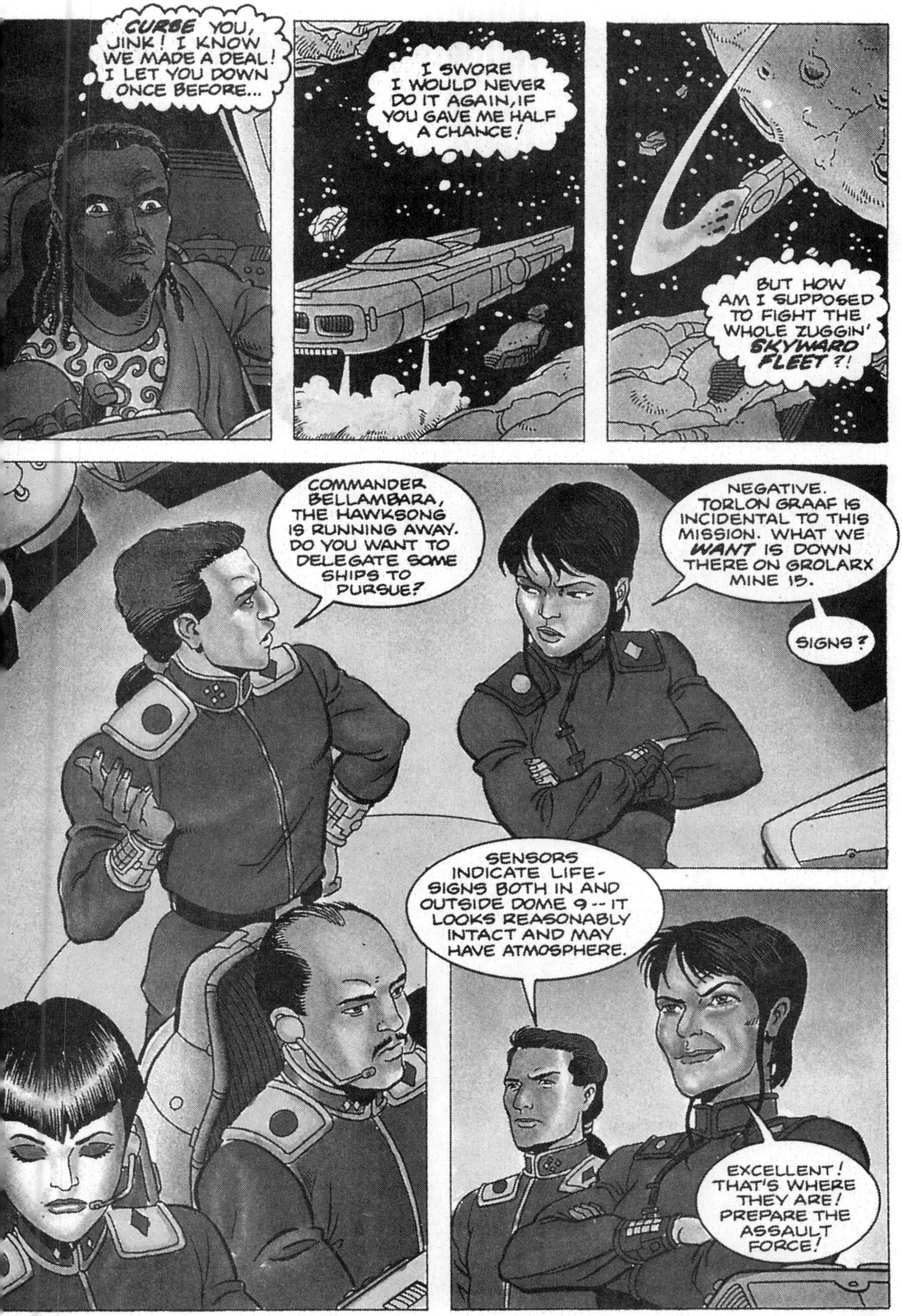
CURSE YOU, JINK! I KNOW WE MADE A DEAL! I LET YOU DOWN ONCE BEFORE...
I SWORE I WOULD NEVER DO IT AGAIN, IF YOU GAVE ME HALF A CHANCE!
BUT HOW AM I SUPPOSED TO FIGHT THE WHOLE ZUGGIN' SKYWARD FLEET?!
COMMANDER BELLAMBARA, THE HAWKSONG IS RUNNING AWAY. DO YOU WANT TO DELEGATE SOME SHIPS TO PURSUE?
NEGATIVE. TORLON GRAAF IS INCIDENTAL TO THIS MISSION. WHAT WE WANT IS DOWN THERE ON GROLARX MINE 15.
SIGNS?
SENSORS INDICATE LIFE-SIGNS BOTH IN AND OUTSIDE DOME 9 -- IT LOOKS REASONABLY INTACT AND MAY HAVE ATMOSPHERE.
EXCELLENT! THAT'S WHERE THEY ARE! PREPARE THE ASSAULT FORCE!

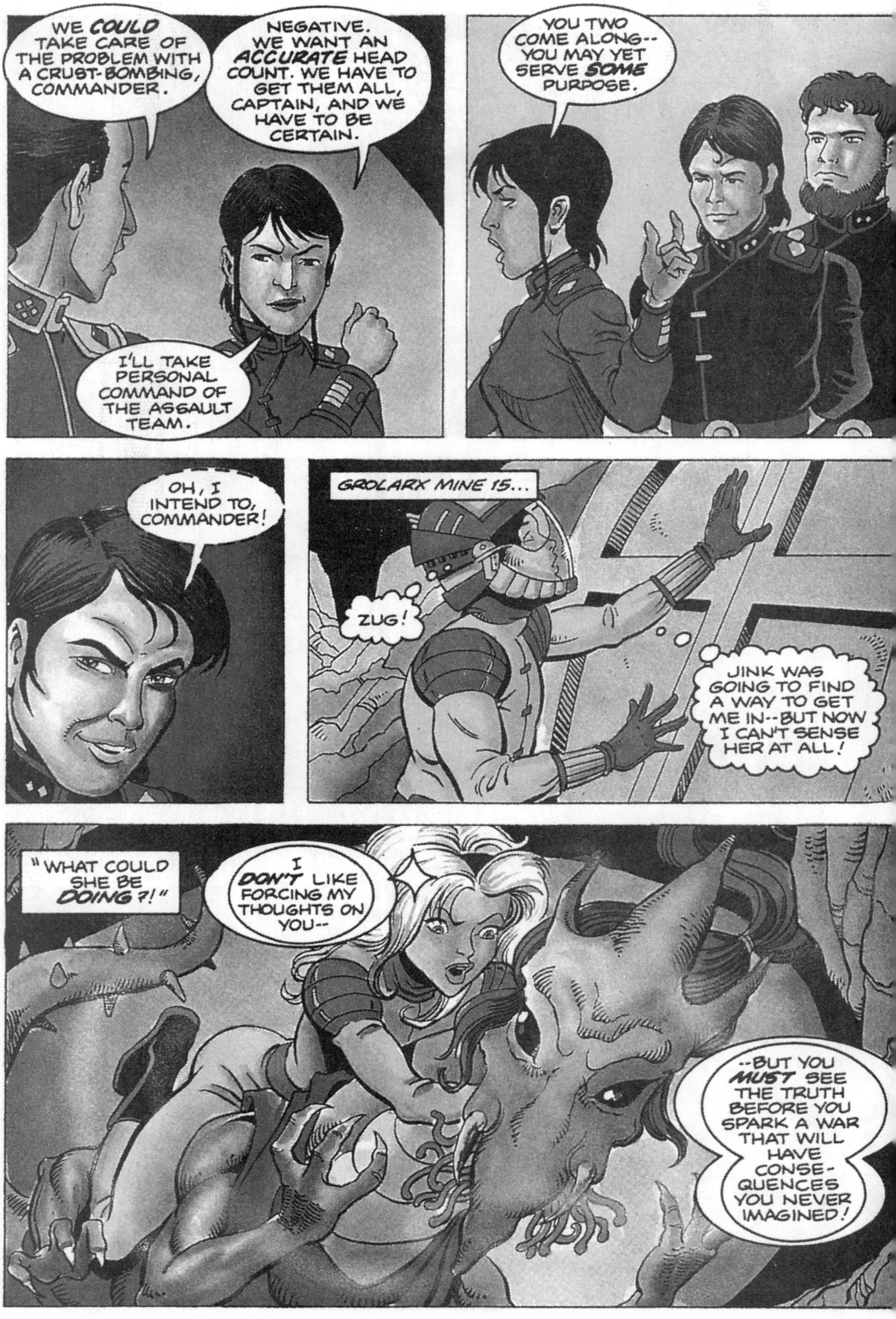

WE COULD TAKE CARE OF THE PROBLEM WITH A CRUST-BOMBING, COMMANDER.
NEGATIVE. WE WANT AN ACCURATE HEAD COUNT. WE HAVE TO GET THEM ALL, CAPTAIN, AND WE HAVE TO BE CERTAIN.
I'LL TAKE PERSONAL COMMAND OF THE ASSAULT TEAM.
YOU TWO COME ALONG-- YOU MAY YET SERVE SOME PURPOSE.
OH, I INTEND TO, COMMANDER!
GROLARX MINE 15...
ZUG!
JINK WAS GOING TO FIND A WAY TO GET ME IN--BUT NOW I CAN'T SENSE HER AT ALL!
"WHAT COULD SHE BE DOING?!"
I DON'T LIKE FORCING MY THOUGHTS ON YOU--
--BUT YOU MUST SEE THE TRUTH BEFORE YOU SPARK A WAR THAT WILL HAVE CONSE-QUENCES YOU NEVER IMAGINED!

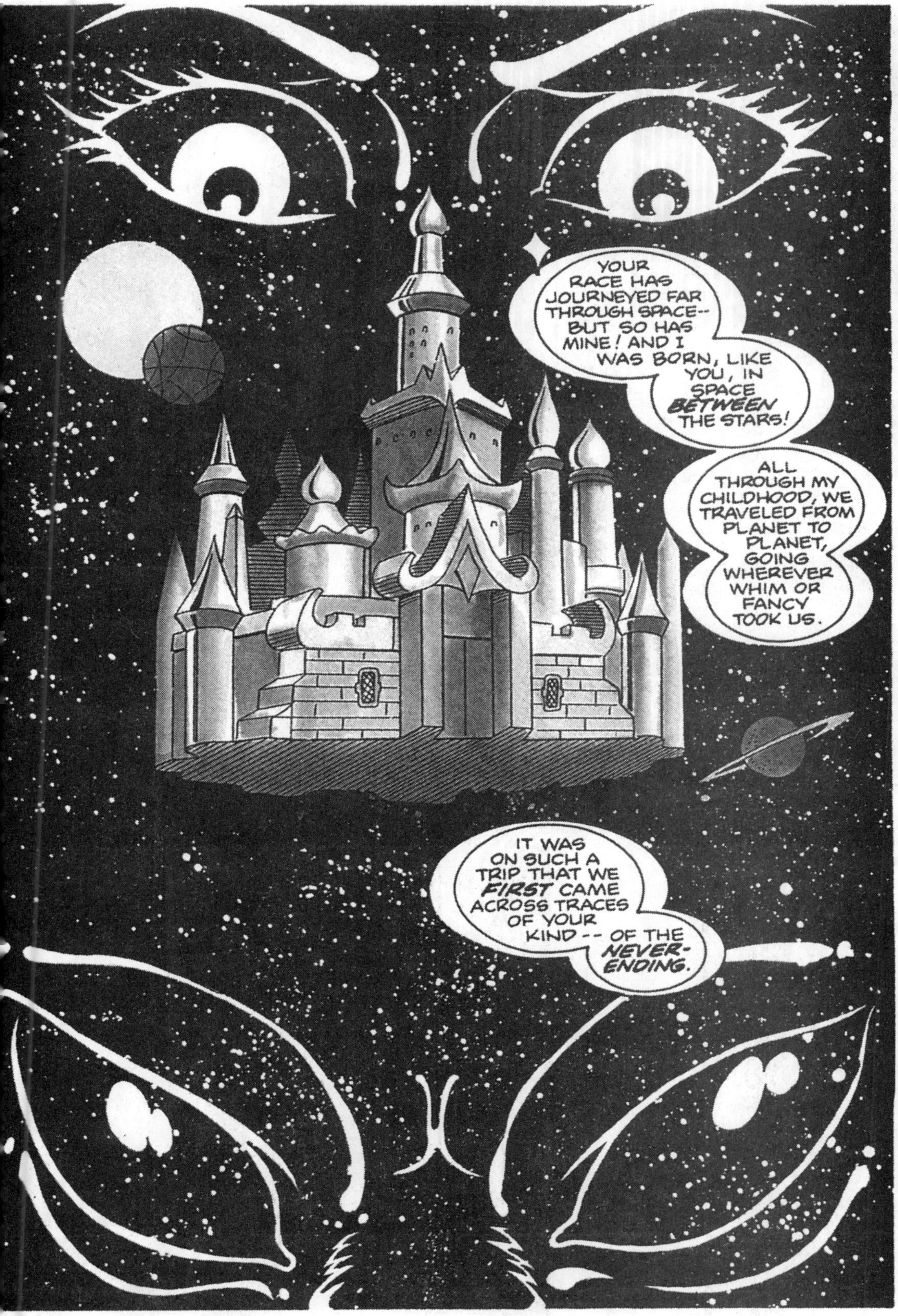
YOUR RACE HAS JOURNEYED FAR THROUGH SPACE-- BUT SO HAS MINE! AND I WAS BORN, LIKE YOU, IN SPACE BETWEEN THE STARS!
ALL THROUGH MY CHILDHOOD, WE TRAVELED FROM PLANET TO PLANET, GOING WHEREVER WHIM OR FANCY TOOK US.
IT WAS ON SUCH A TRIP THAT WE FIRST CAME ACROSS TRACES OF YOUR KIND -- OF THE NEVER-ENDING.

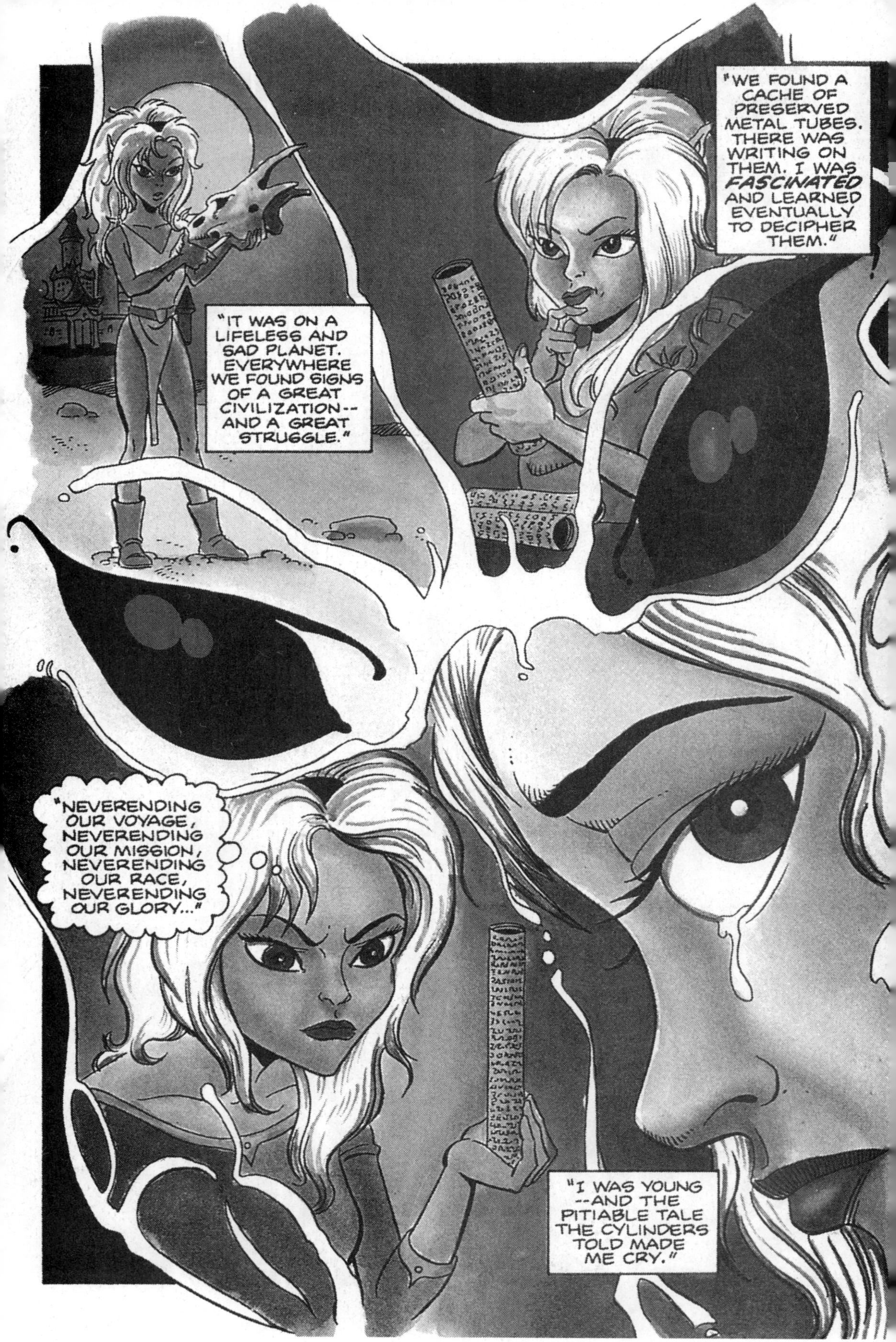
"IT WAS ON A LIFELESS AND SAD PLANET. EVERYWHERE WE FOUND SIGNS OF A GREAT CIVILIZATION--AND A GREAT STRUGGLE."
"WE FOUND A CACHE OF PRESERVED METAL TUBES. THERE WAS WRITING ON THEM. I WAS FASCINATED AND LEARNED EVENTUALLY TO DECIPHER THEM."
"NEVERENDING OUR VOYAGE, NEVERENDING OUR MISSION, NEVERENDING OUR RACE, NEVERENDING OUR GLORY..."
"I WAS YOUNG --AND THE PITIABLE TALE THE CYLINDERS TOLD MADE ME CRY."

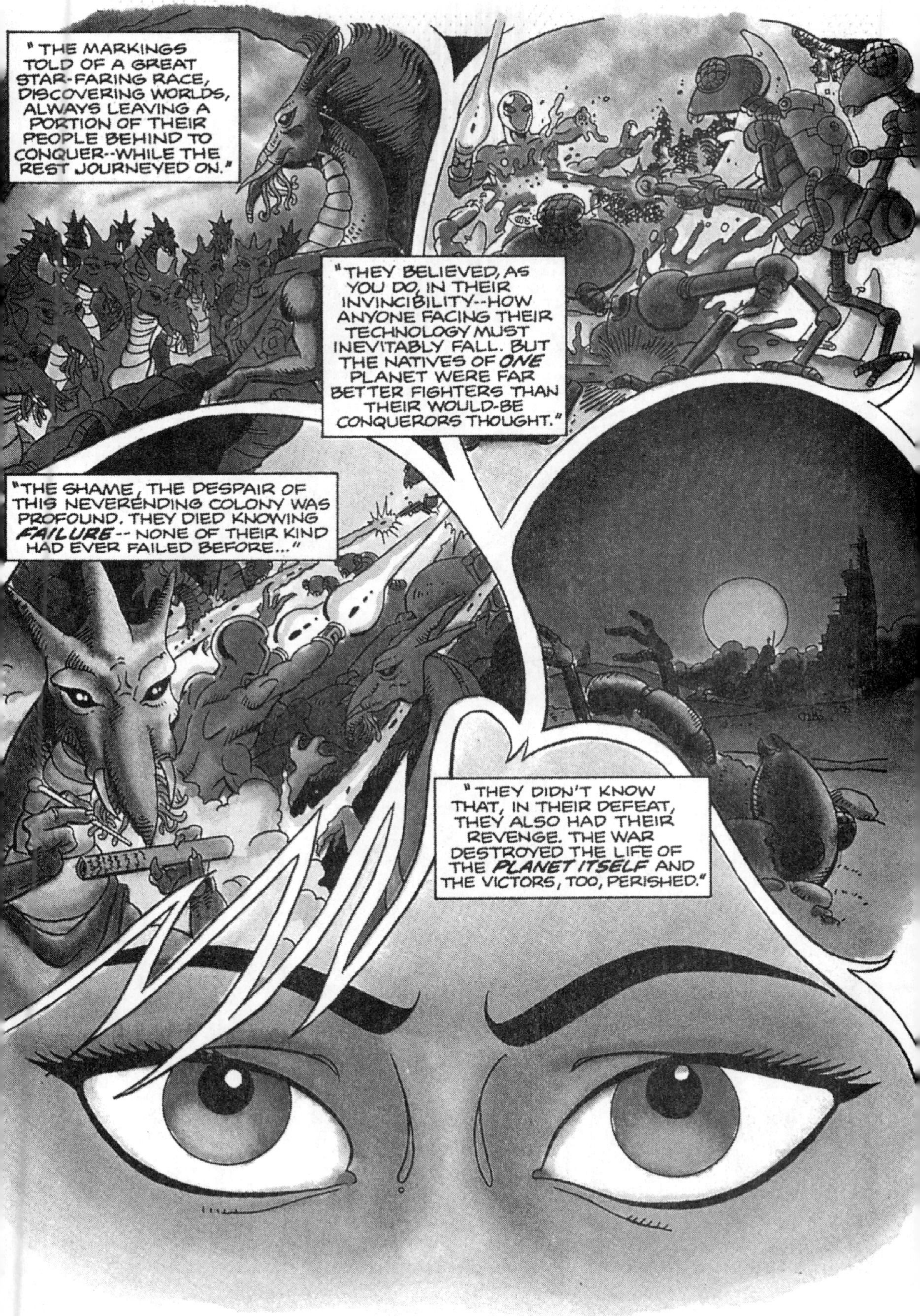
"THE MARKINGS TOLD OF A GREAT STAR-FARING RACE, DISCOVERING WORLDS, ALWAYS LEAVING A PORTION OF THEIR PEOPLE BEHIND TO CONQUER--WHILE THE REST JOURNEYED ON."
"THEY BELIEVED, AS YOU DO, IN THEIR INVINCIBILITY--HOW ANYONE FACING THEIR TECHNOLOGY MUST INEVITABLY FALL. BUT THE NATIVES OF ONE PLANET WERE FAR BETTER FIGHTERS THAN THEIR WOULD-BE CONQUERORS THOUGHT."
"THE SHAME, THE DESPAIR OF THIS NEVERENDING COLONY WAS PROFOUND. THEY DIED KNOWING FAILURE-- NONE OF THEIR KIND HAD EVER FAILED BEFORE..."
"THEY DIDN'T KNOW THAT, IN THEIR DEFEAT, THEY ALSO HAD THEIR REVENGE. THE WAR DESTROYED THE LIFE OF THE PLANET ITSELF AND THE VICTORS, TOO, PERISHED."

"THE CYLINDERS GAVE THE LOCATION OF THE PREVIOUS PLANET COLONIZED--THE ONE THE DEAD ONE WAS MEANT TO CONTACT."

"I WAS ALLOWED TO SEEK THEM OUT-- TO BRING WORD OF WHAT HAD BEFALLEN THEIR SUCCESSORS..."

BUT THE STORY WAS THE SAME. THEY, TOO, HAD DIED OFF. AND SO IT WENT WITH EACH COLONY-- EARLIER AND EARLIER AS WE FOLLOWED UP THE LINE...

NO NO NO NO! THIS CANNOT BE TRUE!

LOOK! TRUE HOLDER BREAKS FREE!

YES! HE REJECTS THE MIND-WITCH'S ATTEMPT TO SNARE HIM AS SHE DID THE GOD-EMPEROR! BUT WE MUST HELP HIM!

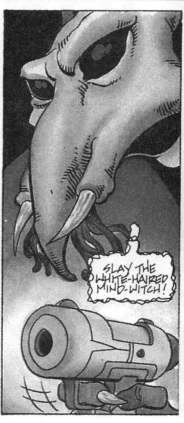

SLAY THE WHITE-HAIRED MIND-WITCH!

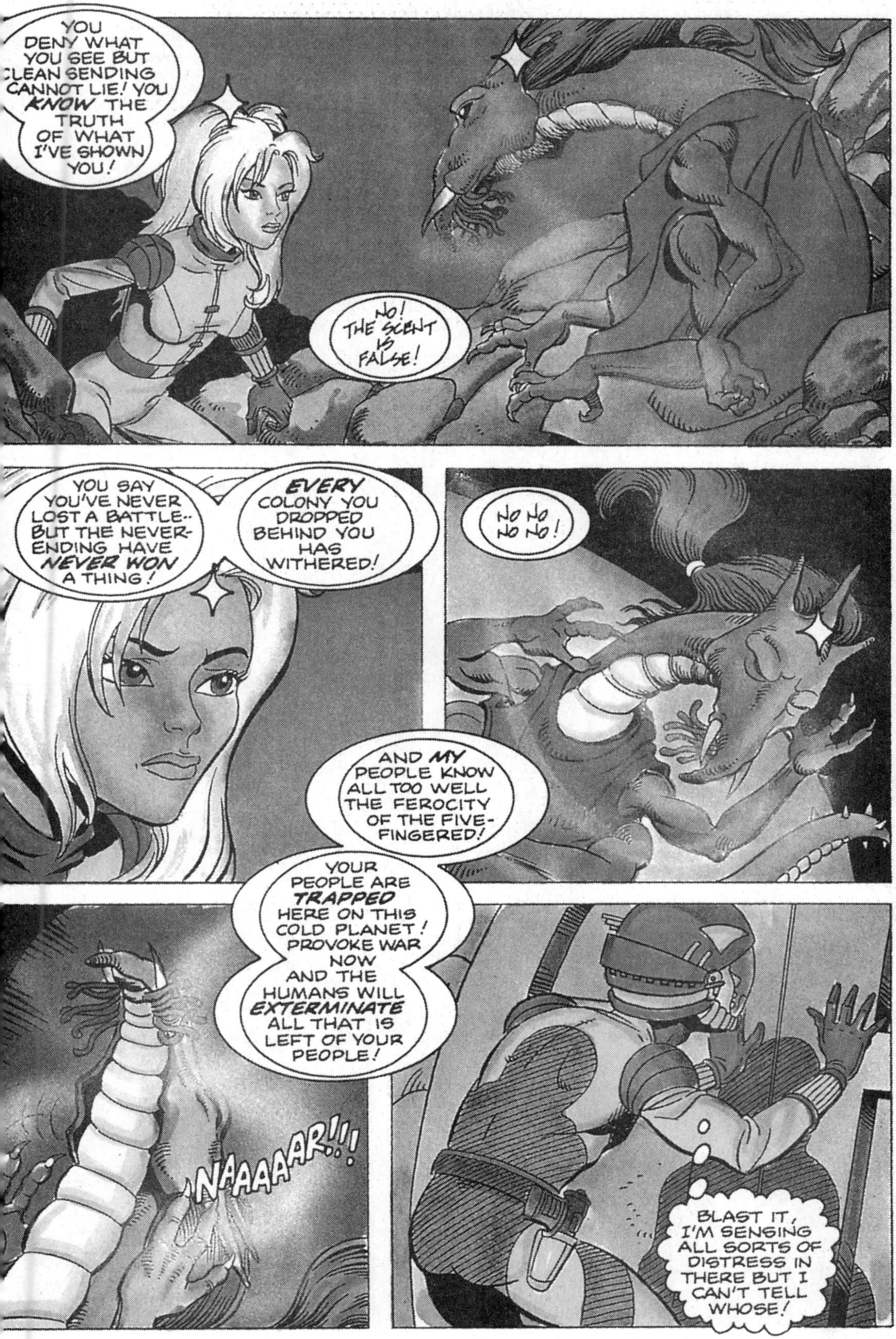
YOU DENY WHAT YOU SEE BUT CLEAN SENDING CANNOT LIE! YOU KNOW THE TRUTH OF WHAT I'VE SHOWN YOU!
NO! THE SCENT IS FALSE!
YOU SAY YOU'VE NEVER LOST A BATTLE.. BUT THE NEVER-ENDING HAVE NEVER WON A THING!
EVERY COLONY YOU DROPPED BEHIND YOU HAS WITHERED!
NO NO NO NO!
AND MY PEOPLE KNOW ALL TOO WELL THE FEROCITY OF THE FIVE-FINGERED!
YOUR PEOPLE ARE TRAPPED HERE ON THIS COLD PLANET! PROVOKE WAR NOW AND THE HUMANS WILL EXTERMINATE ALL THAT IS LEFT OF YOUR PEOPLE!
NAAAAAR!!!
BLAST IT, I'M SENSING ALL SORTS OF DISTRESS IN THERE BUT I CAN'T TELL WHOSE!

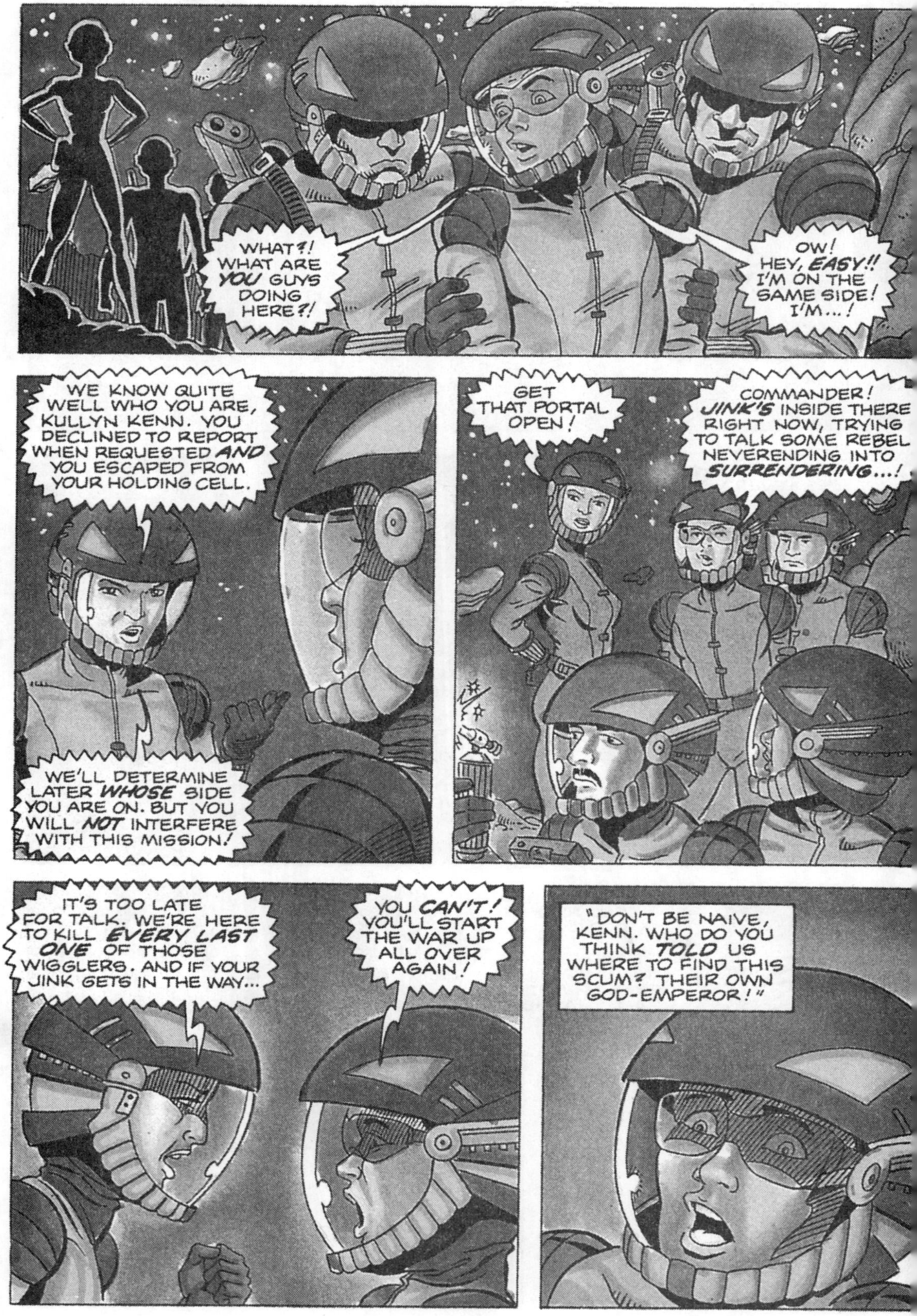
WHAT?! WHAT ARE YOU GUYS DOING HERE?!
OW! HEY, EASY!! I'M ON THE SAME SIDE! I'M...!
WE KNOW QUITE WELL WHO YOU ARE, KULLYN KENN. YOU DECLINED TO REPORT WHEN REQUESTED AND YOU ESCAPED FROM YOUR HOLDING CELL.
WE'LL DETERMINE LATER WHOSE SIDE YOU ARE ON. BUT YOU WILL NOT INTERFERE WITH THIS MISSION!
GET THAT PORTAL OPEN!
COMMANDER! JINK'S INSIDE THERE RIGHT NOW, TRYING TO TALK SOME REBEL NEVERENDING INTO SURRENDERING...!
IT'S TOO LATE FOR TALK. WE'RE HERE TO KILL EVERY LAST ONE OF THOSE WIGGLERS. AND IF YOUR JINK GETS IN THE WAY...
YOU CAN'T! YOU'LL START THE WAR UP ALL OVER AGAIN!
"DON'T BE NAIVE, KENN. WHO DO YOU THINK TOLD US WHERE TO FIND THIS SCUM? THEIR OWN GOD-EMPEROR!"

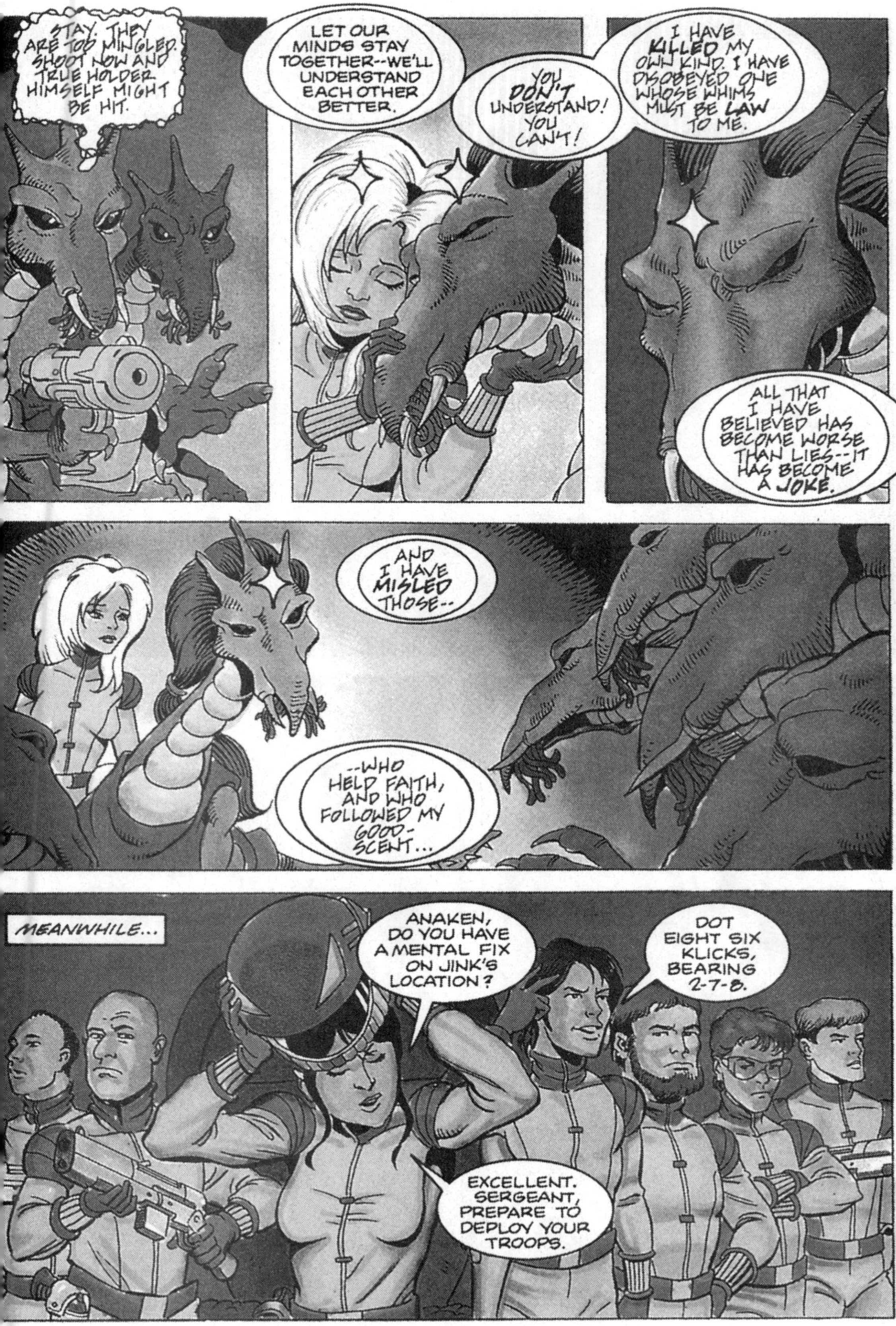
STAY. THEY ARE TOO MINGLED. SHOOT NOW AND TRUE HOLDER HIMSELF MIGHT BE HIT.
LET OUR MINDS STAY TOGETHER--WE'LL UNDERSTAND EACH OTHER BETTER.
YOU DON'T UNDERSTAND! YOU CAN'T!
I HAVE KILLED MY OWN KIND. I HAVE DISOBEYED ONE WHOSE WHIMS MUST BE LAW TO ME.
ALL THAT I HAVE BELIEVED HAS BECOME WORSE THAN LIES--IT HAS BECOME A JOKE.
AND I HAVE MISLED THOSE--
--WHO HELD FAITH, AND WHO FOLLOWED MY GOOD-SCENT...
MEANWHILE...
ANAKEN, DO YOU HAVE A MENTAL FIX ON JINK'S LOCATION?
DOT EIGHT SIX KLICKS, BEARING 2-7-8.
EXCELLENT. SERGEANT, PREPARE TO DEPLOY YOUR TROOPS.

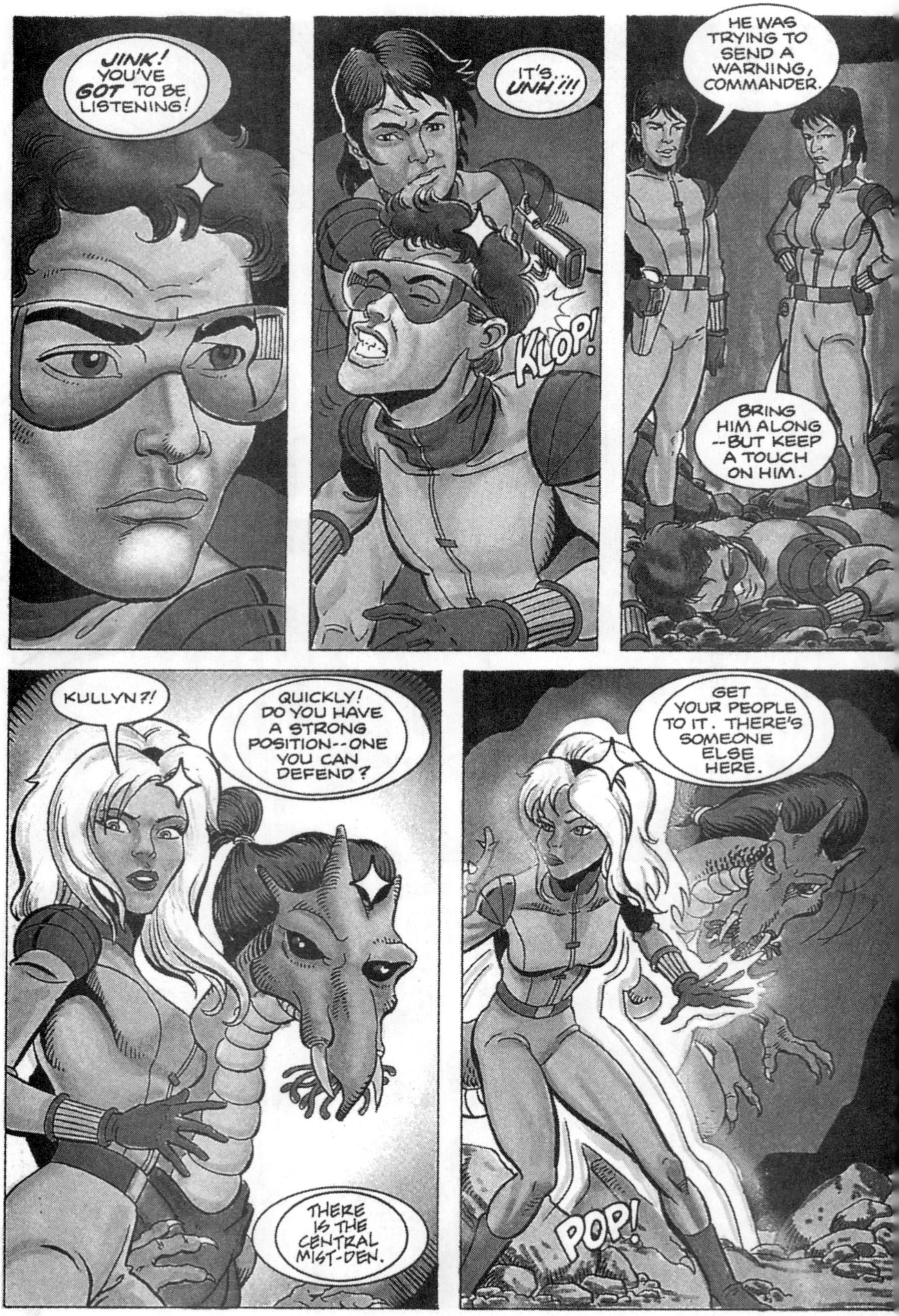
JINK! YOU'VE GOT TO BE LISTENING!
IT'S... UNH!!!
KLOP!
HE WAS TRYING TO SEND A WARNING, COMMANDER.
BRING HIM ALONG --BUT KEEP A TOUCH ON HIM.
KULLYN?!
QUICKLY! DO YOU HAVE A STRONG POSITION--ONE YOU CAN DEFEND?
THERE IS THE CENTRAL MIST-DEN.
GET YOUR PEOPLE TO IT. THERE'S SOMEONE ELSE HERE.
POP!

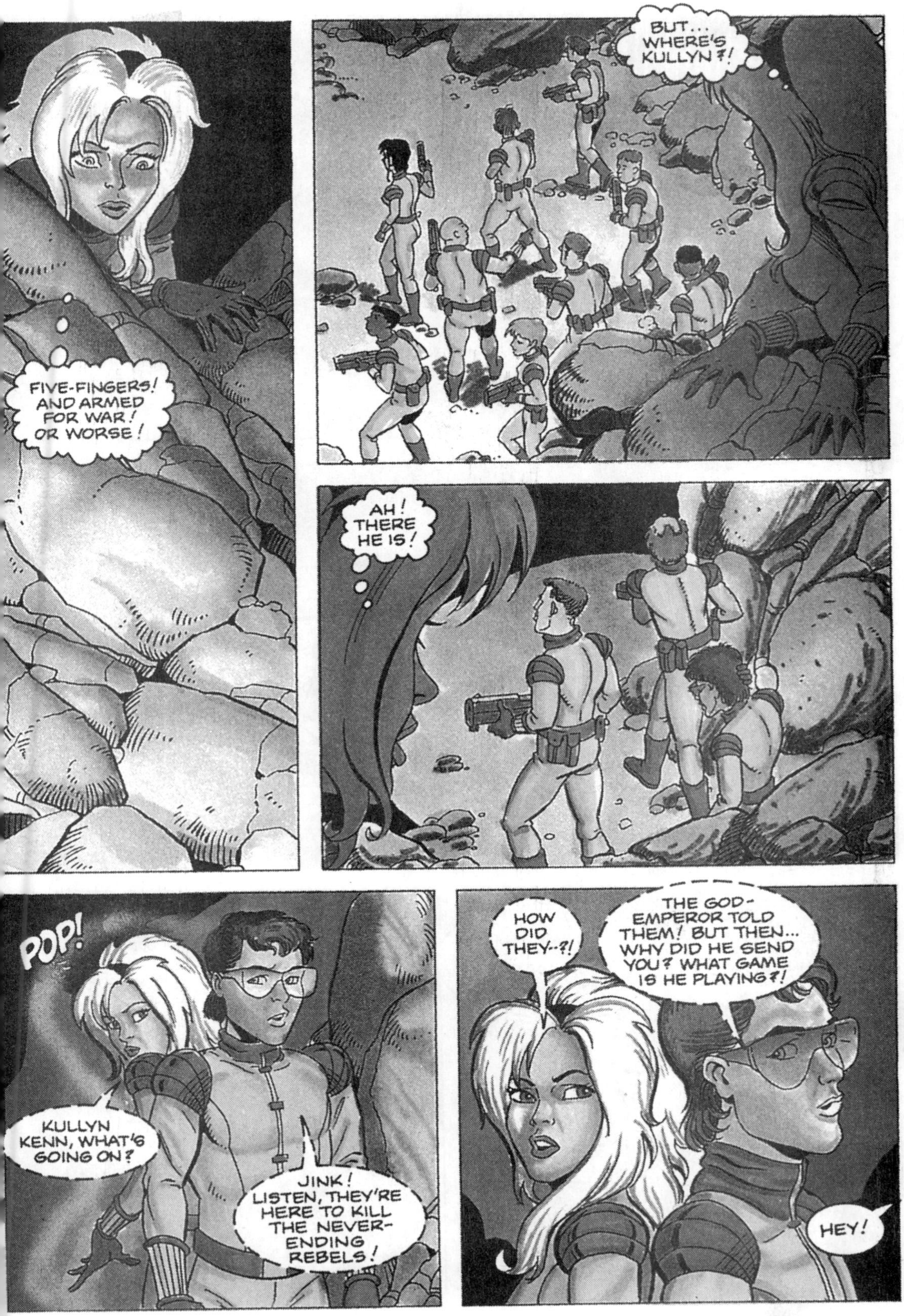
FIVE-FINGERS! AND ARMED FOR WAR! OR WORSE!
BUT... WHERE'S KULLYN ?!
AH! THERE HE IS!
POP!
KULLYN KENN, WHAT'S GOING ON?
JINK! LISTEN, THEY'RE HERE TO KILL THE NEVER-ENDING REBELS!
HOW DID THEY--?!
THE GOD-EMPEROR TOLD THEM! BUT THEN... WHY DID HE SEND YOU? WHAT GAME IS HE PLAYING?!
HEY!

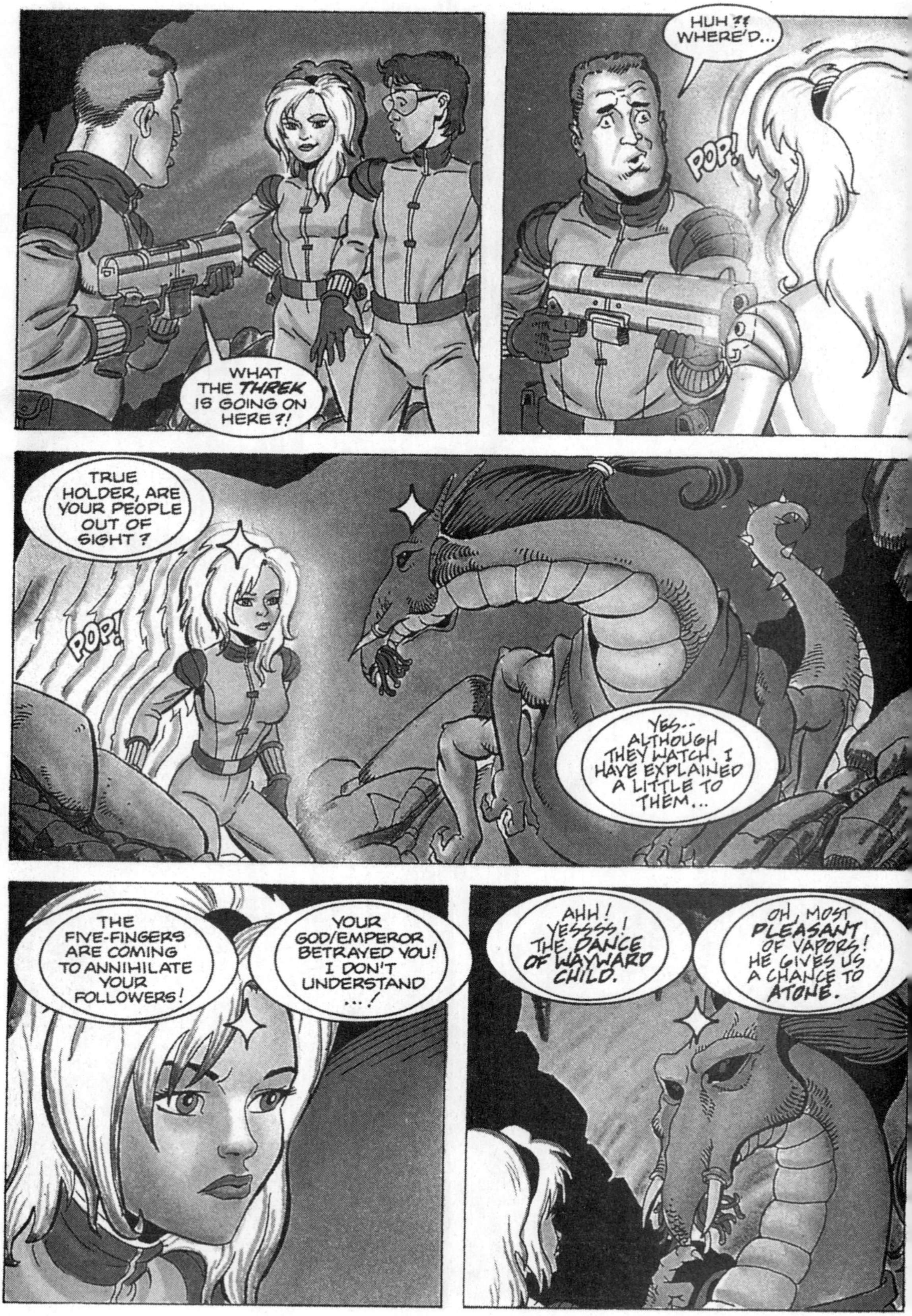
WHAT THE THREK IS GOING ON HERE?!
HUH?! WHERE'D...
POP!
TRUE HOLDER, ARE YOUR PEOPLE OUT OF SIGHT?
POP!
YES.. ALTHOUGH THEY WATCH. I HAVE EXPLAINED A LITTLE TO THEM...
THE FIVE-FINGERS ARE COMING TO ANNIHILATE YOUR FOLLOWERS!
YOUR GOD/EMPEROR BETRAYED YOU! I DON'T UNDERSTAND ...!
AHH! YESSSS! THE DANCE OF WAYWARD CHILD.
OH, MOST PLEASANT OF VAPORS! HE GIVES US A CHANCE TO ATONE.

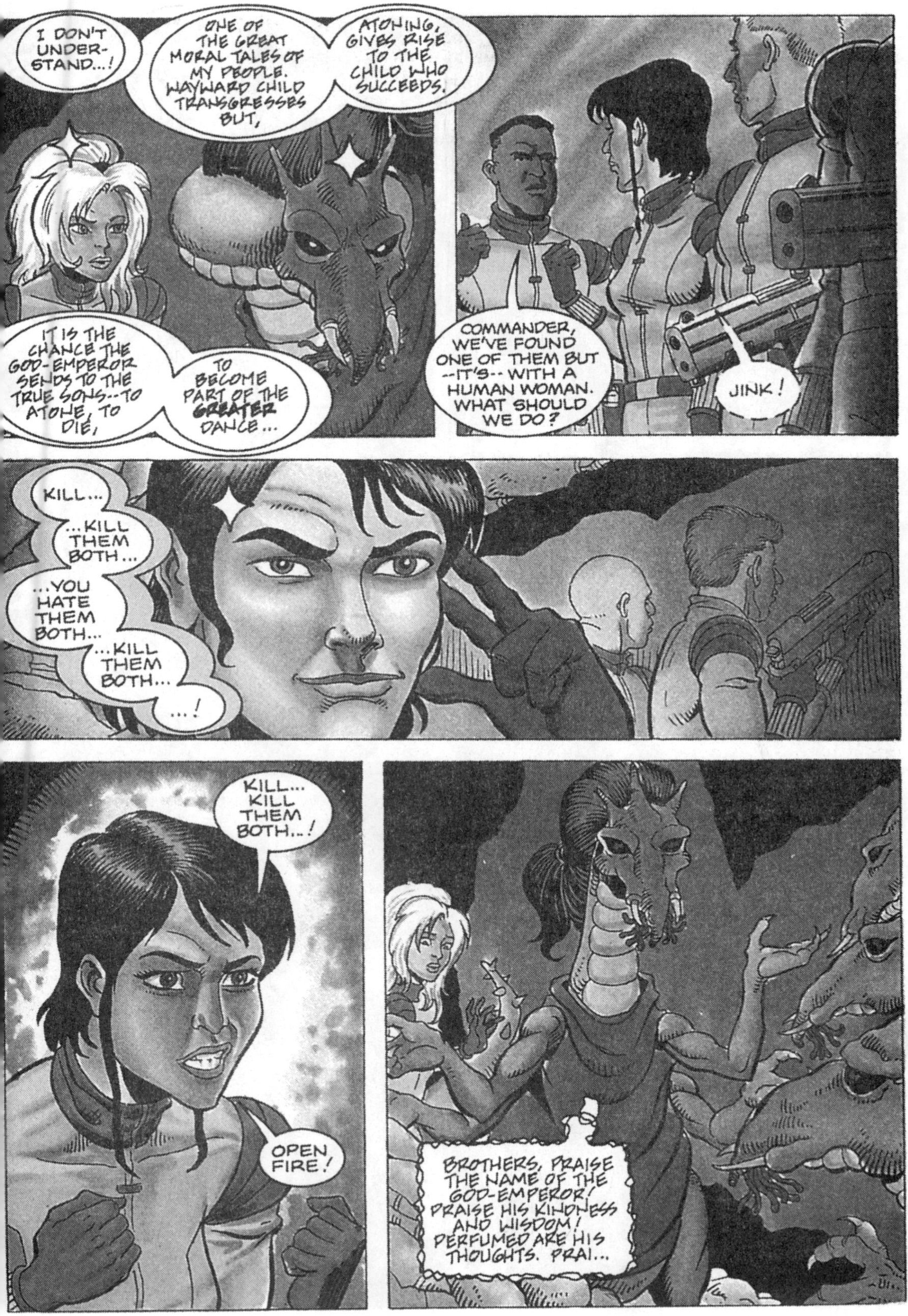
I DON'T UNDER-STAND...!
ONE OF THE GREAT MORAL TALES OF MY PEOPLE. WAYWARD CHILD TRANSGRESSES BUT,
ATONING, GIVES RISE TO THE CHILD WHO SUCCEEDS.
IT IS THE CHANCE THE GOD-EMPEROR SENDS TO THE TRUE SONS--TO ATONE, TO DIE,
TO BECOME PART OF THE GREATER DANCE...
COMMANDER, WE'VE FOUND ONE OF THEM BUT --IT'S-- WITH A HUMAN WOMAN. WHAT SHOULD WE DO?
JINK!
KILL...
...KILL THEM BOTH...
...YOU HATE THEM BOTH...
...KILL THEM BOTH...
...!
KILL... KILL THEM BOTH...!
OPEN FIRE!
BROTHERS, PRAISE THE NAME OF THE GOD-EMPEROR! PRAISE HIS KINDNESS AND WISDOM! PERFUMED ARE HIS THOUGHTS. PRAI...

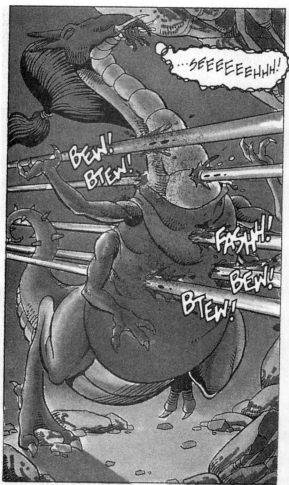

...SEEEEEEHHH!

BEW!
BTEW!

FASH!
BEW!

BTEW!

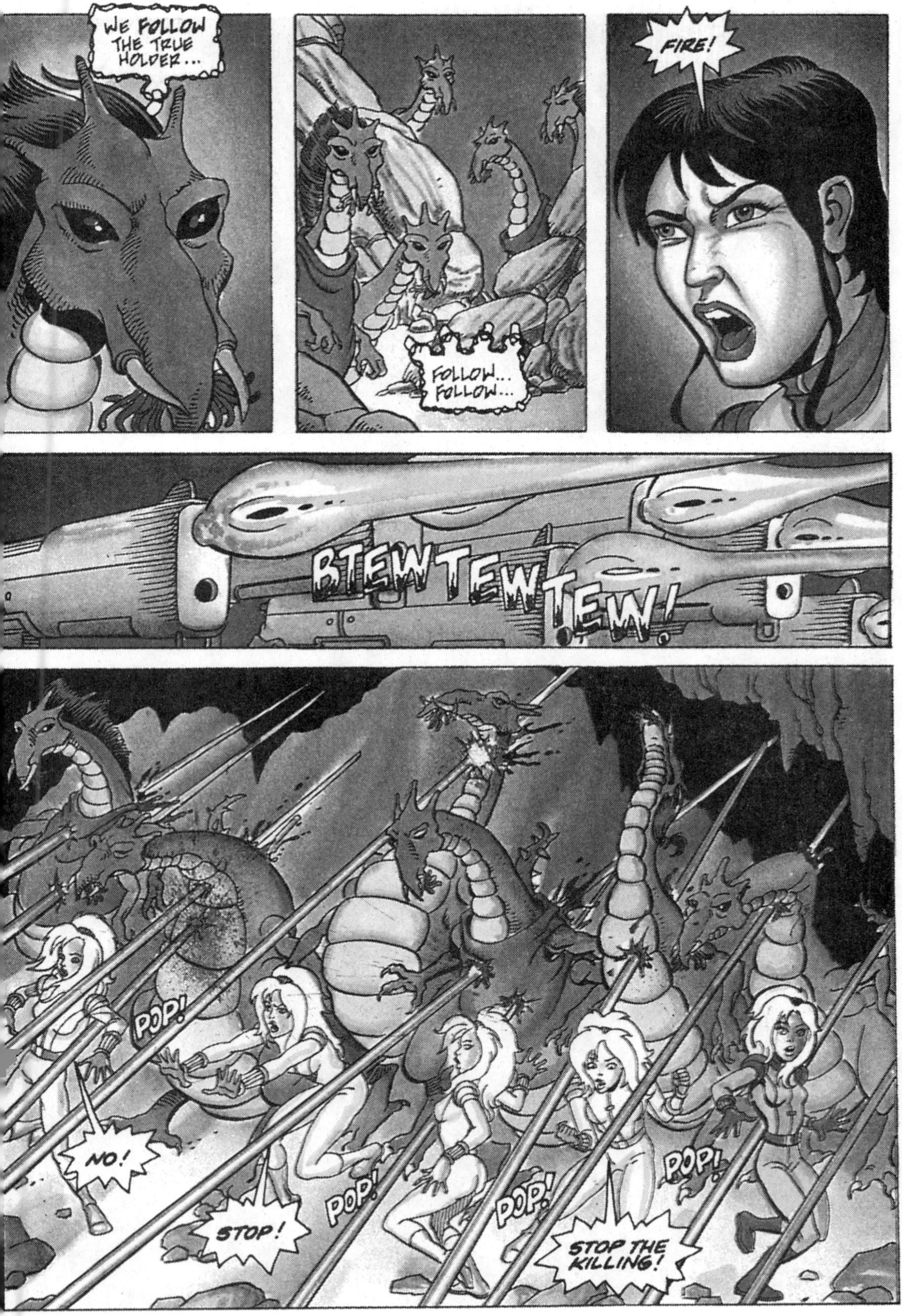
WE FOLLOW THE TRUE HOLDER...
FOLLOW... FOLLOW...
FIRE!
BTEWTEWTEWTEW!
POP!
NO!
STOP!
POP!
POP!
POP!
STOP THE KILLING!

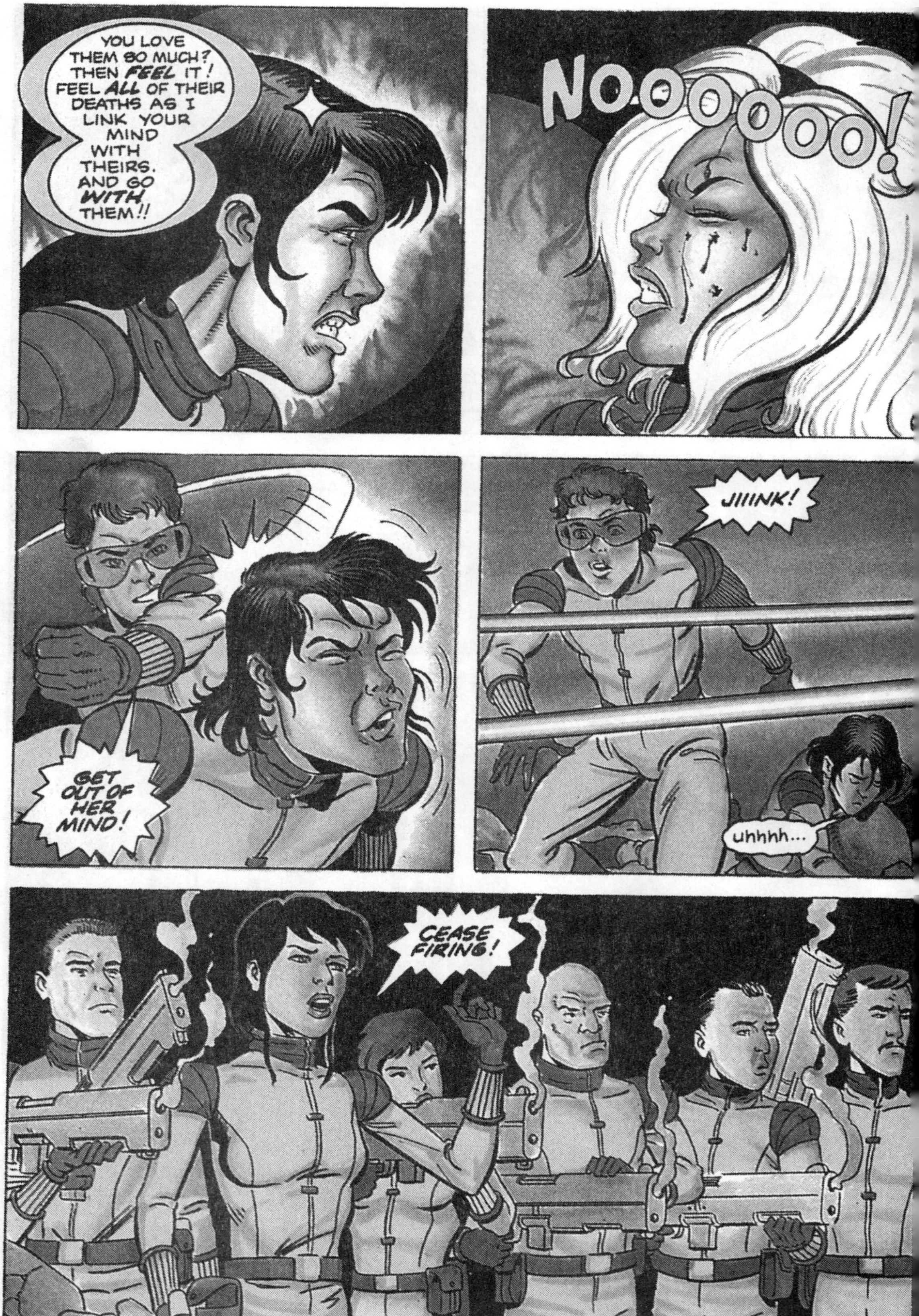
YOU LOVE THEM SO MUCH? THEN FEEL IT! FEEL ALL OF THEIR DEATHS AS I LINK YOUR MIND WITH THEIRS. AND GO WITH THEM!!
NOOOOOOO!
GET OUT OF HER MIND!
JIIINK!
uhhhh...
CEASE FIRING!

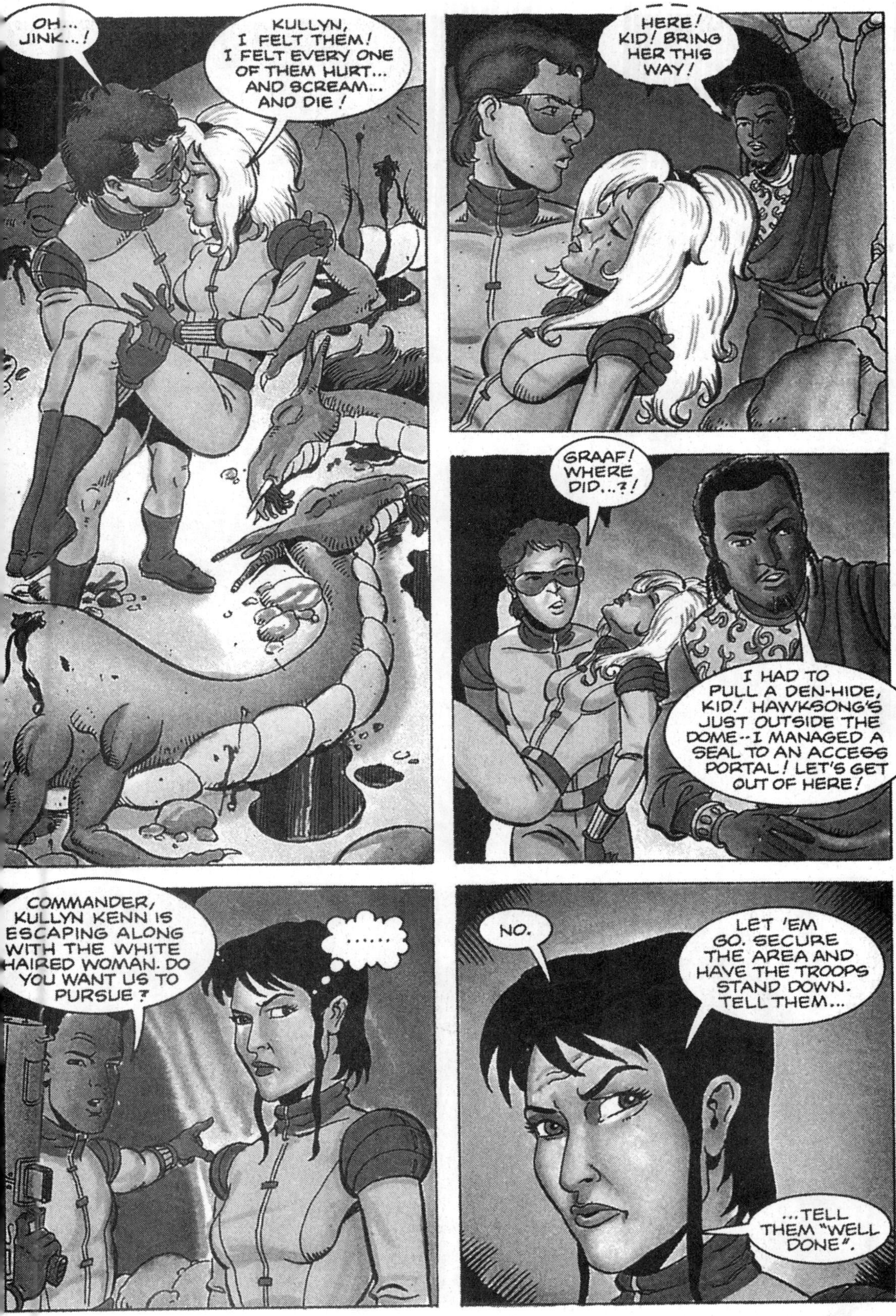
OH... JINK...!
KULLYN, I FELT THEM! I FELT EVERY ONE OF THEM HURT... AND SCREAM... AND DIE!
HERE! KID! BRING HER THIS WAY!
GRAAF! WHERE DID...?!
I HAD TO PULL A DEN-HIDE, KID! HAWKSONG'S JUST OUTSIDE THE DOME--I MANAGED A SEAL TO AN ACCESS PORTAL! LET'S GET OUT OF HERE!
COMMANDER, KULLYN KENN IS ESCAPING ALONG WITH THE WHITE HAIRED WOMAN. DO YOU WANT US TO PURSUE?
......
NO.
LET 'EM GO. SECURE THE AREA AND HAVE THE TROOPS STAND DOWN. TELL THEM...
...TELL THEM "WELL DONE".

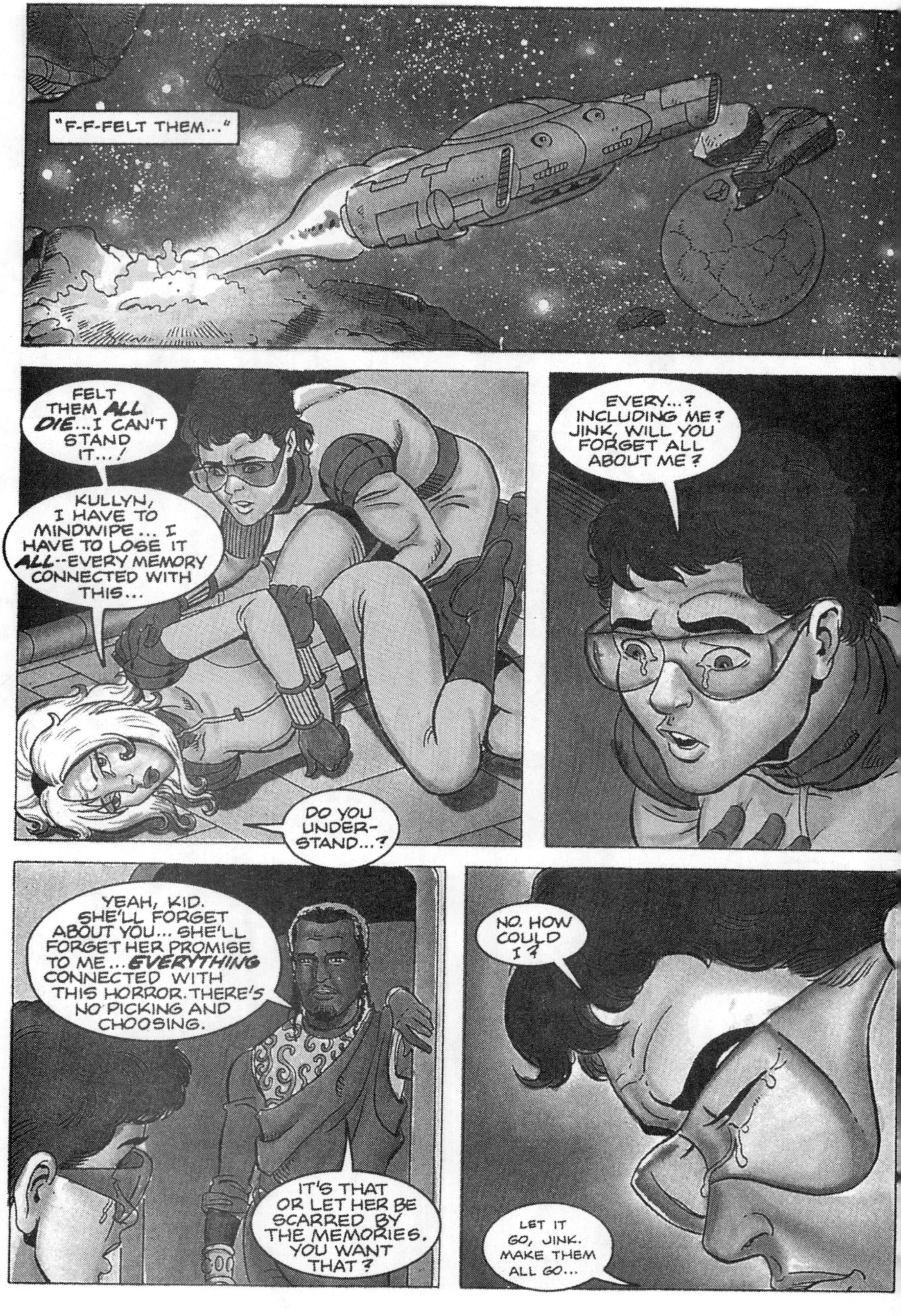
"F-F-FELT THEM..."
FELT THEM ALL DIE...I CAN'T STAND IT...!
KULLYN, I HAVE TO MINDWIPE... I HAVE TO LOSE IT ALL--EVERY MEMORY CONNECTED WITH THIS...
DO YOU UNDER-STAND...?
EVERY...? INCLUDING ME? JINK, WILL YOU FORGET ALL ABOUT ME?
YEAH, KID. SHE'LL FORGET ABOUT YOU... SHE'LL FORGET HER PROMISE TO ME... EVERYTHING CONNECTED WITH THIS HORROR. THERE'S NO PICKING AND CHOOSING.
IT'S THAT OR LET HER BE SCARRED BY THE MEMORIES. YOU WANT THAT?
NO. HOW COULD I?
LET IT GO, JINK. MAKE THEM ALL GO...

THE HEART REMEMBERS WHEN THE MIND FORGETS.

I LOVE YOU, KULLYN.

JINK...?

THAT'S HOW IT GOES, KID. SHE'LL SLEEP ALL THE WAY BACK TO TWO MOON STATION.

SHE'S AT PEACE. YOU WANT TO BE THERE WHEN SHE WAKES UP?

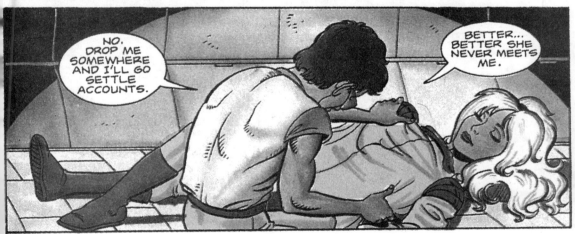

NO. DROP ME SOMEWHERE AND I'LL GO SETTLE ACCOUNTS.

BETTER... BETTER SHE NEVER MEETS ME.

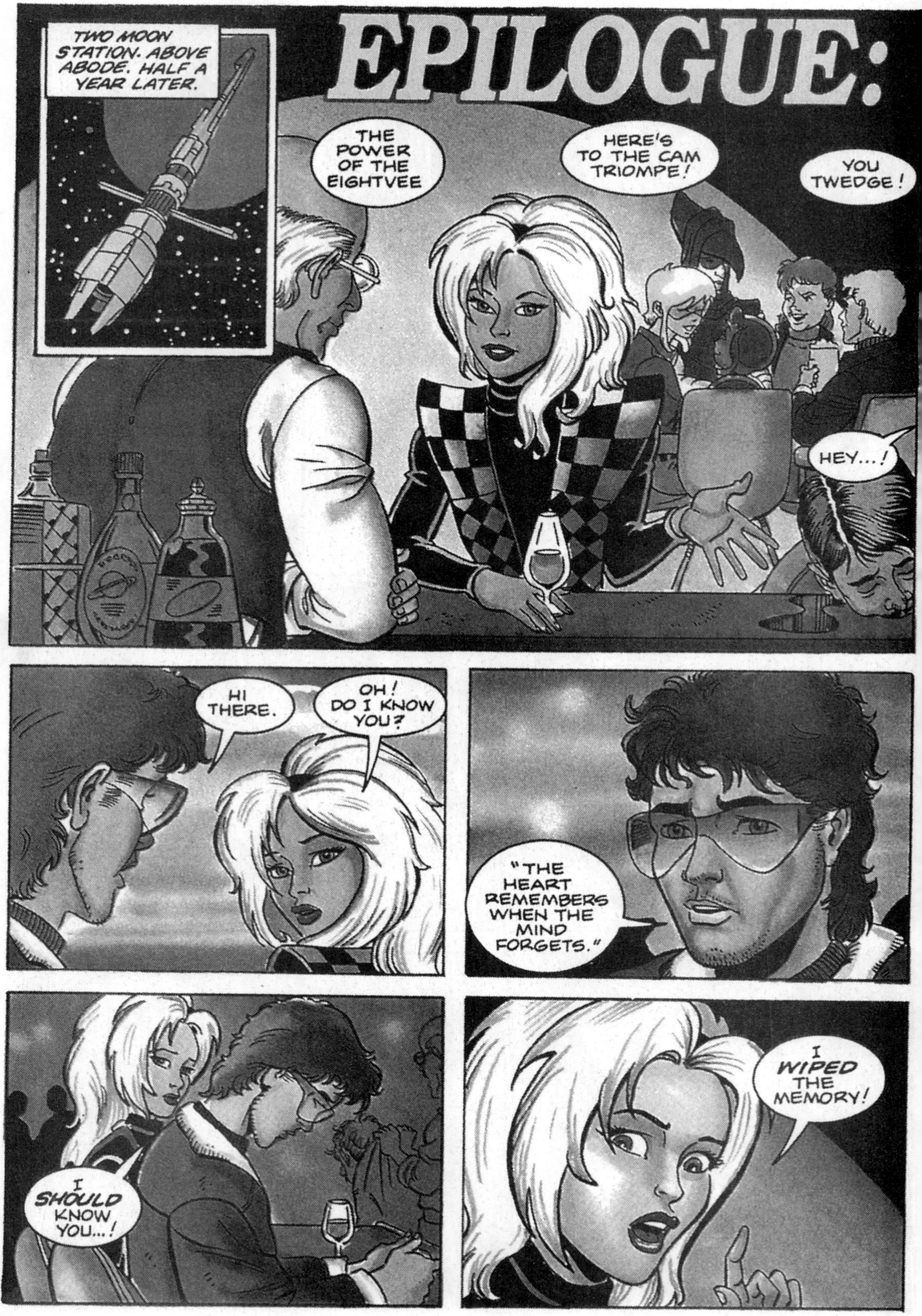
TWO MOON STATION. ABOVE ABODE. HALF A YEAR LATER.
EPILOGUE:
THE POWER OF THE EIGHTVEE
HERE'S TO THE CAM TRIOMPE!
YOU TWEDGE!
HEY...!
HI THERE.
OH! DO I KNOW YOU?
"THE HEART REMEMBERS WHEN THE MIND FORGETS."
I SHOULD KNOW YOU...!
I WIPED THE MEMORY!

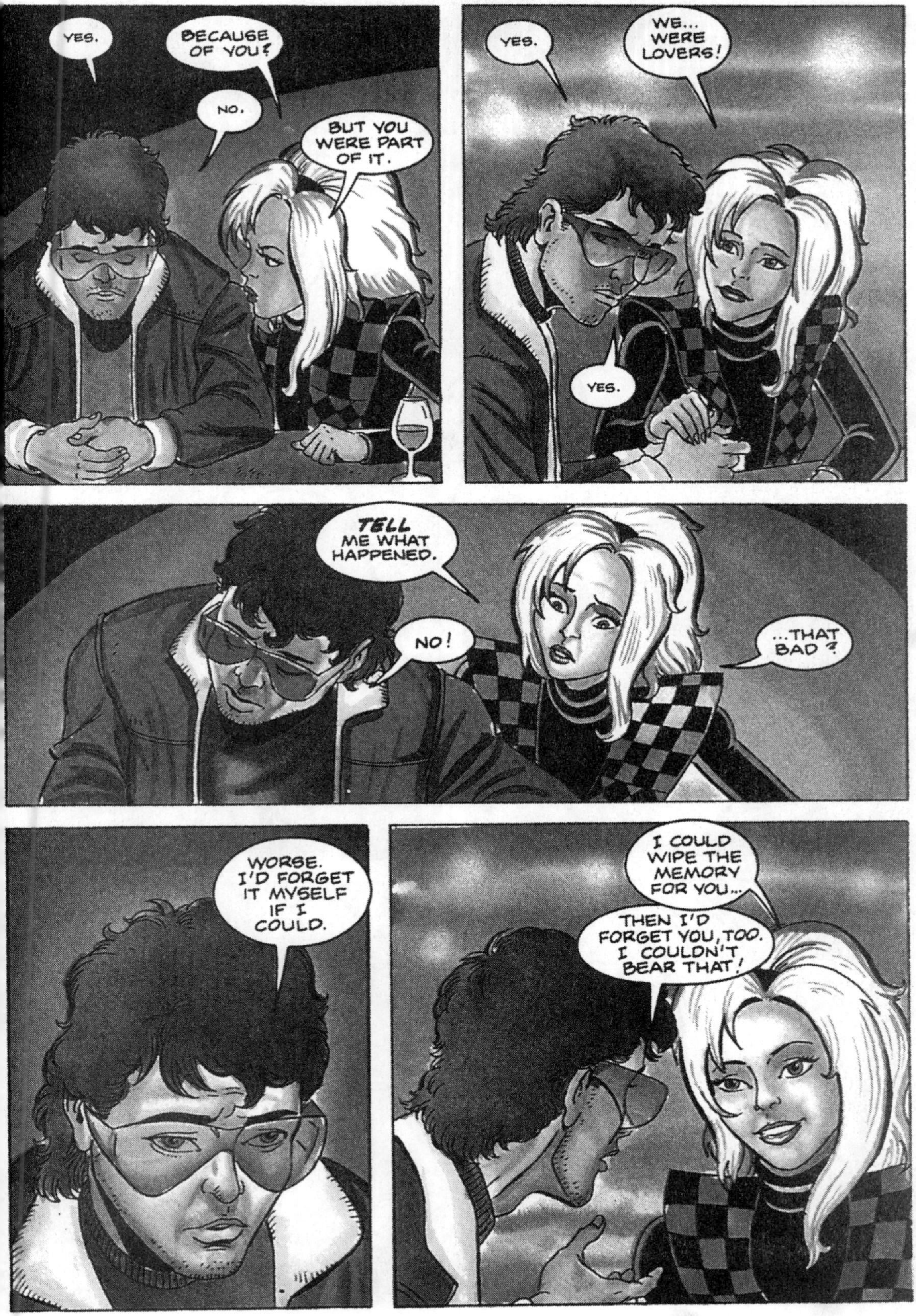
YES.
BECAUSE OF YOU?
NO.
BUT YOU WERE PART OF IT.
YES.
WE... WERE LOVERS!
YES.
TELL ME WHAT HAPPENED.
NO!
...THAT BAD?
WORSE. I'D FORGET IT MYSELF IF I COULD.
I COULD WIPE THE MEMORY FOR YOU...
THEN I'D FORGET YOU, TOO. I COULDN'T BEAR THAT!

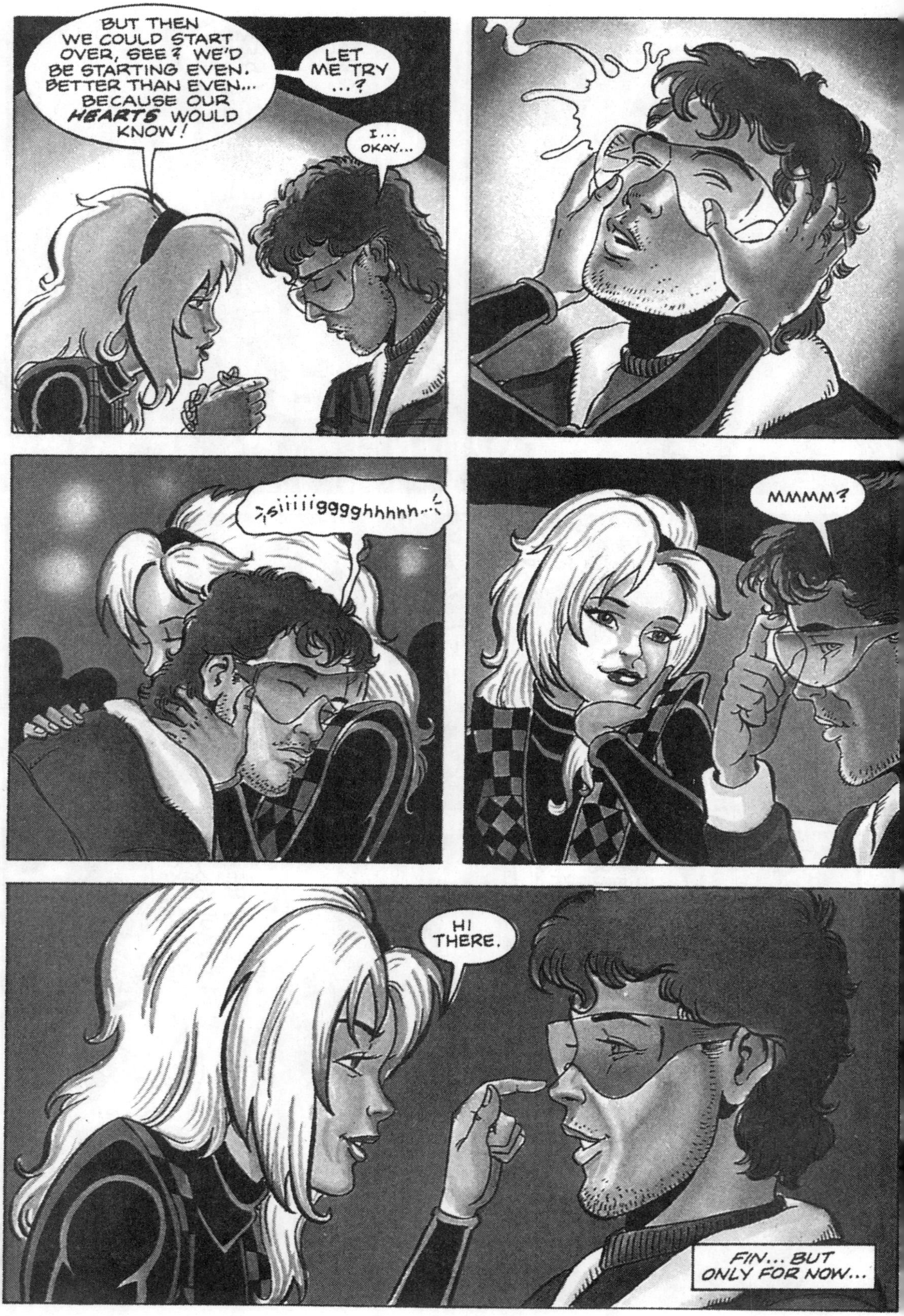

BUT THEN WE COULD START OVER, SEE? WE'D BE STARTING EVEN. BETTER THAN EVEN... BECAUSE OUR HEARTS WOULD KNOW!
LET ME TRY ...?
I... OKAY...
siiiiiggggghhhhh...
MMMM?
HI THERE.
FIN... BUT ONLY FOR NOW...

For the moment, Jink
may rest. However, elsewhere
on Abode an ancient evil stirs...
and will soon awaken in
volume 14a, "Mindcoil."

For now, however, turn the page
to learn more of Jink's story
and how it came to be.

Thinking JiNK

Stories do not spring full-blown into existence. In the case of those Elfquest tales that represent, to us at least, the best and most enjoyable collaborative efforts, story lines took a great deal of hammering into shape. Take Jink for example. Her origins go way back in Wendy's imagination: Her look comes in large part from a character called Vaiya, Daughter of Stone (whose name, by the way, was given minus the "i" to Kahvi's daughter in the original Elfquest saga; nothing gets wasted here!). Jink herself is a pastiche of characters, notably a rakish and racy "Pirate Jenny" type named Luba, who inhabited the same future universe as did Wendy's original Rebels. Ah, connections...

Writer John Ostrander, whom we asked to script the Jink stories, had already made a name for himself in comics as one who could very deftly blend diverse elements — sensuality, horror, emotion, space opera, character interaction and motivation, and a dozen others — just what we wanted for the Jink series. What was needed, back at the beginning, was to bring John onto the world of Abode with which we were familiar — but not totally so. You've already read his take on our "white-haired star-daughter." What follows here are the notes Wendy and Richard prepared — and debated — in one of Jink's first story sessions. The comparison between first take and finished presentation is fascinating. (Most of the notes are by Wendy; the comments in italics are by Richard.) - Ed.

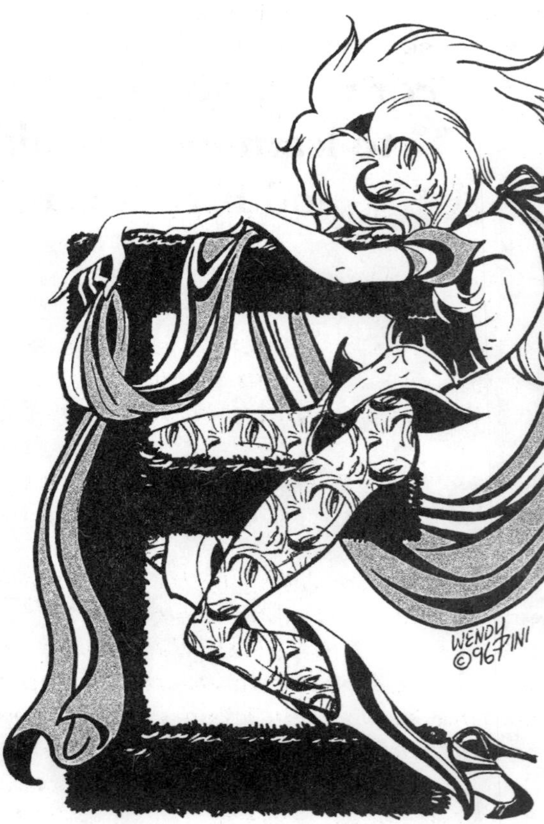
WENDY ©96 PINI

One of the Centers of Abode's world government is located on the continent Iceholt (the equivalent of North America) whose eastern forests once harbored the Wolfriders' original Holt. Kullyn Kenn, an otherwise average human male with some telepathic powers works at that government center.

Years ago it was discovered that certain humans with ESP potential could be plugged into bio-computers and have their powers artificially augmented. A division was formed to oversee the creation of an elite corps of telepaths who refer to themselves irreverently as "Jackups." Kullyn Kenn tried to enter this service, but his repeated sessions with the bio-computers didn't take in any substantial way. The Jackups and their "normal" bosses (some of whom, unknown even to the Jackups, are secretly equipped with "privacy" devices to shut out telepathy) refer to Kenn's type, unkindly, as "Tweaks."

Since any ESP is better than no ESP, Kenn has done different, odd jobs for the government, acting as a human lie-detector or sitting in on diplomatic sessions to catch what the real intentions are under the political jargon. His success rate lately has been about 40% and he's in danger of being fired. Almost as a joke, his superiors offer him one last chance ... If he can find JINK, his butt is saved!

Kullyn Kenn's no dope. He knows there are Jackups who've been on this assignment for months. If she's managed to hide from *them*, why should he have better luck? But he takes the high-tech file on Jink anyway (not quite getting why his savvy bosses mutter "Lucky S.O.B. if you *do* find her...!") and is soon absorbed in learning all he can about this fascinating, elusive female.

The government wants to find her because there's a problem of interplanetary proportions only she can solve. Nearly a century ago, after space exploration had finally pushed to the farthest edge of Abode's solar system, a race of aliens was discovered dwelling on the outermost planet.

(NOTE: Richard wants the science fiction in JINK to be sound and believable, so the origin of these alien invaders, why they're able to exist on this Pluto-like planet — and why they'd even want to ... mineral resources perhaps? — has to be carefully worked out. For my money, they're intergalactic invaders biding their time on that outermost planet, arrogantly preparing at leisure to conquer Abode and its solar system, but then they're caught off guard by Abode's precocious space exploration program. The analogy to Japan, with its long-standing attitude of superiority and isolationism, combined with an aggressive, warlike streak is vital. — Wendy).

(Note 2 — I don't mind a certain amount of "Star Wars" flavor romanticism about this, or in any other title that we do, but I dislike concept/plot holes large enough to drive the Millennium Falcon through. My problems with these aliens is/are:

•They're clearly from outside this solar system so either they (a) have FTL (faster than light) drive or (b) they came in on some kind of "generation ship."

•The problem with FTL travel is that if they were coming in to invade, they'd have known about Abode's own progress in space travel by picking up radio waves and such. Either Abode would be ahead of them or behind them; if Abode were behind, the BEMs would have come right in and taken over. If they were ahead, the BEMs would have gone somewhere else. Either way, it doesn't make for a sensible invasion scenario to me.

•The problem with a generation ship is that it takes a bloody long time to get from there to here. That's OK, if you're absolutely committed to where you're going, even if you don't know what the conditions are like. You'd have to be a real gambler to mount an invasion that way; are these BEMs that odd, psychologically? If the BEMs used a generation ship and 3/4 of the way to Abode's star, started picking up radio signals of progress, they might have said "oh crap" to themselves but kept on going because any deviation in course would have added a ton more time. Once they got to the solar system they would have looked for a place to hole up and build their own resources, hoping that Abode didn't outstrip them. It seems, however, that even so, they've still been discovered... — Richard)

No other planets were thought to be inhabited — how long had these aliens been Abode's comparatively close neighbors while remaining incommunicado? Completely inhuman, weird, beautiful, tentacled (whatever — go as wild with them as you want) these beings proved immediately hostile to visitors, much as the Japanese were when their shores were unexpectedly breached by "foreign devils." Though the aliens appeared technologically advanced (their designs were so far-out there was little point of reference) there was no way to communicate with them. They had no ears or mouths and seemed to speak only through subtle, indecipherable body gestures. With all of their friendly overtures continually repulsed, the humans eventually stopped trying.

(Note 3 — Either this comic title is going to go generally in the direction of the "Retief" stories — which, make no mistake, I like — or liked, before they got repetitive — or they're going to go in some other direction. The Retief stories dealt with alien races in much the same way as this treatment. Author Keith Laumer was with the U.S. Diplomatic Corps for many years and so got to see the "ugly American" mentality at work a lot; he got to see the venal side of the foreign cultures he worked with, too. The one consideration that, in my opinion, has to be taken into account here is that a straight analogy such as "the U.S. was to Japan as Abode is to the BEMs" could trivialize the alienness of these creatures. Their motives must be really well thought out. It's been said that any race capable of mounting interstellar travel must, almost by definition, have outgrown its warlike or imperialistic tendencies. The time scales and expenditures of energy just to make the trip would prohibit such silliness as conquest.
          Of course, if we're giving the critters FTL technology, then they've probably already conquered half the galaxy, so Abode is trash anyway. I both like and dislike giving them FTL drive. If they have it, and they're seen as a threat to Abode, then all the more reason for the government to go after the Rebels when it's discovered that they too can travel FTL — by virtue of the little Palace they acquire. If the BEMs don't have FTL, then the Rebels' having it makes it unique, and again a great prize for the government. I lean toward unique solutions to things — I'm a great believer in the idea that if something's not impossible, and not unique, then it's all over the place and thus quite ordinary. — Richard)

Abode had already colonized its nearest neighboring planets and had many, scattered space stations when the aliens were discovered. A means of rapid interplanetary travel came into use and human outposts sprang up even farther out in the solar system. They began to be attacked by robot ships.

Risking no physical danger themselves, the aliens had perfected extreme long-range guidance systems to the point where their robot warships could threaten Abode itself. But, like the Japanese in World War 2, the aliens never counted on major retaliation. Abode and her ally colonies amassed a huge war fleet capable of launching the equivalent of many H-Bombs at the aliens' Pluto-like world. They were on their way to destroy the robot ships' point of origin along with almost everything else — but hoped they wouldn't have to. The idea of annihilating the first non-humanoid aliens ever discovered went against the world government's most basic ideals.

Jink was found and impressed as ambassador and peace negotiator. With her unequaled telepathic and empathic abilities, only she had a prayer of reaching the aliens and persuading them to surrender. And darned if she didn't succeed, gaining the alien leaders' grudging respect in the process!

That was forty years ago. Since then, diplomatic relations between the aliens and Abode have opened up. The aliens, outwardly in the name of peaceful exchange, have set up trade and cultural centers throughout the solar system. Underneath it all, like the proud Japanese, they're just trying a different, long-term tactic to win the war. These centers are all automated with android replicas of the aliens (who, it is commonly believed, cannot leave their planet) as hosts. Through these androids, humans study the mute creatures' body-language (learning little more, by the inscrutable aliens' deliberate design, than "Hi, how are ya" — an analogy to the immense difficulty Westerners have learning the Japanese language).

But lately something very weird has happened at one or two of these cultural centers — students, and worse, visiting colonial officials, are being murdered in a strange, ritualistic manner. The suspicion is growing that not *all* the alien "hosts" are androids! That's why the government is looking for Jink. If this apparent terrorist activity escalates, it could bring the solar system to the brink of holocaust — and past it!

The stage is now set.

Kullyn Kenn does find Jink, of course (NOTE: there are many places he can look, but I vote for him finding her working as a sort of lumberjack in a hydroponic space forest ten times grander than anything in "Silent Running" — Wendy). Though she is attracted to Kenn because of his minimal telepathy — her nickname for him is "Hunch" — it's not enough to get her to risk investigating the terrorist activity and negotiating with the aliens again. She can't be bothered.

Kenn, hopelessly smitten with Jink but dedicated to duty first, vows to take on the job himself. Half-amused, half worried that he'll get himself killed, Jink secretly follows Kenn as he begins his detective work. To his great peril he learns that a group of live alien terrorists, led by a fanatic, nationalistic "Mishima" type are indeed infiltrating the alien cultural centers to spy, to kill and to avenge the humans' dishonor of their race.

While rescuing Kenn from "Mishima," Jink gets embroiled in spite of herself. The terrorists' cause is noble, but hopeless. Their government, to save face, does not outwardly support them. She and Kenn manage to meet with the "Mishima-type" terrorist leader near one of the alien Cultural Centers and beg him to give up. Kenn says the colonial SkyWard is led by a military commander equally as fanatic as the terrorists — they'll be hunted down and massacred!

"Mishima" does hand-to-tentacle battle with Jink and loses. Still refusing to surrender, he and his band seize the Cultural Center to make an honorable last stand. The SkyWard soon arrives and starts bombing the place. A lot of beautiful and rare alien artifacts in the building get destroyed. "Mishima" gets disheartened and tries to kill himself. Jink stops him and finally seems to get through to him — he agrees to surrender if his followers are allowed to return to their own planet for discipline.

Kenn rushes out and persuades the SkyWard commander to have his men hold their fire. The commander agrees. By telepathically "reading" him, Kenn determines he'll keep his promise. Jink brings the unarmed terrorist leader outside. Her back is to the military as she supports the exhausted "Mishima." Without warning the military fires right *through* Jink, hitting "Mishima." The instant Jink falls, shots are fired by the terrorists inside the building, also right through "Mishima," hitting many of the military.

Ironically the two fanatic leaders had pre-programmed their men with nearly identical orders — except "Mishima" sacrificed himself. The human commander sacrificed Jink. The SkyWard, of course, immediately cuts loose with all its fire power and annihilates the terrorists as they "banzai," alien weapons blazing, out of the building. Kenn manages to run through all this and drag Jink to safety. She's still alive. When the smoke has cleared, Kenn asks the commander, "Why the betrayal?"

"The freaks had to die. She's a freak too — she can heal herself. It's on record. We took a reasonable risk," is the answer.

Now Kenn knows why Jink didn't want to get involved. He also learns that the commander was equipped with a "privacy" device, which is why Kenn read him wrong.

"This is a 'wipe,' isn't it..." Kenn asks Jink.

"You bet."

"But ... you won't remember me."

"No."

Kenn puts his jacket over Jink and walks off, leaving her to do her healing work — including the memory wipe. When she stands up, looking around blankly, she notices his jacket, picks it up, puts it on and walks away.

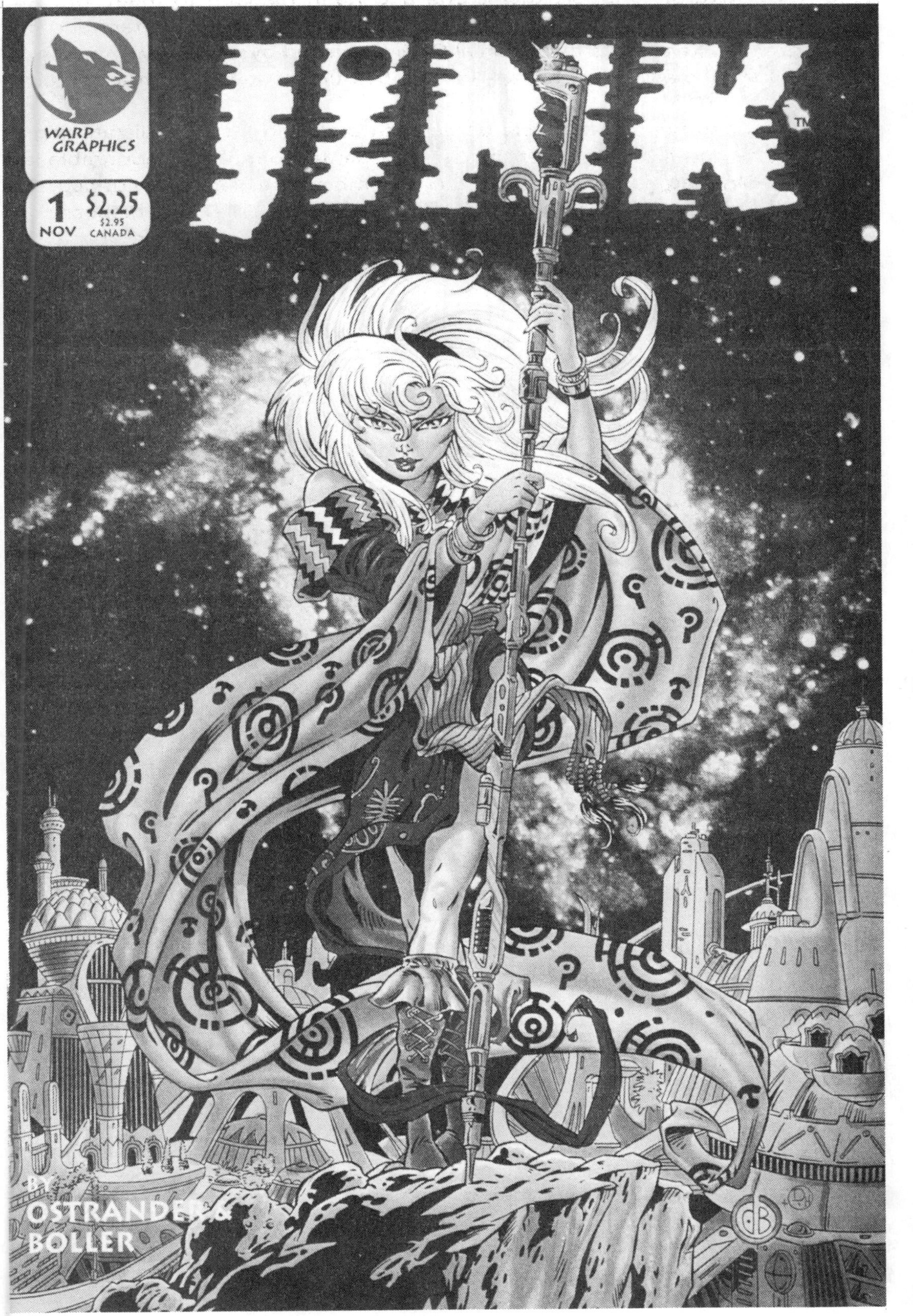
WARP GRAPHICS
JINX™
1 NOV
$2.25
$2.95 CANADA
BY
OSTRANDER &
BOLLER

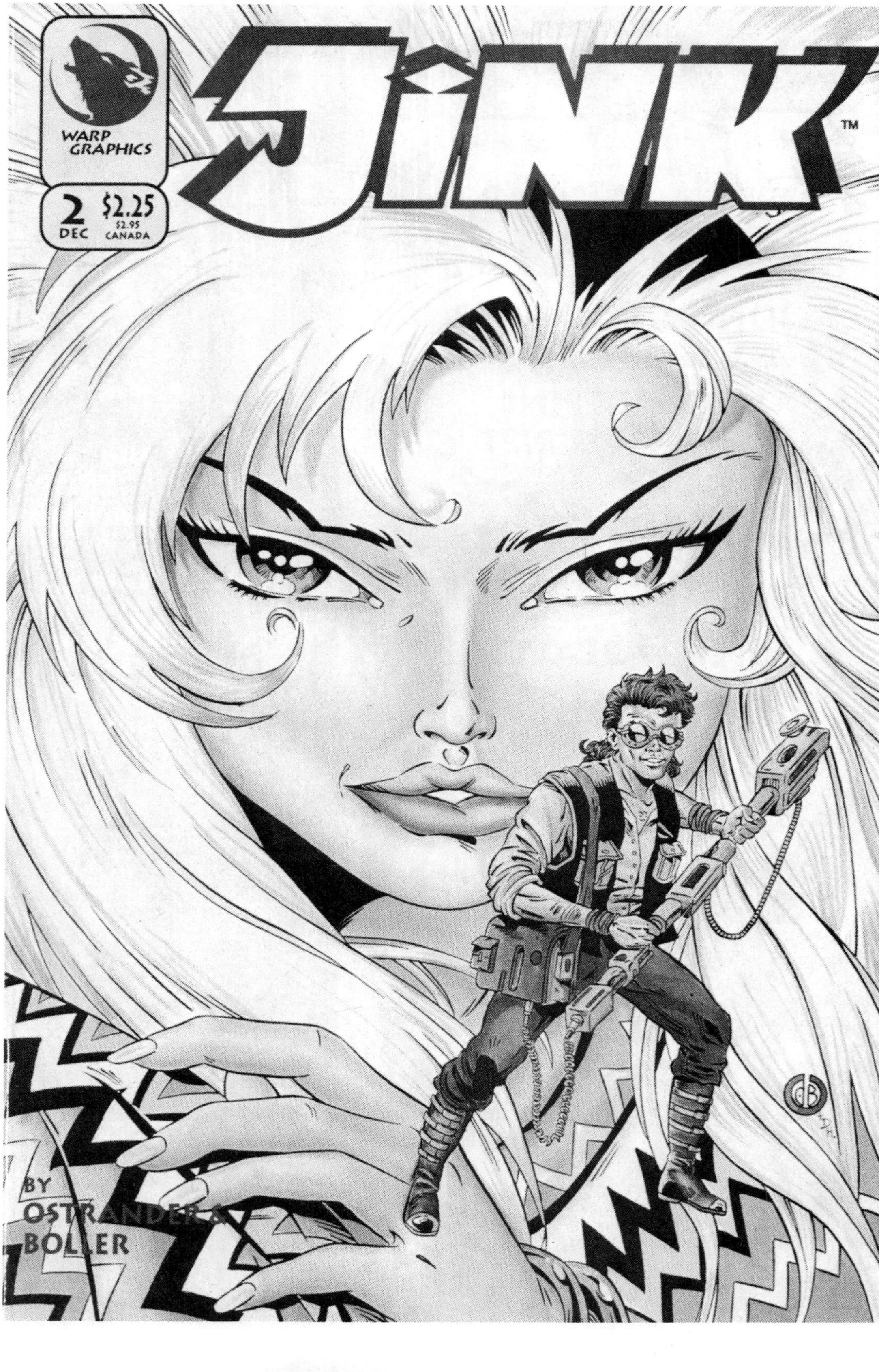
WARP GRAPHICS
JINK™
2 DEC
$2.25
$2.95 CANADA
BY OSTRANDER & BOLLER

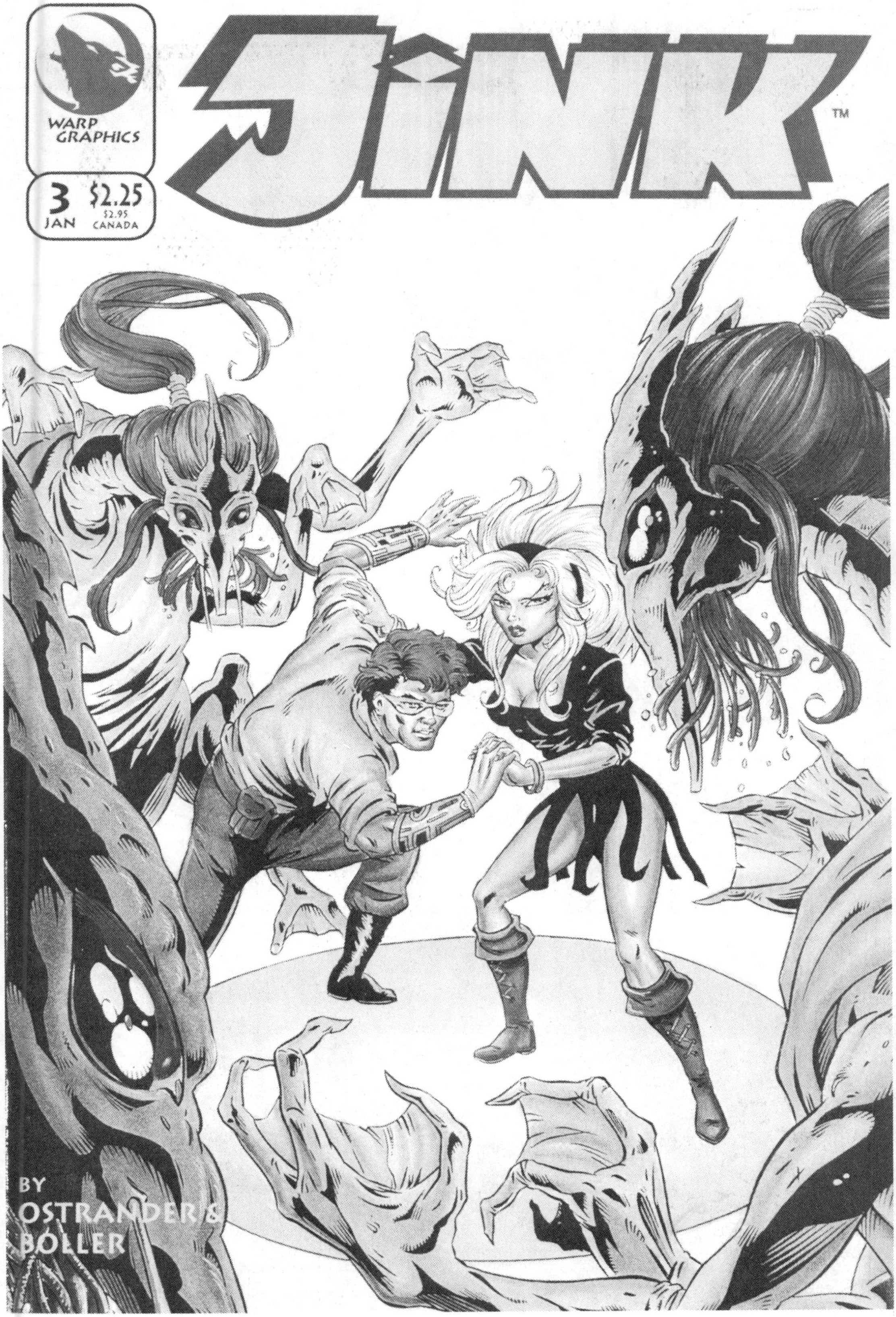
WARP GRAPHICS
JINK™
3 JAN $2.25 $2.95 CANADA
BY OSTRANDER & BOLLER

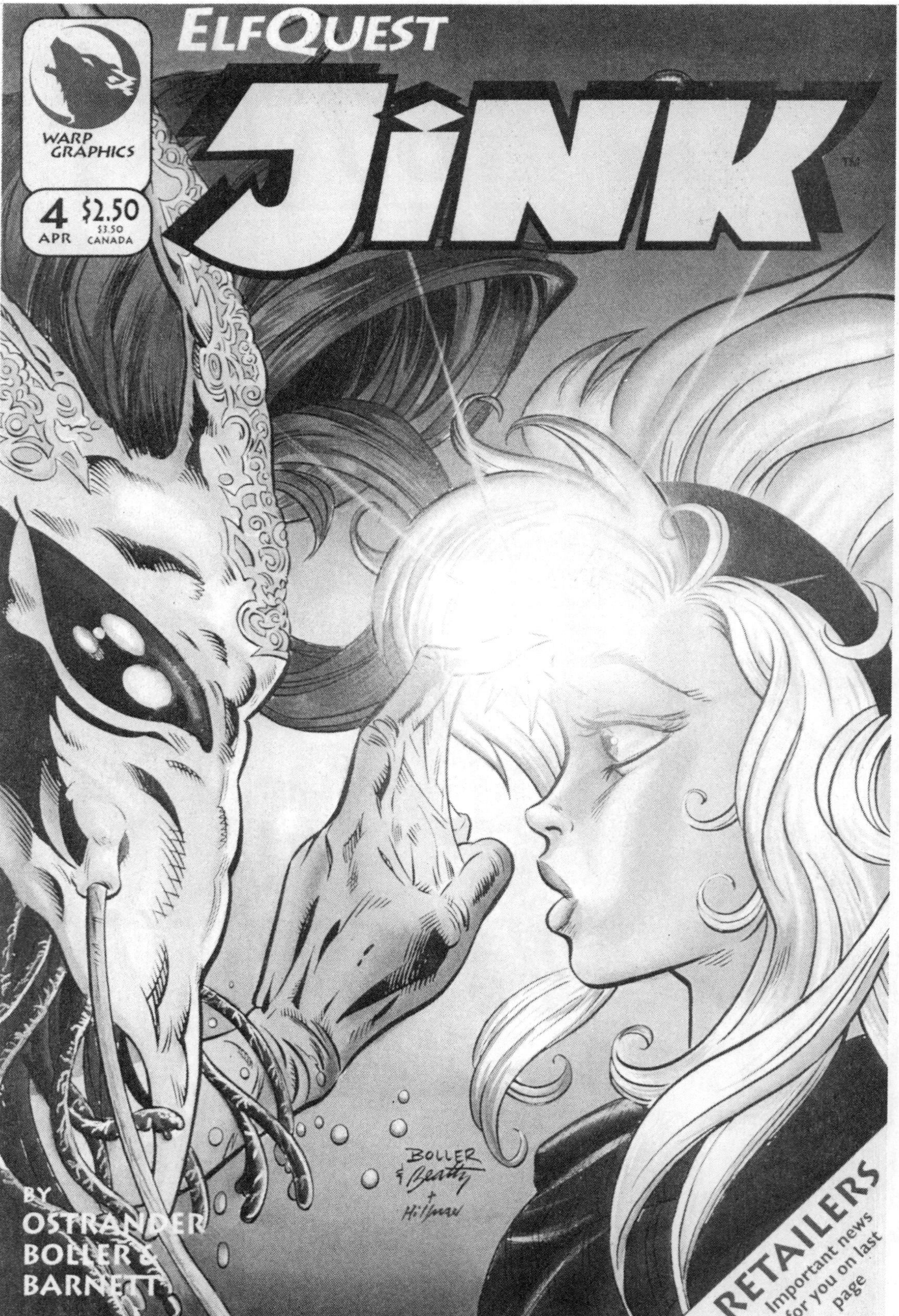

ELFQUEST
JINK
TM
WARP GRAPHICS
4 APR
$2.50
$3.50 CANADA
BOLLER & Beatty + Hillman
BY OSTRANDER BOLLER & BARNETT
RETAILERS
Important news for you on last page

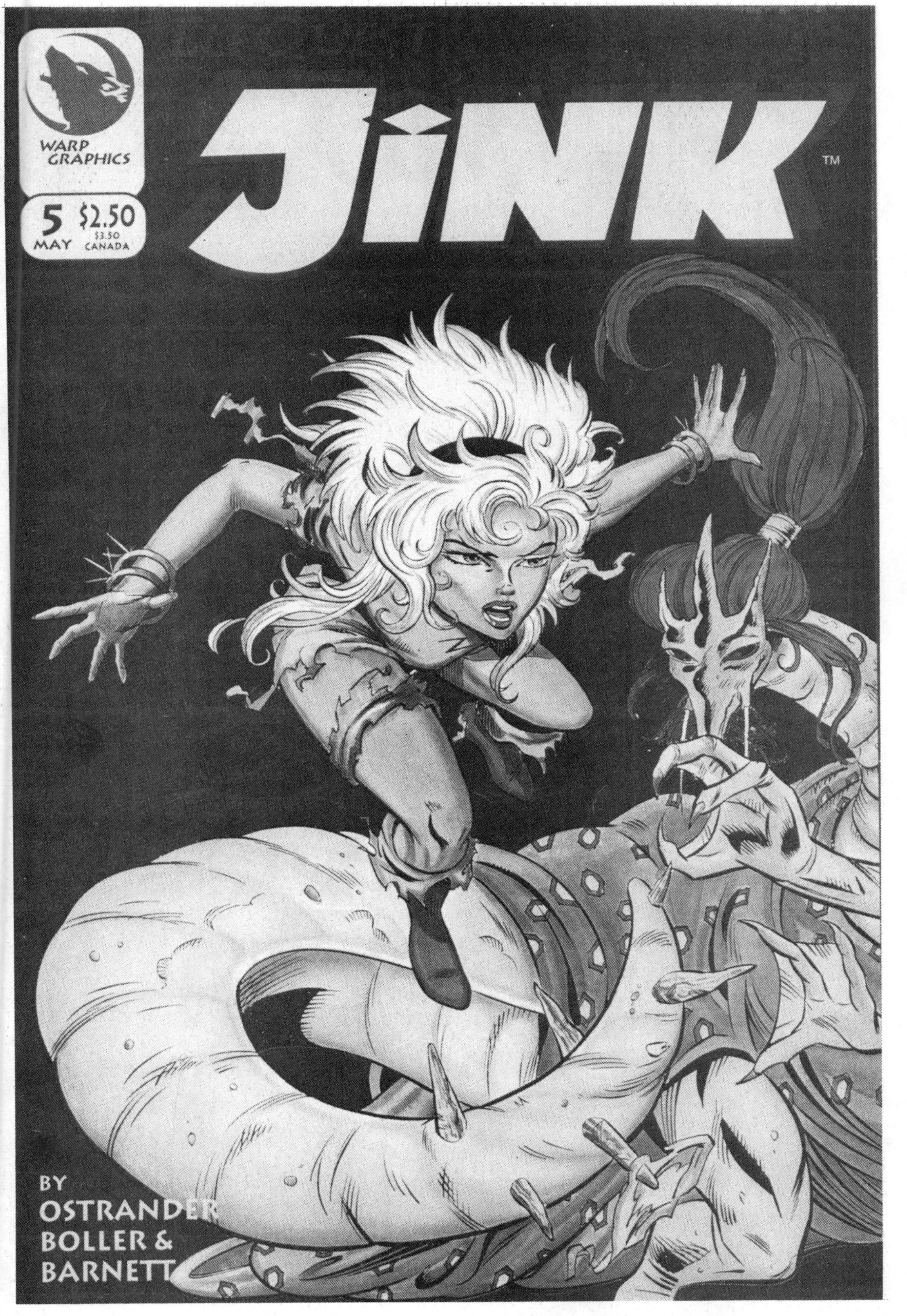
WARP GRAPHICS
JINK™
5 MAY
$2.50
$3.50 CANADA
BY
OSTRANDER
BOLLER &
BARNETT

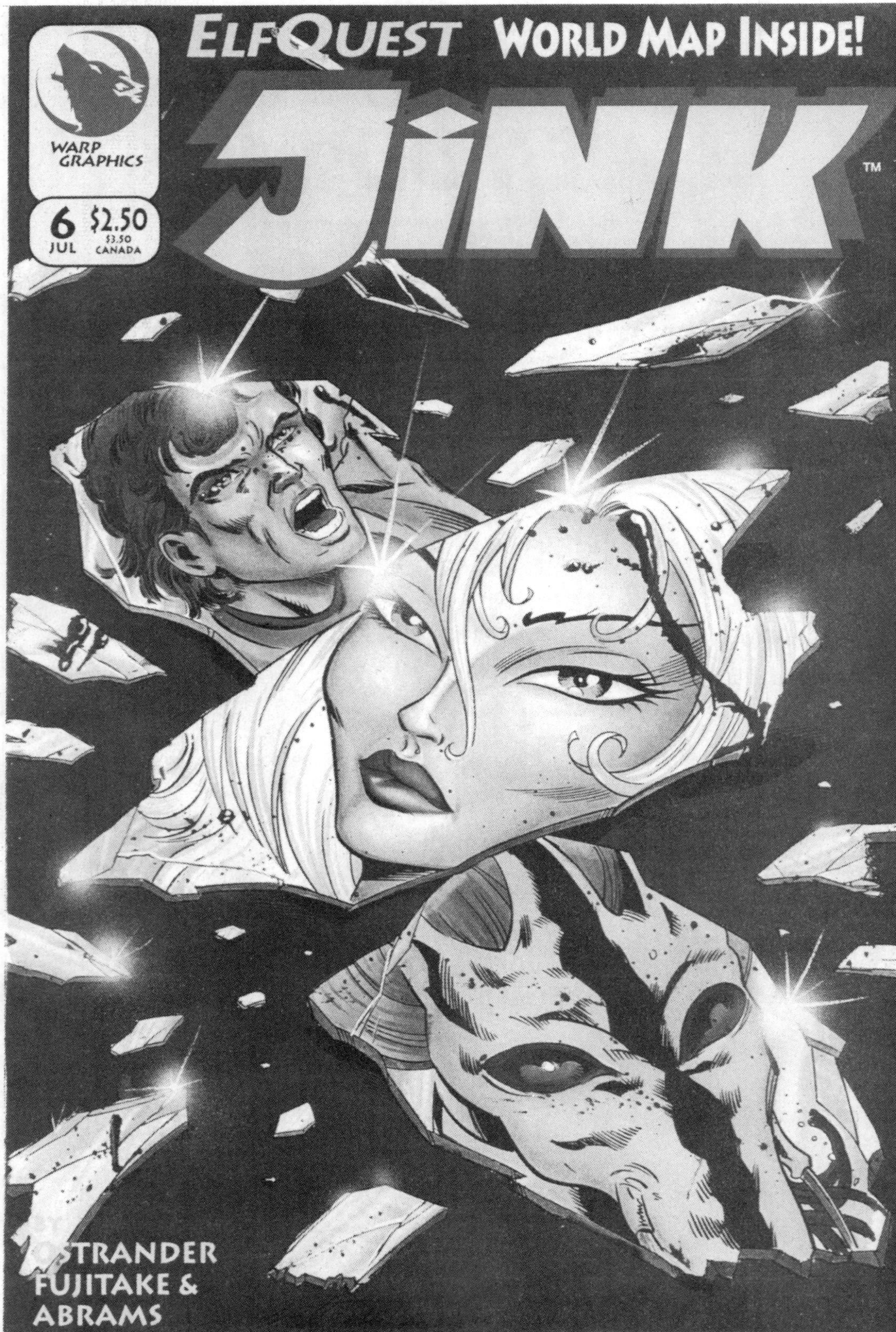
ElfQuest
World Map Inside!
Warp Graphics
6 Jul
$2.50
$3.50 Canada
Jink™
Ostrander
Fujitake &
Abrams